"What can the international community do when a Superpower goes rogue and uses its special status to shield itself from accountability? The question is at the core of this timely and thought-provoking collection by foremost experts in the field of international law."

Stephen Rapp, *former U.S. Ambassador-at-Large for War Crimes Issues, USA*

"These insightful chapters prod us not to forget the most crucial aspects of what should be remembered as a global turning point in the evolution of civil and criminal accountability, reparations, deterrence, and justice for the victims of naked aggression and atrocity."

Harold Hongju Koh, *former Legal Adviser of the U.S. Department of State, USA*

"A compelling book that is essential reading for scholars, practitioners, and diplomats interested in understanding the impact the Ukraine crisis has had on international law and policy and the various options available to deliver comprehensive justice."

Beth Van Schaack, *former U.S. Ambassador-at-Large for Global Criminal Justice, USA*

UKRAINE AND THE LEGAL ACCOUNTABILITY OF RUSSIA

This book explains how the response to Russia's 2022 invasion of Ukraine has transformed international law. It analyzes the significance of the resurrection of the UN General Assembly's Uniting for Peace mechanism, the insertion of the International Criminal Court into world politics at the highest level, and the creation of new types of investigatory mechanisms and tribunals. It explores groundbreaking developments related to war reparations, the crime of aggression and attacks on the environment. And it makes the case that, rather than personifying the failure of international law, the Russia-Ukraine war has demonstrated its continuing relevance and resilience in surprising ways. This work will be compelling reading for academics, researchers and policy-makers working in the areas of International Criminal Law, International Humanitarian Law and the Law of Armed Conflict.

Yvonne Dutton is a Senior Legal Advisor at Public International Law & Policy Group (PILPG), and Professor of Law Emerita at the Robert H. McKinney School of Law, Indiana University, USA.

Michael P. Scharf is the President of the American Branch of the International Law Association and the Joseph C. Hostetler—Baker Hostetler Professor of Law at Case Western Reserve University School of Law, USA, where he served as Dean from 2013–2024.

Milena Sterio is the Charles R. Emrick Jr. - Calfee Halter & Griswold Professor of Law at Cleveland-Marshall College of Law, Cleveland State University, USA, and Managing Director of the Public International Law and Policy Group (PILPG).

Paul R. Williams holds the Rebecca I. Grazier Professorship in Law and International Relations at American University, where he teaches in the School of International Service and at the Washington College of Law, USA. Dr. Williams is also the co-founder of the Public International Law & Policy Group (PILPG).

UKRAINE AND THE LEGAL ACCOUNTABILITY OF RUSSIA

The Emergence of a New Global Order

Edited by Yvonne Dutton, Michael P. Scharf, Milena Sterio and Paul R. Williams

Routledge
Taylor & Francis Group
LONDON AND NEW YORK

Designed cover image: Tomas Ragina/ Getty Images ®

First published 2026
by Routledge
4 Park Square, Milton Park, Abingdon, Oxon OX14 4RN

and by Routledge
605 Third Avenue, New York, NY 10158

Routledge is an imprint of the Taylor & Francis Group, an informa business

British Library Cataloguing-in-Publication Data
A catalogue record for this book is available from the British Library

ISBN: 978-1-032-60221-9 (hbk)
ISBN: 978-1-032-59534-4 (pbk)
ISBN: 978-1-003-45816-6 (ebk)

DOI: 10.4324/9781003458166

Typeset in Galliard
by Deanta Global Publishing Services, Chennai, India

CONTENTS

ABOUT THE EDITORS

Yvonne Dutton

Yvonne Dutton is a Senior Legal Advisor at PILPG. For 12 years, she served as a Professor of Law at the Indiana University Robert H. McKinney School of Law teaching evidence, criminal law, criminal procedure, international criminal law, international law, and comparative law. Professor Dutton graduated from Columbia Law School, where she served on the Columbia Law Review and was a Harlan Fiske Stone Scholar (all years). She also holds a PhD in Political Science from the University of Colorado at Boulder. After graduating from Columbia Law School, Professor Dutton clerked for the Honorable William C. Conner, United States District Judge for the Southern District of New York. Professor Dutton has practiced law as a federal prosecutor in the U.S. Attorney's Office for the Southern District of New York, where she tried narcotics trafficking and organized crime cases. She also practiced as a civil litigator in law firms in New York and California. Professor Dutton's research interests include international criminal law, international human rights law, and maritime piracy. Broadly speaking, her scholarship examines questions about international cooperation and the role and effectiveness of international institutions in deterring and holding accountable those who commit crimes of international concern. In May 2013, her book entitled Rules, Politics, and the International Criminal Court: Committing to the Court was published by Routledge. Professor Dutton has recently been involved with providing technical assistance with the development of framework laws on transitional justice and the harmonization of Ukrainian domestic law with international humanitarian law and the drafting of a legal charter for the Ukrainian peace-building/documentation center.

Michael P. Scharf

In 2024, Michael P. Schar returned to serving as Associate Dean for Global Legal Studies after leading Case Western Reserve University School of Law as Co-Dean for over ten years. He is also the Joseph C. Hostetler—BakerHostetler Professor of Law and serves as a Managing Director of the Public International Law & Policy Group, which he co-founded. Before becoming a law professor, Scharf served in the Office of the Legal Adviser of the U.S. Department of State, where he held the positions of Attorney-Adviser for Law Enforcement and Intelligence, Attorney-Adviser for United Nations Affairs, and delegate to the United Nations Human Rights Commission. In 2004, Scharf trained the judges for the trial of Saddam Hussein and during a sabbatical in 2008, he served as Special Assistant to the Prosecutor of the Cambodia Genocide Tribunal. In February 2022, Scharf presented an Amicus Argument before the Appeals Chamber of the International Criminal Court in The Hague on the question of who has the burden of proof on the insanity defense. Scharf is the author of 20 books, five of which have won national book of the year honors. Since 2012, Scharf has been the producer and host of "Talking Foreign Policy," a radio program broadcast on Cleveland's NPR station and other NPR affiliates across the country, which is also available as a podcast. Scharf is currently the President of the American Branch of the International Law Association and a member of the Executive Council of the American Society of International Law.

Milena Sterio

Milena Sterio, the James A. Thomas Distinguished Professor of Law at Cleveland State University's Cleveland-Marshall College of Law and Managing Director at the PILPG. She is a leading expert on international law, international criminal law and human rights. Sterio leads PILPG's Thought Leadership Initiative. Sterio is one of six permanent editors of the prestigious IntLawGrrls blog, and a frequent contributor to the blog focused on international law, policy and practice. In the spring of 2013, Sterio was selected as a Fulbright Scholar, spending the semester in Baku, Azerbaijan, at Baku State University. While in Baku, she had the opportunity to teach and conduct research on secession issues under international law related to the province of Azerbaijan, Nagorno-Karabakh. Serving as a maritime piracy law expert, she has participated in meetings of the United Nations Contact Group on Piracy off the Coast of Somalia as well as in the work of the United Nations Global Counterterrorism Forum. Sterio has also assisted piracy prosecutions in Mauritius, Kenya and the Seychelles Islands. Sterio is a graduate of Cornell Law School and the University of Paris I, and was an associate in the New York City firm of Cleary, Gottlieb, Steen & Hamilton before joining the ranks of academia full time. She has published seven books and numerous law review articles. Her latest book, "The Syrian Conflict's Impact on International Law," (co-authored with Paul R. Williams and Michael P. Scharf) was published by Cambridge University Press in 2020.

Paul R. Williams

Paul R. Williams holds the Rebecca I. Grazier Professorship in Law and International Relations at American University, where he teaches in the School of International Service and at the Washington College of Law. Dr. Williams is also the co-founder of the Public International Law & Policy Group (PILPG), a pro bono law firm providing legal assistance to states and governments involved in peace negotiations, post-conflict constitution drafting, and the prosecution of war criminals. As a world renowned peace negotiation lawyer, Dr. Williams has assisted over two dozen parties in major international peace negotiations and has advised numerous parties on the drafting and implementation of post conflict constitutions. Several of Dr. Williams' pro bono government clients throughout the world joined together to nominate him for the Nobel Peace Prize. Dr. Williams has served as a Senior Associate with the Carnegie Endowment for International Peace, as well as an Attorney-Adviser for European and Canadian affairs at the U.S. Department of State, Office of the Legal Adviser. He received his J.D. from Stanford Law School and his Ph.D. from the University of Cambridge. Dr. Williams is a sought after international law and policy expert. He is frequently interviewed by major print and broadcast media and regularly contributes op-eds to major newspapers. Dr. Williams has authored eight books on various topics concerning international law, and has published over three dozen scholarly articles on topics of international law and policy. He has testified before the U.S. Congress on a number of occasions relating to specific peace processes, transitional justice, and self-determination. Dr. Williams is a member of the Council of Foreign Relations, and has served as a Counsellor on the Executive Council of the American Society of International Law. In 2010, Paul was awarded the American University School of International Service's Scholar/Teacher of the Year, the School's highest honor for faculty. In 2019, Paul was awarded the Cox International Law Center's Humanitarian Award for Advancing Global Justice. More information about Dr. Williams can be found at www.drpaulrwilliams.com.

LIST OF CONTRIBUTORS

Fatou Bensouda is the former Chief Prosecutor of the International Criminal Court.

Sindija Beta is Legal Officer at Public International Law & Policy Group, Latvia

Mark S. Ellis is Executive Director of the International Bar Association, London, United Kingdom.

Oona A. Hathaway is the Gerard C. and Bernice Latrobe Smith Professor of International Law, Yale Law School and President Elect of the American Society of International Law, USA.

Michael J. Kelly is the Senator Allen A. Sekt Endowed Chair in Law at Creighton University School of Law, USA.

Patrick Keenan is Professor of Law and Heidi Hurd Faculty Scholar at the University of Illinois College of Law, USA.

Kateryna Kyrychenko is Legal Officer at Public International Law & Policy Group, Ukraine.

Maggie M. Mills is a Herbert Hansell Fellow at the Yale Center for Global Legal Challenges.

Greg Noone is Director of the Fairmont State University National Security and Intelligence Program and a Professor of Political Science and Law, USA.

Greta Ramelli is Legal Officer at Public International Law & Policy Group, Italy.

Jennifer Trahan is Clinical Professor and Director of the Concentration in International Law and Human Rights, NYU Center for Global Affairs; Convener, The Global Institute for the Prevention of Aggression, USA.

FOREWORD

by Fatou Bensouda

When Russia invaded Ukraine on February 24, 2022, it set off the largest armed conflict in Europe since WWII. The invasion was accompanied by war crimes and crimes against humanity of the worst sorts. Under Russian President Vladimir Putin's direction, the Russian army kidnapped children and transferred them to Russia for adoption. It systematically attacked hospitals, schools, and residential buildings. It destroyed dams, power stations, and targeted the environment.

Since Russia is a Permanent Member of the United Nations Security Council with a veto as well as the world's largest arsenal of nuclear weapons, some believed the invasion of Ukraine had pushed the international legal system beyond its limits to meaningfully respond. But instead, states, regional and international institutions, and international lawyers rallied to bring accountability in the face of Russian aggression. Sanctions were leveled on Russia, Russian assets were frozen, economic embargoes were imposed, and vast amounts of financial and military aid was funneled to Ukraine. With the Russian economy in free fall, Russia was no longer to prop up the Assad Regime in Syria, which collapsed in December 2024.

In the midst of these countermeasures, the International Criminal Court, of which I served for 18 years first as Deputy Prosecutor and later as Prosecutor, sprang into action. It issued arrest warrants for Putin and his top generals and admirals. Meanwhile, the international community assisted Ukraine in documenting atrocities and enhancing its ability to prosecute perpetrators in person or through in absentia trials. Other states launched their own investigations and prosecutions of Russian perpetrators using universal jurisdiction.

But the worst of Russia's international crimes, the one from which all the others flowed, the crime of aggression, remained outside the jurisdiction of the ICC, and the doctrine of head of state immunity prevented national courts from prosecuting Putin and his foreign minister Sergey Lavrov. So, the international community began to explore novel approaches for a regional or U.N.-established aggression tribunal. As this book goes to press, these efforts are moving relentlessly forward.

This book goes to press as the war enters its fourth year. History is still being written, and how the war will end remains unclear. Nevertheless, with chapters written by several of the world's foremost experts in international accountability, this book provides an in-depth exploration of the novel international responses to Russia's invasion of Ukraine. In this way, it provides a blueprint for responding to war and atrocities committed by the most powerful nations in the world. It documents that the Russian invasion of Ukraine did not destroy the international legal system, rather it strengthened it, in a myriad of surprising ways. And it chronicles the vital role that justice continues to play in achieving peace and security around the globe.

PART I

Setting the Stage

1

INTRODUCTION

by Milena Sterio

The Russian full-scale invasion of Ukraine, which started on February 24, 2022, constitutes a violation of major international criminal law rules, imposes the need for accountability for Russian leaders who orchestrated and ordered the invasion and for the corresponding commission of atrocity crimes, and raises the potential that a new global order – a Grotian Moment – may be emerging. This book discusses the ongoing war in Ukraine through three different lenses: first, the book describes and emphasizes Russian violations of international law; second, the book's contributors argue in favor of the need for accountability, and they propose specific accountability mechanisms; and third, the book suggests that the crisis may be contributing to the emergence of a new global order – a series of Grotian Moments, which are paradigm-shifting developments in international law, typically sparked by a cataclysmic or catastrophic event. The book ends on a suggestion that various events, which have taken place during the Ukraine conflict, may constitute Grotian Moments.

First, Russia has committed major international criminal law violations in Ukraine. Based on relevant information that has been uncovered thus far, it appears that Russian forces have committed war crimes by targeting civilians and civilian buildings and other objectives. It also appears that Russian forces may have committed other violations of the laws of war. In particular, they are reported to have engaged in torture and other mistreatment of civilians, as well as in sexual offenses perpetrated against Ukrainian victims. It may also be argued that Russian forces have committed crimes against humanity in Ukraine, by launching widespread and systematic attacks against civilians. Some have argued that Russians have also committed genocidal acts in

DOI: 10.4324/9781003458166-2

Ukraine by, for example, forcibly transferring Ukrainian children outside of Ukraine and by having them adopted by Russian families in Russia. Finally, Russian leaders have committed the crime of aggression by using force against the political independence, territorial integrity, and sovereignty of Ukraine. Part I of the book sets the stage for Part II's discussion of various accountability options, by outlining the work of the prior international criminal tribunals, starting with Nuremberg, and including the Yugoslavia, Rwanda, Sierra Leone, Cambodia, and Lebanon tribunals, as well as by describing in detail the Ukrainian context, and in particular, the atrocity crimes committed by Russian forces.

In chapter 2, Sterio discusses the arc of accountability by reviewing the history of global criminal justice, starting with Nuremberg and concluding with the establishment of the International Criminal Court (ICC). In addition, Sterio describes other transitional justice efforts such as truth and reconciliation commissions, fact-finding bodies, and investigative mechanisms; according to Sterio, all such efforts combined can provide a blueprint for accountability in Ukraine. In chapter 3, Beta and Ramelli address the Ukraine crisis, by engaging in a detailed narrative of pre-cursors or roots to the Russian full-scale invasion, by analyzing how the war has unfolded over the past three years, and by explaining the role of external actors – states as well as regional and international organizations such as the European Union and NATO. Beta and Ramelli conclude that the war in Ukraine is one of the most consequential conflicts in the 21st century, which will likely have a lasting impact on the evolving geo-political order. And in chapter 4, Scharf addresses how the Ukraine conflict has shaped discussions within the United Nations, with a particular focus on Uniting for Peace resolutions, and how such resolutions, as well as additional action by the United Nations General Assembly, could be utilized in the context of Ukraine.

Second, the commission of heinous crimes requires that accountability be imposed on leaders as well as on direct perpetrators. The International Criminal Court is already investigating the commission of genocide, crimes against humanity, and war crimes in Ukraine but does not have jurisdiction over the crime of aggression. In addition, Ukrainian courts have already prosecuted perpetrators of war crimes, and some have suggested that a specialized war crimes chamber could be constituted within the Ukrainian national system, which would then specialize in the conduct of complex war crimes trials. **Courts** of third states have jurisdiction, under the principle of universal jurisdiction, to prosecute those responsible for the commission of atrocity crimes. Part II of the book explores these various accountability options, as well as issues associated with international or hybrid tribunals and prosecutions, such as legitimacy, immunities, defense rights, the need to prosecute those responsible for sexual- and gender-based violence offenses, as well as other investigative and procedural issues. This Part would also explore related transitional justice issues, such as reparations, lustration, security sector reform, demobilization, and others.

In chapter 5, Keenan focuses on the role of the ICC in accountability efforts in Ukraine. He focuses on Ukraine's declarations to accept the Court's jurisdiction, as well as on the scope of the Court's ongoing investigation in Ukraine; moreover, Keenan addresses the ICC investigation in a broader context, by arguing that the ICC's effort to impose accountability for those responsible for atrocity crimes in Ukraine sends a global deterrence message and positions the Court as a significant accountability agent in the international community. In chapter 6, Trahan focuses on the proposal to create an aggression tribunal for Ukraine. She argues in favor of the establishment of the Special Tribunal on the Crime of Aggression through the United Nations. Trahan also analyzes why accountability for the crime of aggression is crucial, and discusses various other proposals, before concluding that the international model through the Special Tribunal would constitute the most legally sound option. Chapter 7, by Noone and Kyrychenko, focuses on a competing proposal to establish a Ukrainian war crimes chamber. The authors describe other similar models of justice, including the Bosnian War Crimes Chamber, the Iraqi Special Tribunal, and piracy chambers in the courts of Mauritius and The Seychelles; they propose that Ukraine develops a similar war crimes chamber which would prosecute lower-level offenders, which would be positioned within the Ukrainian legal system, and which would be supported by the international community. Such a chamber could, according to Noone and Kyrychenko, close the capacity gap and provide yet another accountability option. In chapter 8, Dutton details the possibility of universal jurisdiction prosecutions in the courts of third states. She examines the underpinnings of universal jurisdiction along with the logistical and at times political challenges associated with universal jurisdiction prosecutions. Dutton then assesses the potential to utilize the courts of third states, under the principle of jurisdiction, to prosecute a select number of defendants who may already be present within the territory of such third states. In chapter 9, Kelly focuses on the prosecution of environmental crimes in Ukraine, before Ukrainian courts and under Ukrainian law. Kelly also discusses the possibility of prosecuting crimes against the environment as war crimes or as ecocide, and he positions both options as valuable accountability efforts in the domestic courts of Ukraine.

Third, scholars have explored the idea that catastrophic or cataclysmic world events may contribute to a rapid development of new norms of customary law; scholars have labeled such moments in history as Grotian Moments. The Russian invasion of Ukraine may constitute such a Grotian Moment, if it contributes to an evolution of new legal norms, or if it causes us to contemplate the existence of a new global order. Part III explores whether the Ukraine crisis is such a Grotian Moment, and whether our global order may be evolving. For example, the Ukraine crisis may cause us to rethink the role of NATO, may contribute to a more realist U.S. foreign policy, may shape the role of the Global South differently, may cause changes within the European system, and may contribute to an increasingly important role for China.

In chapter 10, Hathaway and Mills address reparations, by developing arguments consistent with international law which would force Russia to provide reparations for the war destruction in Ukraine. They thus focus on countermeasures and asset freezes, as well as collective countermeasures for violations of erga omnes norms. They also discuss the possibility of involving the United Nations General Assembly in imposing collective countermeasures against Russia, within the confines of international law, and the implications of such actions on other parts of the world where a similar need for reparations may exist. Chapter 11, by Ellis, focuses on investigating and documenting war crimes, and in particular on innovative ways in which the international community can take an active role in such efforts, such as through new technology. In chapter 12, Williams and Beta address negotiating justice in Ukraine; they focus on how parties to a future peace talk between Ukraine and Russia can negotiate issues of accountability and transitional justice. They also focus on specific positions that Ukraine, Russia, as well as other third parties would be likely to assume at a future peace negotiation, and they argue in favor of accountability as a key ingredient to any successful peace process. Finally, in chapter 13, Scharf provides concluding thoughts by focusing on the concept of Grotian Moments – world events, which cause the rapid development of international law. Scharf describes various Grotian Moments in the post-World War II area, such as those which transpired as a result of the Syrian war. He then discusses the potential for Grotian Moments in the wake of the full-scale invasion of Ukraine by Russia, such as the possibility of using Uniting for Peace resolutions through the General Assembly; the issuance of arrest warrants against heads-of-state by the ICC; the idea of prosecuting the crime of aggression in an ad hoc tribunal; using universal jurisdiction in the courts of third states as a model of accountability; prosecuting crimes against the environment; creating a pathway toward reparations through collective countermeasures; using technology to document atrocity crimes; and negotiating justice in peace agreements.

2

THE ARC OF ACCOUNTABILITY

A History of Global Criminal Justice

By Milena Sterio

Introduction

This chapter analyzes the arc of accountability by focusing on the history of global criminal justice since World War II. Since the Nuremberg and Tokyo tribunals established at the end of World War II, we have witnessed an expansion of the field of international criminal law and justice through the creation of several international and ad hoc criminal tribunals starting in the early 1990s. This growth of international criminal law has solidified the notion that those who commit or order the commission of atrocity crimes bear individual criminal responsibility. Moreover, in addition to the creation of accountability mechanisms, we have witnessed the international community's willingness to further support accountability by establishing evidence-gathering and truth-finding mechanisms.

This chapter provides a comprehensive overview of international criminal tribunals and of the concept of individual criminal responsibility for the commission of atrocity crimes. This chapter discusses the creation of the Nuremberg and Tokyo Tribunals, the relative lack of internationally created accountability mechanisms until the 1990s, and the more recent tribunals such as the Yugoslavia, Rwanda, Sierra Leone, Cambodia, and Lebanon tribunals, as well as the International Criminal Court (ICC). In addition to these international and hybrid mechanisms, this chapter discusses various internationally supported domestic prosecutions, including those for war crimes or other atrocity crimes in Bosnia, Iraq, and Kosovo, and those for maritime piracy prosecutions in Kenya, The Seychelles, and Mauritius. This chapter also analyzes various evidentiary, fact-finding, and truth-seeking mechanisms, such as the Syria and Myanmar Mechanisms, various Commissions of Inquiry, such

DOI: 10.4324/9781003458166-3

as those created for Ukraine, Syria, Libya, Burundi, and the Central African Republic, as well as other fact-finding missions and rapporteurs. Finally, this chapter discusses truth and reconciliation commissions, such as those created in South Africa and several other states, which have been hailed as key transitional justice mechanisms supportive of both accountability and conciliation efforts domestically. The plethora of accountability and transitional justice mechanisms, as described in this chapter, provides significant backdrop and context for the proposition that accountability is necessary for Ukraine – through the ICC's investigation and possible prosecutions, through an ad hoc aggression tribunal created specifically for this situation, through domestic prosecutions, and/or through additional fact-finding and transitional justice mechanisms.

Post-World War II Tribunals: Nuremberg and Tokyo

In the aftermath of World War II, victorious country leaders considered what type of punishment to levy against surviving Nazi leaders. British Prime Minister, Winston Churchill, favored the idea of summary execution, but he was overruled by two other Allied Leaders, Franklin D. Roosevelt and Joseph Stalin. Thus, Allied Leaders ultimately settled on accountability, which lead to the creation of the so-called Nuremberg Tribunal, a precursor to all modern-day international and hybrid accountability mechanisms. "The decision to place the surviving Nazi and Japanese officials on trial, presided over by international military tribunals, established a new precedent in the enforcement of international law and forever changed the meaning of justice in a postwar world."[1] The Nuremberg Tribunal was established through the London Charter of the International Military Tribunal in 1945; the Tribunal was located at Nuremberg, Germany, and its statute provided for the prosecution of three offenses: crimes against peace; crimes against humanity; and war crimes.[2]

Crimes against peace were defined by the London Charter as the planning, preparation, initiation, or waging of a war of aggression in violation of international law.[3] This included the act of starting a war without justification or in violation of treaties. The tribunal emphasized that such actions constituted a serious breach of international norms and principles, particularly those established by the Kellogg-Briand Pact of 1928, which condemned war as a means of resolving disputes. In fact, the definition of crimes against peace at Nuremberg was the precursor for the development of the crime of aggression; it may be argued that the modern-day definition of aggression in the Rome Statute has its origin in Article 6 of the London Charter.[4]

Crimes against humanity were defined as "murder, extermination, enslavement, deportation, and other inhumane acts committed against any civilian population, before or during the war..."[5] This new crime's definition encompassed persecution carried out on political, racial, and religious grounds; the Nuremberg Tribunal was the first-ever tribunal to prosecute individuals on charges of crimes against humanity. Although the modern-day tribunals' definition of crimes against humanity differs from the Nuremberg one in that the former contemplates that crimes against humanity can be committed during war or peace time, it may be argued nonetheless that modern-day tribunals have relied on the Nuremberg definitions of crimes, including crimes against humanity, as a template.[6]

Finally, war crimes were defined in the London Charter as "violations of the laws or customs of war" including "murder, ill-treatment or deportation to slave labour... of civilian population in occupied territory, murder or ill-treatment of prisoners of war... killing of hostages, plunder of public or private property, wanton destruction of cities... or devastation not justified by military necessity."[7] Like in the case of crimes against humanity, modern-day tribunals have significantly expanded the definition of war crimes and have divided war crimes into those committed during international armed conflict versus those committed during non-international armed conflict. Yet, the Nuremberg definition of war crimes formed the basis of any modern-day conception of these crimes, and the Nuremberg prosecutions themselves provided the idea that those who commit such crimes ought to bear individual criminal responsibility.[8]

A total of 24 Nazi government officials were indicted at the Tribunal; the Tribunal ultimately convicted 19 of the defendants; of those convicted, 12 were sentenced to death; three were sentenced to life imprisonment and four to relatively lengthy prison terms. Hermann Goring, one of the most notable convicted defendants, committed suicide the night before his scheduled execution. The Nuremberg Trials lasted 216 days and included the examination of over 100,000 German documents, thousands of photographs, as well as extensive footage of the Nazi atrocities.[9] From 1946 until 1949, a series of twelve additional military tribunals for war crimes against Nazi German leaders were held by the United States. These subsequently prosecuted defendants included 177 high-ranking German leaders who had supported the Nazi regime. Of these 177 defendants, 24 were sentenced to death, 20 to life imprisonment, and 98 to other prison terms; 25 defendants were not found guilty.[10] The combination of the Nuremberg Tribunal, where the most responsible Nazi leaders were prosecuted, and subsequent prosecutions of mid and lower level offenders, resulted in the idea that the imposition of individual criminal responsibility against many of those responsible for the commission of atrocity crimes is both necessary and appropriate. In fact, most post-World War II conflicts' resolutions have resulted in the imposition of some accountability measures on those responsible; Nuremberg may be credited as developing this idea.[11]

In addition to prosecuting German Nazi leaders, the Allied Powers decided to prosecute Japanese leaders as well; the International Military Tribunal for the Far East was thus established in 1946; its statute encompassed war crimes, crimes committed against prisoners of war, and crimes against humanity.[12] However, Allied Leaders agreed not to put the Japanese Emperor Hirohito on trial; this decision affected the Tokyo Trial from its inception as numerous pieces of evidence were censored and not publicly discussed at trial, in order to shield Hirohito from any potential liability. "In a contrast to the trials at Nuremberg, in which photographs and videos of Nazi atrocities were put on public display, the Tokyo Trial was characterized by limited discussions of details."[13] The Tokyo Trial began in 1946 and it ended in 1948; of the 28 Japanese leaders prosecuted, 25 were found guilty; a total of seven were executed by hanging while the remaining 18 were sentenced to various prison terms. After the Tokyo Trial, more than 2,200 additional trials were held in 51 different locations against approximately 5,600 suspected war criminals.[14]

The Nuremberg and Tokyo Trials created a new international standard of justice. First, these trials documented the aggressions, persecutions, and various atrocities ordered by the German and Japanese leaders. Such extensive documentation signified that denial of these atrocities could never become possible in the future, as well as establishing a precedent for the fact that a main function of international criminal trials is the setting of an accurate historical record. Like the Nuremberg and Tokyo Tribunals, subsequent international criminal tribunals have gathered extensive records of the atrocities committed within conflicts which they have investigated. Second, these trials firmly established the idea that heads of state, political and military leaders can bear responsibility for the atrocities which they orchestrated and ordered to be committed. "The postwar world proved that no individual, in spite of the power that many hold, would ever fully avoid accountability under the rule of law."[15] And, perhaps most importantly, these tribunals paved the way for the establishment of future international tribunals which relied on the Nuremberg/Tokyo "precedent" and the idea that political and military leaders ought to endure international criminal responsibility if they wage aggressive wars and commit human rights abuses. Yet, because of relative paralysis in the international community due to the Cold War, no other international criminal tribunals were established until the 1990s when the massive human rights violations in the former Yugoslavia and Rwanda prompted the international community to establish two new tribunals.[16]

The 1990s: Yugoslavia and Rwanda Ad Hoc Tribunals

The International Criminal Tribunal for the former Yugoslavia (ICTY) was created in 1993, pursuant to a Security Council resolution, as a mechanism for the restoration of international peace and security in the Balkans. The tribunal's statute encompassed three substantive crimes: genocide, crimes against humanity, and war crimes. The tribunal was bestowed with prospective jurisdiction starting in 1991, and with territorial jurisdiction over crimes which occurred within the former Yugoslavia. The tribunal's judges were international, and its seat located outside of the conflict area, in The Hague, Netherlands.[17] Thus, the ICTY was the first post-Nuremberg international criminal tribunal, functioning outside of the scope of domestic penal systems, using international judges, prosecutors, and defense attorneys, and applying international law.

The use of the Security Council as a body competent to create a new accountability mechanism was unprecedented, as until this point in time, the Security Council had used more traditional measures toward the restoration of global peace and security, such as sanctions or the use of force against offending actors. Thus, the ICTY itself, in its very first case, dealt with a challenge to its own legitimacy when defendant Tadic argued that the Security Council had acted *ultra vires* in establishing a new ad hoc international criminal tribunal. The ICTY confirmed in the *Tadic* case – perhaps unsurprisingly – that the Security Council had not exceeded its authority and that the tribunal was properly established.[18] In addition to validating the ICTY's existence, the *Tadic* case affirmed the more general idea that new international criminal tribunals could be created as measures aimed at restoring peace and security, and that individual criminal responsibility plays a role in the prevention of future atrocity crimes, as well as in regional stability.[19] The ICTY's notable achievements include the first trial chamber judgment in a case involving more than one accused (the so-called *Celebici* case); the deliverance of the first indictment against a sitting head of state, Slobodan Milosevic; and the first ever indictment of defendants on the grounds of sexual enslavement as a crime against humanity.[20] The tribunal shut down in 2017; over its thirteen years of existence, it indicted 161 individuals, sentenced 90, heard from 4650 witnesses, completed over 10,000 days of trial, and compiled 2.5 million pages of transcripts.[21]

Shortly after the creation of the ICTY, the Security Council acted again in 1994 using its Chapter VII powers to pass a resolution which set up the International Criminal Tribunal for Rwanda (ICTR). Like the ICTY, the ICTR was created as an international criminal tribunal, using international staff and applying international law; like the ICTY, the ICTR was located outside of the conflict country, in neighboring Arusha, Tanzania; like the ICTY, the ICTR's statute contemplated the prosecution of three major atrocity crimes, genocide, crimes against humanity, and war crimes. Similarly to the ICTY, the ICTR's territorial jurisdiction focused on Rwanda only, and its temporal jurisdiction was limited to 1994.[22] The ICTR shut down in 2015 after having completed multiple successful trials. Some of its major milestones include the conviction of Jean-Paul Akayesu on charges of genocide, which constituted the first modern-day conviction of genocide post-Nuremberg; in the same case, the ICTR recognized rape, for the first time ever, as a means for perpetrating genocide. Moreover, the ICTR convicted the first woman ever, Pauline Nyiramasuhuko, of genocide and rape as a crime against humanity. And the ICTR handed down the first verdict by an international tribunal holding members of the media responsible for broadcasts intended to incite acts of genocide.[23]

The ICTR thus used the ICTY precedent to situate itself as a second post-Nuremberg international criminal tribunal and as an ad hoc accountability mechanism capable of contributing to regional peace and security. The coupling of global criminal justice with peace and security is reflected in both the ICTY and the ICTR; such coupling would be further pursued through the creation of subsequent ad hoc and hybrid criminal tribunals as described below. Moreover, despite some of their jurisdictional limitations, it is undisputable that both the ICTY and the ICTR contributed to the development of international criminal law and thereby to the pursuit of global criminal justice.

Permanent International Justice: The Creation of the ICC

The Rome Statute of the International Criminal Court was negotiated in 1998, and the Court became operational in 2002. It is the only permanent international criminal tribunal, and it is in The Hague, Netherlands.[24] The Court originally had jurisdiction over three atrocity crimes: genocide, crimes against humanity, and war crimes. At the Kampala Review Conference in 2010, the crime of aggression was activated and functionally added to the Court's statute.[25] The ICC's temporal jurisdiction starts in 2002 and is prospective, and the Court has jurisdiction over crimes committed on the territory of states parties or by nationals of states parties. In addition, the UN Security Council can refer situations and cases to the ICC regardless of where crimes took place. Cases can also be referred to the ICC by States Parties, and the ICC prosecutor can initiate cases on its own, *sua sponte*. Moreover, the ICC functions based on the principle of complementarity: it is a court of last resort which will initiate investigations only if the relevant country is unable or unwilling to investigate and prosecute.[26]

Thus far, the Court has opened thirty-two cases and has prosecuted ten defendants.[27] Some of its most significant achievements include the conviction of Thomas Lubanga Dyilo for the war crime of using child soldiers; the development of an extensive victim participation regime; the development of several prosecutorial policies, including on the prosecution of the crime of gender persecution and gender-based crimes; the conviction of a defendant for the crime of destruction of cultural property; as well as the most recent prospection on the basis of gender in the Al-Hassan case.[28] Moreover, the ICC has reaffirmed the principle that heads of state are not immune from prosecution before international tribunals; in 2009, the Court thus issued two arrest warrants against the then-President of Sudan, Omar Al-Bashir.[29] Most recently, the ICC has issued arrest warrants against sitting heads of state of Russia and Israel respectively, contributing to the proposition that nobody is above the law, and that accountability for the commission of atrocity crimes attaches to all, including country leaders and presidents.[30]

Although the ICC has been hailed as a significant model of accountability, the Court's most important flaw remains its dependence on state cooperation – the Court can only be as successful as its State Parties allow it to be. "The Court cannot succeed if it is surrounded by hostile states, as all of its investigations depend on the host country's willingness to cooperate with the court."[31] In particular, states have not always cooperated with the ICC regarding the enforcement of arrest warrants; such warrants, especially those against high-profile heads or former heads of state including Al-Bahir, Putin, and Netanyahu, remain outstanding and therefore impede the court's ability to obtain custody of these individuals and to subsequently try them.[32] Moreover, another perceived challenge related to the ICC is the fact that three of the five permanent members of the Security Council, the United States, Russia, and China, have failed to join the Court and have at times actively undermined the Court's ability to function efficiently. Finally, another challenge includes states' ability to walk away from the court – in fact, Burundi and the Philippines have pulled out of the Rome Treaty in 2017 and 2019 respectively.[33]

Overall, the ICC has played a significant role in terms of deterrence, victim support, and the imposition of accountability. "The court's mere existence has… served as a catalyst for accountability."[34] In addition, the ICC complements national judicial systems, especially in countries with weak rule of law, and it promotes the principles of human rights on a global scale, encouraging all nations to uphold these values. The ICC will undoubtedly play an important role in the case of Ukraine. In fact, the Ukraine situation was referred to the court by dozens of member states in 2022; the Prosecutor formally opened an investigation in 2022; as mentioned above, the court has issued arrest warrants against Russia's head of state, Vladimir Putin, as well as five other individuals.[35] Ukraine has accepted the court's jurisdiction through two declarations pursuant to Article 12(3) of the ICC's Rome Statute;[36] in 2024, Ukraine also announced that it had ratified the Rome Statute and would become an ICC member state in 2025.[37] It is extremely likely that the ICC will continue its investigation in Ukraine; unfortunately it remains uncertain whether the Court will be able to obtain custody over the six Russian individuals against whom arrest warrants are currently pending.

Additional Hybrid Tribunals: Sierra Leone, Cambodia, and Lebanon

In addition to the creation of above-described international criminal tribunals, starting in the 1990s the pursuit of global criminal justice has relied on hybrid accountability mechanisms as well. Hybrid tribunals are courts that combine elements of international and national prosecutions. "They employ a mix of international and national judges; they apply both international and domestic criminal laws; they may be located in a host country whose violent past they may be attempting to address; and they strive to fulfill goals of international justice while also helping to promote the growth of the local judiciary, court system, and civil society in general."[38] Hybrid tribunals have been perceived as particularly important in post-conflict situations, where the local judiciary may not be strong enough to handle atrocity prosecutions independently, and where the mix of international and domestic features may produce the best justice outcomes. Some such hybrid tribunals have included the Special Court for Sierra Leone, the Extraordinary Chambers in the Courts of Cambodia, and the Special Tribunal for Lebanon.[39]

The Special Court for Sierra Leone was established in 2002, through an agreement between the United Nations and Sierra Leone. The Court had jurisdiction over atrocities that took place during the Sierra Leonean civil war, starting in 1996; it was in Freetown, Sierra Leone, and it employed a mix of international and local judges. Moreover, the Court's Statute encompassed international crimes as well as Sierra Leonean offenses, specific to the conflict.[40] The Court was able to successfully prosecute the former Liberian President, Charles Taylor, as well as twelve other defendants. The Court closed in 2013 and transitioned to a residual phase.[41] One of the most notable accomplishments of the Special Court for Sierra Leone was its successful conviction of Charles Taylor, through which the Court's judges reaffirmed the principle that heads of state are not immune from prosecution in international courts.[42] This principle is particularly important in the Ukrainian context, as it confirms the idea that Russian leaders like Vladimir Putin can face prosecution in international tribunals, despite their status as heads of state.

The Extraordinary Chambers in the Courts of Cambodia was established in 2003, through an agreement between the United Nations Secretary-General and the Government of Cambodia, in order to prosecute the former leaders of the Khmer Rouge regime for crimes committed between 1975 and 1979.[43] The ECCC, like the Special Court, featured a mix of international and Cambodian judges; its statute encompassed both international and domestic law offenses; in addition, the ECCC featured dual prosecutors, an international and a domestic one. The ECCC transitioned to a residual phase in 2022 after having completed three prosecutions.[44] Although the ECCC has been able to provide a limited level of justice to the victims of the Khmer Rouge regime, it may be argued that this tribunal has been less successful than other hybrids, due to its complex structural features, such as the existence of dual prosecutors, and due to its greater temporal distance from the time period of the commission of the underlying atrocities, as many witnesses as well as defendants were simply too old to participate in criminal justice processes.[45]

The Special Tribunal for Lebanon was created in 2007, pursuant to a United Nations Security Council Resolution; its mandate was to prosecute those responsible for the assassination of former Lebanese prime minister, Rafiq Hariri. The Tribunal was in The Hague, Netherlands, due to security concerns associated with having prosecutions in Lebanon; it featured a statute encompassing Lebanese law offenses as well as the crime of terrorism; it employed a mix of international and Lebanese judges.[46] The Tribunal was unique in that it allowed trials *in absentia*, unlike other international or hybrid tribunals. Indeed, the Tribunal held a trial *in absentia* in *The Prosecutor v. Ayyash et al.* case and sentenced several defendants to life imprisonment.[47] However, the Tribunal was not able to arrest any defendants, and, due this perceived failure, the Tribunal was not able to secure funding and was closed without entering into a residual phase.[48]

The various hybrid tribunals have, like the ICC, played an important role in global criminal justice by complementing the work of national courts and the ICC, and by imposing accountability for the commission of atrocity crimes in different countries and regions pursuant to a hybrid model. This model features an additional advantage over purely international tribunals in that it supports the growth of local judiciaries and, through this type of capacity building, promotes the rule of law and the respect of human rights across various jurisdictions. The hybrid model remains relevant in the Ukrainian context, where significant discussions have already taken place about the possibility of establishing a hybrid tribunal to prosecute the crime of aggression.[49]

Internationalized Tribunals and War Crimes Chambers

An additional model of criminal justice that has developed over the past two decades includes specialized internationally supported war crimes chambers. Examples of such chambers include the Iraqi Special Court, the Bosnian War Chamber, Somali piracy prosecutions in Kenya, Mauritius, and the Seychelles, and the Kosovo Specialist Chambers.

The Iraqi Special Tribunal was established in 2003 through an Iraqi law, supported and approved by the United States, to prosecute Saddam Hussein as well as other Ba'athist regime leaders. The Tribunal was in Baghdad, and it employed domestic judges and applied domestic law; it had jurisdiction over war crimes, crimes against humanity, and genocide, as well as Iraqi law offenses. Although the Tribunal was domestic, it was heavily supported by the international community, and namely the United States. The Tribunal prosecuted and convicted Saddam Hussein of crimes against humanity in 2006; the latter was sentenced to death and executed in late 2006.[50] The Iraqi Special Tribunal is the only internationally supported tribunal to feature the death penalty since Nuremberg, a feature which has drawn significant criticism from the international community. The Iraqi Special Tribunal shut down in 2011.

The Bosnian War Chamber is a specialized domestic chamber within the Bosnian justice system; it has prosecuted war crimes cases that have been transferred to Bosnia by the ICTY as part of its completion strategy, and it has also prosecuted its own cases, stemming from the civil war in the former Yugoslavia during the 1990s. The Chamber employs local judges and applies local law; it is located in the Bosnian capital, Sarajevo.[51] Like similar justice mechanisms, the Chamber has benefitted from extensive international support, and "its processes have been 'internationalized' to ensure procedural quality of prosecutions and to guarantee the delivery of justice pursuant to international standards."[52] As of now, the Bosnian War Chamber has prosecuted over 200 cases and has been perceived as a significant accountability mechanism within the Bosnian national system.

Other examples of internationally supported domestic chambers are the piracy courts in Kenya, Mauritius, and the Seychelles, where captured Somali pirates have been transferred and prosecuted under the respective domestic laws of these countries. These piracy prosecutions benefitted from international assistance by the United Nations Office of Drugs and Crimes, which has provided logistical and financial support, as well as from loaned prosecutors, defense attorneys, interpreters, and other professionals. "In this sense, piracy prosecutions... although conducted in national courts, have been 'internationalized,' due to support and involvement by the United Nations."[53]

Most recently, the Kosovo Specialist Chambers have been established as another model of internationalized domestic justice. The Kosovo Specialist Chambers were created pursuant to an international agreement ratified by the Kosovo Assembly and under Kosovar law; their mandate is to prosecute those responsible for crimes against humanity, war crimes, and other crimes under Kosovo law committed between 1998 and 2000. The Chambers are in The Hague, Netherlands, and employ an international staff of judges, prosecutors, and the registrar.[54] As of today, the Chambers have convicted a total of three defendants; in addition, several trials and/or appellate processes are ongoing, including that of Hashim Thaci, the former senior leader of the Kosovo Liberation Army.[55]

These various internationally supported war crimes chambers and piracy courts represent an additional model of accountability that has been used over the past several decades. "The Nuremberg model of international war crimes prosecutions has been appended in modern times with innovative prosecutorial models, which mix international and domestic law and may be oriented toward both restoring justice and rebuilding peace in war-torn areas."[56] In the Ukraine context, the United States has supported the creation of a domestic aggression tribunal which would be internationally supported, similar to the different models described above.[57] Thus, this type of model, where domestic prosecutions are logistically and financially supported by the international community, remains a viable option for accountability in Ukraine.

Investigative Bodies, Fact-Finding Bodies, and TRCs

To complement the work of various courts and tribunals, the United Nations and other international community actors have created various investigative and fact-finding bodies, commissions of inquiry, and truth and reconciliation commissions; these mechanisms are situation-focused and have limited mandates. Moreover, these mechanisms typically do not focus on accountability but rather complement other accountability bodies by conducting investigations, gathering and processing evidence, and/or performing a truth-seeking or conciliatory role. Some such mechanisms include the two investigative bodies created for Syria and Myanmar respectively, the International, Impartial and Independent Mechanism for Syria (IIIM) and Independent Investigative Mechanism for Myanmar (IIMM); the Commissions of Inquiry for Ukraine, Syria, Libya, Gaza, Burundi, Central African Republic; the fact-finding bodies, such as those in Gaza and Myanmar; UN Special Rapporteurs; as well as truth and reconciliation commissions, such as the South African Truth and Reconciliation Commission (TRC).

The IIIM was created in 2016 through a United Nations General Assembly resolution, with the mandate to collect, preserve, and analyze evidence related to international humanitarian law and human rights violations in Syria. The IIIM aims to support accountability efforts for those responsible for such crimes in Syria. Its work is intended to complement national and international judicial efforts by providing assistance to national and international courts and tribunals that may pursue prosecutions against those responsible for violations in Syria, including sharing evidence and expertise.[58] The IIIM collaborates with various stakeholders, including NGOs, civil society organizations, and international legal experts, to enhance its effectiveness in promoting justice for victims.[59] Overall, the IIIM represents an important step towards accountability in Syria, addressing the widespread impunity for atrocities committed during this prolonged and complex conflict. Its establishment reflects the international community's recognition of the need for justice and the rule of law in the aftermath of such severe human rights violations. Moreover, the IIIM was created through the General Assembly, in the face of Security Council paralysis, due to the Russian and Chinese vetoes related to any efforts to impose accountability on the Syrian leadership, widely perceived as responsible for many of the atrocities committed during the civil war.[60] The establishment of this mechanism therefore reflects the international community's willingness to bypass the Security Council and to act in order to assist accountability efforts in Syria.

The IIMM was established by the United Nations Human Rights Council in 2018. Its purpose is to support efforts to impose accountability on those responsible for serious crimes under international law, including war crimes, crimes against humanity, and genocide, particularly in relation to the Rohingya crisis and other ongoing violence in Myanmar.[61] Like the Syrian IIIM, the IIMM is tasked with collecting, preserving, and analyzing evidence of human rights violations and abuses in Myanmar. While the IIMM addresses a range of violations occurring in Myanmar, it was particularly established in response to the mass atrocities against the Rohingya people, including widespread displacement, violence, and persecution. The mechanism collects testimonies from victims and witnesses, as well as documentation from various sources, to create a comprehensive database of evidence related to violations in Myanmar.[62] Like the IIIM, the IIMM works with various stakeholders, including NGOs, human rights organizations, and international legal experts; it also aids national and international judicial mechanisms, helping to facilitate prosecutions related to the crimes committed in Myanmar.[63] The establishment of the IIMM reflects the international community's commitment to addressing the serious human rights violations in Myanmar and promoting justice for the victims of these atrocities. It aims to ensure that those responsible for crimes are held accountable, even in the absence of a functioning judicial system within Myanmar itself. The IIMM is another example of international community's activism to support accountability, in situations where the Security Council is paralyzed and where atrocity crimes and other serious human rights violations have been committed with widespread impunity.

The Ukraine Commission of Inquiry was established by the United Nations Human Rights Council. The resolution to create the commission was adopted in March 2022 in response to the escalating conflict in Ukraine following Russia's invasion. The commission is tasked with investigating and documenting human rights violations and abuses occurring in Ukraine, with the goal of ensuring accountability for those responsible. It consists of independent experts who gather evidence and testimonies related to the conflict. This commission aims to gather evidence, document incidents of violence, and assess the situation on the ground to ensure accountability for those responsible for violations. The commission comprises independent experts who conduct investigations, collect testimonies from victims and witnesses, and analyze the humanitarian impacts of the conflict.[64] Their findings contribute to reports presented to the United Nations Human Rights Council and may support future legal actions against individuals or entities involved in war crimes or other abuses.[65] The establishment of the commission reflects the international community's commitment to addressing human rights violations in the context of the ongoing conflict in Ukraine.

In addition to the Ukraine one, additional similar commissions of inquiry have been established over the last few decades. The Commission of Inquiry on Syria was established by the United Nations Human Rights Council (UNCHR). It was created in August 2011 in response to the escalating violence and human rights violations occurring during the Syrian civil war. The commission is tasked with investigating and documenting violations of international human rights law in Syria, including war crimes and other abuses, and it reports its findings to the UNHRC and the United Nations General Assembly.[66]

The Commission of Inquiry on Libya was established by the United Nations Human Rights Council. It was created in June 2011 in response to the human rights violations and abuses occurring during the conflict in Libya, particularly during the uprising against then-leader Muammar Gaddafi. The commission's mandate includes investigating violations of international human rights and humanitarian law and providing recommendations to ensure accountability for those responsible for such violations.[67]

The Commission of Inquiry on the 2014 Gaza Conflict was established by the United Nations Human Rights Council. It was created in July 2014 to investigate the events and alleged violations of international humanitarian law during the conflict between Israel and Hamas that occurred during the summer of that year. The commission's mandate included examining the conduct of both parties during the conflict and providing recommendations to prevent future violations and ensure accountability.[68]

The Commission of Inquiry on Burundi was established by the United Nations Human Rights Council in September 2016. It was created in response to the political unrest and escalating human rights violations in Burundi, particularly following the controversial presidential election in 2015. The commission's mandate is to investigate allegations of human rights abuses and violations occurring in the country and to report its findings to the UNHRC.[69]

The International Commission of Inquiry on the Central African Republic was established by the United Nations Security Council. The commission was created in 2013 to investigate serious violations of international humanitarian law and human rights abuses occurring in the Central African Republic amid ongoing conflict and instability. Its mandate includes gathering evidence, documenting crimes, and providing recommendations for accountability and justice in the country.[70]

In addition to the various commissions of inquiry described above, several fact-finding missions have also been created by the United Nations, or other international bodies, to investigate specific incident or situations. Examples include the United Nations Fact-Finding Mission on the 2018 Gaza Protests, which investigated the use of force by Israeli security forces against Palestinian protesters, and the UN Fact-Finding Mission on Myanmar, which investigated human rights violations against the Rohingya population.[71]

Special rapporteurs are typically appointed by the United Nations Human Rights Council; these individuals can investigate and report on human rights situations in specific countries or thematic areas. Examples include the Special Rapporteur on the situation of human rights in North Korea and the Special Rapporteur on the situation of human rights in Myanmar.[72]

The South African Truth and Reconciliation Commission (TRC) was established in 1995 after the end of apartheid to help heal the country and address the human rights violations that occurred during that period. TRC was established by the Government of National Unity, which was formed after the end of apartheid in 1994. The TRC was created through the Promotion of National Unity and Reconciliation Act, passed by the South African Parliament in July 1995. The commission was intended to help the country heal from the wounds of apartheid by uncovering the truth about past human rights violations and promoting reconciliation among South Africans.[73] Archbishop Desmond Tutu was appointed as the chairperson of the TRC. Chaired by Archbishop Desmond Tutu, the TRC aimed to promote national unity and reconciliation by uncovering the truth about past atrocities. A key feature of the TRC included the holding of public hearings, where victims of apartheid-era violence could share their experiences, and perpetrators could confess their actions. This process aimed to provide a platform for truth-telling. The TRC offered conditional amnesty to individuals who fully disclosed their involvement in politically motivated crimes, provided their actions were not gross human rights violations. This was intended to encourage more individuals to come forward. The commission thus documented human rights abuses, including torture, killings, and forced disappearances, creating a historical record of the apartheid era. It also made recommendations for reparations to victims and called for reforms to prevent future violations. This included proposals for the establishment of a Human Rights Commission and changes to law enforcement practices. The TRC produced a comprehensive report detailing its findings, which highlighted the extent of human rights violations and the need for accountability and healing in South African society. It is often cited as a model for transitional justice processes in post-conflict societies, balancing the need for truth, justice, and reconciliation.[74]

In addition to South Africa, other countries have similarly created TRCs. Examples include Argentina (The National Commission on the Disappearance of Persons (CONADEP) (1983–1984), which investigated forced disappearances during the military dictatorship); Chile (the National Commission on Truth and Reconciliation (1990), which examined human rights violations during Augusto Pinochet's regime); Rwanda (the National Unity and Reconciliation Commission (NURC), which was established after the 1994 genocide to promote healing and reconciliation); Canada (the Truth and Reconciliation Commission (2008–2015), which focused on the legacy of residential schools and their impact on Indigenous peoples); Sierra Leone (the Truth and Reconciliation Commission (2002–2004), which investigated the civil war and its atrocities); Liberia (the Truth and Reconciliation Commission (2006–2009), which addressed human rights abuses during the civil wars); Timor-Leste (the Commission for Reception, Truth and Reconciliation (2001–2005), which looked into human rights violations during the Indonesian occupation); Nepal (the Truth and Reconciliation Commission (2014), which was established to address abuses during the civil conflict); and Guatemala (the Commission for Historical Clarification (1997), which investigated human rights violations during the civil war).[75]

These commissions aim to acknowledge past abuses, promote accountability, facilitate reconciliation, and provide a platform for victims to share their experiences. It may be important to consider establishing a TRC for Ukraine; such a TRC could complement other accountability efforts and could thereby provide for a more holistic transitional justice approach.

Conclusion

As this chapter has described and discussed, different accountability and transitional justice models have existed since Nuremberg and Tokyo. On the accountability side, we have witnessed the creation of a permanent international criminal court, as well as a proliferation of international and hybrid tribunals, and internationally supported domestic war crimes and piracy chambers. Such accountability efforts have been coupled with other transitional justice processes, such as commissions of inquiry, fact-finding missions, special rapporteurs, and TRCs. These previous examples provide an important blueprint for justice in Ukraine; subsequent Chapters in this volume will focus on the specifics of different issues relevant to establishing peace and justice in Ukraine.

Notes

1 The National WWII Museum New Orleans, War Crimes on Trial: The Nuremberg and Tokyo Trials, Nov. 24, 2020, available at https://www.nationalww2museum.org/war/articles/nuremberg-and-tokyo-war-crimes-trials.
2 Agreement for the prosecution and punishment of the major war criminals of the European Axis, London, Aug. 8, 1945, available at https://www.un.org/en/genocideprevention/documents/atrocity-crimes/Doc.2_Charter%20of%20IMT%201945.pdf [hereinafter London Charter].
3 *Id.*, Art. 6(a).
4 Compare Agreement for the prosecution and punishment of the major war criminals of the European Axis, Art. 6(a), London, Aug. 8, 1945, available at https://www.un.org/en/genocideprevention/documents/atrocity-crimes/Doc

.2_Charter%20of%20IMT%201945.pdf., with Rome Statute of the International Criminal Court, Art. 8 bis, available at https://www.icc-cpi.int/sites/default/files/2024-05/Rome-Statute-eng.pdf.

5 Agreement for the prosecution and punishment of the major war criminals of the European Axis, Art. 6(c), London, Aug. 8, 1945, available at https://www.un.org/en/genocideprevention/documents/atrocity-crimes/Doc.2_Charter%20of%20IMT%201945.pdf.

6 Trial International, Crimes Against Humanity, available at https://trialinternational.org/topics-post/crimes-against-fhumanity/#:~:text=Crimes%20against%20humanity%20refer%20to,persecution%2C%20enforced%20disappearance%2C%20etc.; *see also* Robert H. Jackson Center, The Influence of the Nuremberg Trial on International Criminal Law, available at https://www.roberthjackson.org/speech-and-writing/the-influence-of-the-nuremberg-trial-on-international-criminal-law/.

7 Agreement for the prosecution and punishment of the major war criminals of the European Axis, Art. 6(b), London, Aug. 8, 1945, available at https://www.un.org/en/genocideprevention/documents/atrocity-crimes/Doc.2_Charter%20of%20IMT%201945.pdf.

8 Robert H. Jackson Center, The Influence of the Nuremberg Trial on International Criminal Law, available at https://www.roberthjackson.org/speech-and-writing/the-influence-of-the-nuremberg-trial-on-international-criminal-law/.

9 The National WWII Museum New Orleans, War Crimes on Trial: The Nuremberg and Tokyo Trials, Nov. 24, 2020, available at https://www.nationalww2museum.org/war/articles/nuremberg-and-tokyo-war-crimes-trials.

10 *Id.*

11 *See, e.g.*, Henry T. King Jr., *The Legacy of Nuremberg*, 34 CASE W. RES. J. INT'L L. 335, 348 (2002) (noting that "[w]hat Nuremberg did was to focus on indignities to the body and spirit of human beings" and concluding that "[t]hese declarations and conventions will remain with us forever as part of the inheritance of Nuremberg").

12 The National WWII Museum New Orleans, War Crimes on Trial: The Nuremberg and Tokyo Trials, Nov. 24, 2020, available at https://www.nationalww2museum.org/war/articles/nuremberg-and-tokyo-war-crimes-trials.

13 *Id.*

14 *Id.*

15 *Id.*

16 Matt Pickles, *Nuremberg war crimes trials 70 years on: a complex legacy*, OXFORD NEWS BLOG, Nov. 20, 2015, available at https://www.ox.ac.uk/news/arts-blog/nuremberg-war-crimes-trials-70-years-complex-legacy.

17 United Nations International Residual Mechanism for Criminal Tribunals, International Criminal Tribunal for the former Yugoslavia, About the ICTY, available at https://www.icty.org/en/about.

18 ICRC, How Does Law Protect in War?, ICTY, The Prosecutor v. Tadic, available at https://casebook.icrc.org/case-study/icty-prosecutor-v-tadic; *see also* ICTY, *The Prosecutor v. Dusko Tadić*, IT-94-1-AR72, Appeals Chamber, Decision, 2 October 1995; available on http://www.un.org.

19 *Id.*

20 United Nations International Criminal Tribunal for the former Yugoslavia, Timeline, available at https://www.icty.org/node/8403.

21 United Nations International Criminal Tribunal for the former Yugoslavia, Infographic: ICTY Facts & Figures, available at https://www.icty.org/node/9590.

22 United Nations International Residual Mechanism for Criminal Tribunals, The ICTR in Brief, available at https://unictr.irmct.org/en/tribunal.

23 United Nations International Residual Mechanism for Criminal Tribunals, ICTR Milestone, available at https://unictr.irmct.org/en/ictr-milestones.

24 *See, e.g.*, Milena Sterio, *The International Criminal Court: Current Challenges and Prospect of Future Success*, 52 CASE W. RES. J. INT'L L. 467 (2020).

25 European Parliament Briefing, International Criminal Court, Achievements and challenges 20 years after the adoption of the Rome Statute, available at https://www.europarl.europa.eu/RegData/etudes/BRIE/2018/625127/EPRS_BRI(2018)625127_EN.pdf.

26 *Id.*

27 International Criminal Court, Cases, available at https://www.icc-cpi.int/cases.

28 *See* Civicus Lens, *20 Years of the International Criminal Court*, July 7, 2022, available at https://lens.civicus.org/20-years-of-the-international-criminal-court/; *see also* Judge Sang-Hyun Song, Past Achievements and Future Challenges of the ICC, Keynote Speech for the 20th Anniversary of the Rome Statute, The Hague, July 17, 2018, available at https://www.icc-cpi.int/sites/default/files/itemsDocuments/20a-ceremony/20180717-sang-speech.pdf (praising the ICC's victim participation regime as a notable achievement).

29 *See, e.g.*, Benjamin Duerr, *Omar Al-Bashir and the Burden of the ICC*, JUSTICEINFO.NET, March 5, 2019, available at https://www.justiceinfo.net/en/40491-omar-al-bashir-and-the-burden-of-the-icc.html.

30 Elise Baker, *The ICC has issued arrest warrants in the Israel-Hamas war. Now what?*, ATLANTIC COUNCIL, Nov. 27, 2024, available at https://www.atlanticcouncil.org/blogs/new-atlanticist/the-icc-has-issued-arrest-warrants-in-the-israel-hamas-war-now-what/.

31 Milena Sterio, *The International Criminal Court: Current Challenges and Prospect of Future Success*, 52 CASE W. RES. J. INT'L L. 467, 478 (2020).

32 Elise Baker, *The ICC has issued arrest warrants in the Israel-Hamas war. Now what?*, ATLANTIC COUNCIL, Nov. 27, 2024, available at https://www.atlanticcouncil.org/blogs/new-atlanticist/the-icc-has-issued-arrest-warrants-in-the-israel-hamas-war-now-what/.

33 European Parliament Briefing, International Criminal Court, Achievements and challenges 20 years after the adoption of the Rome Statute, available at https://www.europarl.europa.eu/RegData/etudes/BRIE/2018/625127/EPRS_BRI(2018)625127_EN.pdf.

34 James A. Goldston, *Don't Give Up on the ICC*, FOREIGN POLICY (Aug. 8, 2019), available at https://foreignpolicy.com/2019/08/08/dont-give-up-on-the-icchague-war-crimes/ [https://perma.cc/PHS4-8XGP].

35 International Criminal Court, Ukraine, available at https://www.icc-cpi.int/situations/ukraine.

36 *Id.*

37 Mikhail Savva, *Ukraine Has Finally Ratified the Rome Statute: Why?*, WILSON CENTER, Sept. 25, 2024, available at https://www.wilsoncenter.org/blog-post/ukraine-has-finally-ratified-rome-statute-why.

38 Milena Sterio, *The Future of Ad Hoc Tribunals: An Assessment of Their Utility Post-ICC*, 19 ILSA J. INT'L COMP. L. 237, 240 (2013).

39 *Id.* at 240–241.

40 *Id.* at 241.

41 Residual Special Court for Sierra Leone, available at https://rscsl.org/#:~:text=The%20Special%20Court%20for%20Sierra%20Leone%20was%20set%20up%20in,1991%2D2002)%20civil%20war (noting that the Residual Special Court

for Sierra Leone was established in order to "oversee the continuing legal obligations of the Special Court for Sierra Leone after its closure in 2013").

42 Milena Sterio, *The Future of Ad Hoc Tribunals: An Assessment of Their Utility Post-ICC,* 19 ILSA J. INT'L COMP. L. 237, 241 (2013).

43 *Id.* at 241–42.

44 Associated Press, After 16 years and 3 convictions, an international tribunal closes down in Cambodia, Sept. 22, 2022, available at https://www.npr.org/2022/09/22/1124432798/cambodia-khmer-rouge-tribunal.

45 For a comprehensive criticism of the ECCC, *see* Heather Ryan, *And Then, Finally, a Judge Wrote the Shameful End of the Khmer Rouge Tribunal,* JUSTICEINFO.NET, Feb. 4, 2022, available at https://www.justiceinfo.net/en/87248-finally-judge-wrote-shameful-end-khmer-rouge-tribunal.html.

46 Milena Sterio, *The Future of Ad Hoc Tribunals: An Assessment of Their Utility Post-ICC,* 19 ILSA J. INT'L COMP. L. 237, 243 (2013).

47 United Nations, UN News, Justice served: Lebanon's Special Tribunal closes, Dec. 31, 2023, available at https://news.un.org/en/story/2023/12/1145217.

48 *Id.*

49 *See, e.g.,* Patrick Butchard, Conflict in Ukraine: A Special Tribunal on the Crime of Aggression, UK Parliament, House of Commons Library, Research Briefing, Aug. 27, 2024, available at https://commonslibrary.parliament.uk/research-briefings/cbp-9968/.

50 Milena Sterio, *The Future of Ad Hoc Tribunals: An Assessment of Their Utility Post-ICC,* 19 ILSA J. INT'L COMP. L. 237, 244–5 (2013).

51 *Id.* at 245.

52 *Id.*

53 *Id.* at 246.

54 Kosovo Specialist Chambers & Specialist Prosecutor's Office, available at https://www.scp-ks.org/en.

55 Kosovo Specialist Chambers & Specialist Prosecutor's Office, Cases, available at https://www.scp-ks.org/en/cases.

56 Id. at 246.

57 Rebecca Hamilton, *An Assessment of the United States' New Position on An Aggression Tribunal for Ukraine,* JUST SECURITY, March 29, 2023, available at https://www.justsecurity.org/85765/an-assessment-of-the-united-states-new-position-on-an-aggression-tribunal-for-ukraine/.

58 International, Impartial and Independent Mechanism, At a Glance, available at https://iiim.un.org/who-we-are/at-a-glance/.

59 International, Impartial and Independent Mechanism, Who We Work With, available at https://iiim.un.org/who-we-work-with/.

60 International, Impartial and Independent Mechanism, At a Glance, available at https://iiim.un.org/who-we-are/at-a-glance/ ("The IIIM was established by the UN General Assembly (UNGA) in 2016 after vetoes in the UN Security Council prevented referral of the Syrian situation to the International Criminal Court (ICC)").

61 Independent Investigative Mechanism for Myanmar, What is the IIMM?, available at https://iimm.un.org/en/what-iimm.

62 Independent Investigative Mechanism for Myanmar, Our process, available at https://iimm.un.org/en/our-process.

63 Independent Investigative Mechanism for Myanmar, Cooperation, available at https://iimm.un.org/en/cooperation.

64 United Nations Human Rights Office of the High Commissioner, Independent International Commission of Inquiry on Ukraine, available at https://www.ohchr.org/en/hr-bodies/hrc/iicihr-ukraine/index.

65 *Id.*
66 United Nations Human Rights Office of the High Commissioner, Independent International Commission of Inquiry on the Syrian Arab Republic, available at https://www.ohchr.org/en/hr-bodies/hrc/iici-syria/independent-international-commission.
67 United Nations Human Rights Office of the High Commissioner, International Commission of Inquiry to investigate human rights violations in Libya releases report, June 1, 2011, available at https://www.ohchr.org/en/press-releases/2011/06/international-commission-inquiry-investigate-human-rights-violations-libya.
68 United Nations Human Rights Council, The United Nations Independent Commission of Inquiry of the 2014 Gaza Conflict, https://www.ohchr.org/en/hr-bodies/hrc/co-i-gaza-conflict/commission-of-inquiry.
69 United Nations Human Rights Council, Commission of Inquiry on Burundi, https://www.ohchr.org/en/hr-bodies/hrc/co-i-burundi/co-i-burundi.
70 United Nations Research Guides, International Commissions of Inquiry, Fact-finding Missions: Africa, available at https://libraryresources.unog.ch/factfinding/africa#s-lg-box-wrapper-11490280.
71 United Nations, The UN Independent Commission of Inquiry on the 2018 Gaza Protests, UN Independent Commission of Inquiry on Protests in Gaza Presents Its Findings – Press Release, Feb. 28, 2019, available at https://www.un.org/unispal/document/un-independent-commission-of-inquiry-on-protests-in-gaza-presents-its-findings-press-release/; United Nations Human Rights Council, Independent International Fact-Finding Mission on Myanmar, available at https://www.ohchr.org/en/hr-bodies/hrc/myanmar-ffm/index.
72 Medecins Sans Frontieres, The Practical Guide to Humanitarian Law, Special Rapporteurs on Human Rights, available at https://guide-humanitarian law.org/content/article/3/special-rapporteurs/.
73 Welcome to the official Truth and Reconciliation Commission Website, available at https://www.justice.gov.za/trc/.
74 United States Institute of Peace, Truth Commission: South Africa, available at https://www.usip.org/publications/1995/12/truth-commission-south-africa.
75 *See, e.g.*, Dalhousie University Libraries, International Human Rights Law, Truth and Reconciliation Commissions, available at https://dal.ca.libguides.com/IHRL/TRC; United States Institute of Peace, Truth Commission Digital Collection, available at https://www.usip.org/publications/2011/03/truth-commission-digital-collection.

3

UKRAINE

The Current Crisis

Greta Ramelli and Sindija Beta

Setting the Stage: Why Ukraine Matters

Prior to February 24, 2022, few people spent their days thinking about Ukraine and how to end the war that had been raging on its territory since 2014. Now, the war in Ukraine has been at the heart of global headlines for several years, and many of the brightest minds in the world are spending their waking hours thinking about how to end it.

When Russia launched its full-scale invasion of Ukraine in February 2022, it immediately became the largest international armed conflict in Europe since World War II and has since dramatically changed the European security landscape.[1] From a continent known for promoting democracy and economic cooperation and relying on the United States for much of its security needs, 2022 marked the beginning of a trend to shore up Europe's own defense and security capacities. Russia's invasion of Ukraine exposed the fragility of the international security architecture, compelling European nations to rethink their defense strategies and accelerate efforts to strengthen their own military capabilities in response to the growing threat on their doorstep.

Located as a bridge between the West and the East, Ukraine is the largest country in Europe by land, sharing borders with seven nations, including four member states of the European Union, Belarus, and Russia. Due to this central position, Ukraine has been a critical transit route for much of Russia's energy flowing into Europe.[2]

With vast natural resources and a large industrial base, Ukraine plays a crucial economic role in Europe and beyond. It is a major agricultural powerhouse, having been named the world's seventh-largest wheat producer prior

DOI: 10.4324/9781003458166-4

to the full-scale invasion and the fifth-largest exporter,[3] supplying crucially needed agricultural goods to states in Europe, Africa, and Asia.[4]

Historically, Ukraine has been a much-contested land, caught between empires, from the Mongols and Polish-Lithuanian Commonwealth to the Russian and Austro-Hungarian empires and later the Soviet Union.[5] Despite the history of foreign domination, the desire for sovereignty and independence has been a driving force in the country's modern political movements, culminating in its declaration of independence from the Soviet Union in 1991.[6] However, Ukraine's path to fully realizing its independence has been fraught with challenges, as its geographic location between Russia and Europe – representing the West – has made it a central point of geopolitical rivalry. Over the years, Ukraine's efforts to forge closer ties with the European Union (EU) and the North Atlantic Treaty Organization (NATO) have clashed with Russian interests, which view Ukraine as a critical buffer zone and a part of its sphere of influence.[7]

The struggle for determining Ukraine's geopolitical positioning between the West and Russia came to a head in 2022 with Russia raining bombs over Ukrainian cities and occupying vast amounts of Ukrainian territory, much of which has since been liberated.[8] The war that followed has brought devastating consequences not only to Ukraine's sovereignty but also to its people. Tens of thousands of people have been killed or injured during the hostilities,[9] over six million Ukrainians have become refugees across Europe,[10] and nearly four million others have been internally displaced within Ukraine.[11] Russia is also accused of having committed numerous atrocity crimes throughout Ukraine, including multiple war crimes, extrajudicial killings, torture, sexual and gender-based violence, and forced displacement and deportations of children, among others.[12] These acts underscore the profound human cost of this war and serve as a stark reminder of the war's tragic and far-reaching consequences.

This chapter will explore the roots of the crisis, tracing Ukraine's tumultuous history, the motivations behind Russia's 2022 full-scale invasion, and the roles of NATO and the EU in shaping the conflict. It will examine Russia's position as a permanent member of the United Nations Security Council and a major global nuclear power, while also addressing the broader global stakes – such as the war's impact on energy and food security – and the pressing issues of justice and accountability.

The Roots of the Crisis

A Tumultuous Past

After the collapse of the Russian Empire, Ukraine, similarly to other smaller nations that had been part of the Empire, pursued its own independence between 1917 and 1920, fighting a bloody war, which it ultimately lost to the Bolshevik forces.[13] Later, Ukraine became one of the 15 Soviet Social Republics (SSRs) of the Union of Soviet Socialist Republics (USSR or Soviet Union) after having been formally incorporated through a 1922 treaty between Russia, Ukraine, Belarus, and Transcaucasia (now Georgia, Armenia, and Azerbaijan).[14] The 1936 Constitution of the USSR, developed on the basis of the 1922 treaty, provided that the USSR was a federal state where each of the 15 SSRs, including the Russian Soviet Federative Socialist Republic, had equal rights.[15] Under the 1936 USSR Constitution, some of the SSRs were further divided into Autonomous Soviet Socialist Republics, autonomous regions, and regions,[16] whereas, under the 1977 USSR Constitution, this structure was slightly amended to include autonomous republics, autonomous regions, and autonomous areas.[17] Although the autonomous structures had some special rights concerning cultural matters, in practice, like the SSRs, all decision-making was dictated by the Communist Party.

The Soviet era entrenched Ukraine as a critical part of the USSR's economic and geopolitical structure. Its fertile lands made it the "breadbasket of the Soviet Union,"[18] while its industrial centers, such as Donetsk and Dnipro, were vital to Soviet production. However, this relationship was far from equal and only fostered Ukrainian people's conviction of their own independent identity.[19]

The early years of Soviet rule saw an attempt to create a "Soviet Ukrainian" identity, which downplayed Ukrainian nationalism and aimed to replace it with a standardized, Soviet-wide identity.[20] The Soviet government maintained strict political control through the Communist Party, limiting the political freedoms of the Ukrainian people. Under leaders like Joseph Stalin, the Soviet government carried out purges, mass arrests, and executions that targeted perceived political enemies and dissenters. Many Ukrainians were affected by these brutal campaigns. The Holodomor in particular was a horrific, man-made famine that occurred during the early 1930s in Ukraine due to Stalin's forced collectivization policies – whereby all landowners were forced to give up their land and join large collective farms (kolkhoz) that produced agricultural goods for all of the USSR. Millions of Ukrainians starved to death during the Holodomor, an event that many among the international community view as a genocide.[21] World War II and a renewed post-war famine took the lives of another 10 million people, including about 1.5 million Ukrainian Jews.[22]

Looking at the history of Crimea, in 1954, the Soviet Union transferred control of the Crimean Peninsula to Ukraine, which was described as a gesture of goodwill between the two populations.[23] The decree with which this transfer was executed itself characterized the move as advisable due to the "territorial inclination of the Crimean Oblast toward the Ukrainian SSR, the commonality of the economy, and close economic and cultural ties between the Crimean Oblast and the Ukrainian SSR".[24] While originally Crimea was afforded the status of an Autonomous Soviet Socialist Republic, it was stripped of this status in 1945, becoming an oblast of the Russian SFSR. As an oblast without any special ethnic or cultural autonomy, it was also incorporated into the Ukrainian SSR. After the declaration of Ukraine's independence, Crimea's autonomous status was restored. The Status of Forces Agreement (1997) and the Kharkiv Agreement (2010) reached after Ukraine's declaration of independence in 1991 again complicated the relationship between Ukraine and Russia on the Crimean Peninsula.[25] The Status of Forces Agreement permitted up to 25,000 Russian soldiers to be stationed at the Sevastopol naval base until 2022, and the Kharkiv Agreement extended the lease through 2042.[26]

The collapse of the Soviet Union in 1991 presented an unprecedented opportunity for Ukraine to assert its sovereignty. In a referendum that December, over 90% of Ukrainians voted for independence, including a majority in regions like Crimea and Donbas.[27] This overwhelming support signaled a strong desire to break free from Moscow's control.

However, Ukraine's post-Soviet journey has been fraught with challenges. After gaining independence, Ukraine inherited the world's third-largest nuclear arsenal from the USSR. Although Ukraine lacked the technical capacity to maintain and control these weapons effectively as the necessary software remained in Russian hands, it created a precarious situation where both Russia and the U.S. wished for all of the weapons Ukraine inherited from the USSR to be transferred to Russia to limit the number of states that possess nuclear weapons.[28] Following a series of agreements and talks throughout the early 1990s, Ukraine finally agreed to transfer its nuclear warheads to Russia, dismantle any remaining nuclear infrastructure, and join the Nuclear Nonproliferation and Strategic Arms Reduction treaties.[29] This concession was secured in exchange for security assurances from the United States, Russia, and the United Kingdom in the Budapest Memorandum on Security Assurances of 1994.[30] The security assurances included a commitment to respect Ukraine's independence, sovereignty, and territorial integrity; not to use force against Ukraine; and to seek immediate United Nations Security Council action to assist Ukraine should it become a victim of aggression.[31]

Further, unlike the Baltic states, which quickly oriented themselves toward the West, Ukraine remained economically, politically, and culturally entangled with Russia. Energy dependency, especially on Russian natural gas, became a tool for Moscow to exert influence.[32] Additionally, Russian leaders, including Vladimir Putin, harbored the view that Ukraine was an inseparable part of the "Russian World" (Russkiy Mir), a notion rooted in shared Eastern Slavic and Orthodox Christian heritage.[33]

Amid these pressures and threats to Ukrainian national identity and independence, Ukrainian nationalism grew stronger, particularly in western Ukraine, where historical ties to Europe and a legacy of resistance to Soviet rulewere more pronounced. This nationalism was not merely a rejection of Russian domination but also a reflection of Ukraine's aspiration to join Western institutions like the EU and NATO, seen as guarantors of democracy and independence.[34]

Ukraine's pivot toward the West intensified after the 2004 Orange Revolution. Triggered by allegations of widespread electoral fraud in the presidential election, the revolution brought millions of Ukrainians to the streets to demand transparency and democratic reforms. The contested election pitted Viktor Yanukovych, a pro-Russian candidate whose campaign was allegedly run by Putin himself,[35] against Viktor Yushchenko, a pro-Western reformist. With sustained public protests, the election results were annulled and a re-run was ordered, leading to Yushchenko's victory.[36] This revolution and eventual election outcome demonstrated the Ukrainian people's shift to the West as opposed to Russia.

Despite the promise of the Orange Revolution, the following years were marked by political instability, economic stagnation, unfulfilled reforms, and disillusionment with Western integration.[37] Corruption remained rampant, and Ukraine struggled to diversify its economy, which was heavily reliant on industries inherited from the Soviet era, such as metallurgy, and domestic competition, which continued to be largely controlled by oligarchs. This economic fragility left Ukraine deeply dependent on Russia, particularly for natural gas.[38] While some progress was made toward EU integration, the slow pace of reforms and internal dysfunction hampered Ukraine's trajectory.[39] By the time Yanukovych was elected President in 2010 in free and fair elections, the strong push for joining NATO and the EU from 2004 had largely dissipated.[40]

During Yanukovych's presidency, Ukraine dropped its ambition to join NATO and signed the Kharkiv Agreement extending the Russian Black Sea Fleet presence in Crimea for 25 years.[41] During this time, Ukraine's democracy was in sharp decline and the social and economic situation only worsened.[42] Yanukovych's policy drift back toward Moscow's orbit eventually imploded in 2013 when his administration announced that Ukraine would postpone the signing of the Association Agreement between Ukraine and the European Union and instead resume dialogue with Russia about joining the Eurasian Customs Union.[43] This decision ignited mass protests in Kyiv's Maidan Independence Square, which have now become widely known as the Maidan Revolution (Euromaidan) or the Revolution of Dignity.

What started as a peaceful protest quickly evolved into a bloody confrontation between the protesters and Yanukovych's forces. The cruel assault on protesters on the night of November 30, 2013, was a catalyst for many to later join the revolution movement.[44] Between November 2013 and February 2014, protesters across all of Ukraine were faced with various forms of persecution, including murders, destruction of property, assault, torture, kidnapping, and arbitrary arrests and detentions.[45] During the Euromaidan, protesters were demanding that the authorities uphold human rights, as well as the resignation of the regime they viewed as corrupt. Many came out wearing Ukrainian and EU symbols signifying the call for aligning with the West.[46] The revolution culminated in Yanukovych's ouster and the establishment of a pro-European interim government.

The upheaval in Kyiv provided the pretext for one of the most consequential events in modern Ukrainian history: Russia's annexation of Crimea in March 2014. Exploiting the political vacuum and instability in Ukraine, Russian forces, disguised as local militias (so-called little green men), occupied key infrastructure in Crimea. This was followed by a hastily organized referendum under dubious conditions, where the majority purportedly voted to join Russia.[47] The international community quickly declared the referendum illegal and adopted sanctions and other diplomatic measures against Russia and Crimea. Putin later admitted that Russian soldiers were involved in the occupation and claimed that Russia was protecting the ethnic Russians in Crimea.[48] Since Ukraine's independence, Crimea remained one of the few locations in Ukraine that constituted an ethnic-Russian majority.[49]

Concurrently, pro-Russian and Russian forces captured the regional administration building in Luhansk and demanded a referendum for independence.[50] By April 2014, these forces had occupied nearly all key Ukrainian administrative buildings within the Donbas cities of Donetsk and Luhansk situated in the two Oblasts of the same respective names.[51] Due to overt and covert Russian interference, Ukrainian armed forces were unable to retake the territory, which self-proclaimed independence in May 2014.[52] With the signing of two failed ceasefire agreements – the Minsk I and Minsk II Agreements in late 2014 and early 2015, the situation settled into a frozen conflict.[53]

The annexation of Crimea and the war in Donbas marked a turning point in Ukraine's internal and external dynamics. Internally, it entrenched ethnic divisions, particularly in eastern regions, strained its economy, and complicated efforts to pursue democratic reforms.[54] Externally, it confirmed the existence of a threat from Russia and complicated its, by then clearly crystallized, goal of joining the EU and NATO.

By the eve of Russia's full-scale invasion in 2022, Ukraine had undergone profound changes. The events of the Orange Revolution, Euromaidan, Crimea's annexation, and the war in Donbas had solidified its identity as a nation striving for full independence from Russia's influence and democracy while grappling with internal hardships and external pressures. Economically, Ukraine was increasingly oriented toward Europe,[55] yet it still bore the scars of corruption and oligarchic influence.[56] Socially, there was a growing sense of national unity and resilience, even as the country faced immense challenges in charting a path forward in the shadow of its powerful neighbor.

What Sparked the Current War?

The roots of Russia's full-scale invasion of Ukraine in 2022 lie in a multifaceted context shaped by historical, geopolitical, and ideological factors. At its core is Russia's long-standing refusal to fully recognize Ukraine as a sovereign, independent nation. This rejection stems from a historical narrative that ties Ukraine's identity to that of Russia, rooted in centuries of shared history, from the Kyivan Rus era to the imperial and Soviet periods. For Russian leaders, particularly Vladimir Putin, Ukraine's independence is not merely a political reality but an ideological affront that challenges the notion of a unified "Russian World" (Russkiy Mir).[57] This belief has driven Putin's rhetoric and policies, portraying Ukraine as an artificial state created by external forces rather than as a nation with its own distinct identity, history, and aspirations.[58]

This ideological framework intersects with Moscow's enduring security concerns and geopolitical strategy. Since the end of the Cold War, Russia has opposed NATO's eastward expansion, viewing it as a betrayal of Western promises allegedly made during the dissolution of the Soviet Union.[59] The incorporation of former Soviet republics (such as the Baltics) and satellite states (Poland, the Czech Republic, Slovakia, Hungary, Romania, Bulgaria) into NATO and the EU, along with growing Western influence in other post-Soviet states (Ukraine, Moldova, Georgia), has been interpreted by the Kremlin as a direct threat to Russia's strategic depth and influence. Ukraine, due to its size, strategic location, and historical significance, holds a particularly sensitive place in this calculus. Although Ukraine was not on the verge of NATO or EU membership, its increasing alignment with Western institutions – such as signing the EU Association Agreement and pursuing stronger ties with NATO – was seen by Moscow as crossing a red line. For Russia, a Ukraine aligned with the EU and NATO symbolized a loss of influence in its so-called "near abroad" and the encroachment of Western military power on its borders.[60] For Russia, its "near abroad" is something less than sovereign, where Moscow wishes to continue exerting influence similarly to how the USSR controlled its satellite states.[61]

Ukraine's aspirations for closer ties with the West did not arise in a vacuum. Since the early 2000s, after years of a volatile economy, pervasive oligarchic influence, and weak democratic institutions that restricted civic space, many Ukrainians began to see integration with the EU as a pathway to reform, modernization, and prosperity. The EU symbolized not only economic opportunity but also the rule of law and democratic accountability – values that contrasted sharply with the corruption and authoritarianism many associated with Russia.[62] NATO, for its part, became increasingly viewed as a vital guarantor of Ukrainian sovereignty, particularly after Russia's annexation of Crimea in 2014 and its involvement in eastern Ukraine.[63] These aspirations, however, exacerbated tensions with Russia, which sought to prevent Ukraine from aligning with Western institutions at all costs.

In fact, Russia's resolve to hinder its "near abroad" from moving closer to Western integration and away from Russia's sphere of influence could already be observed in the late 2000s when a NATO statement promising membership to Ukraine and Georgia at the Bucharest Summit in 2008 was followed by a Russian incursion in Georgia a few months later.[64]

Vladimir Putin's approach to war as a tool of statecraft has been central to Russia's aggression toward Ukraine. His rise to power in the late 1990s was defined by his resolve to crush the Chechen separatist movement, projecting himself as a strong leader capable of restoring Russia's stability after the perceived chaos and weakness of the Yeltsin years. Putin's early presidency focused on consolidating domestic authority and reviving Russian pride. Over time, he expanded this vision into a more aggressive narrative of a "greater Russia," transcending modern borders to unite Russian-speaking and culturally Russian populations, such as those Russian-speaking Ukrainians residing in Crimea and Donbas.[65]

Indeed, even prior to 2022 and also 2014, Ukraine had a substantial political divide between its east and west, with many in the eastern regions continuing to support pro-Russian political parties and preferring more alignment with Russia.[66]

The so-called "Color Revolutions," combined with the large NATO expansion in 2004 where seven former Soviet bloc states (Bulgaria, Estonia, Latvia, Lithuania, Romania, Slovakia, and Slovenia) became NATO members, were pivotal factors in shaping Putin's increasingly aggressive foreign policy. The "Color Revolutions" were democratic uprisings in Georgia (Rose Revolution in 2003), Ukraine (Orange Revolution in 2004), and Kyrgyzstan (Tulip Revolution in 2005). To Moscow, they were a direct challenge to its dominance in its near abroad. The Kremlin viewed these movements as Western-backed conspiracies aimed at weakening Russian influence and promoting regime change. The fear that similar uprisings could inspire domestic dissent drove Putin to adopt a more assertive stance, both domestically and internationally, to prevent further erosion of Russian influence.

Thus, leveraging external threats to foster internal unity, Putin has used military interventions and nationalist rhetoric to distract from domestic challenges, including significant wealth disparities and growing poverty.[67] The narrative of a besieged Russia surrounded by hostile Western powers has served as a tool to rally public support, suppress dissent, and maintain his grip on power.[68]

Such policies have proven relatively successful for Putin as Russia's military actions in Georgia in 2008 and Ukraine in 2014 faced limited international repercussions[69] and achieved their strategic aims in the international arena – to prevent the states from moving closer to NATO and EU membership.

These outcomes could be viewed as having emboldened the Kremlin and set the stage for what took place in 2022.[70]

While the Russian aggression since 2014 ensured that NATO would be even more hesitant to accept Ukraine's membership, it strengthened Ukraine's domestic pro-Western and pro-NATO sentiments, further alienating the Ukrainian public from Russian influence. Volodymyr Zelenskyy, who campaigned and was elected as Ukraine's President in 2019 on a pro-peace platform promising to negotiate with Russia, had shifted his approach slightly by 2021.[71] Zelenskyy launched a policy focused on the reintegration of the occupied territories,[72] actively furthered Ukraine's NATO integration, and adopted a hardline approach toward Moscow, trying to curb any remaining influence on society.[73] For Putin, the combination of Ukraine's increasing Western alignment, Zelenskyy's firm anti-Russia stance, and growing U.S. support under Biden represented a direct challenge to his vision of Russian influence in the region. Putin has repeatedly justified his invasion of Ukraine by accusing the Zelenskyy government of being Nazi and framing the Russian push for a change in Ukraine's government and Ukrainian pro-Western policies as a fight against extremism.[74]

Putin's February 21, 2022, and February 24, 2022,[75] speeches recognizing the independence of Ukrainian self-proclaimed regions and justifying the full-scale invasion drew heavily on this background and tensions. By accusing Ukraine of being controlled by Western powers, framing NATO expansion as an existential threat to Russia, and misusing legal concepts such as genocide and self-defense, Putin launched what he called a "special operation" that has engulfed Ukraine in a devastating, bloody war since. Ultimately, these speeches were not only a justification for the invasion but a reflection of Putin's vision for Russia's place in the world – one that resists the post-Cold War order and seeks to reassert Russian dominance in the region.

How the War Has Evolved

Evolution Between 2014 and 2022

Russia's war in Ukraine did not start on February 24, 2022. It started nearly a decade earlier; however, back then it was restricted to Ukraine's eastern regions. The mass protests that erupted in Kyiv after then President Yanukovych suspended trade and association talks with the EU left a political vacuum that Russia managed to take advantage of to effectively seize administrative buildings in Crimea, stage an illegitimate "referendum", and occupy the peninsula[76] – an act of aggression that would later echo in eastern Ukraine.

The first border crossings of Russian armed forces into Ukraine were, in fact, recorded on February 20, 2014.[77] Later that month, "The Little Green Men", Russian military personnel acting without identification marks, took control of the peninsula. On March 1, 2014, Vladimir Putin openly acknowledged the presence of Russian troops in Ukraine, specifically, Crimea. On March 18, 2014, in response to the purportedly overwhelming support for Crimea's secession in the March 16 referendum, Moscow signed an agreement with the authorities in Crimea on the admission of the peninsula to Russia.[78] Many international organizations and states, including the EU, the UN General Assembly, and the Group of (then) Eight, condemned Russia's actions and refused to recognize Russia's annexation of Crimea.[79]

In April 2014 pro-Russian militants, echoing the tactics used in Crimea, began seizing administrative buildings in the cities of Donetsk, Luhansk, and Kharkiv.[80] Shortly thereafter, Ukraine launched a military operation to reclaim the territories, marking the beginning of the war in Donbas. In May, the Donbas regions of Donetsk and Luhansk organized referendums and declared independence, which was heavily condemned by Ukraine and many Western states.[81]

As the conflict escalated, evidence mounted of Russia's direct involvement in the war in Donbas. After a passenger airplane, Malaysia Airlines Flight MH17, was shot down over eastern Ukraine, the territory controlled by pro-Russian forces, in July 2014, judicial proceedings in the Netherlands confirmed that Russia was militarily supporting the troops fighting Ukraine's military in eastern Ukraine.[82] Throughout 2014, the conflict intensified as Ukraine faced both pro-Russian forces and the Russian army, allegedly ranging between 3,500 and 6,500 soldiers by August 2014.[83] Russian intervention in Ukraine was further confirmed after a Russian convoy of 260 trucks disguised as humanitarian aid was sent to Ukraine in August 2014.[84] It is believed that the use of more overt Russian warfare was a response to indications of a possible Ukrainian retaking of Donbas, which Russia was able to prevent.[85]

In September 2014, the Minsk I Agreement was signed, aiming to establish a ceasefire and outline steps toward a political resolution.[86] However, the ceasefire was short-lived, as both sides accused each other of violations, and fighting resumed. In January 2015, pro-Russian forces supported by Russia launched a new offensive resulting in the capture of the Donetsk International Airport.[87]

By early 2015, the conflict had reached a stalemate, prompting international mediators to negotiate the Minsk II Agreement in February. This agreement sought to create a ceasefire and a demilitarized zone, withdraw all heavy forces, organize local elections, and provide greater autonomy to the Donbas regions of Donetsk and Luhansk.[88] Nonetheless, the implementation of the agreement caused an insurmountable problem[89] and sporadic clashes and ceasefire violations continued. By then, the war had settled into a frozen conflict with Russia maintaining varying degrees of military presence in Ukraine while never openly admitting any involvement up until 2022[90] and skirmishes occurring periodically[91].

In the period after 2015, Russia continued to consolidate its political grip on the territories in Ukraine's east and equipped the pro-Russian forces in Ukraine to convert them into a conventional army.[92]

Meanwhile, Ukraine held the first presidential elections after the ouster of Yanukovych in May 2014, electing a pro-European figure Petro Poroshenko who re-focused Ukraine's efforts on westward integration. In June 2014, he signed the previously stalled partnership agreement with the EU and, in October 2014, pro-Western parties won the parliamentary elections in Ukraine.[93] In the following years, the Ukrainian government took a number of steps to further Ukraine's move toward the EU and NATO.

Tensions flared again in November 2018 with the Kerch Strait incident. Russian forces fired on and seized three Ukrainian naval vessels attempting to pass through the Kerch Strait, a critical waterway connecting the Black Sea to the Sea of Azov. The incident occurred near the recently constructed Kerch Bridge, linking mainland Russia to Crimea, a symbol of Moscow's claim over the annexed territory.[94] Russia accused Ukraine of violating its territorial waters, while Ukraine insisted it had the right to navigate the strait under a 2003 bilateral agreement.[95] The attack injured several Ukrainian sailors and resulted in the capture of 23 crew members, who were detained for months.[96] The incident led to heightened international condemnation of Russia's aggressive tactics and prompted Ukraine to declare martial law for 60 days.[97]

Between 2019 and 2022, geopolitical fault lines hardened further. Ukraine amended its constitution, embedding NATO and EU membership as fundamental objectives.[98] This move sent an unequivocal signal of Ukraine's irreversible westward trajectory, further antagonizing Moscow.

Volodymyr Zelenskyy came to power as Ukraine's President in 2019 with a promise to negotiate with Russia to end the war in Donbas, a policy he actively pursued during the first years of his presidency.[99] Zelenskyy sought to implement confidence-building measures, including prisoner exchanges and ceasefires in Donbas. He was also supportive of organizing local elections in Donbas in compliance with the Minsk II protocol with the goal of reintegrating the territory into Ukraine. However, in July 2020, Ukraine's Verkhovna Rada passed a law mandating that elections could only take place when Russia's temporary occupation is terminated and all forces – withdrawn, a move that Russia opposed.[100] In 2021, Ukraine, under the purview of the Ministry of Reintegration of the Temporarily Occupied Territories, further pursued the adoption of a number of laws and policies on transitional justice with the goal of reintegrating all of the occupied territories, including Crimea, into Ukraine.

On foreign policy, Zelenskyy retained the pro-Western and pro-European stance. In fact, in 2020, Zelenskyy approved a new National Security Strategy for Ukraine reaffirming NATO membership as Ukraine's central goal.[101]

The inauguration of U.S. President Joe Biden in 2021 and renewed transatlantic cooperation provided a favorable backdrop for closer NATO-Ukraine ties, deepening Moscow's hostility. In 2021, Russia began an ominous military buildup along Ukraine's eastern borders, framing it as a defensive measure in response to NATO military exercises. However, Western analysts identified them as a potential prelude to a larger confrontation.[102]

By the fall of 2021, the situation grew increasingly volatile. Nearly 100,000 Russian troops were stationed near Ukraine's borders, their presence accompanied by rhetoric underscoring Moscow's grievances with NATO. On December 17, 2021, Russia presented a contentious set of security demands aimed at "defusing tensions." Chief among these were calls for legally binding assurances that Ukraine would never join NATO and a cessation of NATO military activity in Eastern Europe. These demands were seen by the West as unreasonable.[103]

Throughout 2021, Western nations issued repeated warnings to Moscow to de-escalate its military presence near Ukraine, highlighting the dangers of potential armed conflict. Diplomatic overtures from Washington and NATO sought to manage the rising tensions, albeit with no success.[104]

In the weeks preceding Russia's invasion of Ukraine, a series of events unfolded that underscored the gravity of the situation and the diminishing prospects for a peaceful resolution. Western intelligence began uncovering signs of Russian intentions, including evidence of a plot to install a pro-Kremlin government in Kyiv.[105] Meanwhile, NATO reinforced its eastern borders, and the U.S. placed thousands of troops on alert as Moscow's rhetoric and actions became increasingly aggressive.[106] Diplomatic efforts continued amidst this military buildup; on January 26, the United States and NATO delivered written responses to Russia's demands for de-escalation. While rejecting Moscow's insistence on halting NATO's eastward expansion, they left the door open for discussions on arms control and transparency measures.[107] However, these responses failed to placate the Kremlin.

In 2022, Russia's military buildup near Ukraine's borders had reached nearly 190,000 troops. The early February 2022 military exercises with Belarus, the largest since the Cold War, signaled an imminent threat and raised further alarms among the West and Ukraine.[108]

The tipping point came on February 21, 2022, when President Putin recognized the independence of the breakaway Luhansk and Donetsk People's Republics, formally breaking from the Minsk peace agreements.[109] Three days later, on February 24, Russia launched a full-scale invasion of Ukraine. Putin justified the attack as a "special military operation" aimed at protecting Russian-speaking populations and "demilitarizing and de-Nazifying" Ukraine.[110] The invasion marked a dramatic escalation in a conflict that had simmered for nearly a decade, plunging Europe into its largest war since World War II.

Events Since February 24, 2022

The Russian invasion initially unfolded on multiple fronts: from the north through Belarus, from the east, and from the south via Crimea. The swift and multidirectional advance aimed to encircle Kyiv, decapitate Ukraine's government, and achieve a quick victory. However, this plan encountered heavy resistance from Ukrainian forces, reshaping the trajectory of the war.[111]

In the opening weeks, Russian forces made significant gains, capturing swathes of territory in eastern and southern Ukraine, including the Zaporizhzhia and Kherson regions.[112] The battle for Kyiv, however, became emblematic of Ukraine's resilience. Ukrainian defenders, bolstered by Western-supplied weaponry such as Javelin anti-tank missiles,[113] thwarted Russian advances in urban warfare, forcing Moscow to withdraw from northern Ukraine by early April.[114]

In the east, Russia concentrated its efforts on the Donbas, launching a series of brutal artillery campaigns to take control of key cities like Sievierodonetsk and Lysychansk.[115] These victories came at a high cost, with significant Russian casualties and depleted equipment. By the summer of 2022, the war's momentum had slowed, turning into a grinding war of attrition.[116]

By 2023, the war's dynamics had evolved significantly. Ukraine's military adopted asymmetric tactics, using drones and intelligence to strike deep into Russian-occupied territory and, occasionally, within Russia itself.[117] Nonetheless, the Ukrainian long-anticipated counteroffensive in the summer of 2023 was not able to bring the expected breakthroughs and by November 2023 had reached a stalemate.[118]

Conversely, Russia increasingly relied on mass mobilization and mercenary groups like the Wagner Group to replenish its ranks. This strategy underscored the strain on Russia's professional military forces. The approach changed further after the Wagner Group's brief mutiny attempt in June 2023, which prompted the Russian military to reorganize, reducing reliance on such private entities and focusing on more formalized troop units.[119] Despite numerical advantages, issues such as poor logistics, low morale, and outdated tactics have hampered Russian efforts.[120]

In 2024, Ukraine launched a new phase of the war, executing a bold incursion into Russia's Kursk region, aiming to disrupt key logistical routes and force Russia to reorient its forces from the Donbas region. In this incursion, Ukraine was able to take control of over 1,000 square kilometers of Russian territory. Despite the initial success, in the following months, Russia started to regain some of this territory while also moving further into Ukrainian territory in the Donbas.[121]

In late 2024, further developments in the war saw Russia employing thousands of North Korean soldiers to fight Ukrainian forces in Russia's Kursk region, while several Western states authorized Ukraine's use of long-range weapons deep into Russian territory.[122] The deployment of North Korean soldiers significantly increased the number of foreign fighters supporting Russia in Ukraine, which already included individuals from Central and South Asian states such as Nepal, Syria, Afghanistan, Uzbekistan, Tajikistan, and Kyrgyzstan, along with fighters from Cuba and Serbia.[123] In response to Ukraine's expanded use of Western-provided long-range weapons, Russia lowered the thresholds for the use of nuclear weapons in its military doctrine.[124]

Off the Battlefield

The war's impact has reverberated across the globe, with Europe suffering from economic turmoil amid the disruption of the import of Russian energy supplies. Sanctions and bans on Russian energy exports have driven up energy prices, leading to economic strain and inflation within European countries.[125] Sanctions have also had a substantial impact on the Russian economy, however, they have not been able to significantly hamper Russia's ability to continue its war in Ukraine.[126] Given the widespread cooperation and support from non-Western states, such as China (for trade), Iran (for drones), and North Korea (for missiles and other arms), the impact of sanctions on Russia has been limited.[127]

Ukraine's economy has also been decimated by the ongoing war. Cities and infrastructure have been destroyed, agriculture has been disrupted, and industries have been paralyzed.[128] This devastation has forced Ukraine to rely heavily on Western financial assistance, including loans and aid packages, to maintain basic services and support recovery efforts.[129] The resilience of the Ukrainian people has been tested to its limits as they navigate food shortages, unemployment, and the widespread destruction of their homes and livelihoods.[130]

The war in Ukraine has triggered an unprecedented humanitarian crisis, displacing millions of Ukrainians internally and externally to neighboring countries. Ukrainians face severe challenges accessing basic needs like food, shelter, and healthcare as the armed conflict continues. The war has deeply strained humanitarian aid efforts, creating a dire need for support to address the needs of those affected.[131]

Russian attacks on Ukraine's energy infrastructure have intensified the humanitarian impact, causing widespread power outages and disrupting essential services. This has led to harsh living conditions, particularly during winter, where millions struggle without adequate heating or access to clean water. These targeted strikes have not only worsened immediate suffering but have also complicated relief efforts and hindered Ukraine's recovery.[132]

Moreover, the war has been marked by severe human rights violations and crimes committed by Russian forces. These acts include targeted attacks on civilian objects and areas, resulting in mass casualties and widespread destruction, especially against energy-related infrastructure.[133] Reports of torture, rape[134], mass executions,[135] and other atrocities have emerged, contributing to the immense suffering of the Ukrainian people.

Amidst these reports, numerous accountability efforts have been launched in Ukraine and internationally, representing a landmark commitment to addressing grave violations of international law and fostering justice. These efforts have been notable for their scale and cooperative approach, setting a new precedent in the fight against impunity.[136]

In addition to the ongoing investigations and judicial proceedings, the war has fueled geopolitical realignments and tensions. While some countries have rallied behind Ukraine, providing military and humanitarian assistance, others have carefully navigated their positions to avoid alienating Russia.[137]

The economic and humanitarian impacts of the war, combined with the threat of escalation, have solidified it as a major global issue with long-term repercussions. The conflict has redefined alliances and shifted energy policies. Nevertheless, the road to recovery and peace remains uncertain, with the international community grappling with the question of how to foster a sustainable resolution that upholds sovereignty, justice, and human dignity.

The Global Chessboard: Who's Involved?

On the surface, the war in Ukraine appears to only involve two states, namely, Ukraine and Russia. On deeper analysis, however, this picture is further complicated by the involvement of third parties, in particular NATO and the EU. The role of NATO and the EU in the Russia's war in Ukraine is not limited to their provision of military aid and humanitarian and financial assistance to Ukraine in the ongoing war. The EU and NATO have been involved in Ukraine long before Russia's 2022 full-scale invasion in ways that significantly shaped the geopolitical context and the dynamics of the conflict.

Ukraine's wish to join the EU and NATO is widely considered a key factor in Russia's decision to launch the 2022 full-scale invasion. The primary justification that Russia asserts under international law for its invasion of Ukraine is the right to defend itself from security threats posed by NATO through its influence on Ukraine.[138] Russia claims that its military intervention is necessary to protect the security of its territory and people, as well as the populations of the self-proclaimed separatist regions of Donetsk and Luhansk.[139] Moscow has argued that Ukraine posed a direct threat, citing alleged acts of aggression and plans to join NATO, which Russia perceives as undermining its national security. Furthermore, Russia has invoked the controversial notion of "anticipatory self-defense," suggesting that its actions were preemptive measures to counter future threats.[140] Accordingly, Russia asserts that it had no other option but to invade Ukraine to defend itself from the security threats posed by potential NATO enlargement and NATO presence on its borders. The view that NATO bears responsibility for the armed conflict in Ukraine is commonly referred to in public opinion as "the NATO's fault argument" and has found traction among Russia's allies, certain politicians in Europe, as well as a limited number of academics.[141]

However, the perspective that the Russian aggression against Ukraine stems solely from NATO enlargement oversimplifies the conflict and overlooks broader factors.[142] In particular, this view fails to acknowledge that Russia was unlikely to be satisfied with Ukrainian neutrality as Russia's invasion of Ukraine was part of a bigger geopolitical strategy that is deeply rooted in a historical narrative, aimed at reasserting dominance over regions integral to its national identity and securing its economic interests in Ukraine.[143] Putin's 2021 essay "On the historical unity of Russians and Ukrainians"[144] and previous claims that Ukraine and Russia are one people with "a shared destiny" testify to that.[145]

Russia's interest in maintaining Ukraine under its political and economic sphere of influence or even incorporating it into Russia is further evidenced by Russia's apprehension about Ukraine's potential accession to the EU. Russia's ongoing efforts to infiltrate Ukrainian institutions and political processes, including its interference in Ukraine's elections, highlight its attempts to obstruct Ukraine's progress toward EU integration. These actions reveal Russia's apprehension about the potential economic and trade impacts of Ukraine's alignment with the EU, as well as its broader existential fears.[146]

NATO

NATO is a political and military alliance of countries from Europe and North America established in 1949 to promote democratic values and enable its members to consult and cooperate on security matters. According to its mandate, NATO's primary objective is to facilitate the peaceful resolution of disputes.[147] However, if diplomacy fails, NATO has the military power to undertake collective self-defense operations under Article 5 of the North Atlantic Treaty or crisis management operations under the UN mandate.[148] Collective self-defense is a key principle of the North Atlantic Alliance and revolves around the agreement to defend each other against attacks by third parties. In 2024, of the 32 member countries, 30 are in Europe and two are in North America.

NATO in the Cold War

To fully comprehend NATO's role in today's Russia's war in Ukraine, it is crucial to examine the geopolitical context surrounding its establishment. NATO was established during the aftermath of World War II and the start of the Cold War specifically to monitor and potentially react to security threats posed by the defeated Germany and the strengthened Soviet Union. In 1947, France and the United Kingdom signed the Treaty of Dunkirk to regulate mutual assistance in case of attacks by Germany and the Soviet Union. In 1948, this alliance was expanded through the Treaty of Brussels to include the Benelux countries (which at that time were forming the European Economic Community, a Predecessor of the EU). In 1949, the alliance was expanded to other European countries and North America, leading to the establishment of NATO.

Throughout the Cold War, NATO's primary focus remained collective defense against the Soviet Union and its satellite states, driven by the ideological and military confrontation between the Western democratic nations and the communist Soviet sphere. Since 1955, when the Warsaw Pact – a military alliance among communist countries to counter NATO's influence – was signed, NATO has operated as its counterweight. Multiple Cold War crises underscored the need for NATO, including the Korean War (1950–1953), the Berlin Blockade (1961), and the Cuban Missile Crisis (1962). However, with the dissolution of the Soviet Union in 1991, NATO's role evolved significantly from its original Cold War focus on countering the Soviet Union.

In the post-Cold War era, NATO mainly engaged in crisis management, cooperative security efforts, and partnerships aimed at maintaining peace and stability in the post-Cold War environment. In the 1990s, NATO had a strong presence in the Balkans, managing peacekeeping operations stemming from the conflicts in the former Yugoslavia. In Bosnia and Herzegovina, NATO led the Implementation Force (IFOR) and Stabilization Force (SFOR) missions to enforce the Dayton Peace Agreement. In Kosovo, NATO established NATO's Kosovo Force (KFOR) in 1999 to maintain security and stability following its intervention during the Kosovo War. KFOR is still active, ensuring a safe environment in the region and the protection of ethnic groups. In 2001, NATO's Article 5 was invoked for the first and, thus far, only time in response to the terrorist attacks in the U.S.[149] Thereafter, NATO troops were deployed to Afghanistan as part of the well-known International Security Assistance Force (ISAF) operation. In 2011, NATO conducted its Operation Unified Protector to enforce a United Nations Security Council Resolution aimed at protecting civilians during the Libyan Civil War.

Development of NATO-Ukraine Relations

NATO-Ukraine relations can be summarized in six key steps: Initial Engagement (1991–1994); Deepening Cooperation (1997–2004); Fluctuations During the Kuchma Era (1994–2005); The Orange Revolution and Increased Western Alignment (2004–2010); The Yanukovych Era and Cooling Relations (2010–2014); The Turning Point – Euromaidan Revolution (2013–2014).

Initial Engagement (1991–1994)

Since the collapse of the Soviet Union, NATO-Ukraine relations progressed from cautious engagement to growing cooperation, reflecting Ukraine's desire to align more closely with the West, which is also enshrined in the Constitution of Ukraine.[150] However, this growing cooperation was influenced by domestic political changes in Ukraine and varying levels of interest among NATO members. The first form of cooperation between Ukraine and NATO, since Ukraine had gained independence following the collapse of the Soviet Union, came in 1991, when Ukraine joined the North Atlantic Cooperation Council (since 1997 – the Euro-Atlantic Partnership Council).[151] In 1994, Ukraine became the first former Soviet republic to join NATO's Partnership for Peace (PfP) program, aimed at building trust and cooperation between NATO and non-member states. In the same year, Ukraine aligned itself with NATO's non-proliferation initiative by signing the Budapest Memorandum on Security Assurances with the United States, the United Kingdom, and Russia.[152] While the Budapest Memorandum was not a NATO initiative, it met NATO's interests in nuclear non-proliferation.

Deepening Cooperation (1997–2004)

Cooperation between Ukraine and NATO deepened between 1997 and 2004 as a result of new agreements and joint military training. On 9 July 1997, Ukraine signed the Charter on a Distinctive Partnership between Ukraine and the North Atlantic Treaty Organization, formalizing Ukraine's relationship with NATO and establishing the NATO-Ukraine Commission (NUC) to facilitate dialogue and cooperation.[153] The Charter recognizes Ukraine's sovereignty and role in guaranteeing European security. Additionally, Ukraine participated in numerous NATO-led military exercises and peacekeeping operations, such as KFOR and the NATO-led invasion of Afghanistan.

Fluctuations During the Kuchma Era (1994–2005)

President Leonid Kuchma continued and intensified efforts to strengthen ties with NATO, although the administration sought to balance NATO engagement with maintaining good relations with Russia. Under Kuchma, Ukraine declared NATO membership a long-term goal but refrained from making concrete commitments. However, progress in cooperation between Ukraine and NATO was paused following scandals regarding widespread allegations of corruption and authoritarian practices.

The Orange Revolution and Increased Western Alignment (2004–2010)

The 2004 Orange Revolution brought President Viktor Yushchenko to power, marking a shift toward a more pro-Western foreign policy. Yushchenko actively pursued closer ties with NATO and the EU. In particular, in 2008, Ukraine expressed its desire to join NATO and requested a Membership Action Plan (MAP), which is a structured program to help aspiring members prepare for NATO membership. This is viewed as a formal step toward NATO membership. However, at the 2008 NATO Summit in Bucharest, NATO members were divided over Ukraine's request. While some countries, such as the United States, supported granting Ukraine a MAP, others, particularly France and Germany, opposed it. Their reluctance was primarily based on concerns about how granting Ukraine a MAP would be perceived by Russia, which strongly opposed NATO's eastward expansion. These countries feared that moving forward with Ukraine's membership process could provoke Russia and destabilize the region. The 2008 NATO summit in Bucharest resulted in a compromise: Ukraine was promised eventual membership but was not granted a MAP at that time.[154] This left Ukraine in an ambiguous position: Ukraine was officially recognized as a future NATO member but there was no agreed timeline or plan for its actual membership. Ukrainian public opinion was divided over Ukraine's attempts to become a NATO member, with the opposition being primarily located in the eastern and southern regions.

The Yanukovych Era and Cooling Relations (2010–2014)

Viktor Yanukovych declared Ukraine a "non-aligned" country, seeking to balance Ukraine's relationships with both Russia and the West but effectively halting efforts to join NATO. This approach was a sharp departure from the pro-Western policies of his predecessor, Viktor Yushchenko, who had actively pursued NATO membership following the 2004 Orange Revolution. Yanukovych's non-alignment policy reflected his desire to ease tensions with Russia, which strongly opposed NATO's expansion and past Ukrainian efforts to join NATO. It was also aligned with Yanukovych's domestic political strategy, as many of his supporters in eastern and southern Ukraine were skeptical of NATO and maintained closer cultural and political ties to Russia. Accordingly, in 2010 the Ukrainian parliament, dominated by Yanukovych's allies, passed legislation declaring non-alignment as a core component of its foreign policy.[155] Key components of this policy included (1) renunciation of NATO membership goals; (2) no membership in military alliances, and (3) balanced relations. Despite the non-alignment declaration, Ukraine maintained limited cooperation with NATO, as the two sides had established long-standing ties under frameworks like the 1997 NATO-Ukraine Charter on a Distinctive Partnership. For example, it still contributed troops to NATO-led operations, including the ISAF in Afghanistan, and to some degree it continued its modernization efforts in line with NATO standards.

The Turning Point – Euromaidan Revolution (2013–2014)

Sparked by Yanukovych's decision to reject an EU Association Agreement in favor of closer ties with Russia, massive protests led to his ouster in early 2014 (Euromaidan Revolution). Russia viewed the revolution as a Western-backed coup threatening its influence over Ukraine and quickly exploited the political chaos for its own geopolitical interests. In March 2014, Russian troops, many disguised as local militias (little green men), occupied the Crimean Peninsula. The international community condemned Russia's illegal annexation of Crimea. Also, NATO condemned Russia's actions[156] and started to intensify its support for Ukraine, providing political backing, capacity-building programs, and increased military cooperation. This period marked a decisive shift in Ukraine's orientation toward Euro-Atlantic integration.

NATO's Role Following Russia's Annexation of Crimea

Until Russia's annexation of Crimea, there was a widely held view that NATO, as a product of the Cold War, had become less relevant in the post-Soviet era. Many argued that NATO's primary purpose – to counterbalance the Soviet Union – was obsolete, and its continued existence risked provoking unnecessary tensions with Russia.[157] However, a notable shift in NATO's engagement came with Russia's annexation of Crimea in 2014. Russia's annexation of Crimea in 2014 underscored that the alliance's role as a counterbalance to Russian aggression was far from obsolete, a view that was further confirmed by the security threats posed by Russia's large-scale aggression in 2022.

Following Russia's annexation of Crimea, NATO members pledged to allocate 2% of their gross domestic product (GDP) to defense spending by 2024.[158] They also agreed to strengthen NATO's presence in the Alliance's eastern region through the NATO Enhanced Forward Presence (EFP) initiative. This initiative was designed to reassure and protect NATO's eastern members, particularly those bordering Russia or near the conflict in Ukraine,[159] by deploying four multinational battalion-sized battlegroups in Estonia, Latvia, Lithuania, and Poland. Beyond the EFP, NATO enhanced its air policing missions, increased naval patrols in the Baltic and Black Seas, and expanded its cyber defense initiatives.

NATO's Role Post-2022 Russian Aggression

Russia's full-scale invasion of Ukraine in February 2022 has profoundly impacted NATO's role and engagement in Europe, redefining its strategic priorities and reinvigorating its perceived role as a protector of regional security and a deterrent of Russia's aggression. The invasion brought a level of cohesion among NATO members that had been lacking in previous years. Disputes over burden-sharing and strategy were temporarily set aside as allies united to condemn Russia's actions and respond collectively.

With regard to the situation in Ukraine, NATO invoked Article 4, signaling heightened concern from its members located near Russia, and coordinated efforts to address the crisis politically, economically, and militarily. This unity reaffirmed NATO's original mission of collective defense under Article 5 and dispelled lingering doubts about its strategic focus.

One of the most striking consequences of Russia's 2022 invasion was the accelerated expansion of NATO membership. Finland and Sweden, long known for their neutrality, abandoned decades of non-alignment and applied for membership, which was granted in 2023 and 2024 respectively.[160] This marked a significant geopolitical shift, driven by heightened security concerns in the face of Russian aggression. Finland's accession extended NATO's direct border with Russia, while Sweden's advanced military capabilities bolstered NATO's presence in the Baltic Sea region. These new memberships demonstrate that NATO's deterrence role remains a powerful incentive for countries seeking security guarantees.

Contrary to what everyone expected and what Russian officials had expressed previously, as Finland and Sweden declared they would become NATO members, Putin announced that he did not view it as a threat to Russia.[161] As some have argued, Russia's reaction to Finland and Sweden's NATO membership demonstrates that Russia's ambitions in Ukraine go further than solely protecting Russia from NATO. According to this view, Russia's long-term objective has been to maintain Ukraine in its sphere of influence, if not direct incorporation into the Russian state, which is evidenced by Russia's continuous infiltrations into Ukrainian institutions.[162]

In response to the invasion, NATO also dramatically increased its military presence on its eastern flank. Additional battle groups were deployed to Romania, Bulgaria, Slovakia, and Hungary, complementing the existing EFP in Poland and the Baltic states. The alliance also enhanced its air and naval patrols, particularly in the Black Sea and Baltic regions, while prepositioning equipment and troops to improve readiness for any potential escalation.

The crisis spurred significant increases in defense spending among NATO members. The commitment for allies to allocate 2% of their GDP to defense – a benchmark that has been inconsistently met – gained renewed urgency.[163] Germany announced a landmark €100 billion investment in military modernization, reversing decades of underfunding.[164] Other European nations such as Poland and the Baltic states similarly accelerated their defense investments, acquiring advanced systems to deter Russian aggression. The United States,

NATO's largest contributor, reinforced its leadership by deploying additional troops to Europe, significantly raising its presence.[165]

At the strategic level, NATO updated its Strategic Concept at the Madrid Summit in 2022, explicitly identifying Russia as the "most significant and direct threat" to Euro-Atlantic security.[166] This marked a stark departure from earlier concepts that sought a more cooperative relationship with Moscow. NATO also unveiled a new force model aimed at having 300,000 troops at high readiness, a significant increase over previous capabilities, reflecting the alliance's determination to adapt to emerging threats.[167]

As for Ukraine's military defense, NATO has provided unprecedented support. Member states have supplied advanced weaponry, including HIMARS rocket systems, air defense platforms, and armored vehicles, to bolster Ukraine's defensive capabilities. Training programs and non-lethal assistance, such as medical supplies and cyber defense tools, have further enhanced Ukraine's resilience. NATO's establishment of a Defense Contact Group has streamlined coordination among allies, ensuring efficient and sustained support for Ukraine.

Additionally, NATO has intensified its efforts to integrate hybrid threat countermeasures into its defense planning. Energy security has emerged as a critical focus, with NATO supporting efforts to diversify energy supplies and protect critical infrastructure from potential sabotage.

Ukraine's NATO Membership Process

Discussions over Ukraine's accession to NATO are ongoing and multifaceted, influenced by continuing geopolitical tensions, potential peace negotiations with Russia, and NATO's broader strategic considerations. Since 2022, Ukraine's push for membership has undoubtedly intensified and Ukraine continues to make progress in aligning its military and political structures with NATO standards. Efforts include enhanced defense sector reforms and modernized military capabilities, which NATO closely monitors. However, significant hurdles remain. Some member states remain cautious about extending a formal membership invitation due to fears of escalating the conflict with Russia and potential implications for Article 5 of NATO's treaty, which mandates collective defense.

Recently, the NATO Parliamentary Assembly called for Ukraine's accession "as soon as possible," signaling broad political support among some members.[168] Despite this, the necessary consensus among all NATO members for extending a formal invitation to Ukraine is far from secured. NATO Secretary-General Mark Rutte has been prioritizing providing immediate military aid to Ukraine over addressing the timeline for full membership. This approach reflects NATO's desire to strengthen Ukraine's defense capabilities while navigating the complex political realities of enlargement.

European Union

The European Union (EU) is a political and economic union comprising 27 European countries that work together to promote integration, cooperation, and shared prosperity across the continent. Established in its current form by the Treaty of Maastricht, which was signed in 1992 and entered into force in 1993, the EU is a unique supranational organization designed to foster peace, stability, and economic growth through collective governance and shared policies.

Overview of Ukraine-EU Relations since 1991

Since the collapse of the Soviet Union in 1991 and the establishment of the European Union in its current form in 1993, relations between Ukraine and the EU have undergone significant evolution. The partnership has progressed from initial diplomatic engagement to deeper political, economic, and security cooperation, with pivotal moments of alignment and friction shaped by Ukraine's complex geopolitical position between Europe and Russia. Ukraine-EU relations can be summarized into six main phases as discussed below: Early Engagement and Partnership (1991–2004); The Orange Revolution and European Aspirations (2004–2010); Cooling Relations During the Yanukovych Era (2010–2014); Post-Euromaidan Period and Conflict with Russia (2013–2019); Intensifying Partnership and Resilience Amidst Russian Aggression (2019–2022); and Post-2022: Full-Scale Russian Invasion.

Early Engagement and Partnership (1991–2004)

Initial relations with the EU focused on fostering stability, democracy, and economic reform. In 1994, the EU and Ukraine signed a Partnership and Cooperation Agreement (PCA), which came into force in 1998.[169] This agreement laid the groundwork for political dialogue, trade cooperation, and support for Ukraine's transition to a market economy.[170] Throughout the 1990s, the EU also provided technical assistance through programs like TACIS (Technical Assistance to the Commonwealth of Independent States) to aid Ukraine's institutional and economic reforms.[171] However, there was no clear roadmap for EU membership during this period.

The Orange Revolution and European Aspirations (2004–2010)

Ukraine's relations with the EU took a significant turn during and after the Orange Revolution (2004–2005), which was sparked by public protests against election fraud and signaled Ukraine's desire for stronger ties with the

West. The EU supported Ukraine's democratic aspirations and acknowledged its geopolitical importance as the political situation appeared to open a window of opportunity for strengthening Ukraine-EU relations.[172] In this context, in 2005, the EU and Ukraine adopted the European Neighbourhood Policy (ENP) Action Plan, outlining steps to enhance political, economic, and sectoral cooperation.[173] During this period, Ukraine sought closer economic integration, leading to early discussions about a potential Deep and Comprehensive Free Trade Area (DCFTA). Despite Ukraine's clear interest and ambition to join the EU, EU member states remained cautious, focusing on partnership initiatives rather than offering a membership process.

Cooling Relations During the Yanukovych Era (2010–2014)

The election of President Viktor Yanukovych in 2010 led to a period of tension in EU-Ukraine relations as Ukraine oscillated between European integration and closer ties with Russia. While initially pursuing the EU Association Agreement, Yanukovych's administration ultimately rejected it under pressure from Moscow and, instead, signed agreements for closer economic ties with Russia. Generally, Yanukovych's political strategy aligned more with Russian influence, which strained relations with the EU.[174]

Post-Euromaidan Period and Conflict with Russia (2013–2019)

After the widespread Euromaidan protests and the ouster of Yanukovych in 2014, Ukraine signed the EU-Ukraine Association Agreement which included a Deep and Comprehensive Free Trade Area (DCFTA).[175] This agreement symbolized Ukraine's commitment to European integration and facilitated economic cooperation between the EU and Ukraine.

In this period, Ukraine's relationship with the EU deepened significantly, despite the backdrop of the annexation of Crimea by Russia and the ongoing conflict in Eastern Ukraine. The signing of the EU-Ukraine Association Agreement in 2014 was a turning point that introduced a framework for closer political association and economic integration.

In 2016, the Deep and Comprehensive Free Trade Area (DCFTA) came into provisional application, eliminating tariffs on most goods and aligning Ukraine's regulations with EU standards in areas like trade, customs, competition, and public procurement.[176] This alignment strengthened Ukraine's economic ties with the EU, which became its largest trading partner by 2019.

In 2017, the EU granted Ukrainian citizens visa-free travel to the Schengen Area for short stays, a highly symbolic achievement that reinforced Ukraine's European orientation.[177]

Additionally, since 2014, the EU has provided substantial financial and technical support to Ukraine, focusing on governance, anti-corruption measures, and judicial reforms. Initiatives like the EU Advisory Mission (EUAM) Ukraine were launched to support civilian security reform.[178]

As for security cooperation, while not a member of NATO, Ukraine has also increased its security dialogue and cooperation with the EU, particularly through the EU's Common Security and Defence Policy (CSDP) initiatives.

Intensifying Partnership and Resilience Amidst Russian Aggression (2019–2022)

Under President Zelenskyy, who took office in 2019, Ukraine-EU relations gained momentum. Amidst escalating tensions with Russia, the EU emerged as a steadfast partner in supporting Ukraine's sovereignty and territorial integrity. Since 2019, Ukraine and the EU continued to deepen economic ties, with the DCFTA serving as a vehicle for closer alignment with EU standards and regulations.

In parallel, the EU maintained pressure on Ukraine to implement critical reforms, including judicial independence, anti-corruption measures, and decentralization, reinforcing past efforts and initiatives taken since 2014. The EU's financial support was often tied to the successful implementation of these reforms.

Post-2022: Full-Scale Russian Invasion

The full-scale Russian invasion of Ukraine in February 2022 was a seismic event that further transformed Ukraine-EU relations. The crisis galvanized unprecedented levels of support from the EU, marking a new phase in their partnership.

EU's Role Post-2022 Russian Aggression

The 2022 full-scale Russian invasion of Ukraine marked a historic turning point in Ukraine-EU relations, leading to unprecedented changes in political, economic, security, and humanitarian dynamics. Most notably, since 2022, Ukraine has received an unprecedented level of security and military support. The EU has provided direct military support to Ukraine through the European Peace Facility (EPF), an EU instrument aimed at enhancing its ability to prevent conflicts, promote peace, and strengthen international security.[179] Such support includes funding for both lethal military equipment and supplies. Between 2022 and 2024, the EU mobilized €6.1 billion under the EPF to respond to Ukraine's defense needs.[180] Additionally, in March 2024, the EU decided to increase the financial ceiling of the EPF by €5 billion, by establishing a dedicated Ukraine Assistance Fund.[181] With this operation, the total financial support allocated via the EPF currently amounts to €11.1 billion. Complementarily, in 2022, the EU launched the Military Assistance Mission in support of Ukraine (EUMAM Ukraine) with the aim of strengthening the capabilities and resilience of the Ukrainian armed forces and enhancing the protection of the civilian population.[182]

In addition to security and military support, the EU has implemented its most extensive sanctions package in history, targeting Russia's economy, energy sector, and key individuals, while reducing its own dependence on Russian energy. These sanctions were added to those already imposed on Russia since 2014 following the annexation of Crimea and the lack of implementation of the Minsk agreements.[183] Individual sanctions targeted key leaders and individuals responsible for supporting Russia's invasion of Ukraine or those who benefit from such actions. In addition to sanctions against Russia, the EU adopted sanctions against Russia's allies, Belarus, Iran, and North Korea.[184] Overall, by imposing such sanctions and limitations, the EU mainly aimed to weaken Russia's ability to finance its military aggression against Ukraine by isolating it from the global financial system.

Additionally, since 2022, there have been increasing efforts to reinforce Ukraine's European identity and promote its integration. In June 2022, the EU granted Ukraine official candidate status. This was a monumental decision reflecting strong political solidarity and long-term commitment to Ukraine's EU membership. While EU membership requires Ukraine's stabilization of its territorial integrity and long-term security, which are highly dependent on the current armed conflict with Russia, Ukraine has already started working towards other components of the membership process. In particular, initiatives have been implemented to reform governance systems, enhance the rule of law, and combat corruption, while building a resilient, market-oriented economy capable of integrating into the EU's single market.

Ukraine's candidate status has implications not only for Ukraine but also for the EU and the wider region. Being the second largest country in Europe, Ukraine's membership will enhance the EU's geopolitical reach and resilience; however, it represents an important challenge for the EU, as its accession requires careful planning and adaptation within the EU itself, including budgetary and institutional adjustments.

Finally, the EU has played a key role in humanitarian assistance. The EU activated the Temporary Protection Directive. The Temporary Protection Directive was adopted following the conflicts in former Yugoslavia and was triggered for the first time to offer quick and effective assistance to people fleeing the war in Ukraine.[185] Through the Temporary Protection Directive, the EU has provided millions of Ukrainian refugees access to housing, healthcare, education, and work opportunities in EU member states.[186] This swift and unified response highlighted the EU's commitment to supporting Ukrainians in their time of need. In addition to this, the EU delivered significant humanitarian aid to address the needs of displaced persons within Ukraine, including food, medical supplies, and emergency shelter.

The Stakes for the World

Russia's war on Ukraine has had profound global repercussions, affecting security, energy markets, food systems, and the international legal order. Russia's aggression against Ukraine has tested the resilience of the international legal order, exposed economic vulnerabilities, and reshaped priorities for nations worldwide. On the other hand, it inadvertently strengthened EU cohesion and initiated a wave of solidarity for Ukraine.[187]

Given Russia's pivotal role as a major exporter of oil and natural gas, the war has inevitably destabilized energy markets.[188] Sanctions and supply disruptions have caused price volatility, energy shortages, and economic strain, particularly in Europe. This has prompted countries to diversify energy supplies and accelerate investments in renewable energy, reshaping global energy dependencies. The crisis has also underscored the strategic vulnerabilities of overreliance on single suppliers, driving a reevaluation of energy security strategies across Europe.

In addition to energy, the conflict has disrupted global food security. Ukraine and Russia are key exporters of grains and sunflower oil, and the war has caused significant disruptions to these supply chains, leading to spiking food prices and exacerbating hunger in vulnerable regions. These shortages have fueled instability, particularly in fragile states, and highlighted the need for diversified agricultural supply chains to enhance resilience.[189]

Nuclear security has also come into focus, with Russia's veiled threats of nuclear weapons use raising concerns about the erosion of decades-old nonproliferation norms.[190] The targeting of Ukrainian nuclear facilities, such as Zaporizhzhia, has underscored the risks of conflicts in nuclearized regions and the potential for catastrophic accidents. This has sparked discussions on deterrence and the global implications of nuclear policies.

The war is also testing the strength of the global legal order. Russia's invasion has blatantly violated the sovereignty of Ukraine, challenging fundamental principles of international law. Allegations of war crimes and the targeting of civilians have intensified calls for accountability through mechanisms like the International Criminal Court (ICC). Efforts to prosecute Russian leaders for crimes of aggression and war crimes are pushing the limits of international legal frameworks, while discussions about repurposing frozen Russian assets for Ukraine's reconstruction have raised complex legal questions about sovereignty and property rights.

The global response, including unprecedented sanctions targeting Russia's economy and elites, represents a significant shift in how international law intersects with economic measures. The effectiveness of these actions will set a precedent for addressing future conflicts. A failure to enforce accountability risks emboldening other powers to disregard international norms, while robust actions could strengthen the rule of law.

Ultimately, the stakes of the Ukraine war extend far beyond the immediate conflict. It has disrupted critical systems, tested the resilience of international institutions, and set the stage for future geopolitical dynamics. Its outcome will influence how nations address aggression, safeguard global stability, and uphold the principles of international law in the decades to come.

Concluding Thoughts

The war in Ukraine represents one of the most consequential conflicts of the 21st century, with ramifications that extend far beyond the region. At its core, it is a struggle for sovereignty, democracy, survival, and self-determination, fought against the backdrop of geopolitical rivalries, historical legacies, and systemic challenges to the international order. For Ukraine, this war is not only about defending its territorial integrity but also about affirming its identity as a sovereign nation capable of determining its political future, aligned with the values of freedom and democracy. For the world, the conflict has become a litmus test for the resilience of international norms, the stability of global security systems, and the collective ability to respond to aggression.

The global stakes of this war are immense. Energy markets, food security, and nuclear stability have all been profoundly disrupted, exposing vulnerabilities that demand urgent attention. The war has also highlighted the importance of cohesive international action, both in holding aggressors accountable and in ensuring support for those defending their sovereignty. Efforts to address the war's humanitarian, economic, and legal dimensions have underscored the necessity of a robust and adaptable international framework capable of responding to contemporary challenges.

At the same time, the crisis has catalyzed unprecedented unity, cohesion, and resilience among Ukraine's allies. The EU, NATO, and other international actors have rallied to support Ukraine, signaling a reinvigoration of multilateral cooperation and underscoring the need for such mechanisms of cooperation to exist. This moment of solidarity, while born out of tragedy, demonstrates the enduring relevance of collective action in confronting global threats.

As the war continues, its outcome will shape the geopolitical landscape for decades to come. It will determine the future of Ukraine's integration into Europe, the strength of the international legal order, and the balance of power in the global system. More fundamentally, it will test the world's resolve to uphold the principles of sovereignty, justice, and human dignity in the face of aggression.

Notes

1 Orsolya Ráczová, *Implications of the Ukraine Conflict for Europe* (Apr. 2023), GLOBSEC, https://www.globsec.org/sites/default/files/2023-04/globsec-orsolya-intempl-final.pdf.
2 "Ukraine Conflict: A Crossroads for Europe and Russia," *Council on Foreign Relations*, https://www.cfr.org/backgrounder/ukraine-conflict-crossroads-europe-and-russia.
3 Foreign Agricultural Service, *Ukraine: Factsheet* (Apr. 2022), https://fas.usda.gov/sites/default/files/2022-04/Ukraine-Factsheet-April2022.pdf.
4 "Agricultural Exports from Ukraine by Product and Destination," *Statista*, https://www.statista.com/statistics/1383828/agricultural-exports-ukraine-by-product-and-destination/.
5 "Origins and History of Ukraine," *Ukraine.ua*, https://ukraine.ua/explore/origins-history-of-ukraine/.
6 Matthew L. Bindon et al., *Understanding Ukraine's Security Challenges: A Historical and Strategic Perspective*, 6 *LSE Public Policy Rev.* (2022), https://ppr.lse.ac.uk/articles/10.31389/lseppr.90.
7 "Ukraine Conflict: A Crossroads for Europe and Russia," *Council on Foreign Relations*, https://www.cfr.org/backgrounder/ukraine-conflict-crossroads-europe-and-russia/.
8 "Ukraine Conflict: A Crossroads for Europe and Russia," *Council on Foreign Relations*, https://www.cfr.org/backgrounder/ukraine-conflict-crossroads-europe-and-russia/.
9 "Ukraine War Casualties," *Statista*, https://www.statista.com/statistics/1293492/ukraine-war-casualties/.
10 "Ukrainian Refugees by Country," *Statista*, https://www.statista.com/statistics/1312584/ukrainian-refugees-by-country/.
11 "Ukraine Emergency," *UNHCR*, https://www.unrefugees.org/emergencies/ukraine/.
12 Office for Democratic Institutions and Human Rights, *Report on Violations and Abuses of International Humanitarian and Human Rights Law, War Crimes and Crimes Against Humanity, Related to the Arbitrary Deprivation of Liberty of Ukrainian Civilians by the Russian Federation* (Apr. 19, 2024), https://www.osce.org/files/f/documents/f/4/567367_0.pdf.
13 Dr. Björn Alexander Düben, There is No Ukraine: Fact-Checking the Kremlin's Version of Ukrainian History, *LSE International History Blog* (July 1, 2020), https://blogs.lse.ac.uk/lseih/2020/07/01/there-is-no-ukraine-fact-checking-the-kremlins-version-of-ukrainian-history/.
14 "History of the Soviet Union," *History.com*, A&E Television Networks, https://www.history.com/topics/european-history/history-of-the-soviet-union.
15 Joseph Stalin, *The Constitution of the USSR* (Dec. 5, 1936), in *Works*, Vol. 14 (Red Star Press Ltd. 1978), https://www.marxists.org/reference/archive/stalin/works/1936/12/05.htm.
16 Joseph Stalin, *The Constitution of the USSR* (Dec. 5, 1936), in *Works*, Vol. 14 (Red Star Press Ltd. 1978), Chapter II, https://www.marxists.org/reference/archive/stalin/works/1936/12/05.htm.
17 Constitution of the Union of Soviet Socialist Republics, Chapters 8–11 (1977), https://www.marxists.org/history/ussr/government/constitution/1977/constitution-ussr-1977.pdf.
18 Sujan Chinoy, et.al., *Ukraine War: Military Perspectives and Strategic Reflections*, Institute for Defence Studies, 15 (2024), https://www.idsa.in/wp-content/uploads/2024/05/ukraine-war-book.pdf.

19 Sujan Chinoy et al., *Ukraine War: Military Perspectives and Strategic Reflections*, Institute for Defence Studies, 15 (2024), https://www.idsa.in/wp-content/uploads/2024/05/ukraine-war-book.pdf.
20 Serhy Yekelchyk. *Stalinist Patriotism as Imperial Discourse: Reconciling the Ukrainian and Russian "Heroic Pasts," 1939–45, Kritika: Explorations in Russian and Eurasian History*, 3 (2002), https://muse.jhu.edu/pub/28/article/18733.
21 *Holodomor: Parliament Recognises Soviet Starvation of Ukrainians as Genocide*, European Parliament News (2022), https://www.europarl.europa.eu/news/en/press-room/20221209IPR64427/holodomor-parliament-recognises-soviet-starvation-of-ukrainians-as-genocide.
22 Sujan Chinoy et al., *Ukraine War: Military Perspectives and Strategic Reflections*, Institute for Defence Studies, 15 (2024), https://www.idsa.in/wp-content/uploads/2024/05/ukraine-war-book.pdf.
23 Alexander Puzanov. (1954, February 5). *Decree Of The Russian Soviet Federative Socialist Republic Council Of Ministers, 'Concerning The Transfer Of The Crimean Oblast' From The RSFSR to the UKSSR'.* Wilson Center Digital Archive, https://digitalarchive.wilsoncenter.org/document/119634.
24 Alexander Puzanov. (1954, February 5). *Decree Of The Russian Soviet Federative Socialist Republic Council Of Ministers, 'Concerning The Transfer Of The Crimean Oblast' From The RSFSR to the UKSSR'.* Wilson Center Digital Archive, https://digitalarchive.wilsoncenter.org/document/119634.
25 Alwishewa, Hiruni. "Revisiting Crimea and the Utility of International Law." Opinio Juris. Internationa Commission of Jurists, March 7, 2022, http://opinio-juris.org/2022/03/08/revisiting-crimea-and-the-utility-of-international-law/.
26 Hiruni Alwishewa. "Revisiting Crimea and the Utility of International Law." Opinio Juris. International Commission of Jurists, March 7, 2022, http://opiniojuris.org/2022/03/08/revisiting-crimea-and-the-utility-of-international-law/.
27 U.S. Commission on Security and Cooperation in Europe, Ukraine's Referendum on Independence and Presidential Election (Dec. 1, 1991), https://www.csce.gov/wp-content/uploads/2016/06/120191UkraineReferendum.pdf.
28 Sujan Chinoy et al., *Ukraine War: Military Perspectives and Strategic Reflections*, Institute for Defence Studies, 20 (2024), https://www.idsa.in/wp-content/uploads/2024/05/ukraine-war-book.pdf.
29 Arms Control Association, Ukraine: Nuclear Weapons and Security Assurances at a Glance (last updated Dec. 2022), https://www.armscontrol.org/factsheets/ukraine-nuclear-weapons-and-security-assurances-glance.
30 United Nations, Memorandum on Security Assurances in Connection with Ukraine's Accession to the Treaty on the Non-Proliferation of Nuclear Weapons, U.N. Doc. S/1994/1399 (Dec. 19, 1994), https://www.securitycouncilreport.org/atf/cf/%7B65BFCF9B-6D27-4E9C-8CD3-CF6E4FF96FF9%7D/s_1994_1399.pdf.
31 United Nations, Memorandum on Security Assurances in Connection with Ukraine's Accession to the Treaty on the Non-Proliferation of Nuclear Weapons, U.N. Doc. S/1994/1399 (Dec. 19, 1994), https://www.securitycouncilreport.org/atf/cf/%7B65BFCF9B-6D27-4E9C-8CD3-CF6E4FF96FF9%7D/s_1994_1399.pdf.
32 European Parliament, Energy as a tool of foreign policy of authoritarian states, in particular Russia (2018), https://www.europarl.europa.eu/RegData/etudes/STUD/2018/603868/EXPO_STU(2018)603868_EN.pdf.

33 "Russkiy Mir: On the Genesis of a Geopolitical Concept and Its Effects on Ukraine," *German Council on Foreign Relations*, https://dgap.org/en/events/russkiy-mir-russian-world.
34 "A Short History of Ukrainian Nationalism and Its Tumultuous Relationship with Russia," *The Conversation*, March 17, 2022, https://theconversation.com/a-short-history-of-ukrainian-nationalism-and-its-tumultuous-relationship-with-russia-179346.
35 Anders Åslund, *The Orange Revolution, 2004*, in *How Ukraine Became a Market Economy and Democracy*, 182 (Peterson Institute for International Economics), https://www.piie.com/publications/chapters_preview/4273/07iie4273.pdf.
36 "How Ukraine's Orange Revolution Shaped Twenty-First Century Geopolitics," *Atlantic Council*, November 21, 2022, https://www.atlanticcouncil.org/blogs/ukrainealert/how-ukraines-orange-revolution-shaped-twenty-first-century-geopolitics/.
37 "Ukraine's Orange Revolution and Referendum," *Council on Foreign Relations*, https://www.cfr.org/expert-brief/ukraines-orange-revolution-referendum.
38 "Ukraine's Economy Since 1991," *Carnegie Endowment for International Peace*, March 2012, https://carnegieendowment.org/research/2012/03/the-underachiever-ukraines-economy-since-1991?lang=en.
39 "Ukraine's Orange Revolution and Referendum," *Council on Foreign Relations*, https://www.cfr.org/expert-brief/ukraines-orange-revolution-referendum.
40 "Ukraine's Orange Revolution and Referendum," *Council on Foreign Relations*, https://www.cfr.org/expert-brief/ukraines-orange-revolution-referendum.
41 "External Influences on Ukraine's European Integration," *Brookings Institution*, April 1, 2013, https://www.brookings.edu/articles/external-influences-on-ukraines-european-integration/.
42 Matviichuk, *The Price of Freedom. Public Report by human rights organizations on crimes against humanity committed during Euromaidan (November 2013 – February 2014)*, Human Rights and Justice Program Initiative of the International Renaissance Foundation, 7 (2015), https://www.europarl.europa.eu/cmsdata/267948/Matviichuk_Ukrainian%20NGO's.EuroMaidan.November%202013-February2014.Eng..pdf.
43 "Ukraine's Struggle for Independence in Russia's Shadow," *Council on Foreign Relations*, https://www.cfr.org/timeline/ukraines-struggle-independence-russias-shadow.
44 Matviichuk, *The Price of Freedom. Public Report by human rights organizations on crimes against humanity committed during Euromaidan (November 2013 – February 2014)*, Human Rights and Justice Program Initiative of the International Renaissance Foundation, 14 (2015), https://www.europarl.europa.eu/cmsdata/267948/Matviichuk_Ukrainian%20NGO's.EuroMaidan.November%202013-February2014.Eng..pdf.
45 Matviichuk, *The Price of Freedom. Public Report by human rights organizations on crimes against humanity committed during Euromaidan (November 2013 – February 2014)*, Human Rights and Justice Program Initiative of the International Renaissance Foundation, 10 (2015), https://www.europarl.europa.eu/cmsdata/267948/Matviichuk_Ukrainian%20NGO's.EuroMaidan.November%202013-February2014.Eng..pdf.
46 Matviichuk, *The Price of Freedom. Public Report by human rights organizations on crimes against humanity committed during Euromaidan (November 2013 – February 2014)*, Human Rights and Justice Program Initiative of the International Renaissance Foundation, 16 (2015), https://www.europarl.europa.eu/cmsdata/267948/Matviichuk_Ukrainian%20NGO's.EuroMaidan.November%202013-February2014.Eng..pdf.

47 "Lessons from Russia's Operations in Crimea and Eastern Ukraine," *RAND Corporation*, May 9, 2017, https://www.rand.org/pubs/research_reports/RR1498.html.
48 "Seven Years Since Russia's Illegal Annexation of Crimea," *European External Action Service*, March 18, 2021, https://www.eeas.europa.eu/eeas/seven-years-russia%E2%80%99s-illegal-annexation-crimea_en; "Ukraine's Struggle for Independence in Russia's Shadow," *Council on Foreign Relations*, https://www.cfr.org/timeline/ukraines-struggle-independence-russias-shadow.
49 "Results of the 2001 Ukrainian Census: Nationality in Crimea," *State Statistics Committee of Ukraine*, http://2001.ukrcensus.gov.ua/eng/results/general/nationality/Crimea/.
50 "Lessons from Russia's Operations in Crimea and Eastern Ukraine," *RAND Corporation*, May 9, 2017, https://www.rand.org/pubs/research_reports/RR1498.html.
51 "Lessons from Russia's Operations in Crimea and Eastern Ukraine," *RAND Corporation*, May 9, 2017, https://www.rand.org/pubs/research_reports/RR1498.html.
52 "Lessons from Russia's Operations in Crimea and Eastern Ukraine," *RAND Corporation*, May 9, 2017, https://www.rand.org/pubs/research_reports/RR1498.html.
53 "What Are the Minsk Agreements on the Ukraine Conflict?" *Reuters*, February 21, 2022, https://www.reuters.com/world/europe/what-are-minsk-agreements-ukraine-conflict-2022-02-21/.
54 "Peace in Ukraine III: The Costs of the War in Donbas," *International Crisis Group*, https://www.crisisgroup.org/europe-central-asia/eastern-europe/ukraine/261-peace-ukraine-iii-costs-war-donbas.
55 Darvas, Zsolt et al., *European Union of Ukraine's Potential Future Accession*, 17 (Bruegel Report No. 02/24, April 2024), https://www.bruegel.org/system/files/2024-04/Report%2002.pdf.
56 Darvas, Zsolt et al., *European Union of Ukraine's Potential Future Accession*, 28 (Bruegel Report No. 02/24, April 2024), https://www.bruegel.org/system/files/2024-04/Report%2002.pdf.
57 "Address by President Vladimir Putin on Russian-Ukrainian Relations," *Kremlin.ru*, February 21, 2022, http://en.kremlin.ru/events/president/news/66181.
58 "There Is No Ukraine: Fact-Checking the Kremlin's Version of Ukrainian History," *LSE International History Blog*, July 1, 2020, https://blogs.lse.ac.uk/lseih/2020/07/01/there-is-no-ukraine-fact-checking-the-kremlins-version-of-ukrainian-history/.
59 "Ukraine: The History Behind Russia's Claim That NATO Promised Not to Expand to the East," *The Conversation*, January 10, 2022, https://theconversation.com/ukraine-the-history-behind-russias-claim-that-nato-promised-not-to-expand-to-the-east-177085.
60 Ekman, Per, *Foreign Policy After Empire: Explaining Georgia's and Ukraine's International Orientation from Independence until 2021,* 17 (Uppsala University, 2024), https://uu.diva-portal.org/smash/get/diva2:1888235/FULLTEXT01.pdf; Darvas, Zsolt et al., *European Union of Ukraine's Potential Future Accession,* 34 (RAND Corporation, 2024), https://www.rand.org/content/dam/rand/pubs/research_reports/RRA400/RRA444-3/RAND_RRA444-3.pdf.
61 Ekman, Per, *Foreign Policy After Empire: Explaining Georgia's and Ukraine's International Orientation from Independence until 2021,* 17 (Uppsala University, 2024), https://uu.diva-portal.org/smash/get/diva2:1888235/FULLTEXT01.pdf.

62 Olga Onuch, *Ukrainians' Unwavering Path Toward the EU* (Carnegie Endowment for International Peace, June 2024), https://carnegieendowment.org/research/2024/06/ukrainians-unwavering-path-toward-the-eu?lang=en&center=europe.

63 Pifer, Steven, *Ukraine's Long Path Toward NATO* (American Diplomacy, August 2024), https://americandiplomacy.web.unc.edu/2024/08/ukraines-long-path-toward-nato/.

64 "Was It Inevitable? A Short History of Russia's War on Ukraine," *The Guardian*, March 11, 2022, https://www.theguardian.com/world/2022/mar/11/was-it-inevitable-a-short-history-of-russias-war-on-ukraine.

65 Sujan Chinoy et al., *Ukraine War: Military Perspectives and Strategic Reflections*, Institute for Defence Studies, 18, 19 (2024), https://www.idsa.in/wp-content/uploads/2024/05/ukraine-war-book.pdf.

66 Kofman, Michael et al., *Lessons from Russia's Operations in Crimea and Eastern Ukraine* 49 (RAND Corporation, May 9, 2017), https://www.rand.org/pubs/research_reports/RR1498.html.

67 *Socioeconomic inequality in Russia* (European Parliament, 2018), https://www.europarl.europa.eu/RegData/etudes/ATAG/2018/620225/EPRS_ATA(2018)620225_EN.pdf.

68 Ramani, Samuel Nathan, *Post-Soviet Region and Middle East: A Quest for Domestic Legitimacy*, 314–15 (DPhil thesis, University of Oxford, March 2021), https://ora.ox.ac.uk/objects/uuid:f6eb56b1-456e-46a8-ac89-532b499bff49/files/d6108vb419; Likhotal, Alexey, *Root Causes of the Russian Invasion*, 5 (Cadmus Journal, July 2022), https://www.cadmusjournal.org/files/pdfreprints/vol4issue6/Root-Causes-of-the-Russian-Invasion-ALikhotal-The-War-in-Ukraine-July-2022.pdf.

69 Likhotal, Alexey, *Root Causes of the Russian Invasion*, 8 (Cadmus Journal, July 2022), https://www.cadmusjournal.org/files/pdfreprints/vol4issue6/Root-Causes-of-the-Russian-Invasion-ALikhotal-The-War-in-Ukraine-July-2022.pdf.

70 Likhotal, Alexey, *Root Causes of the Russian Invasion* (Cadmus Journal, July 2022), https://www.cadmusjournal.org/files/pdfreprints/vol4issue6/Root-Causes-of-the-Russian-Invasion-ALikhotal-The-War-in-Ukraine-July-2022.pdf; "How Russia and Ukraine's Tangled Histories Led to War," *Tufts Now*, January 22, 2024, https://now.tufts.edu/2024/01/22/how-russia-and-ukraines-tangled-histories-led-war.

71 Mearsheimer, John J., *The Causes and Consequences of the Ukraine War* (CIRSD, Summer 2022), https://www.cirsd.org/en/horizons/horizons-summer-2022-issue-no.21/the-causes-and-consequences-of-the-ukraine-war.

72 "Decree No. 117/2021 on the Strategy of De-Occupation and Reintegration of the Temporarily Occupied Territory of the Autonomous Republic of Crimea," *President of Ukraine*, March 24, 2021, https://ppu.gov.ua/en/press-center/today-president-of-ukraine-volodymyr-zelenskyy-signed-decree-117-2021-of-march-24-2021-on-the-strategy-of-de-occupation-and-reintegration-of-the-temporarily-occupied-territory-of-the-autonomous-republ/.

73 Mearsheimer, John J., *The Causes and Consequences of the Ukraine War* (CIRSD, Summer 2022), https://www.cirsd.org/en/horizons/horizons-summer-2022-issue-no.21/the-causes-and-consequences-of-the-ukraine-war.

74 "Putin Says Ukraine Goals Will Be Achieved as He Repeats Neo-Nazi Claims," *Al Jazeera*, September 30, 2024, https://www.aljazeera.com/news/2024/9/30/putin-says-ukraine-goals-will-be-achieved-as-he-repeats-neo-nazi-claims.

75 "Address by President Vladimir Putin on the Situation in Donbass and Security of Russia," *Kremlin.ru*, February 24, 2022, http://en.kremlin.ru/events/president/news/67843.

76 "Understanding the Situation in Ukraine from 2014 to 24 February 2022," *French Ministry for Europe and Foreign Affairs*, updated June 2022, https://www.diplomatie.gouv.fr/en/country-files/ukraine/situation-in-ukraine-what-is/understanding-the-situation-in-ukraine-from-2014-to-24-february-2022/.

77 "Chronology of the Occupation of Crimea," *Crimea Platform*, https://crimea-platform.org/en/occupation-chronology/.

78 "Chronology of the Occupation of Crimea," *Crimea Platform*, https://crimea-platform.org/en/occupation-chronology/.

79 Walker, Nigel, *Conflict in Ukraine: A Timeline (2014 – Eve of 2022 Invasion)* (House of Commons Library, August 22, 2023), https://researchbriefings.files.parliament.uk/documents/CBP-9476/CBP-9476.pdf.

80 Walker, Nigel, *Conflict in Ukraine: A Timeline (2014 – Eve of 2022 Invasion)* (House of Commons Library, August 22, 2023), https://researchbriefings.files.parliament.uk/documents/CBP-9476/CBP-9476.pdf.

81 Walker, Nigel, *Conflict in Ukraine: A Timeline (2014 – Eve of 2022 Invasion)* (House of Commons Library, August 22, 2023), https://researchbriefings.files.parliament.uk/documents/CBP-9476/CBP-9476.pdf.

82 "Criminal Investigation by the Joint Investigation Team (JIT)," *Prosecution Service of the Netherlands*, https://www.prosecutionservice.nl/topics/mh17-plane-crash/criminal-investigation-jit-mh17.

83 "Ten Years of War and Russification in Ukraine's Donbas," *France 24*, April 8, 2024, https://www.france24.com/en/europe/20240408-ukraine-donbas-ten-years-of-war-russification-russia-donetsk-luhansk.

84 Walker, Nigel, *Conflict in Ukraine: A Timeline (2014 – Eve of 2022 Invasion)* (House of Commons Library, August 22, 2023), https://researchbriefings.files.parliament.uk/documents/CBP-9476/CBP-9476.pdf.

85 "Ten Years of War and Russification in Ukraine's Donbas," *France 24*, April 8, 2024, https://www.france24.com/en/europe/20240408-ukraine-donbas-ten-years-of-war-russification-russia-donetsk-luhansk; Kofman, Michael et al., *Lessons from Russia's Operations in Crimea and Eastern Ukraine,* 44 (RAND Corporation, May 9, 2017), https://www.rand.org/pubs/research_reports/RR1498.html.

86 "Results of Consultations of the Trilateral Contact Group on the Implementation of the Peace Plan of the President of Ukraine, P. Poroshenko, and the Initiatives of the President of Russia, V. Putin," *Peace Agreements*, September 1, 2014, https://www.peaceagreements.org/viewmasterdocument/1363.

87 "Ukraine Crisis: Timeline of Events," *BBC News*, https://www.bbc.com/news/world-europe-30931105.

88 "Package of Measures for the Implementation of the Minsk Agreements," February 12, 2015, *available at* https://horlogedelinconscient.fr/wp-content/uploads/2020/09/Minsk-2-Full-text-UNIAN.pdf.

89 "Minsk-2 Agreement," *Chatham House*, May 2020, https://www.chathamhouse.org/2020/05/minsk-conundrum-western-policy-and-russias-war-eastern-ukraine-0/minsk-2-agreement.

90 "Ten Years of War and Russification in Ukraine's Donbas," *France 24*, April 8, 2024, https://www.france24.com/en/europe/20240408-ukraine-donbas-ten-years-of-war-russification-russia-donetsk-luhansk.

91 Kofman, Michael et al., *Lessons from Russia's Operations in Crimea and Eastern Ukraine* 45 (RAND Corporation, May 9, 2017), https://www.rand.org/pubs/research_reports/RR1498.html.

92 Kofman, Michael et al., *Lessons from Russia's Operations in Crimea and Eastern Ukraine* 45 (RAND Corporation, May 9, 2017), https://www.rand.org/pubs/research_reports/RR1498.html.
93 Walker, Nigel, *Conflict in Ukraine: A Timeline (2014 – Eve of 2022 Invasion)* (House of Commons Library, August 22, 2023), https://researchbriefings.files.parliament.uk/documents/CBP-9476/CBP-9476.pdf.
94 "The Kerch Strait Incident," *International Institute for Strategic Studies*, November 2018, https://www.iiss.org/publications/strategic-comments/2018/the-kerch-strait-incident/.
95 "Ukraine Conflict: Timeline of Key Events," *BBC News*, https://www.bbc.com/news/world-46345317.
96 "The Kerch Strait Incident," *International Institute for Strategic Studies*, November 2018, https://www.iiss.org/publications/strategic-comments/2018/the-kerch-strait-incident/.
97 "Consequences of the Incident in the Sea of Azov," *Centre for Eastern Studies (OSW)*, November 26, 2018, https://www.osw.waw.pl/en/publikacje/analyses/2018-11-26/consequences-incident-sea-azov.
98 "Constitution of Ukraine," *Verkhovna Rada of Ukraine*, June 28, 1996, https://zakon.rada.gov.ua/laws/show/en/254%D0%BA/96-%D0%B2%D1%80.
99 "Zelenskiy's First Year: He Promised Sweeping Changes. How's He Doing?" *Radio Free Europe/Radio Liberty*, https://www.rferl.org/a/zelenskiys-first-year-he-promised-sweeping-changes-how-s-he-doing-/30576329.html.
100 "Conflict Management in Donbas: Elections Could Not Be," *CIDOB*, December 2020, https://www.cidob.org/publicaciones/conflict-management-donbas-elections-could-not-be.
101 "Relations with Ukraine," *NATO*, https://www.nato.int/cps/en/natohq/topics_37750.htm.
102 "Russian and Ukrainian Spring 2021 War Scare," *Center for Strategic and International Studies (CSIS)*, https://www.csis.org/analysis/russian-and-ukrainian-spring-2021-war-scare.
103 "Russia Issues List of Demands Amid Tensions with NATO and Ukraine," *The Guardian*, December 17, 2021, https://www.theguardian.com/world/2021/dec/17/russia-issues-list-demands-tensions-europe-ukraine-nato.
104 Walker, Nigel, *Conflict in Ukraine: A Timeline (2014 – Eve of 2022 Invasion)* (House of Commons Library, August 22, 2023), https://researchbriefings.files.parliament.uk/documents/CBP-9476/CBP-9476.pdf.
105 "Confusion Over UK Claim That Putin Plans Coup in Ukraine," *The Guardian*, January 22, 2022, https://www.theguardian.com/world/2022/jan/22/confusion-over-uk-claim-that-putin-plans-coup-in-ukraine.
106 "NATO Reinforces Eastern Borders as Ukraine Tensions Mount," *The Guardian*, January 24, 2022, https://www.theguardian.com/world/2022/jan/24/nato-reinforces-eastern-borders-as-ukraine-tensions-mount.
107 "US and NATO Deliver Responses to Russian Demands Over Ukraine," *Al Jazeera*, January 26, 2022, https://www.aljazeera.com/news/2022/1/26/us-nato-deliver-responses-to-russian-demands-over-ukraine.
108 "Ukraine: Russia and Belarus Hold Joint Military Exercises," *CNN*, February 10, 2022, https://edition.cnn.com/2022/02/10/europe/ukraine-russia-news-thursday-military-exercises-intl/index.html.
109 "On the Recognition of the Donetsk People's Republic and the Lugansk People's Republic," *Kremlin.ru*, February 21, 2022, http://en.kremlin.ru/events/president/news/67829.

110 "February 24, 2022: The Day Russia Invaded Ukraine," *France 24*, February 14, 2023, https://www.france24.com/en/live-news/20230214-february-24-2022-the-day-russia-invaded-ukraine.
111 "Russia's War in Ukraine: Military and Intelligence Aspects," *Congressional Research Service*, September 14, 2023, https://crsreports.congress.gov/product/pdf/R/R47068.
112 "Ukraine War: EU Leaders Agree €50bn Support Package for Ukraine," *BBC News*, https://www.brookings.edu/articles/the-russia-ukraine-war-at-three-months/.
113 "Fact Sheet on U.S. Security Assistance for Ukraine: Roll-Up as of April 21, 2022," *U.S. Department of Defense*, https://www.defense.gov/News/Releases/Release/article/3007664/fact-sheet-on-us-security-assistance-for-ukraine-roll-up-as-of-april-21-2022/.
114 "Russia's War in Ukraine: Military and Intelligence Aspects," *Congressional Research Service*, September 14, 2023, https://crsreports.congress.gov/product/pdf/R/R47068.
115 "Ukraine: Donbas, Ten Years of War and Russification," *France 24*, April 8, 2024, https://www.france24.com/en/europe/20240408-ukraine-donbas-ten-years-of-war-russification-russia-donetsk-luhansk.
116 "Russia's War in Ukraine: Military and Intelligence Aspects," *Congressional Research Service*, 10, September 14, 2023, https://crsreports.congress.gov/product/pdf/R/R47068.
117 "Russia's War in Ukraine: Military and Intelligence Aspects," *Congressional Research Service*, 27, September 14, 2023, https://crsreports.congress.gov/product/pdf/R/R47068.
118 "Conflict in Ukraine," *Council on Foreign Relations*, https://www.cfr.org/global-conflict-tracker/conflict/conflict-ukraine.
119 "Russian Military Objectives and Capacity in Ukraine Through 2024," *Royal United Services Institute (RUSI)*, https://www.rusi.org/explore-our-research/publications/commentary/russian-military-objectives-and-capacity-ukraine-through-2024.
120 "Brass Tacks: Why Russia's Military Fails to Reform," *European Council on Foreign Relations (ECFR)*, https://ecfr.eu/publication/brass-tacks-why-russias-military-fails-to-reform/.
121 "Ukraine Has Lost Over 40% of Territory in Russia's Kursk Region," *Reuters*, November 23, 2024, https://www.reuters.com/world/europe/ukraine-has-lost-over-40-russias-kursk-region-counter-attacks-senior-kyiv-2024-11-23/.
122 "Ukraine: A Year of War," *BBC News*, https://www.bbc.com/news/articles/cx2nrlq1840o.
123 "Putin's Foreign Legion: Foreigners Fighting in the War with Ukraine," *OSW (Centre for Eastern Studies)*, February 20, 2024, https://www.osw.waw.pl/en/publikacje/analyses/2024-02-20/putins-foreign-legion-foreigners-fighting-war-ukraine.
124 "Russia's Use of a Nuclear-Capable Missile Marks a Significant Escalation in Ukraine Conflict," *CNN*, November 22, 2024, https://carnegieendowment.org/russia-eurasia/politika/2024/11/russia-new-nuclear-threat?lang=en.
125 "Ukraine: What's the Global Economic Impact of Russia's Invasion?" *Economics Observatory*, https://www.economicsobservatory.com/ukraine-whats-the-global-economic-impact-of-russias-invasion.
126 "What Are the Sanctions on Russia and Have They Affected Its Economy?" *BBC News*, February 23, 2024, https://www.bbc.com/news/world-europe-60125659.

127 "How Russia Has Managed to Shake Off the Impact of Sanctions with a Little Help from Its Friends," *The Conversation*, https://theconversation.com/how-russia-has-managed-to-shake-off-the-impact-of-sanctions-with-a-little-help-from-its-friends-223632.
128 "Ukraine: What's the Global Economic Impact of Russia's Invasion?" *Economics Observatory*, https://www.economicsobservatory.com/ukraine-whats-the-global-economic-impact-of-russias-invasion.
129 "World Bank Emergency Financing Package for Ukraine," *World Bank*, https://www.worldbank.org/en/country/ukraine/brief/world-bank-emergency-financing-package-for-ukraine.
130 "Ukraine: What's the Global Economic Impact of Russia's Invasion?" *Economics Observatory*, https://www.economicsobservatory.com/ukraine-whats-the-global-economic-impact-of-russias-invasion.
131 "1000 Days of Russia's Full-Scale War on Ukraine: 5 Facts You Need to Know," *European Civil Protection and Humanitarian Aid Operations*, https://civil-protection-humanitarian-aid.ec.europa.eu/news-stories/stories/1000-days-russias-full-scale-war-ukraine-5-facts-you-need-know_en.
132 "1000 Days of Russia's Full-Scale War on Ukraine: 5 Facts You Need to Know," *European Civil Protection and Humanitarian Aid Operations*, https://civil-protection-humanitarian-aid.ec.europa.eu/news-stories/stories/1000-days-russias-full-scale-war-ukraine-5-facts-you-need-know_en.
133 "Report of the Independent International Commission of Inquiry on Ukraine," *Office of the United Nations High Commissioner for Human Rights*, October 25, 2024, https://www.ohchr.org/sites/default/files/documents/hrbodies/hrcouncil/coiukraine/A_79_4632_AUV.pdf.
134 "Report of the Independent International Commission of Inquiry on Ukraine," *Office of the United Nations High Commissioner for Human Rights*, October 25, 2024, https://www.ohchr.org/sites/default/files/documents/hrbodies/hrcouncil/coiukraine/A_79_4632_AUV.pdf.
135 "Report of the Secretary-General on the Situation in Ukraine," *United Nations*, December 2022, https://documents.un.org/doc/undoc/gen/n22/637/72/pdf/n2263772.pdf.
136 See more in the following chapters of this book.
137 "Demystifying the Enemy: Putin's Geopolitical Calculus and the War in Ukraine," *Georgetown Journal of International Affairs*, August 28, 2024, https://gjia.georgetown.edu/2024/08/28/demystifying-the-enemy-putins-geopolitical-calculus-and-the-war-in-ukraine/.
138 Peter Hilpold, *Justifying the Unjustifiable: Russia's Aggression against Ukraine, International Law, and Carl Schmitt's "Theory of the Greater Space" ("Großraumtheorie")*, 22 Chinese Journal of International Law (2023), https://doi.org/10.1093/chinesejil/jmad039.
139 Roy Allison, *Russia's Case for War against Ukraine: Legal Claims, Political Rhetoric, and Instrumentality in a Fracturing International Order*, 71 Problems of Post-Communism, Taylor and Francis Online (2024), https://doi.org/10.1080/10758216.2023.2254915.
140 Masahiko Asada, *The War in Ukraine under International Law: Its Use of Force and Armed Conflict Aspects*, 26 International Community Law Review (2024), https://brill.com/view/journals/iclr/26/1-2/article-p5_2.xml.
141 "Why NATO Expansion Explains Russia's Actions in Ukraine," *Australian Institute of International Affairs*, https://www.internationalaffairs.org.au/australianoutlook/why-nato-expansion-explains-russias-actions-in-ukraine/.
142 "The Russian-Ukrainian War: NATO Fault Thesis Proponents Can't Explain Why It's Genocidal," *Australian Institute of International Affairs*, https://www

.internationalaffairs.org.au/australianoutlook/the-russian-ukrainian-war-nato-fault-thesis-proponents-cant-explain-why-its-genocidal/.
143 "Ukraine: Conflict at the Crossroads of Europe and Russia," CFR (Council on Foreign Relations), February 14, 2023, https://www.cfr.org/backgrounder/ukraine-conflict-crossroads-europe-and-russia.
144 "Putin's Article: 'On the Historical Unity of Russians and Ukrainians'," *OSW (Centre for Eastern Studies)*, July 13, 2021, https://www.osw.waw.pl/en/publikacje/analyses/2021-07-13/putins-article-historical-unity-russians-and-ukrainians.
145 Stent, A. (2019). *Putin's World: Russia Against the West and With the Rest.* New York: Hachette Book Group. p. 131.
146 "The Russian-Ukrainian War: NATO Fault Thesis Proponents Can't Explain Why It's Genocidal," *Australian Institute of International Affairs*, https://www.internationalaffairs.org.au/australianoutlook/the-russian-ukrainian-war-nato-fault-thesis-proponents-cant-explain-why-its-genocidal/.
147 North Atlantic Treaty art. 1, Apr. 4, 1949, 63 Stat. 2241, 34 U.N.T.S. 243.
148 North Atlantic Treaty art. 5, Apr. 4, 1949, 63 Stat. 2241, 34 U.N.T.S. 243.
149 "Collective defence and Article 5," *NATO* https://www.nato.int/cps/ie/natohq/topics_110496.htm.
150 "Would Ukraine Breach its own Constitution if it Dropped its NATO Bid?," *Verfassungsblog*, https://verfassungsblog.de/would-ukraine-breach-its-own-constitution-if-it-dropped-its-nato-bid/.
151 "Cooperation with NATO," *Ministry of Foreign Affairs of Ukraine*, https://mfa.gov.ua/cooperation-nato.
152 Budapest Memorandum, Dec. 5, 1994, OSCE Conference Agreements.
153 "15 years of Distinctive Partnership between NATO and Ukraine," *NATO*, https://www.nato.int/cps/en/natohq/news_89037.htm.
154 Bucharest Summit Declaration, *NATO*, https://www.nato.int/cps/ua/natohq/official_texts_8443.htm.
155 "Ukraine's parliament votes to abandon Nato ambitions," *BBC*, https://www.bbc.com/news/10229626.
156 "NATO Secretary General's Remarks at the Press Conference Following the NATO Summit in Wales," *NATO*, September 5, 2014, https://www.nato.int/cps/en/natolive/news_107716.htm.
157 "Reducing Tensions Between Russia and NATO," *Council on Foreign Relations*, March 2017, https://cdn.cfr.org/sites/default/files/pdf/2017/03/CSR_79_Marten_RussiaNATO.pdf.
158 "The Politics of 2 Percent: NATO and the Security Vacuum in Europe," *Carnegie Europe*, September 2, 2015, archived July 12, 2018, https://web.archive.org/web/20180712221337/https://carnegieeurope.eu/2015/09/02/politics-of-2-percent-nato-and-security-vacuum-in-europe-pub-61139.
159 "NATO's Military Presence in the East of the Alliance," *NATO*, https://www.nato.int/cps/en/natohq/topics_136388.htm.
160 "How Sweden and Finland went from neutral to Nato," *BBC*, https://www.bbc.com/news/world-europe-61397478.
161 "Russia on NATO Enlargement to Sweden and Finland," *Polish Institute of International Affairs*, https://www.pism.pl/publications/russia-on-nato-enlargement-to-sweden-and-finland.
162 "The Russian-Ukrainian War: NATO Fault Thesis Proponents Can't Explain Why It's Genocidal," *Australian Institute of International Affairs*, https://www.internationalaffairs.org.au/australianoutlook/the-russian-ukrainian-war-nato-fault-thesis-proponents-cant-explain-why-its-genocidal/.

163 "Secretary General Welcomes Unprecedented Rise in NATO Defence Spending," *NATO*, February 14, 2024, https://www.nato.int/cps/en/natohq/news_222664.htm.
164 "Special Fund for the Federal Armed Forces," *Bundesregierung*, https://www.bundesregierung.de/breg-en/news/special-fund-federal-armed-forces-2047910.
165 "Fact Sheet: U.S. Contributions to NATO Deterrence and Defense," *The White House*, July 11, 2024, https://www.whitehouse.gov/briefing-room/statements-releases/2024/07/11/fact-sheet-u-s-contributions-to-nato-deterrence-and-defense/.
166 "NATO 2022 Strategic Concept," *NATO*, June 29, 2022, https://www.nato.int/cps/en/natohq/topics_210907.htm.
167 "NATO's New Force Model: A Watershed Step for the Alliance's Deterrence, Defence and Crisis Management Missions in a Complex Euro-Atlantic Security Landscape," *Atlantic Forum*, https://www.atlantic-forum.com/atlantica/natos-new-force-model-a-watershed-step-for-the-alliances-deterrence-defence-and-crisis-management-missions-in-a-complex-euro-atlantic-security-landscape.
168 NATO Parliamentary Assembly calls for Ukraine's accession 'as soon as possible,' *Kyiv Independent*, https://kyivindependent.com/nato-parliamentary-assembly-ukraine/.
169 "European Commission Press Release: PCA with Ukraine enters into force," *European Commission*, February 27, 1998, https://ec.europa.eu/commission/presscorner/detail/en/ip_98_198.
170 "EU-Ukraine Partnership and Cooperation Agreement," *CORDIS*, June 14, 1994, archived November 17, 2022, https://cordis.europa.eu/article/id/2672-euukraine-partnership-and-cooperation-agreement.
171 "European Commission Memorandum: EU Relations with Ukraine," *European Commission*, February 18, 1992, https://ec.europa.eu/commission/presscorner/detail/en/memo_92_54.
172 Roth, Mathias. "EU-Ukraine Relations after the Orange Revolution: The Role of the New Member States." *European Security* 16, no. 2 (2007): 177–198. https://www.tandfonline.com/doi/full/10.1080/15705850701641023.
173 "EU-Ukraine – Strengthening the Strategic Partnership," *European Commission*, https://ec.europa.eu/commission/presscorner/detail/en/memo_05_57.
174 "EU-Ukraine Relations: what developments have there been since the election of Viktor Yanukovych?," *Foundation Robert Schuman*, https://www.robert-schuman.eu/en/european-issues/0214-eu-ukraine-relations-what-developments-have-there-been-since-the-election-of-viktor-yanukovych.
175 "EU-Ukraine Deep and Comprehensive Free Trade Area," *European Commission*, https://trade.ec.europa.eu/access-to-markets/en/content/eu-ukraine-deep-and-comprehensive-free-trade-area.
176 "EU-Ukraine Deep and Comprehensive Free Trade Area," *European Commission*, https://trade.ec.europa.eu/access-to-markets/en/content/eu-ukraine-deep-and-comprehensive-free-trade-area.
177 "Visas: Council confirms agreement on visa liberalisation for Ukrainians," *Council of the EU*, https://www.consilium.europa.eu/en/press/press-releases/2017/03/02/visa-liberalisation-ukraine/pdf.
178 "EUAM UKRAINE: European Union Advisory Mission for Civilian Security Sector Reform in Ukraine - Civilian Mission," *European Union Advisory Mission for Civilian Security Sector Reform Ukraine (EUAM Ukraine)*, https://www.eeas.europa.eu/euam-ukraine/euam-ukraine-european-union-advisory-mission-civilian-security-sector-reform-ukraine-civilian_und_en.

179 "European Peace Facility," *Council of the European Union*, https://www.consilium.europa.eu/en/policies/european-peace-facility/.
180 "European Peace Facility: EU Support to Ukraine," *Council of the European Union*, https://www.consilium.europa.eu/en/policies/european-peace-facility/#ukraine.
181 "European Peace Facility: EU Support to Ukraine," *Council of the European Union*, https://www.consilium.europa.eu/en/policies/european-peace-facility/#ukraine.
182 "European Peace Facility: EU Support to Ukraine," *Council of the European Union*, https://www.consilium.europa.eu/en/policies/european-peace-facility/#ukraine.
183 "Sanctions Against Russia Explained," *Council of the European Union*, https://www.consilium.europa.eu/en/policies/sanctions-against-russia-explained/#sanctions.
184 "Sanctions Against Russia Explained," *Council of the European Union*, https://www.consilium.europa.eu/en/policies/sanctions-against-russia-explained/#sanctions.
185 "Temporary Protection," *European Commission*, https://home-affairs.ec.europa.eu/policies/migration-and-asylum/common-european-asylum-system/temporary-protection_en.
186 "Temporary Protection," *European Commission*, https://home-affairs.ec.europa.eu/policies/migration-and-asylum/common-european-asylum-system/temporary-protection_en.
187 "Seven ways Russia's war on Ukraine has changed the world," *Chatham House*, https://www.chathamhouse.org/2023/02/seven-ways-russias-war-ukraine-has-changed-world.
188 "Consequences of the War in Ukraine: The Economic Fallout," *Rand*, https://www.rand.org/pubs/commentary/2023/03/consequences-of-the-war-in-ukraine-the-economic-fallout.html.
189 Tarek Ben Hassen & Hamid El Bilali, *Impacts of the Russia-Ukraine War on Global Food Security: Towards More Sustainable and Resilient Food Systems?* 2022, https://pmc.ncbi.nlm.nih.gov/articles/PMC9368568/.
190 "Threat of Nuclear Weapons Use 'Grave Danger That We Must Resist with All Our Might', Disarmament Affairs Official Tells General Assembly," *United Nations*, https://press.un.org/en/2024/ga12619.doc.htm.

4

THE RUSSIAN INVASION OF UKRAINE AND THE RESPONSE OF THE UNITED NATIONS

By Michael P. Scharf

Introduction

After the disintegration of the Soviet Union in 1991, foreign policy experts optimistically declared that the world had entered the "post-Cold War age."[1] Within the UN Security Council, it was a period of unprecedented collaboration and accomplishment.[2] In the few years that followed, the UN Security Council adopted more Chapter VII resolutions (condemning international law violations, establishing peace-keeping forces, imposing sanctions, authorizing force, establishing No Fly Zones and Safe Areas, and creating investigative commissions and international criminal tribunals) than in the preceding five decades since the creation of the United Nations.[3] But that period of cooperation lasted less than twenty years.[4]

During the Syrian conflict, starting in 2010, Russia vetoed thirteen Security Council Resolutions that would have condemned the Syrian government's atrocities, created a commission to investigate Syria's use of chemical weapons, and referred the matter to the International Criminal Court.[5] In this context, the Guardian newspaper reported in 2015 that "[t]he United States has warned that Russia's continued blanket use of its UN veto will jeopardize the [S]ecurity [C]ouncil's long-term legitimacy and could lead the U.S. and like-minded countries to bypass it as a decision-making body."[6] As the U.S. Permanent Representative to the UN told the Guardian: "It's a Darwinian universe here. If a particular body reveals itself to be dysfunctional, then people are going to go elsewhere."[7]

Then, in February 2022, Russia's massive invasion of neighboring Ukraine ushered in a full-on return of a new Cold War.[8] The invasion and international response were described as "a major breaking point in history."[9] Five

DOI: 10.4324/9781003458166-5

days after the invasion, 11 members of the UN Security Council adopted a U.S.-drafted Resolution invoking the authority of the 1950 "Uniting for Peace" Resolution[10] and calling for an emergency session of the UN General Assembly to take action to respond to Russia's aggression in circumvention of Russia's veto at the Security Council.[11] At that emergency session, on March 2, 2022, the UN General Assembly adopted Resolution ES-11/1 by a vote of 141 in favor, 5 opposed, and 35 abstentions.[12] The Resolution characterized Russia's action as "aggression … in violation of Article 2(4) of the Charter" and demanded that Russia "immediately, completely and unconditionally withdraw all of its military forces from the territory of Ukraine within its internationally recognized borders."[13] This was the first time in three decades that the Security Council and General Assembly had utilized the "Uniting for Peace" mechanism – a process designed to end-run a Security Council veto. Together with the General Assembly's creation of the IIIM in 2016, the use of the Uniting for Peace process to condemn Russia's aggression in 2022 represented a major shift in power away from the Security Council and to the General Assembly, with potentially broad and long-term implications.

This chapter chronicles the causes and consequences of that power shift. First, it surveys the history of the adoption of the Uniting for Peace Resolution and its historic uses. Next, it explores the adoption of Resolution ES-11/1, focusing on the reinterpretation of the UN Charter reflected by those developments. It then examines the subsequent General Assembly Resolutions adopted under its Uniting for Peace authority and the possible future Uniting for Peace resolutions related to the Ukraine conflict. Finally, it concludes by analyzing the likely legal and institutional consequences of these developments.

The History of the Uniting for Peace Resolution

Security Council Deadlock During the Cold War

After the failure of the League of Nations (1920–1945), the countries that negotiated the UN Charter in San Francisco in May–June 1945 formed the new organization around a potent Security Council, made up of the five most powerful states (the Permanent Members)[14] and a handful of others elected on a rotating basis. While the General Assembly would include every member of the organization with an equal vote, the Security Council would have the primary responsibility within the UN system for the maintenance of international peace and security, as well as enforcement of international law.[15]

As the price demanded for their support of the new organization,[16] the Permanent Members were accorded a veto over all substantive matters before the Security Council.[17] The delegates at San Francisco granted the veto power to the Permanent Five because of "a tremendous amount of confidence in the certainty that the veto shall not be applied except in exceptional cases."[18] But that confidence was misplaced. The creation of the United Nations corresponded with the dawn of the Cold War.[19] It was a period marked by gridlock in the Security Council, which was prevented by the Permanent Member veto from intervening to halt atrocities and bloodshed in a variety of conflict areas around the world.[20] During the Cold War period, the Soviet Union vetoed 122 Resolutions, the United States vetoed 80, Britain vetoed 32, France vetoed 20, while China vetoed none.[21]

Security Council deadlock during the Cold War went through two phases. In the first (1946–1965), when most of the members of the United Nations were West-leaning States, the Soviet Union vetoed 106 resolutions, while the United States vetoed none.[22] In the second phase (1966–1989), during which a number of former colonies joined the United Nations as newly independent States, the United States vetoed 67 Security Council Resolutions (most related to Israel), while the Soviet Union vetoed just 13.[23]

The frequent use of the veto, especially in cases where UN action could halt humanitarian disasters, has eroded the legitimacy of the United Nations Security Council. Over the years, there have been numerous proposals to amend the UN Charter to make it more difficult for the Permanent Five to exercise their veto power.[24] But Charter amendment requires the consent of the Permanent Five, so all proposals that would weaken the veto have been met with their opposition and have gone nowhere, leading scholars to decry that the "veto is essentially immune from reform."[25]

The Creation and Early Uses of the Uniting for Peace Resolution

At the height of the Cold War, the Uniting for Peace Resolution was created to enable the General Assembly to act quickly in an international crisis in the face of Security Council paralysis due to a Permanent Member veto. The brainchild of the United States, the Resolution was adopted by the General Assembly on November 3, 1950, in response to the Soviet Union's veto of resolutions addressing North Korea's aggression against South Korea.[26]

In June 1950, the Security Council had initially authorized Members of the United Nations to "furnish such assistance to the Republic of Korea as may be necessary to repel the armed attack and to restore international peace and security in the area."[27] That resolution was not vetoed by the Soviet Union (an ally of North Korea) because at the time the Soviet Union was boycotting the meetings of the Security Council in an effort to compel the Council to seat the communist government of Beijing rather than the Nationalist Government of Taiwan as China. This turned out to be an enormous diplomatic blunder since the other members of the Council and later the International Court of Justice[28] took the position that being absent was not the same as a non-concurring vote for purposes of exercising the Permanent Member veto.[29]

When the Soviet delegation returned to the Security Council in August 1950, it voted against a United States draft resolution condemning the continued defiance of the United Nations by the North Korean authorities.[30] In order to overcome this impasse, the United States proposed that the General Assembly adopt the Uniting for Peace Resolution.[31] The United States knew that this would dilute the power of its veto, but up to that point in time it had never used the veto and viewed the continued authorization to fight the Korean War as a more important consideration.

The Uniting for Peace Resolution allows the General Assembly to immediately consider matters in which the Security Council has failed in its duty to maintain international peace and security due to the use of the veto.[32] It can do so when asked by a majority of the members of the Security Council (this procedure is not subject to the veto), or upon its own decision to take up the matter with a two-thirds vote. If the Assembly is not in session, the Uniting for Peace process allows it to convene an emergency session. Then, with an affirmative vote of a two-thirds majority of members present, the General Assembly may issue recommendations it deems necessary to restore international peace and security.

In its initial use of this authority, on February 1, 1951, the General Assembly adopted Resolution 498(V), calling upon states to support continued UN military action in Korea, including repelling Chinese aggression. To date, this is the only time the General Assembly has called for use of force under the Uniting for Peace Resolution.[33] There is scholarly debate, however, about whether the 1951 General Assembly Resolution was based on the underlying right of collective self-defense, merely constituted a confirmation of an existing Security Council authorization to use force or represented an independent authorization to take enforcement measures.[34]

The Uniting for Peace Resolution was next used in 1956 when Egypt nationalized the Suez Canal, prompting Britain, France, and Israel to attack Egypt with the objective of regaining Western control of the Canal and remove the Egyptian President from power.[35] The UK and France vetoed Security Council resolutions mandating the immediate withdrawal of armed forces. Invoking the Uniting for Peace Resolution, the United States called for an emergency Special Session of the General Assembly. The Assembly convened and adopted Resolution 997, calling for an immediate ceasefire and withdrawal of all foreign forces, an arms embargo, the reopening of the Suez Canal, and the placement of UN peacekeeping forces to monitor the situation.[36] Within a week of the Resolution's adoption, Britain and France withdrew their armed forces.[37]

General Assembly Resolution 997 demonstrated that the General Assembly could take up a matter that the Security Council had been debating despite Article 12 of the UN Charter. That article states that "while the Security Council is exercising in respect of any dispute or situation the recommendations with regard to that dispute or situation unless the Security Council so requests."[38] In the 2004 Construction of a Wall Case, the International Court of Justice confirmed that the interpretation of Article 12 has evolved through state practice, and that there was no bar "for the General Assembly to deal in parallel with the same matter [as the Security Council] concerning the maintenance of international peace and security."[39]

General Assembly Resolution 997 also indicated the wide panoply of powers that could be exercised by the General Assembly under the Uniting for Peace Resolution, which were traditionally viewed as belonging exclusively to the Security Council. Importantly, the Resolution did not purport to authorize force or enforcement action. Nor has any subsequent General Assembly Resolution invoking the Uniting for Peace Resolution.

Under the UN Charter, the General Assembly can only "recommend" the use of force, not "authorize" it as the Security Council is empowered to do.[40] This is significant because Article 2(4) of the UN Charter prohibits use of force except in self-defense or when authorized by the Security Council.[41] In the "Certain Expenses" advisory opinion of 1962, the International Court of Justice noted that under the UN Charter, only the Security Council can authorize enforcement by coercive action against an aggressor.[42] This suggests that the Uniting for Peace Resolution can only be used to call for use of force in a situation in which the UN Charter would permit collective self-defense to respond to an armed attack.[43] However, some scholars argue that a General Assembly recommendation for use of force under the Uniting for Peace process can have the same legal affect as a Security Council authorization because the prohibition on the use of force binds members and not the United Nations organization.[44] Thus, where the organization delegates authority to use force through a recommendation, such force will not run afoul of the Article 2(4) prohibition.[45]

Between its first use in 1951 and its revival in 2022, the Uniting for Peace Resolution had been invoked only eleven times – seven times at the request of a majority of members of the Security Council and five times unilaterally by the General Assembly. In each case, the General Assembly recommended non-use of force measures, such as: establishing a consensual peace keeping force (Suez Canal, 1950), establishing a commission of inquiry (Hungary, 1956), calling for the withdrawal of foreign troops from Jordan and Lebanon (1958), calling for an embargo of weapons to the Congo (1960), calling for the rescission by Israel of unilateral measures in Jerusalem (1967), providing assistance to East Pakistani refugees (1971), calling for the withdrawal of foreign troops from Afghanistan (1980), calling for the withdrawal of Israel from territories occupied since 1967 (1980), condemning South Africa for the occupation of Namibia and calling for assistance to the liberation struggle (1981), calling on members to apply sanctions on Israel (1982), and requesting an advisory opinion of the ICJ on the legal consequences of the construction of a wall in the occupied Palestinian territory (1997).[46]

The Soviet Union considered the Uniting for Peace mechanism to be an illegitimate usurpation by the General Assembly of powers reserved to the Security Council. It therefore refused to pay its assessed share for the peacekeeping forces authorized by the General Assembly for the Middle East (1958) and Congo (1960). In an advisory opinion that has been described "as a paradigm shift in the character of the UN,"[47] the International Court of Justice determined that the expenses for the peacekeeping forces created by the General Assembly under the Uniting for Peace process were expenses of the organization that the Soviet Union was obligated to pay.[48] In so doing, the Court confirmed the power of the General Assembly to authorize peacekeeping forces with the consent of the territorial state, saying that the power of the Security Council to take action to maintain or restore international peace and security "is primary, not exclusive."[49] To support its opinion, the International Court of Justice articulated a broad approach to the implied powers doctrine, noting that "when the Organization takes action which warrants the assertion that it was appropriate for the fulfilment of one of the stated purposes of the United Nations, the presumption is that such action is not ultra vires the Organization.[50]

Is the Uniting for Peace Resolution Still Relevant Today?

Until the 2022 Ukraine crisis, the Security Council had not referred any matter under the Uniting for Peace procedure since 1982, and the General Assembly had not unilaterally invoked it since 1997.[51] Professor Christian Tomuschat believes this reluctance reflected concern that the Uniting for Peace Resolution "has a potential that could subvert the well-equilibrated balance of power within the United Nations."[52] This concern led the Soviet Union and later Russia to continuously object to the Resolution as authorizing the General Assembly to act in an ultra vires manner.[53] Meanwhile, after the Uniting for Peace Resolution was used in 1967, 1980, 1982, and 1997 to condemn and recommend sanctions against Israel, the United States soured on its utility. These concerns explain the dearth of times the Resolution has been invoked, and the length of time that transpired since its last use until 2022.

Moreover, Larry Johnson, former Deputy Legal Counsel of the United Nations, has argued that the Uniting for Peace Resolution is no longer needed.[54] He points out that since the General Assembly is now in session year-round, the Uniting for Peace Resolution is not necessary to call a special session.[55] He notes that the International Court of Justice confirmed in the "Wall" case that there is no bar to the General Assembly taking up a matter of which the Security Council is seized with or without invoking the Uniting for Peace Resolution.[56] He argues that since the General Assembly has exercised the powers of the Uniting for Peace Resolution a number of times without invoking the Resolution, such as in calling for voluntary sanctions, the Resolution is not a necessary predicate to such action.[57] And with respect to the General Assembly recommending the use of force pursuant to the Uniting for Peace Resolution, Johnson argues that the Assembly can do so only within the limited context of supporting the exercise by States of their inherent right to individual or collective self-defense under Article 51 of the Charter.[58]

The General Assembly's Creation of the IIIM

The Cold War began its return eight years before the Russian invasion of Ukraine, stemming from events in Syria, a close ally of Russia. Despite significant evidence of atrocity crimes being committed in the ongoing civil war in Syria – particularly by government forces – the UN Security Council was paralyzed by the Russian veto, unable to take any steps towards accountability. In May 2014, Russia vetoed a Security Council resolution that would have referred the situation in Syria to the International Criminal Court.[59] Later, Russia vetoed a Security Council resolution that would have established an investigative mechanism to document Syrian use of chemical weapons and other atrocities.[60] In all, Russia vetoed 13 resolutions to prevent accountability of the Syrian government since the outbreak of the Syrian civil war.[61]

In contrast, in the 1990s, the Security Council first condemned atrocities in the former Yugoslavia and Rwanda, then established an investigative commission to document them, and finally created ad hoc tribunals to prosecute the perpetrators.[62] Also, ten years later, the Security Council referred the situations in The Sudan and Libya to the ICC for prosecution.[63] But in Syria, the Security Council could do absolutely nothing. This led the United States Representative to bluntly declare: "The United States is disgusted that a couple of members of this Council continue to prevent us from fulfilling our sole purpose here, which is to address an ever-deepening crisis in Syria and a growing threat to regional peace and security. For months, this Council has been held hostage by a couple of members."[64]

Enter Liechtenstein's UN Ambassador Christian Wenaweser, who had formerly served as President of the International Criminal Court's Assembly of State Parties. In the fall of 2016, Ambassador Wenaweser hatched a bold plan for an end-run around the Security Council that did not involve invoking the disfavored Uniting for Peace Resolution. For months, Wenaweser canvassed UN delegates, arguing: "We have postponed any meaningful action on accountability too often and for too long."[65] Commenting on the outsized role Wenaweser played, Harvard Law Professor Alex Whiting writes, "the short history of international criminal justice, from Nuremberg to the present, is full of heroic individuals and their improbable and creative ideas that have pushed the project forward."[66]

Galvanized by Ambassador Wenaweser's efforts, on December 21, 2016, the United Nations General Assembly took a historic step in establishing a mechanism to investigate and preserve evidence of international crimes in Syria, the first time the Assembly has established such a body.[67] Despite objection by Russia, the General Assembly adopted Resolution 71/248 by a vote of 105 to 15 with 52 abstentions, creating the International, Impartial and Independent Mechanism to Assist in the Investigation and Prosecution of Those Responsible for the Most Serious Crimes under International Law Committed in the Syrian Arab Republic since March 2011, known in shorthand as the IIIM.[68]

The IIIM is empowered to collect evidence from other bodies including the Independent International Commission of Inquiry established by the Human Rights Council, and to conduct its own investigations "including interviews, witness testimony, documentation, and forensic material."[69] The General Assembly Resolution directs the IIIM to analyze the collected evidence and prepare files of evidence that could be provided to "national, regional or international courts or tribunals that have or may in the future have jurisdiction over these crimes, in accordance with international law."[70]

This was the first time in history that the General Assembly established an investigative body to assemble and analyze evidence of international crimes for the purpose of preserving evidence for future international or domestic trials. Its authority to do so was questioned by Russia. During the debate on the resolution and subsequently in a note verbale dated February 8, 2017, the Russian Government complained that "the General Assembly acted ultra vires – going beyond its powers as specified" in the UN Charter.[71] Specifically, Russia argued that

> a number of powers vested in the mechanism under [R]esolution 71/248, including those of "analys[ing] evidence" and "prepar[ing] files," are prosecutorial in nature. However, prosecutions, criminal investigations and support of criminal investigations are not among the functions of the General Assembly. It cannot create an organ that has more powers than the General Assembly itself.[72]

There was a time when it was not settled whether the Security Council itself had the power to establish a prosecutorial institution, let alone whether the General Assembly could do so. But that question was answered in the affirmative by the Appeals Chamber of the Yugoslavia Tribunal in 1995 based on the extraordinary powers vested in the Security Council under Chapter VII of the UN Charter to maintain international peace and security.[73] The General Assembly has much more limited powers, and they do not include the power to prosecute international crimes. Yet, it is not clear that the powers of the IIIM are "prosecutorial in nature" in the sense that they entail the prosecution of individuals, a power that could only be conferred by the Security Council. Rather, the Resolution and Secretary General's report describe a "prosecutorial" body only in respect to the standards that will be adopted by the IIIM when collecting and analyzing evidence. If one views the IIIM not as a sort of investigative judge or prosecutor but simply as a fact-finding body that will adhere to a criminal law standard in performing its functions, its creation seemed to be squarely within the powers of the General Assembly. In this respect the IIIM is not much different than the several commissions established by the General Assembly-created Human Rights Council to investigate international criminal law violations in Palestine (2006), Lebanon (2006), Darfur (2006), Libya (2011), Cote d'Ivoire (2011), Syria (2012), Eritrea (2014), DPRK (2014), and Ethiopia (2021).[74]

Article 10 of the UN Charter gives the General Assembly the power to "discuss" and make "recommendations" concerning "any questions or matters within the scope of the present Charter or relating to the powers and functions of any organs provided for in the present Charter."[75] As such, it is within the mandate of the General Assembly to consider questions of threats to peace and security in Syria and whether a referral to the ICC or the establishment of an ad hoc tribunal is warranted. Further, Article 22 of the Charter empowers the General Assembly to "establish such subsidiary organs as it deems necessary for the performance of its functions."[76] Therefore, the General Assembly has the authority to establish a "subsidiary organ" to collect and assess the available evidence of international crimes in Syria in order to inform the General Assembly's discussion and recommendations on these matters. On the other hand, the evidence collected by the IIIM would undeniably not be used solely (or even primarily) for the purpose of the General Assembly's discussion and recommendations, but it is not clear that additional uses of the information would render the creation of the IIIM beyond the power of the General Assembly.

Whatever the merits of Russia's legal argument, the establishment of this novel institution by the General Assembly clearly evinces a fundamental power shift away from the Security Council and to the General Assembly caused by the international community's frustration with the abuse of the veto to prevent action to deal with international atrocities. In providing a legal justification for this power shift, Professor Jennifer Trahan of New York University argues

> [t]he veto power is being abused in a way never anticipated when the Charter was drafted, and in a way that is at odds with other bodies of international law (such as the highest level jus cogens norms) and the "purposes and principles" of the UN Charter, with which the Security Council

(including its Permanent Members) are bound, under article 24.2 of the Charter, to act in accordance.[77]

To some, this extraordinary action by the General Assembly confirmed Larry Johnson's view that the Uniting for Peace Resolution was no longer necessary. The power of the General Assembly was ascending without it.

Humanitarian Intervention: The Bombing of the Syrian Chemical Weapons Facilities

In its 2001 report on "Responsibility to Protect," the International Commission on Intervention and State Sovereignty opined that the General Assembly could play an important role in legitimizing force to halt atrocities where the Security Council is prevented from doing so by the veto.[78] But fearing a slippery slope in which the Responsibility to Protect principle would be used in conjunction with the Uniting for Peace Resolution to target certain States (such as Israel), the "responsibility to protect" concept as adopted by the Assembly in the 2005 World Summit Outcome Resolution does not contemplate the Assembly recommending that States use coercive force to stop a State from committing atrocity crimes against its own population.[79]

This explains why the General Assembly did not invoke the Uniting for Peace Resolution in the context of Syrian use of chemical weapons against the Syrian population from 2013 to 2018. With the Security Council paralyzed and the General Assembly not perceived as a viable option, on April 14, 2018, the United States, United Kingdom, and France acted on their own in conducting airstrikes against three Syrian chemical weapons facilities.[80] They justified their use of force as necessary to prevent the Assad regime from continuing to use chemical weapons against the Syrian population in the context of Security Council paralysis to establish accountability for this international crime. Before the Syrian airstrikes, most countries and experts had taken the position that there was no international law right of humanitarian intervention under customary international law or the UN Charter except when authorized by the UN Security Council.[81]

This was confirmed in 1999, when Russia blocked the Security Council from authorizing force against Serbia to safeguard Kosovar Albanians in the Serb province of Kosovo from ethnic cleansing, and NATO launched a 78-day bombing campaign against Serbia without Security Council authorization. The United States and United Kingdom justified the action as a sui generis act to save hundreds of thousands of lives.[82] The UN described it as "unlawful but legitimate."[83] In the years since the 1999 NATO airstrikes, countries have used force for humanitarian purposes without Security Council authorization on several other occasions, including the U.S.–UK imposition of a no-fly zone over Iraq to protect the Marsh Arabs from Saddam Hussein's reprisals,[84] the Russian invasion of South Ossetia, Georgia ostensibly to protect ethnic Russians living there from attack,[85] and the U.S. airstrikes against the ISIS terrorist group to save the besieged Yazidis on Mount Sinjar, Iraq.[86] But never before the April 14, 2018 airstrikes against Syria had humanitarian use of force been accompanied by a clear legal justification based on a right of humanitarian intervention.

In contrast to the prior cases, the countries participating in the April 2018 airstrikes on Syria embraced a common legal justification – humanitarian intervention – rather than cite only factual considerations that render the use of force morally defensible as they had in the past. The United Kingdom was the most explicit of the three, telling the Security Council that its actions were legally justified on the basis of "humanitarian intervention" in the context of preventing use of chemical weapons when the Security Council had been paralyzed by a Permanent Member's veto.[87] It stated that "[a]ny State is permitted under international law, on an exceptional basis, to take measures in order to alleviate overwhelming humanitarian suffering."[88]

The United Kingdom's position was that humanitarian intervention in such cases without Security Council authorization would not be in violation of Article 2(4) of the UN Charter because that provision only prohibits the use of force that is "against the territorial integrity or political independence of any state" and "inconsistent with the Purposes of the United Nations."[89] Humanitarian intervention, the United Kingdom argued, is consistent with the Charter's Purposes and Principles, which include "maintaining international peace and security," "promoting and encouraging respect for human rights," and "sav[ing] succeeding generations from the scourge of war." According to the United Kingdom, humanitarian intervention in response to use of chemical weapons is not seeking to threaten the integrity of a state or bring about political change, but only to save lives and enforce the global ban on chemical weapons.[90] The United Kingdom's argument would have been strengthened if the General Assembly had authorized the action under the Uniting for Peace Resolution, thereby rendering it a collective action taken by the UN rather than by just three States.[91]

For its part, the United States told the Security Council that "[t]he United States is deeply grateful to the United Kingdom and France for their part in the coalition to defend the prohibition of chemical weapons. We worked in lock step: we were in complete agreement" (emphasis added).[92] As such, the United States can be held to have implicitly adopted the rationale of the United Kingdom.[93] This is particularly significant because the United States has never recognized a right of humanitarian intervention outside of Security Council authorization under international law.

Out of a total of seventy states that publicly commented on the airstrikes at the United Nations or elsewhere, only a small handful of countries questioned their legality.[94] This suggests that the United Kingdom, France and the

United States could have easily garnered the votes of two-thirds the General Assembly to obtain authorization under the Uniting for Peace Resolution if they had decided to go that route. Such action would have avoided the possibility of mixed motives and self-interests. As one author has observed, "the most effective safeguard that the developing world has against unilateral misuse of force by those with the military capabilities is by an unbiased U.N. authorization of collective force."[95]

The implications of the April 2018 airstrikes are far-reaching. Like the creation of the IIIM, the growing recognition of a right of humanitarian intervention without Security Council authorization represents a fundamental power shift from the Security Council – which had historically been viewed as holding the keys to the use of force – to coalitions of states who assert a right to act to save lives when the Council is paralyzed.

Russia's 2022 Invasion of Ukraine: Reemergence of the Uniting for Peace Mechanism

Resolution ES-11/1

While the United States had been wary of resorting to the Uniting for Peace Resolution for the past fifty years,[96] in response to Russia's invasion of Ukraine in February 2022 the United States decided the time was right to dust off the Resolution and once again put it to use. On February 27, 2022, eleven members of the Security Council voted in favor of the U.S.-sponsored resolution calling for an emergency session of the General Assembly under the Uniting for Peace process; only Russia opposed, while three members abstained (China, India and the United Arab Emirates).[97] Twenty-four hours later, in an emergency session broadcast live around the world, an overwhelming number of States joined together to express their collective disapprobation of the Russian aggression.

Ukraine's Representative, who introduced the Resolution, said that "for almost a week, his country has been fighting missiles and bombs. Half a million people have fled as the Russian Federation tries to deprive his country of the right to exist, carrying out a long list of war crimes."[98] The U.S. Representative urged countries to vote in favor of the Resolution, saying her country "is choosing to stand with the Ukrainian people and will hold the Russian Federation accountable for its actions."[99] The Representative of the European Union, speaking for the 28 EU States, added: "This is not just about Ukraine, this is not just about Europe, this is about defending an international order based on rules. … Today's historic vote clearly shows the Russian Federation's isolation from the rest of the international community."[100]

The Special Session resulted in the adoption of Resolution ES-11/1 by a large majority – 141 in favor, five against and 35 abstentions.[101] The resolution did not go as far as some of the prior Uniting for Peace Resolutions. It did not call for sanctions, peacekeepers, or collective use of force. But it did return to a legal characterization that the General Assembly had long avoided by declaring the Russian invasion to constitute an act of "aggression"[102] – recognized as a crime under international law.[103] Specifically, the resolution deplored "in the strongest terms the "aggression by the Russian Federation against Ukraine in violation of Article 2(4) of Charter" and condemned Russia's declaration as to the necessity of this "special military operation."[104]

Resolution ES-11/1 further demanded Russia to "cease its use of force against Ukraine" as well as to "immediately, completely and unconditionally withdraw all of its military forces from the territory of Ukraine within its internationally recognized borders."[105] It also condemned "all violations of international humanitarian law and violations and abuses of human rights," demanding that parties to the conflict "fully comply with their obligations under international humanitarian law to spare the civilian population."[106]

The finding that Russia committed aggression in Ukraine has already had an effect in the *Ukraine v. Russia case*, where the International Court of Justice drew upon Resolution ES-11/1 to support the ordering of provisional measures to protect the rights of Ukraine from being subject to the use of force by Russia based on false allegations of genocide under the Genocide Convention.[107] And it could be of legal relevance in criminal cases in either domestic courts or an ad hoc tribunal prosecuting Russian leaders for the crime of aggression.[108]

Resolutions ES-11/2 through ES-11/6

In the months following the adoption of ES-11/1, the General Assembly has resorted to the "Uniting for Peace" mechanism to reconvene five additional times in emergency session to adopt resolutions in response to the evolving situation in Ukraine. On March 24, 2022, it adopted a resolution on the humanitarian consequences of aggression against Ukraine.[109] On April 7, 2022, it adopted a resolution suspending the rights of membership of Russia in the Human Rights Council.[110] On October 12, 2022, it adopted a resolution rejecting the sham plebiscites and illegal Russian annexation of territory in Eastern Ukraine.[111] And on November 14, 2022, it adopted a resolution establishing a claims register in The Hague to compile state and individual compensation claims against Russia related to the war in Ukraine.[112]

The most recent resolution, ES-11/6, was adopted on the one-year anniversary of the Russian invasion of Ukraine.[113] This resolution, sponsored by Ukraine, underscores the need to reach a comprehensive, just and lasting peace in Ukraine as soon as possible "in line with the Charter of the United Nations." This phrase was interpreted to mean an agreement respecting the internationally recognized borders of Ukraine prior to Russia's invasion.[114]

The Resolution was adopted by a vote of 141 in favor and 7 opposed with 32 abstentions after the Assembly rejected proposed amendments that would have watered down the resolution proposed by Russia's staunch ally, Belarus.[115] Importantly, the resolution "emphasizes the need to ensure accountability for the most serious crimes under international law committed on the territory of Ukraine through appropriate, fair and independent investigations and prosecutions at the national or international level." Two weeks later, the International Criminal Court issued arrest warrants for Russian President Vladimir Putin and his Commissioner for Children's Rights, Maria Alekseyevna Lvova-Belova, charging them with the war crime of abduction and deportation of Ukraine children for adoption in Russia.[116]

What is likely to come next?

The drawback of writing about an evolving situation is that there are likely to be new developments before the book is even published. Resolutions ES-11/1 through 11/6 are unlikely to be the General Assembly's final word on the Ukraine situation. Rather, it is anticipated that the Resolutions will be a door opener to a variety of possible collective actions by the General Assembly as the crisis unfolds in the months and years ahead. For example, the General Assembly's finding in Resolution ES-11/1 that the "rights and benefits" of membership[117] entail good faith obligations could provide a foundation for future claims that the Russian government has not acted in accordance with the expectations incumbent on a UN member state. While the General Assembly cannot unilaterally suspend Russia from the UN Security Council and General Assembly through Article 5 of the UN Charter,[118] it could potentially use that finding to reject Russia's credentials and block Russian diplomats from participating in UN bodies. Usually, credentials challenges involve competing government claims to represent the State, but there is precedent for the General Assembly to factor in a regime's adherence to the UN Charter in assessing whether to accept or reject credentials. The credentials of the South African apartheid regime were thus rejected for many years by the General Assembly due to its "flagrant violation" of the UN Charter.[119]

Another way in which the General Assembly's determinations might assist the international community's response to Russia's invasion of Ukraine is in supporting the legal justification and coalescing political will for the continuation and strengthening of sanctions against Russia. In response to Russia's war of aggression against Ukraine, the United States, European Union, and several other states have imposed the most comprehensive economic sanctions ever leveled on a major world power.[120] Individual sanctions (including freezing of assets and restrictions on travel) have now been imposed on more than a thousand Russian decision-makers in key political and economic positions.

Almost 50% of the Russian central bank's foreign exchange reserves have been frozen, and Western banks have been prohibited from undertaking transactions with it, making it extremely difficult for Russia to service debt. Other Russian banks have been removed from the SWIFT system, making international transactions more difficult for Russian companies. Russian airlines have been banned from European and U.S. airspace; their aircraft are no longer being maintained and they cannot obtain parts. In addition, Russian energy and arms companies can no longer receive loans from Western banks. Key technologies for aviation, shipping, and raw material extraction and processing are subject to an export ban.[121] While Russia has the monetary reserves and revenue from continuing oil and gas exports to fund its military operations, "it may not be able to arm it as easily if sanctions continue."[122] Restrictions on imports of aviation parts and high-tech goods mean that Russia will "have very limited ability to make tanks, missiles...and fighter jets."[123]

Russia is the world's second-largest exporter of crude oil, accounting for most of its foreign trade.[124] Significantly, the United States and EU States have agreed to ban imports of Russian coal, gas, and petroleum, but with transitional periods for countries that are particularly affected and exemptions for pipeline deliveries.[125] Despite these sanctions, Russia exported $97.7 billion worth of fossil fuels in the first 100 days since its invasion of Ukraine, at an average of $977 million per day.[126] Most of the Russian oil, gas, and coal went to China, India, Turkey, Japan, South Korea, and Egypt, which have not imposed bans on Russian oil.[127] Through these exports, Russia is keeping its economy afloat. This demonstrates an axiom of trade sanctions – they don't work well unless they are applied universally, as they were against Iran in the early 2000s.[128]

The General Assembly has used the Uniting for Peace Resolution in the past to call upon members to impose diplomatic sanctions and trade embargoes as a countermeasure to induce compliance with international law by a law-breaking State.[129] For States questioning the legitimacy of such sanctions, the General Assembly could play a useful role certifying that the conditions for the valid invocation of the law of countermeasures under Article 49 of the International Law Commission's Draft Articles on State Responsibility (proportionality, proper purpose, and temporal limitation) have been met.[130]

Finally, in collaboration with Ukraine, acting under the Uniting for Peace Resolution, the General Assembly could establish a "hybrid tribunal" to prosecute the Crime of Aggression as described in the below Chapter by Jennifer Trahan. Such a court has been proposed by a number of experts and organizations.[131] The International Criminal Court can prosecute war crimes, crimes against humanity, and genocide committed by Russian nationals in Ukraine because the Ukraine government lodged a declaration accepting the Court's jurisdiction over such crimes since 2013.[132] But a separate international, hybrid, or internationalized tribunal is needed because the

International Criminal Court does not have jurisdiction over Russian aggression under the terms of the 2010 Kampala Aggression Amendment to the ICC Statute.[133] Moreover, although Ukraine has a criminal statute granting Ukrainian courts jurisdiction over the Crime of Aggression,[134] Ukraine on its own would not be able to prosecute the top Russian leaders because of the doctrine of Head of State Immunity, which does not apply to international courts.[135]

As discussed above, the General Assembly's powers are limited to making recommendations, as confirmed by the International Court of Justice in the *Certain Expenses case*, and the General Assembly lacks the ability to take enforcement action, which is the exclusive prerogative of the Security Council.[136] As the International Criminal Tribunal for the Former Yugoslavia's Appeals Chamber made clear in the *Tadić* case, the establishment of a criminal tribunal is a form of such coercive or enforcement action.[137] But the General Assembly's past practice has indicated a way around those limitations. The General Assembly can support an exercise of criminal jurisdiction possessed by one or more UN Member States. The foremost example is the GA's creation of the Extraordinary Chambers in the Courts of Cambodia (ECCC). In the case of the ECCC, the General Assembly introduced a resolution recommending the UN Secretary General to enter into a bilateral agreement with the Government of Cambodia for establishing a criminal tribunal,[138] and subsequently, the resolution establishing the ECCC was approved by the General Assembly.[139]

Conclusion

The Security Council and General Assembly's resort to the Uniting for Peace mechanism for the first time since 1982 reflects the failure of the Security Council to fulfill its responsibility to respond to threats to international peace and security in the context of the Ukraine crisis. With the Security Council paralyzed once again by the veto during a new Cold War, institutional power has shifted to the General Assembly.

The United States conceived the Uniting for Peace mechanism during the Korean War to end-run the Soviet veto and supported its use for several decades thereafter. But after the Uniting for Peace mechanism began to be used to sanction Israel notwithstanding U.S. vetoes at the Security Council, the United States concluded that the mechanism should be relegated to the dustpan of history, where it remained unused for 30 years. The dawn of a new Cold War, sparked by Russia's invasion of Ukraine, changed the calculus. In resorting to the Uniting for Peace mechanism in 2022, the United States had little to lose because the General Assembly through diplomatic practice and International Court of Justice decisions, had slowly amassed the power to act on matters of which the Security Council was seized, to recommend imposition of sanctions, and to create investigative bodies and hybrid tribunals without invoking the Uniting for Peace Resolution.

While resorting to the Uniting for Peace mechanism might not have been necessary in light of the General Assembly's recent practice, the foundation of the Uniting for Peace Resolution imbued Resolution ES-11/1 with tremendous symbolic value, and the Resolution's determination that Russia had committed an unprovoked act of aggression had an immediate impact on the Russia-Ukraine International Court of Justice case and set the stage for subsequent actions by the General Assembly under the Uniting for Peace mechanism. Additional General Assembly actions using the mechanism might include a credentials challenge to suspend the Russian delegation from participation at the United Nations, endorsement of diplomatic and economic sanctions, and the creation of a hybrid tribunal to prosecute Russian leaders for the crime of aggression.

Although it is not clear at the time of this writing that the votes exist for the General Assembly to adopt such actions, an axiom of international diplomacy is that events on the ground can quickly alter votes at the United Nations. A major atrocity, or Russian use of chemical or tactical nuclear weapons, for example, would dramatically alter the diplomatic terrain. In such a case, the Uniting for Peace mechanism, now as in 1950, will play a historic role.

What is clear is that the Ukraine crisis has been the catalyst for a major power shift at the United Nations. If, as the U.S. Representative to the UN described it, "[i]t's a Darwinian universe here,"[140] we are witnessing great leaps in the evolution of the modern United Nations. Because of Ukraine, the United Nations will never be the same. The series of General Assembly resolutions based on the Uniting for Peace mechanism in 2022–2024 represent a fundamental reinterpretation of the UN Charter, with potentially significant implications beyond the Russia-Ukraine war. Not long after, the General Assembly used the mechanism to adopt a resolution on May 10, 2024, upgrading Palestine's participation in the United Nations,[141] and another on September 18, 2024, calling on States to take measures to prevent their nationals, companies, and entities under their jurisdiction from engaging in activities that support or sustain Israel's occupation of Palestine.[142] If, as Western States had long feared, the Uniting for Peace mechanism was a Pandora's box, the box is now open.

Notes

1 Charles William Maynes and William G. Hayland, THE NATURE OF THE POST-COLD WAR WORLD (Strategic Studies Institute, U.S. Army War College, 1993) (Maynes was the editor of *Foreign Policy* and Hayland was the editor of *Foreign Affairs*), available at: https://www.globalsecurity.org/military/library/report/1993/ssi_maynes-hyland.pdf.

2 *See generally* Kenneth Manusama, The United Nations Security Council in the Post-Cold War Era: Applying the Principle of Legality (2006).
3 *Id.*
4 Michael P. Scharf, Milena Sterio, and Paul R. Williams, The Syria Conflict's Impact on International Law (2020).
5 Michael P. Scharf, Milena Sterio, and Paul R. Williams, The Syria Conflict's Impact on International Law (2020).
6 Julian Borger and Bastien Inzaurralde, *Russian Vetoes are Putting UN Security Council Legitimacy at Risk, US Says*, The Guardian, September 23, 2015.
7 *Id.*
8 Elliott Abrams, *The New Cold War*, Council on Foreign Relations, March 3, 2022, available at: https://www.cfr.org/blog/new-cold-war-0 (Abrams served as President George W. Bush's Deputy National Security Advisor for Global Democracy Strategy); John Simpson, *Ukraine invasion: Is this a new Cold War*, BBC News, February 24, 2022 (Simpson is the World Affairs Editor of the BBC), available at: https://www.bbc.com/news/world-europe-60515342; Travis Andersen, *Does Russia's invasion of Ukraine signal the start of a new Cold War?* The Boston Globe, March 2, 2022, available at: https://www.msn.com/en-us/news/world/does-russias-invasion-of-ukraine-signal-the-start-of-a-new-cold-war-foreign-policy-specialists-weigh-in/ar-AAUwzIQ.
9 Dan De Luce, A new Cold War without rules: U.S. braces for a long-term confrontation with Russia, NBC News,
March 6, 2022 (quoting Mary Elise Sarotte, professor of history at the Johns Hopkins University School of Advanced International Studies), available at: https://www.nbcnews.com/news/investigations/new-cold-war-rules-us-braces-long-term-confrontation-russia-rcna18554.
10 The Uniting for Peace Resolution, Resolution 377 (V) (1950), November 3, 1950.
11 UNSC Res. 2623 (2022), available at: https://www.securitycouncilreport.org/un-documents/document/s-res-2623.php.
12 UNGA Res. ES-11/1 (2022), available at: https://documents-dds-ny.un.org/doc/UNDOC/LTD/N22/272/27/PDF/N2227227.pdf?OpenElement (States opposing were Belarus, North Korea, Eritrea, Russia, and Syria).
13 *Id.* at Operative Paras. 2 and 4.
14 The Permanent Members of the Security Council are China (originally Nationalist China and now the People's Republic of China), France, the Soviet Union (now Russia), the United Kingdom, and the United States.
15 UN Charter, arts. 41, 42, and 94.
16 Joseph M. Isanga, *Resurgent Cold War and U.N. Security Council Reform Opportunities*, 47 Denver J. Int'l L. 73, 82 (2019).
17 UN Charter, Art. 27.
18 Commission III Security Council, Verbatim Minutes of the First Meeting of Commission III, Doc. 943 III/5 (June 13, 1945), reprinted in 11 Documents of the United Nations Conference on International Organization, San Francisco 13 (1945), at 165 (quoting the address of Mr. Lleras Camargo of Colombia).
19 Coined by George Orwell in 1945, the term "Cold War" has been used to describe the open yet restricted rivalry that developed after World War II between the United States and the Soviet Union and their respective allies. The Cold War was waged from 1945 to 1991 on political, economic, and propaganda fronts, with fighting confined to conventional weapons between proxy nations and insurgent groups. Britannica, *Cold War*, available at: https://www.britannica.com/event/Cold-War.

20 Jan Wouters and Tom Ruys, *Security Council Reform: A New Veto for a New Century*, 44 Mil. L. & L War Rev. 139 (2005).
21 Joseph M. Isanga, *Resurgent Cold War and U.N. Security Council Reform Opportunities*, 47 Denver J. Int'l L. 73, 84 (2019).
22 Joseph M. Isanga, *Resurgent Cold War and U.N. Security Council Reform Opportunities*, 47 Denver J. Int'l L. 73, 88 (2019).
23 *Id.*
24 See Frederic L. Kirgis, Jr., *The Security Council's First Fifty Years*, 89 Am. J. Int'l L. 506 (1995); Richard Butler, *Bewitched, Bothered, and Bewildered: Repairing the Security Council*, 78 Foreign Affairs 9 (1999); John D. Caron, *The Legitimacy of the Collective Authority of the Security Council*, 87 Am. J. Int'l L. 552 (1993).
25 John D. Caron, *The Legitimacy of the Collective Authority of the Security Council*, 87 Am. J. Int'l L. 552, 569 (1993).
26 Christian Tomuschat, *Uniting for Peace*, United Nations Audiovisual Library of International Law, 2008, available at: https://legal.un.org/avl/pdf/ha/ufp/ufp_e.pdf.
27 Christian Tomuschat, *Uniting for Peace*, United Nations Audiovisual Library of International Law, 2008, available at: https://legal.un.org/avl/pdf/ha/ufp/ufp_e.pdf.
28 Legal Consequences for States of the Continued Presence of South Africa in Namibia (South West Africa) notwithstanding Security Council Resolution 276 (1970), Advisory Opinion, I.C.J. Reports 1971, p. 16, at para. 22.
29 UN Charter, Art. 27 ("Decisions of the Security Council on all [substantive] matters shall be made by an affirmative vote of nine members including the concurring votes of the permanent members").
30 Christian Tomuschat, *Uniting for Peace*, United Nations Audiovisual Library of International Law, 2008, available at: https://legal.un.org/avl/pdf/ha/ufp/ufp_e.pdf.
31 Christian Tomuschat, *Uniting for Peace*, United Nations Audiovisual Library of International Law, 2008, available at: https://legal.un.org/avl/pdf/ha/ufp/ufp_e.pdf.
32 The Uniting for Peace Resolution, Resolution 377 (V) (1950), November 3, 1950, provides: "If the Security Council, because of lack of unanimity of the permanent members, fails to exercise its primary responsibility for the maintenance of international peace and security in any case where there appears to be a threat to the peace, breach of the peace, or act of aggression, the General Assembly shall consider the matter immediately with a view to making appropriate recommendations to Members for collective measures, including in the case of a breach of the peace or act of aggression the use of armed force when necessary, to maintain or restore international peace and security. If not in session at the time, the General Assembly shall therefore meet in emergency special session within twenty-four hours of the request. Such emergency special session may be called if requested by the Security Council on the vote of any seven members [nine since 1965], or by a majority of the Members of the United Nations."
33 Michael Ramsden, *Uniting for MH17*, 7 Asian J. Int'l L. 1, 16 (2016).
34 Larry D. Johnson, *Uniting for Peace: Does it Still Serve any Useful Purpose?* 108 Am. J. Int'l L. 106, 112 (2014).
35 Asian Udoh, *Case Study: Invoking the "Uniting for Peace" Resolution of 1950 to Authorize the Use of Humanitarian Military Interventions and Prevent Mass Atrocities in Syria*, 23 Willamette J. Int'l & Dispute Res. 187, 211 (2015).
36 Asian Udoh, *Case Study: Invoking the "Uniting for Peace" Resolution of 1950 to Authorize the Use of Humanitarian Military Interventions and Prevent Mass Atrocities in Syria*, 23 Willamette J. Int'l & Dispute Res. 187, 211 (2015).

37 Asian Udoh, *Case Study: Invoking the "Uniting for Peace" Resolution of 1950 to Authorize the Use of Humanitarian Military Interventions and Prevent Mass Atrocities in Syria*, 23 Willamette J. Int'l & Dispute Res. 187, 211 (2015).
38 UN Charter, Art. 12.
39 Legal Consequences of the Construction of a Wall in the Occupied Palestinian Territory, Advisory Opinion, 2004 I.C.J. 138 (July 9).
40 Christian Tomuschat, *Uniting for Peace*, United Nations Audiovisual Library of International Law, 2008, available at: https://legal.un.org/avl/pdf/ha/ufp/ufp_e.pdf.
41 UN Charter Arts. 51 (armed force in self-defense) and 42 (armed force authorized by the Security Council).
42 Certain Expenses of the United Nations (Article 17, Paragraph 2 of the Charter), Advisory Opinion, 1962 ICJ REP. 151, 163 (July 20).
43 UN Charter, Art. 51.
44 Andrew Carswell, Unblocking the UN Security Council: The Uniting for Peace Resolution, 18 J. Conflict & Security L. 453, 461 (2013); Ved Nanda, *Challenges to the Security Council Veto: The Security Council Veto in the Context of Atrocity Crimes, Uniting for Peace, and the Responsibility to Protect*, 51 Case Western Res. J. Int'l L. 119, 139 (2020).
45 Andrew Carswell, Unblocking the UN Security Council: The Uniting for Peace Resolution, 18 J. Conflict & Security L. 453, 461 (2013); Ved Nanda, *Challenges to the Security Council Veto: The Security Council Veto in the Context of Atrocity Crimes, Uniting for Peace, and the Responsibility to Protect*, 51 Case Western Res. J. Int'l L. 119, 139 (2020).
46 Security Council Report, Security Council Deadlocks and Uniting for Peace: An Abridged History, October 2013, available at https://www.securitycouncilreport.org/atf/cf/%7B65BFCF9B-6D27-4E9C-8CD3-CF6E4FF96FF9%7D/Security_Council_Deadlocks_and_Uniting_for_Peace.pdf; Larry D. Johnson, *Uniting for Peace: Does it Still Serve any Useful Purpose?* 108 Am. J. Int'l L. 106, 112 (2014).
47 Laishram Malem Mangal, *Case Commentary on Certain Expenses of the United Nations Advisory Opinion of 20 July 1962*, Research Gate, July 2020, available at: https://www.researchgate.net/publication/342719409_Case_Commentary_Certain_expenses_of_the_United_Nations_Advisory_Opinion_of_20_July_1962-converted.
48 Certain Expenses of the United Nations (Article 17, paragraph 2 of the Charter), 1962 ICJ REP. 151, (July 20), available at: https://www.icj-cij.org/en/case/49/advisory-opinions.
49 Certain Expenses of the United Nations (Article 17, paragraph 2 of the Charter), 1962 ICJ REP. 151, (July 20), at p. 16, available at: https://www.icj-cij.org/en/case/49/advisory-opinions.
50 Certain Expenses of the United Nations (Article 17, paragraph 2 of the Charter), 1962 ICJ REP. 151, 168 (July 20), available at: https://www.icj-cij.org/en/case/49/advisory-opinions.
51 Ved Nanda, *Challenges to the Security Council Veto: The Security Council Veto in the Context of Atrocity Crimes, Uniting for Peace, and the Responsibility to Protect*, 51 Case Western Res. J. Int'l L. 119, 141 (2020).
52 Christian Tomuschat, *Uniting for Peace*, United Nations Audiovisual Library of International Law, 2008, available at: https://legal.un.org/avl/pdf/ha/ufp/ufp_e.pdf.
53 Asian Udoh, *Case Study: Invoking the "Uniting for Peace" Resolution of 1950 to Authorize the Use of Humanitarian Military Interventions and Prevent Mass Atrocities in Syria*, 23 Willamette J. Int'l & Dispute Res. 187, 217 (2015).

54 Larry D. Johnson, *Uniting for Peace: Does it Still Serve any Useful Purpose?* 108 Am. J. Int'l L. 106, 112 (2014).
55 Larry D. Johnson, *Uniting for Peace: Does it Still Serve any Useful Purpose?* 108 Am. J. Int'l L. 106, 112 (2014).
56 Larry D. Johnson, *Uniting for Peace: Does it Still Serve any Useful Purpose?* 108 Am. J. Int'l L. 106, 112 (2014).
57 Larry D. Johnson, *Uniting for Peace: Does it Still Serve any Useful Purpose?* 108 Am. J. Int'l L. 106, 112 (2014).
58 Larry D. Johnson, *Uniting for Peace: Does it Still Serve any Useful Purpose?* 108 Am. J. Int'l L. 106, 112 (2014).
59 I. Black, *Russia and China Veto UN Move to Refer Syria to International Criminal Court*, The Guardian, 22 May 2014.
60 *Russia's 12 Vetoes on Syria*, RTE, April 11, 2018, available at: https://www.rte.ie/news/world/2018/0411/953637-russia-syria-un-veto/.
61 *Russia's 12 Vetoes on Syria*, RTE, April 11, 2018, available at: https://www.rte.ie/news/world/2018/0411/953637-russia-syria-un-veto/.
62 *See generally*, Milena Sterio and Michael Scharf, The Legacy of Ad Hoc Tribunals in International Criminal Law (2019).
63 Security Council Press Release, Security Council Refers Situation in Darfur, Sudan, to Prosecutor of International Criminal Court, March 31, 2005, https://www.un.org/press/en/2005/sc8351.doc.htm; Situation in Libya, ICC-01/11, available at: https://www.icc-cpi.int/libya.
64 UN SCOR., 67th Sess., 6711th mtg., at 5, UN Doc. S/PV.6711 (Feb. 4, 2014).
65 Michelle Nichols, *UN Creates Team to Prepare Cases on Syria War Crimes*, Reuters, December 21, 2016, available at: https://www.reuters.com/article/us-mideast-crisis-syria-warcrimes-idUSKBN14A2H7?il=0.
66 Alex Whiting, *An Investigation Mechanism for Syria: The General Assembly Steps Ito the Breach*, 15 Journal of International Criminal Justice 231, (2017).
67 Alex Whiting, *An Investigation Mechanism for Syria: The General Assembly Steps Ito the Breach*, 15 Journal of International Criminal Justice 231 (2017).
68 UN Doc. A/71/L.48, 21 December 2016.
69 The Secretary-General, *Report of the Secretary General on the Implementation of the resolution establishing the International, Impartial and Independent Mechanism to Assist in the Investigation and Prosecution of Persons Responsible for the Most Serious Crimes under International Law Committed in the Syrian Arab Republic since March 2011*, UN Doc. A/71/755, 19 January 2017, at §12.
70 UN Doc. A/71/L.48, 21 December 2016, at § 4.
71 The Secretary-General, *Note verbale dated 8 February 2017 from the Permanent Mission of the Russian Federation to the United Nations addressed to the Secretary General*, UN Doc. A/71/793, 14 February 2017.
72 *Id.*
73 Prosecutor v. Tadic, Case No. IT-94-1-T (Trial Chamber, Decision on the Defense Motion: Jurisdiction of the Tribunal, 10 August 1995), affirmed, Prosecutor v. Tadic, Case No. IT-94-1-AR72 (Appeals Chamber, Decision on the Defense Motion for Interlocutory Appeal on Jurisdiction, 2 Oct. 1995); Virginia Morris and Michael P. Scharf, The International Criminal Tribunal for Rwanda, Vol. 1 at 95–97 (1998).
74 Michael Ramsden, Uniting Against Impunity: The UN General Assembly as a Catalyst for Action at the ICC, 66 Int'l & Comp. L. Quarterly 893 (2017); International Commission of Human Rights Experts on Ethiopia. See: https://www.ohchr.org/en/hr-bodies/hrc/ichre-ethiopa/index.
75 UN Charter, Article 10.
76 UN Charter, Article 22.

77 Jennifer Trahan, *Russia's Illegitimate Veto*, Opinio Juris (Apr. 23, 2018), https://opiniojuris.org/2018/04/23/the-narrow-case-for-the-legality-of-strikes-in-syria-and-russias-illegitimate-veto/. Trahan argues that there are three ways in which the Russian veto of the proposal to refer the matter of Syria to the International Criminal Court, or to at least establish an international investigative mechanism for Syria, was incompatible with the UN Charter. First, the veto power derives from the UN Charter, which is subsidiary to *jus cogens* norms. Thus, a veto that violates *jus cogens* norms, or permits the continued violation of *jus cogens* norms, would be illegal. The Charter (and veto power) must be read in a way that is consistent with *jus cogens*. Second, the veto power derives from the UN Charter, which states in Article 24(2) that the Security Council "[in] discharging [its] duties ...shall act in accordance with the Purposes and Principles of the United Nations." A veto in the face of a credible draft resolution aimed at curtailing or alleviating the commission of genocide, crimes against humanity or war crimes does not accord with the Charter's purposes and principles. And finally, a permanent member of the Security Council that utilizes the veto power also has other treaty obligations, such as those under the Genocide Convention, which contains an obligation to "prevent" genocide. A Permanent Member's use of the veto that would enable genocide, or allow its continued commission, would violate that state's legal obligation to "prevent" genocide. A similar argument can be made as to allowing the perpetration of at least certain war crimes, such as "grave breaches" and violations of Common Article 3 of the 1949 Geneva Conventions.

For a contrary view, see Mohamed Helal, *On the Legality of the Russian Vetoes and the Harsh Realities of International Law, A Rejoinder to Professor Jennifer Trahan*, Opinio Juris, May 4, 2018, available at: http://opiniojuris.org/2018/05/04/on-the-legality-of-the-russian-vetoes-in-the-un-security-council-and-the-harsh-reality-of-international-law-a-rejoinder-to-professor-jennifer-trahan/.

78 Rep. of the Int'l Comm'n. on Intervention and State Sovereignty, *The Responsibility to Protect* (Dec. 2001).

79 2005 World Summit Outcome, GA Res. 60/1 (Sept. 16, 2005).

80 Michael P. Scharf, *Striking a Grotian Moment: How the 2018 Airstrikes on Syria Changed International Law Related to Humanitarian Intervention*, 19.2 Chicago Journal of International Law 586–614 (2019).

81 Michael P. Scharf, *How the War on ISIS Changed International Law*, 48 Case Western Reserve Journal of International Law 15–68 (2016).

82 U.S. Secretary of State Madeleine Albright, Press Conference with Russian Foreign Minister Igor Ivanov, Singapore, 26 July 1999, available at: http://secretary.state.gov./www/statements/1999/990726b.html; UK Prime Minister Tony Blair, UK Parliamentary Debates, Commons, 26 April 1999, co 30.

83 Independent Int'l Comm'n on Kosovo, The Kosovo Report: Conflict, International Response, Lessons Learned 4 (2000).

84 HC Deb 26 February 2001 vol 363 cc 620–34.

85 Brian Barbour and Brian Gorlick, *"Embracing the Responsibility to Protect": A Repertoire of Measures Including Asylum for Potential Victims*, 20 International Journal of Refugee Law 533, 559 (2008).

86 Helene Cooper and Michael D. Schear, *Militants' Seige on Mountain in Iraq is Over, Pentagon Says*, The New York Times, August 14, 2014, available at: http://www.nytimes.com/2014/08/14/world/middleeast/iraq-yazidi-refugees.html?_r=0; Helene Cooper, Mark Landler, and Alissa J. Rubin, *Obama Allows Limited Airstrikes on ISIS*, The New York Times, August 7, 2014, available at: http://www.nytimes.com/2014.08/08/world/middleeast/obama-weighs-military-strikes-to-aid-trapped-iraqis-officials-say.html.

87 A policy paper issued by the UK Prime Minister's Office stated: "The UK is permitted under international law, on an exceptional basis, to take measures in order to alleviate overwhelming humanitarian suffering. The legal basis for the use of force is humanitarian intervention...." Alonso Gurmendi Dunkelberg, Rebecca Ingber, Priya Pillai, and Elvina Pothelet, *Mapping States Reactions to the Syria Strikes of April 2018*, Just Security, April 22, 2018, available at: https://www.justsecurity.org/55157/mapping-states-reactions-syria-strikes-april-2018/.

88 Provisional Verbatim Record of the Security Council, Threats to International Peace and Security: The Situation in the Middle East, UN Doc. S/PV.8233, April 14, 2018.

89 Richard Ware, *Briefing Paper: The Legal Basis for Air Strikes Against Syrian Government Targets*, House of Commons Library, April 16, 2018, available at: https://researchbriefings.parliament.uk/ResearchBriefing/Summary/CBP-8287.

90 Richard Ware, *Briefing Paper: The Legal Basis for Air Strikes Against Syrian Government Targets*, House of Commons Library, April 16, 2018, available at: https://researchbriefings.parliament.uk/ResearchBriefing/Summary/CBP-8287.

91 Andrew Carswell, *Unblocking the UN Security Council: The Uniting for Peace Resolution*, 18 J. Conflict & Security L. 453, 461 (2013); Ved Nanda, *Challenges to the Security Council Veto: The Security Council Veto in the Context of Atrocity Crimes, Uniting for Peace, and the Responsibility to Protect*, 51 Case Western Res. J. Int'l L. 119, 139 (2020).

92 Provisional Verbatim Record of the Security Council, Threats to International Peace and Security: The Situation in the Middle East, UN Doc. S/PV.8233, April 14, 2018.

93 International Law Commission, Draft Articles on State Responsibility, Art. 11 (2008), available at: http://legal.un.org/ilc/texts/instruments/english/commentaries/9_6_2001.pdf (citing international cases where a State's unequivocal acknowledgment and adoption of another's position will render the State retroactively responsible for it).

94 Fifty-six separate states and NATO (consisting of 28 member states) – for a total of over seventy countries – publicly expressed opinions about the April 14, 2018 airstrikes. Alonso Gurmendi Dunkelberg, Rebecca Ingber, Priya Pillai, and Elvina Pothelet, *Mapping States Reactions to the Syria Strikes of April 2018*, Just Security, April 22, 2018, available at: https://www.justsecurity.org/55157/mapping-states-reactions-syria-strikes-april-2018/.

95 Asian Udoh, *Case Study: Invoking the "Uniting for Peace" Resolution of 1950 to Authorize the Use of Humanitarian Military Interventions and Prevent Mass Atrocities in Syria*, 23 Willamette J. Int'l & Dispute Res. 187, 223–224 (2015).

96 The last time the United States proposed General Assembly action under the Uniting for Peace Resolution was in response to the Soviet invasion of Afghanistan in 1980. Security Council Report, Security Council Deadlocks and Uniting for Peace: An Abridged History, October 2013, available at https://www.securitycouncilreport.org/atf/cf/%7B65BFCF9B-6D27-4E9C-8CD3-CF6E4FF96FF9%7D/Security_Council_Deadlocks_and_Uniting_for_Peace.pdf.

97 Ukraine: Vote on Draft "Uniting for Peace" Resolution*: What's In Blue: Security Council Report

98 UN Press Release, Eleventh Emergency Special Session, 2 March 2022, available at:
https://press.un.org/en/2022/ga12407.doc.htm.

99 UN Press Release, Eleventh Emergency Special Session, 2 March 2022, available at:
https://press.un.org/en/2022/ga12407.doc.htm.
100 UN Press Release, Eleventh Emergency Special Session, 2 March 2022, available at:
https://press.un.org/en/2022/ga12407.doc.htm.
101 UNGA Res. ES-11/1 (2022), available at: https://documents-dds-ny.un.org/doc/UNDOC/LTD/N22/272/27/PDF/N2227227.pdf?OpenElement.
102 UNGA Res. ES-11/1 (2022), available at: https://documents-dds-ny.un.org/doc/UNDOC/LTD/N22/272/27/PDF/N2227227.pdf?OpenElement.
103 *See* Michael Scharf, Universal Jurisdiction and the Crime of Aggression, 53 Harv. Int'l L. J. 358–389 (2012), available at: https://harvardilj.org/wp-content/uploads/sites/15/2012/10/HLI201.pdf.
104 UNGA Res. ES-11/1 (2022), Operative Para. 2 and Preamble Para. 10, available at: https://documents-dds-ny.un.org/doc/UNDOC/LTD/N22/272/27/PDF/N2227227.pdf?OpenElement.
105 UNGA Res. ES-11/1 (2022), Operative Para. 4, available at: https://documents-dds-ny.un.org/doc/UNDOC/LTD/N22/272/27/PDF/N2227227.pdf?OpenElement.
106 UNGA Res. ES-11/1 (2022), Operative Para. 12, available at: https://documents-dds-ny.un.org/doc/UNDOC/LTD/N22/272/27/PDF/N2227227.pdf?OpenElement.
107 Allegations of Genocide under the Convention on the Prevention and Punishment of the Crime of Genocide (Ukraine v. Russian Federation), Order of 15 March 2022, available at: https://www.icj-cij.org/en/case/182/orders.
108 *See* Michael Scharf, Universal Jurisdiction and the Crime of Aggression, 53 Harv. Int'l L. J. 358–389 (2012), available at: https://harvardilj.org/wp-content/uploads/sites/15/2012/10/HLI201.pdf.
109 UN Doc. A/RES/ES-11/2, 24 March 2022 (adopted by a vote of 140 in favor, 5 against, 38 abstentions).
110 UN Doc. A/RES/ES-11/3, 7 April 2022 (adopted by a vote of 93 in favor, 24 against, 58 abstentions).
111 UN Doc. A/RES/ES-11/4, 12 October 2022 (adopted by a vote of 143 in favor, 5 against, 35 abstentions).
112 UN Doc. A/RES/ES-11/5, 24 November 2022 (adopted by a vote of 94 in favor, 14 against, and 74 abstentions).
113 UNGA Res. ES-11/6 (2023) 23 February 2023 (adopted by a vote of 141 in favor, 7 against, 32 abstentions), available at: https://www.securitycouncilreport.org/atf/cf/%7B65BFCF9B-6D27-4E9C-8CD3-CF6E4FF96FF9%7D/a_res_es_11_6.pdf.
114 Statement of the Secretary-General, UN Press Release, 22 February 2023, available at: https://press.un.org/en/2023/ga12491.doc.htm?_gl=1*7ru2ne*_ga*MTA0NDc4NDE4OC4xNjk1NDgwNTAx*_ga_TK9BQL5X7Z*MTY5NTQ4MDUwMC4xLjEuMTY5NTQ4MjY1Mi4wLjAuMA.
115 UN Press Release, 23 February 2023, available at: https://press.un.org/en/2023/ga12492.doc.htm?_gl=1*17pgpvn*_ga*MTA0NDc4NDE4OC4xNjk1NDgwNTAx*_ga_TK9BQL5X7Z*MTY5NTQ4MDUwMC4xLjEuMTY5NTQ4MjgxNi4wLjAuMA.
116 ICC Press Release, Situation in Ukraine: ICC judges issue arrest warrants against Vladimir Vladimirovich Putin and Maria Alekseyevna Lvova-Belova, March 17, 2023, available at: https://www.icc-cpi.int/news/situation-ukraine-icc-judges-issue-arrest-warrants-against-vladimir-vladimirovich-putin-and.

117 UNGA Res. ES-11/1 (2022), Preamble Para. 3, available at: https://documents-dds-ny.un.org/doc/UNDOC/LTD/N22/272/27/PDF/N2227227.pdf?OpenElement.
118 UN Charter, Art. 5 (suspension requires a recommendation by the Security Council followed by a decision by the General Assembly).
119 Raymond Suttner, *Has South Africa been Illegally Excluded from the United Nations General Assembly?* 17, The Compar. & Int'l L. J. of Southern Africa 279–301 (1984).
120 Stefan Meister and David Jalivand, *Sanctions Against Russia*, June 8, 2022, available at: https://dgap.org/en/research/publications/sanctions-against-russia.
121 Stefan Meister and David Jalivand, *Sanctions Against Russia*, June 8, 2022, available at: https://dgap.org/en/research/publications/sanctions-against-russia.
122 Ashish Valentine, Are sanctions actually hurting Russia's economy?, National Public Radio, July 1, 2022, available at: https://www.npr.org/2022/07/01/1109033582/are-sanctions-actually-hurting-russias-economy-heres-what-you-need-to-know.
123 *Id.*
124 Yahoo Finance, Who is still Buying Russian Oil and Gas?, July 3, 2022, available at: https://finance.yahoo.com/news/still-buying-russian-oil-gas-150000467.html?guccounter=1&guce_referrer=aHR0cHM6Ly93d3cuYmluZy5jb20v&guce_referrer_sig=AQAAALc7hUsjHpvOb5KwAGqLOwUva0-dkNhMLbR7aYK1VDnT-UWIsY3loBUR1CXjcM0FQuWCXg8gf3cmRA1ozywINtPodI4C1eDpLFpfcd5TlBjX0AakrmIunx5a9sgGVSlMS74IiEZyfcq-Fnp-zemUNpg9K6L8mvfP8TrKq2D1z4ES.
125 Stefan Meister and David Jalivand, *Sanctions Against Russia*, June 8, 2022, available at: https://dgap.org/en/research/publications/sanctions-against-russia.
126 *Who is still Buying Russian Oil and Gas?*, Yahoo Finance, July 3, 2022, available at: https://finance.yahoo.com/news/still-buying-russian-oil-gas-150000467.html?guccounter=1&guce_referrer=aHR0cHM6Ly93d3cuYmluZy5jb20v&guce_referrer_sig=AQAAALc7hUsjHpvOb5KwAGqLOwUva0-dkNhMLbR7aYK1VDnT-UWIsY3loBUR1CXjcM0FQuWCXg8gf3cmRA1ozywINtPodI4C1eDpLFpfcd5TlBjX0AakrmIunx5a9sgGVSlMS74IiEZyfcq-Fnp-zemUNpg9K6L8mvfP8TrKq2D1z4ES; Nicolla Conte, *Who's Still Buying Fossil Fuels from Russia*, June 22, 2022, available at: https://elements.visualcapitalist.com/importers-of-russian-fossil-fuels/.
127 *Who is still Buying Russian Oil and Gas?*, Yahoo Finance, July 3, 2022.
128 *Sanctions on Iran*, Council on Foreign Relations, July 15, 2015, available at: https://www.cfr.org/backgrounder/international-sanctions-iran.
129 Security Council Report, Security Council Deadlocks and Uniting for Peace: An Abridged History, October 2013, available at https://www.securitycouncilreport.org/atf/cf/%7B65BFCF9B-6D27-4E9C-8CD3-CF6E4FF96FF9%7D/Security_Council_Deadlocks_and_Uniting_for_Peace.pdf; Larry D. Johnson, *Uniting for Peace: Does it Still Serve any Useful Purpose?* 108 Am. J. Int'l L. 106, 112 (2014).
130 International Law Commission, Draft Articles on State Responsibility (2001) (Art. 49), available at https://legal.un.org/ilc/texts/instruments/english/commentaries/9_6_2001.pdf; Michael Ramsden, *Uniting for Peace, the Emergency Special Session on Ukraine*, Harvard International Law Journal Online (2022).
131 On April 28, 2022, the Parliamentary Assembly of the Council of Europe (PACE) adopted a resolution proposing the establishment of an ad-hoc international tribunal to investigate and prosecute the crimes of Russia's military aggression in Ukraine, available at https://www.coe.int/en/web/portal/-/pace-calls-for-an-ad-hoc-international-criminal-tribunal-to-investigate-war-crimes-in-ukraine;

Statement Calling for the Creation of a Special Tribunal for the Punishment of the Crime of Aggression Against Ukraine, March 4, 2022, available at https://gordonandsarahbrown.com/wp-content/uploads/2022/03/Combined-Statement-and-Declaration.pdf; Jennifer Trahan, Just Security, Mar. 7, 2022, available at: https://www.justsecurity.org/80545/u-ngeneral-assembly-should-recommend-creation-of-crime-of-aggression-tribunal-for-ukraine-nuremberg-is-not-themodel/.

132 See First and Second Declarations lodged by Ukraine, dated November 2013 and April 2014, available at https://www.icc-cpi.int/ukraine.

133 Rome Statute for an International Criminal Court, Arts. 8 Bis, 15 Bis (5). Since Russia is not a party to the ICC Statute and has not accepted the Aggression Amendment, Russian nationals cannot be prosecuted by the ICC for the Crime of Aggression unless the Security Council refers the case.

134 Article 437 of the Ukrainian Criminal Code states that (1) "planning, preparation or waging of an aggressive war or armed conflict, or conspiring for any such purposes, - shall be punishable by imprisonment for a term of seven to twelve years" and (2) "conducting an aggressive war or aggressive military operations, - shall be punishable by imprisonment for a term of ten to fifteen years."

135 Arrest Warrant of 11 April 2000 (Dem. Rep. Congo v. Belg.), Judgment, 2002 I.C.J. 3 (Feb. 14), available at: https://www.icj-cij.org/case/121

136 Certain Expenses of the United Nations, Advisory Opinion, 1962 I.C.J 151, 165 (July 20).

137 Prosecutor v. Tadic, Case No. IT-94-1-I, Decision on Defence Motion for Interlocutory Appeal on Jurisdiction, ¶ 37–40, 44 (Int'l Crim. Trib. for the Former Yugoslavia Oct. 2, 1995). Since the ICTY was created under Article 41 of the Charter by the Security Council, the passage is dicta as applied to the General Assembly creation of a Tribunal. Professor Michael Ramsden has argued that the General Assembly would have the implied power to create such a tribunal under Article 22 of the UN Charter. See Michael Ramsden, *Uniting for MH17*, 7 Asian J. Int'l L. 1, 11 (2016).

138 Agreement Between the United Nations and the Royal Government of Cambodia Concerning the Prosecution Under Cambodian Law of Crimes Committed During the Period of Democratic Kampuchea, available at: https://www.eccc.gov.kh/sites/default/files/legal-documents/Agreement_between_UN_and_RGC.pdf.

139 Resolution 57/228 of May 13, 2003, http://www.unakrt-online.org/sites/default/files/documents/A-Res-57-228B.pdf.

140 Julian Borger and Bastien Inzaurralde, *Russian Vetoes are Putting UN Security Council Legitimacy at Risk, US Says*, The Guardian, September 23, 2015.

141 UN News, May 10, 2024, available at: https://news.un.org/en/story/2024/05/1149596.

142 UN News, September 28, 2024, available at: https://news.un.org/en/story/2024/09/1154496.

PART II

Options for Accountability

5

UKRAINE AND THE INTERNATIONAL CRIMINAL COURT

By Patrick Keenan

Introduction

Less than a week after Russia invaded Ukraine on February 24, 2022,[1] Karim Khan, the Prosecutor of the International Criminal Court, announced that his office would open an investigation into the situation in Ukraine.[2] By this time, the ICC was no stranger to the effects of Russia's ongoing threats and attacks on Ukraine, having considered allegations of atrocity crimes in Ukraine on two earlier occasions. But the investigation after Russia's invasion in 2022 marked a turning point in the ICC's history with Ukraine. This Chapter will discuss how the ICC came to have jurisdiction over the situation in Ukraine, how Prosecutor Khan's current investigation has unfolded, what makes it distinctive, and what is missing from the investigation so far.

At the time that Russia invaded Ukraine and the conflict commenced, neither Ukraine nor Russia were States Parties to the Rome Statute, which meant that Ukraine did not have the legal authority to refer itself to the ICC. However, well before Russia's invasion in 2022, Ukraine had agreed to accept the ICC's jurisdiction, which has given the ICC the authority to investigate and possibly prosecute people who commit crimes against humanity, genocide, and war crimes in Ukraine.

Before moving on, a note on the terms used in the ICC. A situation in the ICC refers to the collection of possible crimes that are connected by geography and the time period in which they allegedly occurred. When the ICC Office of the Prosecutor (OTP) investigates a situation, it investigates all possible atrocity crimes in the situation over which the ICC could have jurisdiction, regardless of who in the conflict committed them. It is entirely possible

DOI: 10.4324/9781003458166-7

for the Prosecutor to pursue charges against wrongdoers from both (or all) sides in a conflict if the facts and circumstances warrant it.

A case refers to the charges against an individual defendant that the Prosecutor will seek to bring to trial. Cases in the ICC proceed in well-defined stages. A preliminary examination is the first important formal stage and happens when a situation comes to the attention of the Prosecutor. At this stage, the Prosecutor's job is to determine if there is a "reasonable basis to proceed with an investigation" into the situation. Rome Statute Art. 15(2). The Prosecutor must consider whether any cases brought would meet the ICC's jurisdictional requirements, whether proceeding is in the interests of justice, and whether the alleged crimes are of sufficient gravity. Rome Statute Art. 53. At the preliminary examination stage, the Prosecutor relies on information from the states involved, news reports, reports from international organizations or non-governmental organizations, and other sources. The Prosecutor does not have investigative powers at this point.

How a situation moves from the preliminary examination to an investigation, the next formal stage, depends on how the situation came to the attention of the Prosecutor. At the investigation stage, the Prosecutor assembles a full investigative team, including hiring investigators who speak the local languages, identifies sources of evidence, engages with victims and witnesses, and analyzes the underlying legal issues that are likely to arise, which determines the process by which the case proceeds. A situation involving possible atrocity crimes can be referred to the ICC in one of three ways: referral from the Prosecutor on his or her own motion under Article 13(c), referral from a State Party under Article 13(a), or referral from the United Nations Security Council under Article 13(b). If the case is referred to the ICC by a State Party or by the UN Security Council, the prosecutor may move from the preliminary examination stage to the investigation stage directly, without permission from the Court. But if the Prosecutor wishes to initiate a case on his or her own initiative under Article 13(c), the Prosecutor must receive authorization from a Pre-Trial Chamber of the Court before beginning an investigation.

The ICC's Jurisdiction Over the Situation in Ukraine

Ukraine's Acceptance of ICC Jurisdiction before Russia's Invasion

Until January 1, 2025, Ukraine was not a State Party to the Rome Statute, but it accepted the ICC's jurisdiction over crimes under the Rome Statute well before Russia's 2022 invasion. Under Article 12(3) of the Rome Statute, any state may accept the jurisdiction of the ICC with respect to alleged crimes in its territory or by its nationals by filing a declaration with the Registrar of the ICC. The declaration does not make a state a party to the Rome Statute, but it does authorize the Prosecutor to begin a preliminary examination, which may lead to a request by the Prosecutor to open an investigation *proprio motu* under Article 15. A request to open an investigation *proprio motu* requires approval by a Pre-Trial Chamber, which could delay the proceedings.

Ukraine has filed two such declarations accepting the ICC's jurisdiction on two occasions. The first was in February 2014, after Russia's annexation of Crimea. Ukraine's 2014 declaration accepted the ICC's jurisdiction over crimes committed on the territory of Ukraine between November 21, 2013, and February 22, 2014.[3] The second declaration was open-ended and was sufficient to authorize the Prosecutor's actions in 2022. On September 8, 2015, Ukraine accepted the ICC's jurisdiction over crimes against humanity and war crimes committed on its territory.[4] The declaration stated that the ICC's jurisdiction was over crimes committed beginning February 20, 2014, and had no end date.

Referrals by States Parties after Russia's Invasion

The 2015 declaration was in force, and authorized the Prosecutor's preliminary investigation, when Russia invaded Ukraine in February 2022. This declaration would have been sufficient for the Prosecutor to proceed but would have required the Prosecutor to seek authorization from a Pre-Trial Chamber before opening an investigation. To avoid delay, the Prosecutor invited States Parties to refer the situation in Ukraine to his office, which would then permit the Prosecutor to proceed with an investigation without seeking permission from a Pre-Trial Chamber.[5] After the Prosecutor's invitation, 41 states formally referred the situation in Ukraine to the Prosecutor. This permitted the Prosecutor to open an investigation directly, without any delay occasioned by having to seek approval from a Pre-Trial Chamber.

Scope of the ICC's Jurisdiction

When a State Party refers a situation to the ICC, or a state accepts the ICC's jurisdiction, the Prosecutor is permitted to investigate alleged crimes committed by anyone in the territory during the relevant time period. Even if Ukraine's acceptance of jurisdiction in 2015 and the referrals from States Parties in 2022 were motivated by Russia's allegedly illegal actions, the Prosecutor has the authority to fully investigate alleged crimes committed by anyone, not just Russia.

Referrals and the acceptance of jurisdiction can limit the geographic and temporal scope of the Prosecutor's investigation. In the case of Ukraine, Prosecutor Khan has stated that his office has the authority to investigate alleged crimes committed from November 21, 2013 (the starting date in Ukraine's 2014 declaration) onward, with no terminal date.[6] The investigation can cover alleged crimes committed on any part of the territory of

Ukraine. Again, the geographic scope is determined by the scope of Ukraine's acceptance of jurisdiction.

Determining the crimes over which the ICC has jurisdiction is more complicated. In its 2014 declaration, Ukraine does not indicate any particular crimes. However, in the 2015 declaration, Ukraine specifically mentions crimes against humanity and war crimes, but not genocide. Prosecutor Khan has indicated that, because of the terms of the State Party referrals, his office has the authority to investigate any of the original crimes of the Rome State: genocide, crimes against humanity, and war crimes.[7]

The ICC's History with the Situation in Ukraine

The ICC first became involved with issues around Ukraine in 2014, after Ukraine accepted the Court's jurisdiction over alleged crimes committed from November 21, 2013, to February 22, 2013.[8] This stemmed from alleged crimes committed during the Maidan protest movement in 2013–2014. Then-ICC Prosecutor Fatou Bensouda opened a preliminary examination into these events to determine if the ICC had jurisdiction over any alleged crimes within the Rome Statute.[9] Prosecutor Bensouda concluded in November 2015 that the ICC did not have jurisdiction over the alleged crimes. First, she concluded that, because there was no armed conflict in Ukraine at the time, there was no possibility of charging war crimes.[10] Next, she concluded that the allegations did not amount to crimes against humanity because the alleged crimes were not sufficiently systematic.[11]

While Prosecutor Bensouda was considering the first set of allegations, Ukraine accepted the ICC's jurisdiction a second time, on September 8, 2015.[12] This declaration did not have a temporal limit, meaning Ukraine's acceptance of jurisdiction would remain extant indefinitely. On September 29, 2015, Prosecutor Bensouda announced an extension of the preliminary examination of the Situation in Ukraine to the new allegations.[13] The OTP continued to monitor events in Ukraine, gather evidence, and assess the legal issues until 2020.[14] On December 11, 2020, Prosecutor Bensouda concluded her preliminary examination and announced that there was a reasonable basis to believe that war crimes and crimes against humanity had been committed in Ukraine, and that the Rome Statute's criteria for opening an investigation had been met.[15] Because there was a planned transition from Prosecutor Bensouda to newly-elected Prosecutor Karim Khan in 2021, the OTP decided to wait for Prosecutor Khan's tenure to begin before determining how to proceed with the Ukraine investigation.[16] The OTP remained engaged with authorities in Ukraine and preserved possible evidence, but did not advance the case. That was the status quo when Russia invaded Ukraine in 2022.

The ICC Prosecutor's Ongoing Investigation in Ukraine

Russia invaded Ukraine on February 24, 2022, and the next day the new ICC Prosecutor, Karim Khan,[17] reminded all sides that his office had the authority to exercise jurisdiction over any crimes within the Rome Statute committed on the territory of Ukraine (apart from the crime of aggression).[18] Just four days after the invasion, on February 28, 2022, Khan announced that he would seek to open an investigation into possible crimes against humanity, genocide, and war crimes in Ukraine.[19] Prosecutor Khan stated then that, based on the available evidence and the previous preliminary examination, there was a reasonable basis to proceed with an investigation.[20] The current investigation covers possible crimes against humanity, genocide, and war crimes committed by any person on any part of the territory of Ukraine from November 21, 2013 onward.

As of July 2024, the ICC has issued arrest warrants against six individuals accused of war crimes or crimes against humanity. On March 17, 2023, Pre-Trial Chamber II issued arrest warrants against Russian President Vladimir Putin and Maria Lvova-Belova, Russia's Commissioner for Children's Rights. Putin and Lvova-Belova are accused of the war crimes of unlawful deportation of children and unlawfully transferring children from occupied areas of Ukraine to Russia. The theory of liability is that Putin committed these crimes with or through others and that he failed to exercise proper control over his civilian and military subordinates, who physically perpetrated the alleged crimes. The theory of liability for Lvova-Belova is that she acted with or through others to commit the alleged offenses.

Since the initial charges against Putin and Lvova-Belova, Prosecutor Khan has announced that he has sought and been granted arrest warrants for four additional suspects, all of whom are members of the Russian military leadership. They are all alleged to have committed war crimes and crimes against humanity for their roles in directing attacks against civilians or civilian objects and similar offenses. All are alleged to have directly committed the offenses or committed them jointly with or through others. All four suspects are among the highest-ranking members of the Russian military: Sergei Kobylash is a general in the Russian Armed Forces, Viktor Sokolov is an admiral in the Russian Navy, Sergei Shoigu is Minister of Defense of the Russian Federation, and Valery Gerasimov is Chief of the General Staff of the Russian Armed Forces and First Deputy Minister of Defense.

Seeking the arrest of a sitting head of state can raise difficult legal issues. The simple fact that the ICC Prosecutor would target a sitting head of state is extraordinary, although not unprecedented. The ICC Prosecutor previously sought the arrest of Sudan's then-president Omar Al-Bashir for alleged crimes against humanity, genocide, and war crimes in Darfur. Al-Bashir argued that the international law doctrine of head-of-state immunity should exempt him from criminal process. Under Article 27(1) of the Rome Statute, an individual's official capacity does not exempt him or her from criminal liability. After significant litigation, the ICC Appeals Chamber held that Article 27(1) means the ICC also does not recognize immunity from arrest.[21] The Appeals Chamber held that head-of-state immunity from prosecution has never been recognized as a bar to the jurisdiction of an international court. Thus, even if a head of state were immune from criminal process in a domestic court, he or she would not be immune in an international court like the ICC.

Beyond the immunity issue, Putin's arrest warrant raises issues around the obligation of ICC States Parties to cooperate with the Court. The ICC does not have a police force that it can use to arrest suspects. Instead, it relies on the cooperation of States Parties, who agreed under the Rome Statute to cooperate fully with the Court in its investigations and prosecutions. Article 89 of the Rome Statute permits the ICC to request that a state arrest and surrender a suspect and requires States Parties to do so (subject to protections for the accused person). Thus, if Putin, or any of the accused persons in Ukraine situation, travels to an ICC State Party, that state would be obligated to arrest him or her. But in practice, as noted in Chapter 2, there have been many instances of States Parties refusing to arrest accused persons. The most notorious example of non-cooperation has been in the case of Omar Al-Bashir. Despite the existence of multiple arrest warrants, Al-Bashir has traveled to several States Parties without being arrested. In reality, the only way that Putin or the other defendants is likely to be arrested is if someone in Russia with the power to turn them over the ICC does so or if they travel to a state willing to arrest them. If the suspects remain in Russia, and Putin remains in power, the likelihood of their arrest is virtually zero.

Prosecutorial Strategy

So far, Prosecutor Khan's approach to Ukraine investigation has been to seek the arrest of Putin and others at the very center of Russian decision-making about the war. This is consistent with the mission of the ICC and the OTP's own policies, which purport to guide prosecutorial strategy in all cases. The ICC was created to end "impunity for the perpetrators" of "the most serious crimes of concern to the international community."[22] To accomplish this, the ICC Prosecutor targets "the individuals who are allegedly most responsible" for crimes covered by the Rome Statute.[23] By targeting Putin, Lvova-Belova, and Russia's military leadership, Prosecutor Khan signaled that he believed that they were the lead architects of the alleged crimes in Ukraine.

The choice of crimes for the initial charges was certainly not random. The ICC Prosecutor has emphasized the need to focus on crimes against children and for sexual and gender-based violence. This commitment is reflected in two new OTP policies and in Prosecutor Khan's approach to Ukraine investigation. Prosecutor Khan also chose to focus on particularly heinous crimes and vulnerable victims. Putin and Lvova-Belova are alleged to have directed a program that took children from Ukraine and unlawfully transferred them to Russia. Although there are many credible reports of widespread atrocities in Ukraine, those affecting children are surely among the most serious. In his Policy on Children,[24] Prosecutor Khan wrote that the victimization of children and their role as stakeholders has been "largely overlooked or ignored."[25] By choosing to focus on Putin and Lvova-Belova from the outset, Prosecutor Khan signaled that the ICC would attempt to hold accountable the highest leadership of Russia's alleged crimes and to protect the most vulnerable victims of those crimes.

It is not yet possible to determine which incidents gave rise to the other arrest warrants, but it is clear from the charges that the focus is on civilian victims. The OTP's Policy on the Crime of Gender Persecution[26] updates the OTP's 2014 Policy Paper on Sexual and Gender-Based Crimes[27] and states that sexual and gender-based crimes are among the "gravest crimes" addressed by the Rome Statute. In his statements about Ukraine investigation, Prosecutor Khan has repeatedly emphasized the need to pay particular attention to allegations of sexual and gender-based crimes. For example, when Khan announced an agreement with the Eurojust, the European Union Agency for Criminal Justice Cooperation, on practical guidelines for documenting international crimes, he stated that one of the benefits of the program would be to make the ICC a more effective forum for prosecuting crimes of sexual violence.[28] Similarly, after meeting with Ukrainian President Volodymyr Zelensky, Khan stated that there must be "zero tolerance" sexual or gender-based violence.[29] To date, Prosecutor Khan has not released sufficient information about the incidents underlying the arrest warrants against Gerasimov, Kobylash, Shoigu, and Sokolov to determine if they involve sexual or gender-based violence, but it is clear that these issues are at the forefront of the investigation.

Complementarity and Collaboration with Domestic Investigative Processes

The relationship of the OTP's investigation and ongoing ICC proceedings and the host country government's own legal processes is delicate. The ICC is a court of last resort. If there are legitimate domestic proceedings going on about the same or substantially the same conduct, the ICC may not proceed with its case. This principle is established in Article 1 of the Rome Statute, which provides that the Court "shall be complementary to national criminal jurisdictions." Under Article 17 of the Rome Statute, the ICC is permitted to exercise jurisdiction only if the national jurisdiction is unwilling or unable to do so (along with other conditions). States may object to an ICC proceeding on the grounds that the state is investigating or has investigated or prosecuted the same or substantially similar conduct. This happened with respect to the ICC's investigation into the situation in Iraq when the ICC and the United Kingdom investigated substantially the same conduct. The OTP concluded that there was a reasonable basis to believe that forces from the United Kingdom had committed war crimes in Iraq, but also found that there was no evidence that the UK was unwilling to genuinely carry out an investigation even though no one was prosecuted in the UK for the alleged crimes.[30]

The situation in Ukraine presents a stark contrast. The government of Ukraine has welcomed and encouraged the ICC investigation. President Zelensky has met with Prosecutor Khan and urged the ICC to pursue its investigation in Ukraine.[31] Indeed, Zelensky asked that Khan open an office of the ICC Prosecutor in Ukraine.[32] The OTP has deployed dozens of investigators and forensic experts to Ukraine to pursue the ICC's investigation and to support the investigations of Ukrainian authorities.[33] This has occurred even though the Ukrainian Prosecutor General, the country's top prosecutor, has initiated investigations into more than 100,000 suspected crimes related to Russia's invasion.[34] The Prosecutor General's office created a web portal through which any member of the public can report alleged Russian crimes and even submit evidence of those crimes.[35] Despite Ukraine's own ongoing investigations, the government has welcomed the involvement of the ICC.

Indeed, the situation in Ukraine might serve as a model of what is often called positive complementarity.[36] In this model, the ICC Prosecutor "relies on national and international networks [] and participates in a system of international cooperation" to encourage "genuine national proceedings."[37] The OTP and Ukrainian authorities have cooperated closely during the investigation. When Khan announced the arrest warrants against Putin and Lvova-Belova, he cited the essential role played by the Ukrainian Prosecutor General in the investigation to that point.[38] Prosecutor Khan has repeatedly visited Ukraine and met with Ukrainian authorities and ordinary citizens to ensure effective cooperation and to assure victims and survivors that the ICC is vigorously investigating the situation.[39]

In addition to the important diplomatic and signaling effect of cooperation, there are significant practical considerations. By collaborating closely with Ukrainian personnel and ordinary people, the OTP will be able to more effectively gather and ensure the security and chain of custody of evidence, locate photographic and video evidence of crimes, and develop relationships with advocates for victims and survivors. By establishing these relationships and processes from the beginning of the case, while simultaneously ensuring an independent and legitimate prosecution, the ICC increases the likelihood that all charges will be supported by compelling evidence and that the charges brought reflect the harms actually inflicted on victims and survivors.

An important part of the OTP's cooperation with Ukrainian authorities and ordinary people has been to teach people how to gather evidence. This effort has included work with Ukrainian law enforcement personnel to strengthen their evidence-gathering procedures.[40] The OTP has also worked closely with ordinary Ukrainians to enlist them in the effort to document possible international crimes and preserve evidence of them in a way that will contribute to future prosecutions. This work has involved multiple meetings with Ukrainians during Prosecutor Khan's visits and training for Ukrainian citizens.[41] Prosecutor Khan's practice of working closely with Ukrainian citizens aligns with many elements of the OTP's Strategic Plan.[42] In June 2023, the ICC announced the adoption of a new Strategic Plan,[43] which contained several goals that align with the approach to the Ukraine investigation. In Strategic Goal 4, the OTP pledged to "deepen its engagement" with civil society organizations and local communities.[44] Strategic Goal 7 pledged to increase the field presence of the OTP in situation countries to better identify evidence and better understand the underlying situation.[45]

The Role of Technology

The OTP's new Strategic Plan stated that the OTP intended to enhance its ability to identify and use "digital, documentary, video, and audio material"[46] and Prosecutor Khan appears to have fully implemented this in Ukraine investigation. The ICC has created a dedicated portal through which anyone with access to the internet may contact the OTP about alleged atrocities.[47] The portal allows users to describe the incident, provide a location using the interactive map, and attach photos or videos of alleged crimes. The ICC's dedicated portal is not a substitute for direct engagement with affected communities, but still offers ordinary people a means by which to contact investigators to report alleged crimes.[48]

The expanded use of technology and user-generated evidence raises legal and prudential issues. The Rome Statute sets out the basic rules for the admissibility of evidence before the ICC. Under Article 69(4), the Court determines the admissibility of evidence based on three principal criteria: the relevance of the evidence, its probative value, and the risk that the evidence will cause prejudice to a fair trial or a fair evaluation of the testimony of a witness.[49] Different Trial Chambers have framed this inquiry slightly differently. For example, one Trial Chamber held that the general rule is that "all prima facie relevant evidence is admissible subject to the Chamber's discretion to exclude relevant evidence" based on other provisions of the Rome Statute or general principles of law, as provided by Article 21.[50] A different Trial Chamber stated that "for an item to be admitted into evidence it must satisfy the three-part test under which it must (i) be relevant to the case; (ii) have probative value; and (iii) be sufficiently relevant and probative as to outweigh any prejudicial effect its admission may cause."[51] Regardless of the precise framing, admissibility depends on relevance, probative value, and risk of improper prejudice. Despite this, it is not yet clear how the Court might treat user-generated evidence.

By creating a portal for ordinary people, the ICC is keeping pace with others involved in international criminal justice. Ukraine's Prosecutor General has created a dedicated portal through which users may submit evidence of atrocity crimes.[52] The portal is both a means for the public to submit evidence and a way for the Prosecutor General to educate the public about what war crimes are and the kinds of evidence that is most useful. The portal gives examples of war crimes and includes a checklist of characteristics that might apply. It asks users to click on a map to indicate where the incident occurred and to state exactly when it occurred. Importantly, it also includes a way for users to upload photographic and video files showing alleged crimes or their aftermath. Even London's Metropolitan Police has a website for uploading evidence of crimes anywhere, with a Ukrainian language portal that includes the assurance that it will accept evidence of crimes anywhere in the world. Even beyond the user-generated evidence submitted to prosecutors, there are also thousands of social media posts showing alleged atrocities. Some of these have been collected in places like the Eyes on Russia map, a crowdsourced online map that links to tweets and other social media posts purporting to show atrocities, locates the incidents on a map of Ukraine, and documents when they allegedly happened. Because the OTP is working in close collaboration with so many others, it is at least possible that all this evidence could come to the attention of the ICC. When court proceedings begin, Prosecutor Khan will confront a problem that many prosecutors never face: what to do with the mountain of evidence of atrocities which has come from private citizens, advocacy groups, and others who do not work for the ICC as investigators.

Separate from the legal issues are political or prudential issues that may arise with the increased engagement with citizen-investigators. For example, how will Prosecutor Khan describe his case selection priorities? Individuals submit user-generated evidence for many reasons, but among those reasons is surely the notion that the evidence will be used to prosecute and punish those responsible for the harms. How will Prosecutor Khan justify what he is not prosecuting or the evidence he is not using? The scale of war crimes and crimes against humanity is enormous; there are likely thousands of potential cases that the OTP could pursue. Some of Prosecutor Khan's case selection principles are well known. For example, when he considers which of the many cases the OTP should prosecute in any situation, Prosecutor Khan considers whether the suspects have been prosecuted by a state for their crime, how the prosecutions will affect victims, and whether the prosecutions could contribute to the prevention of crimes. These are reasonable criteria, but even if they are neutrally applied, they will result in perhaps thousands of unprosecuted crimes. Prosecutor Khan would be wise to publish a Ukraine-specific case selection policy to supplement the existing Policy Paper on Case Selection and Prioritization. In the end, the OTP's seeming embrace of technology is a salutary step toward modernization of the ICC and will help maintain the ICC's relevance and efficiency, but it comes with legal and prudential risks.

The ICC Process in Context

Prosecutor Khan's current investigation does not and cannot cover all possible charges in the Ukraine situation. Most significantly, the ICC does not have jurisdiction over the crime of aggression in the situation in Ukraine. Under the Rome Statute, the crime of aggression has a unique jurisdictional scheme. The crime of aggression was added to the Rome Statute only after the approval of amendments to the statute, which went into effect in 2018. Under this specific jurisdictional regime, the UN Security Council has essentially the same power to refer aggression to the ICC as it does with other crimes. But the rules for referrals by States Parties and *proprio motu* jurisdiction are very different. For jurisdiction stemming from a referral or by the Prosecutor *proprio motu*, the Prosecutor must seek authorization to proceed from a Pre-Trial Chamber. In addition, the ICC may not exercise jurisdiction over the nationals of a non-State Party or regarding actions occurring on the territory of a non-State Party, even if the aggression is against a State Party. This means that the ICC Prosecutor is not permitted to prosecute allegations of the crime of aggression in the situation in Ukraine. The ICC's lack of jurisdiction over the crime of aggression does not mean that the OTP can play no role in addressing Russia's illegal invasion of Ukraine. The OTP is part of multiple joint investigation processes. Evidence gathered by the OTP can be shared with Ukrainian prosecutors and with other authorities in other states that might be able to attempt a prosecution for the crime of aggression.

Prosecuting Aggression Outside the ICC

There is no straightforward way to prosecute the crime of aggression when it is committed by a member of the UN Security Council—such as Russia. First, a Security Council member would block any attempt to refer it to the ICC, and joining the ICC's aggression regime is entirely optional. In addition, the crime of aggression is a leadership crime. Under the current state of international law, only those individuals who are in a position to effectively control or otherwise direct the military actions of a state may be prosecuted.[53] In the case of Ukraine, that group includes Putin and likely several of the other individuals already wanted by the ICC, all of whom are in a position to avoid prosecution in the ICC or elsewhere if they refrain from traveling outside Russia or states friendly to Russia.

These impediments to prosecutions for the crime of aggression are compounded by the absence of a forum in which an aggression prosecution could take place.[54] The UN Charter assigned to the Security Council the primary responsibility for upholding the UN Charter's requirement that states refrain from waging war absent legal reason. But the UN Charter did not create a forum through which the Security Council could punish those who violate the Charter. There have been serious debates among state representatives, advocates, and scholars about the possibility of creating an ad hoc tribunal for the crime of aggression.[55] Such a tribunal could be a complement to the ICC with jurisdiction only over aggression and not crimes against humanity, genocide, or war crimes. There are several ways in which such a tribunal could come into existence, a full exploration of which is beyond the scope of this Chapter. But it is important to note that the many of the proposals envision a role for the UN, likely acting through the General Assembly, and for Ukraine itself. Indeed, Chapter 6 discusses various of these proposals in significant detail, while Chapter 7 discusses a proposal for a War Crimes Chamber within Ukraine (with a draft Statute for a High War Crimes Court for Ukraine included in the Appendix).

Prosecuting Aggression by Other Names

The crime of aggression is *sui generis*, but those who commit it often also commit other crimes. The other crimes under the Rome Statute have their roots in human rights law or in *jus in bello*, the body of law that governs ongoing armed conflicts. In contrast, the crime of aggression is rooted in *jus ad bellum*, the body of law governing the legality of the use of force in the first place.[56] The crime of aggression is also generally limited to the actions of government leaders, not ordinary members of belligerent forces or even relatively high-level commanders. Despite these differences and limitations, the lack of ICC jurisdiction over the crime of aggression does not mean that those who might have been charged with it will escape criminal punishment. As discussed above, those already wanted by the ICC include many of the leaders of Russia's military decision-making establishment. The ICC arrest warrants do not mention aggression, but they do target those who likely would be charged with aggression if it were possible to do so. This is even more relevant in the ICC because the OTP has stated that its policy is to target those most responsible for the crimes under its jurisdiction.[57] There is substantial overlap between those who are able to direct a state's policies with respect to the initiation of a war and the waging of that war, at least in the case of Russia.

What Is Missing (So Far) from the Prosecutor's Investigation

The full set of charges stemming from Russia's attack on Ukraine are not yet clear, so it is premature to thoroughly critique the OTP's decision to omit one crime or another. Nonetheless, there are at least two categories of crimes that do not appear to have been charged. First, despite allegations that Russian forces are committing genocide in Ukraine, Prosecutor Khan has not sought arrest warrants for genocide. Second, there do not appear to be any charges to date that target environmental crimes, which the OTP has suggested would be a focal point in future prosecutions.

Genocide

There have been credible allegations that Russian forces have committed genocide in Ukraine. The UN Human Rights Council Commission of Inquiry on Ukraine has repeatedly reported that, based on its continuing investigation, it was concerned about allegations of genocide.[58] It also reported that some of the rhetoric transmitted in Russian state media might constitute incitement to genocide, a separate crime.[59] The former Prosecutor General of Ukraine has argued that there was substantial evidence that Russia was committing genocide in Ukraine based on the number of people killed, the means by which they were killed, and statements by Russian authorities and troops.[60]

The crime of genocide is intentionally difficult to prosecute. Genocide is a distinct category of crime over which the ICC has jurisdiction under the terms of Ukraine's acceptance of jurisdiction. Genocide is a unique crime that stands apart from crimes against humanity or war crimes. The Rome Statute defines genocide as any one of a specified list of acts committed "with the intent to destroy, in whole or in part, a national, ethnical, racial or religious group, as such." Art. 6. That definition is taken directly from the Convention on the Prevention and Punishment of the Crime of Genocide. The ICC Elements of Crimes, adopted by the ICC Assembly of States Parties in 1998, elaborate on the crimes listed in the Rome Statute, and add an element not found in the Rome Statute. The underlying conduct must occur "in the context of a manifest pattern of similar conduct directed against" the targeted group or "was conduct that could itself effect such destruction." Elements of Crimes, Art. 6(a). The ICC has not had occasion to expound at length on the evidence necessary to prove that a defendant acted with the intent to destroy one of the specified groups, as such. Cases from the ICTY set a high bar for such evidence, requiring it to be manifest and virtually beyond question. (*Jelisic*, Dec. 14, 1999; *Mladic*, June 8, 2021). That there is a high bar for prosecuting genocide certainly does not mean that it is impossible, even in the case of Ukraine.

The ICC Prosecutor has charged Putin and Lvova-Belova with crimes against humanity for forcibly transferring children from Ukraine to Russia. That conduct, if proven, would certainly meet the legal criteria for crimes against humanity. But the same conduct may also support a charge of genocide. The Rome Statute lists forcibly "transferring children" from the targeted group to another group as an act of genocide. Indeed, the former Prosecutor General of Ukraine argued from the earliest days of the war that the transfer of children amounted to genocide.[61] Despite this, the ICC Prosecutor chose to charge the conduct as a crime against humanity instead of genocide, perhaps because he was not satisfied that there was sufficient evidence of intent to destroy to meet the very high standard required in international criminal law. Regardless of the reason, whether any Russian officials are eventually charged with genocide will be one of the key legacies of the ICC's handling of the situation in Ukraine.

Environmental Crimes

On June 6, 2023, the Nova Kakhovka Dam on the Dnieper River was destroyed, sending a torrent of water downstream.[62] The Kakhovka Reservoir, above the dam, was rapidly depleted, inundating the surrounding area. Tens of thousands of people lost access to clean water and thousands more saw their villages flooded.[63] The dam provided power and clean water to more than 700,000 people in the surrounding area, and provided the water that farmers needed to irrigate hundreds of thousands of acres of agricultural land.[64] After the dam was destroyed, credible evidence quickly emerged that Russian forces were responsible, although there is not yet definitive proof of this.[65]

In 2023, Prosecutor Khan launched a new initiative to create a policy covering environmental crimes, something he promised to do in his 2023–24 strategic plan.[66] The focus of the environmental crimes initiative is to develop a policy to address crimes that are "committed by means of, or that result in, environmental damage."[67] The destruction of the Nova Kakhovka Dam appears to be precisely the kind of case the new policy would be intended to address.

The Rome Statute provides several ways for a prosecutor to address environmental crimes, especially when the environmental damage is caused by the destruction of a dam or other built infrastructure.[68] For example, Article 8(2)(b)(iv) provides a straightforward way to prosecute the case as a war crime. Under that provision, serious "violations of the laws and customs" of war governing international armed conflicts include intentional attacks committed in the knowledge that the attack will cause "widespread, long-term and severe damage to the natural environment" that is excessive to the military advantage gained. The statute places three requirements on the evidence of environmental damage: it must be widespread, long-term, and severe.[69] That certainly appears to be the case with the Nova Kakhovka Dam. The damage was extraordinarily widespread and severe. The flood caused by the dam's destruction submerged more than 600 square kilometers and damaged or destroyed thousands of homes and buildings.[70] More than 100,000 people were directly affected, and many more were indirectly impacted.[71] A report by the government of Ukraine and the UN estimates the destruction of the dam and devastation caused by the flood caused over $13 billion in damage and losses.[72] And the damage appears to be long-term, with civilians continuing to struggle to rebuild and recover many months after the event.[73] Of course, the OTP will be required to produce evidence of every element of the crime and it is not possible to determine whether that will be possible based solely on media reports. But as with genocide, whether this conduct is addressed by the ICC will be a key part of its legacy.

To date, most reporting suggests that Russian forces are responsible for the dam's destruction,[74] which would be consistent with Russia's apparent strategy of targeting civilian infrastructure in Ukraine.[75] There have also been reports that it is not clear who destroyed the dam, leaving open the possibility that it was done by Ukrainian forces (or even another actor).[76] Russia denies responsibility and there have been reports that Ukrainian forces may have destroyed the Nord Stream pipelines in the Baltic Sea, a somewhat similar kind of attack for which Russia was initially blamed.[77] For the ICC, the affiliation of those who destroyed the Nova Kakhovka Dam is irrelevant. The ICC has jurisdiction over the crime, assuming it was a crime, under the terms of Ukraine's acceptance of jurisdiction. When the OTP investigates a situation, it does not focus on just one party to the conflict; it can investigate any actor who commits crimes over which it has jurisdiction. In the case of the Nova Kakhovka Dam, this means the ICC would have the power to prosecute the wrongdoers regardless of whether they turn out to be Russian, Ukrainian, or from somewhere else.[78]

Conclusion: What the ICC Investigation Communicates

The consequences of the ICC's involvement in the situation in Ukraine are not purely legal or limited to the suspects charged with crimes. The work and choices of the OTP communicate meaning to the people of Ukraine, the international community, and potential wrongdoers in Russia and beyond, and the ICC Prosecutor appears to be mindful of this reality.[79] In his public statements about the situation, Prosecutor Khan has stated that the ICC's role is to reduce suffering and make clear that potentially wrongdoers will be held legally responsible for their actions.[80] This deterrence argument is familiar to policymakers and scholars of criminal justice, international and domestic, and is notoriously difficult to measure.[81] So far, Putin has indicated that he is not concerned about the ICC's arrest warrant and does not recognize the

ICC's legitimacy.[82] It is impossible to determine whether the arrest warrants for high-level leaders might cause lower-level decision makers to behave differently, but Prosecutor Khan clearly believes this is possible.

Another message that Prosecutor Khan has articulated is that the work of the ICC amounts to an act of solidarity with the victims of international crimes in Ukraine.[83] Prosecutor Khan's actions can show ordinary Ukrainians that what Russia is doing to them is deeply wrongful and that the international community is paying attention. Signaling to people who are suffering terrible attacks, many directed against the most vulnerable civilians, that they have not been forgotten far from a sufficient response, but it may be a small but important measure of support. Prosecutor Khan has framed his support in moral terms, but there are also practical reasons that the OTP must remain closely connected to ordinary people in Ukraine. Prosecutor Khan needs citizens to provide the evidence that his team will need to prove the charges. If civilians see the OTP as a partner in accountability, Prosecutor Khan's job will be more manageable.

The final message that Prosecutor Khan has been eager to emphasize is that the ICC will not be intimidated by a powerful state.[84] Russia is a permanent member of the UN Security Council and has significant geopolitical reach. By seeking to hold the leaders of Russia's war efforts responsible for their illegal actions, Prosecutor Khan can communicate to other states that the ICC does not just target states in Africa or other states without political power.[85] This is especially important after the ICC's difficulties with the Afghanistan investigation.[86] In that situation, a Pre-Trial Chamber refused to permit a prosecution to go forward, one that would have looked at the role of US forces alleged to have committed war crimes in Afghanistan. The Pre-Trial Chamber concluded that the investigation was not in the interests of justice because the United States would refuse to provide essential evidence, which would stymie the investigation and absorb resources that could go to other investigations. Eventually the Appeals Chamber reversed, and Prosecutor Khan was permitted to go forward,[87] but not before the ICC was subjected to withering criticism for appearing to have acted out of fear of the US.[88]

Finally, Prosecutor Khan has been careful to emphasize that his investigation and the possibility of prosecutions in the ICC are not the only means by which wrongdoers can be held accountable for the ongoing atrocities in Ukraine. Prosecutor Khan has stressed the significant role of Ukraine's domestic processes, and emphasized the role that other states can play regarding legal accountability. The legal processes cannot, and will not, be the only components of the process of healing and rebuilding Ukraine after Russia's assault and the widespread violence and destruction of the war. The ICC's investigation and eventual prosecutions, as important as they are, is just one part of what will need to be a comprehensive transitional justice process.

Notes

1 Russia Attacks Ukraine, N.Y. Times, Feb. 24, 2022, https://www.nytimes.com/live/2022/02/24/world/russia-attacks-ukraine.
2 Office of the Prosecutor, *Statement of ICC Prosecutor, Karim A.A. Khan QC, on the Situation in Ukraine: "I have decided to proceed with opening an investigation,"* International Criminal Court, Feb. 28, 2022, https://www.icc-cpi.int/news/statement-icc-prosecutor-karim-aa-khan-qc-situation-ukraine-i-have-decided-proceed-opening.
3 Embassy of Ukraine, Declaration, Apr. 9, 2014, https://www.icc-cpi.int/sites/default/files/itemsDocuments/997/declarationRecognitionJuristiction09-04-2014.pdf.
4 Minister for Foreign Affairs of Ukraine, Statement, Sept. 8, 2014, https://www.icc-cpi.int/sites/default/files/iccdocs/other/Ukraine_Art_12-3_declaration_08092015.pdf#search=ukraine.
5 Office of the Prosecutor, *Statement of ICC Prosecutor, Karim A.A. Khan QC, on the Situation in Ukraine: "I have decided to proceed with opening an investigation,"* International Criminal Court, Feb. 28, 2022, https://www.icc-cpi.int/news/statement-icc-prosecutor-karim-aa-khan-qc-situation-ukraine-i-have-decided-proceed-opening.
6 Office of the Prosecutor, *Statement of ICC Prosecutor, Karim A.A. Khan QC, on the Situation in Ukraine: Receipt of Referrals from 39 States Parties and the Opening of an Investigation*, March 2, 2022, https://www.icc-cpi.int/news/statement-icc-prosecutor-karim-aa-khan-qc-situation-ukraine-receipt-referrals-39-states.
7 *Id.*
8 Embassy of Ukraine, Declaration, Apr. 9, 2014, https://www.icc-cpi.int/sites/default/files/itemsDocuments/997/declarationRecognitionJuristiction09-04-2014.pdf.
9 Office of the Prosecutor, *Press Release: The Prosecutor of the International Criminal Court, Fatou Bensouda, opens a preliminary examination in Ukraine*, Apr. 25, 2014, https://www.icc-cpi.int/news/prosecutor-international-criminal-court-fatou-bensouda-opens-preliminary-examination-ukraine.
10 Office of the Prosecutor, Report on Preliminary Examination Activities (2015), Nov. 12, 2015, ¶ 89, https://www.icc-cpi.int/sites/default/files/iccdocs/otp/OTP-PE-rep-2015-Eng.pdf.
11 *Id.* at ¶¶ 90–91, 101.
12 Minister for Foreign Affairs of Ukraine, Statement, Sept. 8, 2014, https://www.icc-cpi.int/sites/default/files/iccdocs/other/Ukraine_Art_12-3_declaration_08092015.pdf.
13 Office of the Prosecutor, Report on Preliminary Examination Activities (2015), Nov. 12, 2015, ¶ 79, https://www.icc-cpi.int/sites/default/files/iccdocs/otp/OTP-PE-rep-2015-Eng.pdf.
14 Office of the Prosecutor, Report on Preliminary Examination Activities 2020, Dec. 14, 2020, ¶ 248–251, https://www.icc-cpi.int/sites/default/files/items-Documents/2020-PE/2020-pe-report-eng.pdf.
15 Report of the International Criminal Court, UN Doc. A/76/293, Aug. 24, 2021, ¶ 55, https://www.icc-cpi.int/sites/default/files/itemsDocuments/A_76_293_E.pdf.
16 Office of the Prosecutor, Report on Preliminary Examination Activities 2020, Dec. 14, 2020, ¶ 89, https://www.icc-cpi.int/sites/default/files/itemsDocuments/2020-PE/2020-pe-report-eng.pdf.

17 International Criminal Court, Press Release: Mr Karim Asad Ahmad Khan QC sworn in today as the Prosecutor of the International Criminal Court, June 16, 2021, https://www.icc-cpi.int/news/mr-karim-asad-ahmad-khan-qc-sworn-today-prosecutor-international-criminal-court.

18 Office of the Prosecutor, *Statement of ICC Prosecutor, Karim A.A. Khan QC, on the Situation in Ukraine: "I have been closely following recent developments in and around Ukraine with increasing concern."*, Feb. 25, 2022, https://www.icc-cpi.int/news/statement-icc-prosecutor-karim-aa-khan-qc-situation-ukraine-i-have-been-closely-following.

19 Office of the Prosecutor, *Statement of ICC Prosecutor, Karim A.A. Khan QC, on the Situation in Ukraine: "I have decided to proceed with opening an investigation,"* International Criminal Court, Feb. 28, 2022, https://www.icc-cpi.int/news/statement-icc-prosecutor-karim-aa-khan-qc-situation-ukraine-i-have-decided-proceed-opening.

20 *Id.*

21 *Prosecutor v. Omar Hassan Ahmad Al-Bashir*, Case No. ICC-02/05-01/09, *Judgment*, ¶ 1 (Appeals Chamber, May 6, 2019).

22 Rome Statute of the International Criminal Court (Rome Statute), Preamble, July 17, 1998, 2187 U.N.T.S. 3.

23 International Criminal Court, About the Office of the Prosecutor, https://www.icc-cpi.int/about/otp.

24 Office of the Prosecutor, Policy on Children, Dec. 2023, https://www.icc-cpi.int/sites/default/files/2023-12/2023-policy-children-en-web.pdf.

25 Office of the Prosecutor, Policy on Children ¶ 3, Dec. 2023, https://www.icc-cpi.int/sites/default/files/2023-12/2023-policy-children-en-web.pdf.

26 Office of the Prosecutor, Policy on the Crime of Gender Persecution, Dec. 7, 2023, https://www.icc-cpi.int/sites/default/files/2022-12/2022-12-07-Policy-on-the-Crime-of-Gender-Persecution.pdf.

27 Office of the Prosecutor, Policy Paper on Sexual and Gender-Based Crimes, June 2014, https://www.icc-cpi.int/sites/default/files/iccdocs/otp/OTP-Policy-Paper-on-Sexual-and-Gender-Based-Crimes--June-2014.pdf.

28 Office of the Prosecutor, Press Release: ICC Prosecutor and Eurojust launch practical guidelines for documenting and preserving information on international crimes, Sept. 21, 2022, https://www.icc-cpi.int/news/icc-prosecutor-and-eurojust-launch-practical-guidelines-documenting-and-preserving-information.

29 Anthony Deutsch & Stephen Farrell, ICC Insists on "Zero Tolerance" of Crimes Against Children in Ukraine, Reuters, Mar. 16, 2022, https://www.reuters.com/article/world/icc-insists-on-zero-tolerance-of-crimes-against-children-in-ukraine-idUSKCN2LD1RX/.

30 Office of the Prosecutor, Situation in Iraq/UK Final Report, Dec. 9, 2020, ¶ 1, https://www.icc-cpi.int/sites/default/files/itemsDocuments/201209-otp-final-report-iraq-uk-eng.pdf.

31 President of Ukraine, Press Release: President of Ukraine Met with the Prosecutor of the International Criminal Court, Feb. 28, 2023, https://www.president.gov.ua/en/news/prezident-ukrayini-zustrivsya-z-prokurorom-mizhnarodnogo-kri-81349.

32 *Id.*

33 Office of the Prosecutor, Statement: ICC Prosecutor Karim A.A. Khan QC announces deployment of forensics and investigative team to Ukraine, welcomes strong cooperation with the Government of the Netherlands, May 17, 2022, https://www.icc-cpi.int/news/icc-prosecutor-karim-aa-khan-qc-announces-deployment-forensics-and-investigative-team-ukraine.

34 Reuters, Ukraine Probing over 122,000 Suspected War Crimes, Says Prosecutor, Feb. 23, 2024, https://www.reuters.com/world/europe/ukraine-probing-over-122000-suspected-war-crimes-says-prosecutor-2024-02-23/.
35 Office of the Prosecutor General, Evidence Portal, https://warcrimes.gov.ua/en.
36 Patryk I. Labuda, International Criminal Tribunals and Domestic Accountability: In the Court's Shadow 27 (2023).
37 Office of the Prosecutor, Report on Prosecutorial Strategy, at 5, Sept. 14, 2006, https://www.icc-cpi.int/sites/default/files/NR/rdonlyres/D673DD8C-D427-4547-BC69-2D363E07274B/143708/ProsecutorialStrategy20060914_English.pdf.
38 Office of the Prosecutor, Statement by Prosecutor Karim A. A. Khan KC on the issuance of arrest warrants against President Vladimir Putin and Ms Maria Lvova-Belova, Mar. 17, 2023, https://www.icc-cpi.int/news/statement-prosecutor-karim-khan-kc-issuance-arrest-warrants-against-president-vladimir-putin.
39 Office of the Prosecutor, Statement, ICC Prosecutor Karim A. A. Khan KC concludes fourth visit to Ukraine: "Amidst this darkness, the light of justice is emerging," Mar. 7, 2023, https://www.icc-cpi.int/news/icc-prosecutor-karim-khan-kc-concludes-fourth-visit-ukraine-amidst-darkness-light-justice.
40 Office of the Prosecutor, Statement: ICC Office of the Prosecutor hosts roundtable event on forensic support and field deployment, Mar. 25, 2024, https://www.icc-cpi.int/news/icc-office-prosecutor-hosts-roundtable-event-forensic-support-and-field-deployment.
41 Office of the Prosecutor, Statement of ICC Prosecutor, Karim A.A. Khan QC, on his visits to Ukraine and Poland: "Engagement with all actors critical for effective, independent investigations," Mar. 16, 2022, https://www.icc-cpi.int/news/statement-icc-prosecutor-karim-aa-khan-qc-his-visits-ukraine-and-poland-engagement-all-actors.
42 Office of the Prosecutor, Strategic Plan 2023–2025 (Strategic Plan), https://www.icc-cpi.int/sites/default/files/2023-08/2023-strategic-plan-otp-v.3.pdf.
43 Office of the Prosecutor, Press Release: International Criminal Court Launches Strategic Plans for 2023–2025, June 14, 2023, https://www.icc-cpi.int/news/international-criminal-court-launches-strategic-plans-2023-2025.
44 Office of the Prosecutor, Strategic Plan, ¶¶ 46–49, https://www.icc-cpi.int/sites/default/files/2023-08/2023-strategic-plan-otp-v.3.pdf.
45 *Id.* at ¶¶ 65–67.
46 *Id.* at ¶¶ 42–43.
47 The portal is available at https://otplink.icc-cpi.int/.
48 International Criminal Court, OPTLink, https://otplink.icc-cpi.int/.
49 Article 69(4) reads in full: "The Court may rule on the relevance or admissibility of any evidence, taking into account, inter alia, the probative value of the evidence and any prejudice that such evidence may cause to a fair trial or to a fair evaluation of the testimony of a witness, in accordance with the Rules of Procedure and Evidence."
50 Prosecutor v. Ruto and Sang, Trial Chamber V(A), Decision on the Prosecution's Request for Admission of Documentary Evidence, No. ICC-01/09/-01/11 (June 10, 2014), ¶ 15.
51 Prosecutor v. Bemba, Trial Chamber III, Decision on the Admission into Evidence of Items Deferred in the Chamber's "Decision on the Prosecution's Application for Admission of Materials into Evidence Pursuant to Article 64(9) of the Rome Statute," No. ICC-01/05-01/08 (June 27, 2013), ¶ 9.
52 Office of the Prosecutor General, Evidence Portal, https://warcrimes.gov.ua/en.
53 *See, e.g.*, Rome Statute, Art. 8 *bis* ("'crime of aggression' means the planning, preparation, initiation or execution, by a person in a position effectively to exercise

control over or to direct the political or military action of a State, of an act of aggression which, by its character, gravity and scale, constitutes a manifest violation of the Charter of the United Nations").

54 In this part, I draw on the comprehensive article on the topic by Prof. Jennifer Trahan. Jennifer Trahan, *The Need for an International Tribunal on the Crime of Aggression Regarding the Situation in Ukraine*, 46 Fordham J. Int'l L. 671 (2023). Professor Trahan discusses the need for an aggression tribunal further in her chapter below.

55 *Id. at* 683–684.

56 Jocelyn Getgen Kestenbaum, *Closing Impunity Gaps for the Crime of Aggression*, 17 Chicago J. Int'l L. 51, 62–63 (2016), https://chicagounbound.uchicago.edu/cgi/viewcontent.cgi?article=1701&context=cjil.

57 Astrid Reisinger Coracini & Pal Wrange, *The Specificity of the Crime of Aggression*, in The Crime of Aggression: A Commentary, (Claus Kress & Stefan Barriga, eds, April 2017).

58 Human Rights Council, Report of the Independent International Commission of Inquiry on Ukraine, Mar. 18, 2024, U.N. Doc. A/HRC/55/66, https://www.ohchr.org/sites/default/files/documents/hrbodies/hrcouncil/coiukraine/a-hrc-55-66-aev.pdf; Human Rights Council, Oral Update of the Independent International Commission of Inquiry on Ukraine, Sept. 24, 2023, https://www.ohchr.org/sites/default/files/documents/hrbodies/hrcouncil/coiukraine/20230923-Oral-Update-IICIU-EN.pdf.

59 Human Rights Council, Report of the Independent International Commission of Inquiry on Ukraine, Mar. 18, 2024, U.N. Doc. A/HRC/55/66, https://www.ohchr.org/sites/default/files/documents/hrbodies/hrcouncil/coiukraine/a-hrc-55-66-aev.pdf.

60 Ashish Kumar Sen, United States Institute of Peace, Is Russia Committing Genocide in Ukraine?, Sept. 21, 2022, https://www.usip.org/publications/2022/09/russia-committing-genocide-ukraine.

61 Yale School of Public Health, Russia's Systematic Program for the Re-Education & Adoption of Ukraine's Children, at 6–7, Feb. 14, 2023, https://hub.conflictobservatory.org/portal/sharing/rest/content/items/97f919ccfe524d31a241b53ca44076b8/data.

62 Andrew E. Kramer, et al., Destroyed Ukrainian Dam Floods War Zone and Forces Residents to Flee, N.Y. Times, June 6, 2023, https://www.nytimes.com/2023/06/06/world/europe/ukraine-dam-destroyed-flood.html.

63 United Nations Office for the Coordination of Humanitarian Affairs, Flash Update: Ukraine – Destruction of Kakhovka Dam, June 16, 2023, https://reports.unocha.org/en/country/ukraine/flash-update/1Xfih2k5WjajTAzfgaS62L/.

64 United Nations Office for the Coordination of Humanitarian Affairs, Flash Update: Destruction of Kakhovka Dam, June 22, 2023, https://www.unocha.org/publications/report/ukraine/ukraine-humanitarian-impact-and-response-flash-update-8-destruction-kakhovka-dam-22-jun-2023-enuk.

65 James Glanz, et al., Why the Evidence Suggests Russia Blew Up the Kakhovka Dam, N.Y. Times, June 16, 2023, https://www.nytimes.com/interactive/2023/06/16/world/europe/ukraine-kakhovka-dam-collapse.html.

66 Office of the Prosecutor, Statement: The Office of the Prosecutor launches public consultation on a new policy initiative to advance accountability for environmental crimes under the Rome Statute, Feb. 16, 2024, https://www.icc-cpi.int/news/office-prosecutor-launches-public-consultation-new-policy-initiative-advance-accountability-0; Office of the Prosecutor, Strategic Plan, ¶ 57, https://www.icc-cpi.int/sites/default/files/2023-08/2023-strategic-plan-otp-v.3.pdf.

67 Office of the Prosecutor, Statement: The Office of the Prosecutor launches public consultation on a new policy initiative to advance accountability for environmental crimes under the Rome Statute, Feb. 16, 2024, https://www.icc-cpi.int/news/office-prosecutor-launches-public-consultation-new-policy-initiative-advance-accountability-0.
68 Thomas Obel Hansen, Could the Nova Kakhovka Dam Destruction Become the ICC's First Environmental Crimes Case, Just Security, June 8, 2023, https://www.justsecurity.org/86862/could-the-nova-kakhovka-dam-destruction-become-the-iccs-first-environmental-crimes-case/.
69 Thomas Obel Hansen, Could the Nova Kakhovka Dam Destruction Become the ICC's First Environmental Crimes Case, Just Security, June 8, 2023, https://www.justsecurity.org/86862/could-the-nova-kakhovka-dam-destruction-become-the-iccs-first-environmental-crimes-case/.
70 United Nations, Ukraine, Post-Disaster Needs Assessment, 2023 Kakhovka Dam Disaster, Ukraine, Oct. 2023, https://ukraine.un.org/sites/default/files/2023-10/PDNA%20Final%20and%20Cleared%20-%2016Oct.pdf.
71 *Id.*
72 *Id.*
73 Jeffrey Gettleman, The Never-Ending Nightmare of Ukraine's Dam Disaster, N.Y. Times, Sept. 3, 2023, https://www.nytimes.com/2023/09/03/world/europe/ukraine-dam-flooding-damage.html.
74 James Glanz, et al., Why the Evidence Suggests Russia Blew Up the Kakhovka Dam, N.Y. Times, June 16, 2023, https://www.nytimes.com/interactive/2023/06/16/world/europe/ukraine-kakhovka-dam-collapse.html.
75 Armed Conflict Location & Event Data Project, Still Under Fire: The Evolving Fate of Civilians in Ukraine, Feb. 22, 2024, https://acleddata.com/acleddatanew/wp-content/uploads/2024/03/Ukraine-2nd-anniversary-study.pdf.
76 Patrick Wintour, Russia Floundering in "Mud of Lies" Over Kakhovka Dam Destruction, Ukraine Tells UN, The Guardian, June 6, 2023, https://www.theguardian.com/world/2023/jun/07/russia-accused-of-floundering-in-lies-at-un-security-council-after-claiming-ukraine-behind-dam-destruction.
77 James Glanz, et al., Destroyed Ukrainian Dam Floods War Zone and Forces Residents to Flee, N.Y. Times, June 6, 2023, https://www.nytimes.com/2023/06/06/world/europe/ukraine-dam-destroyed-flood.html; Niha Masih, Who Blew Up the Nord Stream Pipelines? What We Know One Year Later, Wash. Post, Sept. 25, 2023, https://www.washingtonpost.com/world/2023/09/25/nord-stream-pipeline-explosion-update-russia-ukraine/; Adam Entous, et al., Intelligence Suggests Pro-Ukrainian Group Sabotaged Pipelines, U.S. Officials Say, N.Y. Times, Mar. 7, 2023, https://www.nytimes.com/2023/03/07/us/politics/nord-stream-pipeline-sabotage-ukraine.html.
78 Office of the Prosecutor, Statement of ICC Prosecutor Karim A.A. Khan KC: Applications for Arrest Warrants in the Situation in the State of Palestine, May 20, 2024, https://www.icc-cpi.int/news/statement-icc-prosecutor-karim-aa-khan-kc-applications-arrest-warrants-situation-state.
79 See generally, Carsten Stahn, Justice as Message (2020).
80 Office of the Prosecutor, Statement: ICC Prosecutor Karim A.A. Khan QC Visits Kharkiv, Ukraine on 15 June 2022, June 17, 2022, https://www.icc-cpi.int/news/icc-prosecutor-karim-khan-qc-visits-kharkiv-ukraine-15-june-2022; Office of the Prosecutor, Statement of ICC Prosecutor, Karim A.A. Khan QC, at the Arria-Formula meeting of the UN Security Council on "Ensuring accountability for atrocities committed in Ukraine", Apr. 27, 2022, https://www.icc-cpi.int/news/statement-icc-prosecutor-karim-aa-khan-qc-arria-formula-meeting-un-security-council-ensuring.

81 United Nations, Press Release: International Criminal Court's Success Will Be Legacy for Future Generations, Secretary-General Says at Inauguration of Its Permanent Premises, Apr. 19, 2016, https://press.un.org/en/2016/sgsm17685.doc.htm; Benjamin J. Appel, "In the Shadow of the International Criminal Court: Does the ICC Deter Human Rights Violations?" 62 *J. Conflict Resolution* 3 (2018).

82 Marlise Simons & Anushka Patil, International Criminal Court Issues Arrest Warrant for Putin, N.Y. Times, Mar. 17, 2023, https://www.nytimes.com/live/2023/03/17/world/russia-ukraine-putin-news#the-international-criminal-court-issues-an-arrest-warrant-for-putin.

83 Office of the Prosecutor, Statement of ICC Prosecutor, Karim A.A. Khan QC, on his visits to Ukraine and Poland: "Engagement with all actors critical for effective, independent investigations," Mar. 16, 2022, https://www.icc-cpi.int/news/statement-icc-prosecutor-karim-aa-khan-qc-his-visits-ukraine-and-poland-engagement-all-actors; Office of the Prosecutor, Statement: ICC Prosecutor Karim A.A. Khan QC announces deployment of forensics and investigative team to Ukraine, welcomes strong cooperation with the Government of the Netherlands, May 17, 2022, https://www.icc-cpi.int/news/icc-prosecutor-karim-aa-khan-qc-announces-deployment-forensics-and-investigative-team-ukraine.

84 Office of the Prosecutor, Statement by Prosecutor Karim A. A. Khan KC on the issuance of arrest warrants against President Vladimir Putin and Ms Maria Lvova-Belova, Mar. 17, 2023, https://www.icc-cpi.int/news/statement-prosecutor-karim-khan-kc-issuance-arrest-warrants-against-president-vladimir-putin.

85 Oumar Ba, A Truly International Criminal Court: Why the New Prosecutor Should Look Beyond Africa, Foreign Affairs, June 18, 2021, https://www.foreignaffairs.com/articles/africa/2021-06-18/truly-international-criminal-court.

86 *See generally* Sara L. Ochs, The United States, the International Criminal Court, and the Situation in Afghanistan, 95 Notre Dame L. Rev. Reflection 89 (2019).

87 Situation in the Islamic Republic of Afghanistan, Case No. ICC-02/17 OA4, Judgment on the Appeal Against the Decision on the Authorization of an Investigation into the Situation in the Islamic Republic of Afghanistan (Appeals Chamber, Mar. 5, 2020), https://www.icc-cpi.int/sites/default/files/CourtRecords/CR2020_00828.PDF.

88 Human Rights Watch, ICC, Afghanistan Inquiry Can Resume, Oct. 31, 2022, https://www.hrw.org/news/2022/10/31/icc-afghanistan-inquiry-can-resume.

6

PROPOSALS FOR THE FORMATION OF A CRIME OF AGGRESSION TRIBUNAL

for the Situation of Ukraine

*by Jennifer Trahan**

Introduction

Since the spring of 2022, a variety of proposals have surfaced for pursuing accountability for the crime of aggression related to the situation of Ukraine. The aggression of course commenced earlier, with the 2014 invasion and attempted annexation of Crimea, but calls for criminal accountability became pronounced after the full-scale invasion of February 24, 2022. At the time of writing, no one proposal for accountability for the crime has prevailed and it is currently unclear whether an aggression-specific tribunal will be established, although a significant number of states have made the commitment to creating one and there is still time to develop a successful proposal. To the author, it is imperative to establish the strongest and most legitimate tribunal possible, as nothing else would be an appropriate response to a flagrant assault not only on Ukraine but the international legal order.

This chapter traces, at the time of writing, competing proposals for developing a stand-alone aggression-specific tribunal for the situation of Ukraine. They include: (a) pooling the domestic jurisdictions of several countries; (b) creating a regional tribunal; (c) establishing a Special Tribunal on the Crime of Aggression ("STCoA") through the United Nations; (d) forming an internationalized chamber within the Ukrainian system; and (e) utilizing the domestic jurisdiction of a third state (e.g., such as a court within the Netherlands). The author will include her views on why, of these proposals, the STCoA is the best model and should be chosen. It is, however, possible that another model will emerge and be the one implemented. In the long-run, states that support accountability for the crime of aggression also need to amend the Rome Statute[1] of the International Criminal Court ("ICC") and bring the

DOI: 10.4324/9781003458166-8

ICC's jurisdiction over the crime in line with the ICC's jurisdiction over its other crimes so that similar situations may be prosecuted there in the future.[2]

The imperative of accountability for the crime of aggression

Initially, it is significant to acknowledge that the various competing proposals all share the view that there must be accountability for the crime of aggression being committed against Ukraine. Indeed, a "Core Group" of states (approximately 40 as of this writing) have expressly made that commitment.[3] The goal of accountability for the crime of aggression is expressly also supported by the Council of Europe, the European Commission, the Parliamentary Assembly of NATO,[4] and numerous domestic parliaments,[5] with the UN General Assembly supporting the goal of accountability more generally.[6] Unsurprisingly, the Government of Ukraine strongly supports the call for criminal accountability for the crime of aggression and establishing an aggression-specific tribunal.[7]

Solid precedent exists for prosecuting the crime of aggression. It was the central focus of the prosecutions before the International Military Tribunal ("IMT") at Nuremberg and the International Military Tribunal for the Far East ("IMTFE") (Tokyo).[8] However, at the international level, prosecutions thereafter languished. The crime resurfaced though in 1998 in the ICC's Rome Statute as one of the crimes over which the ICC would have jurisdiction.[9] The definition of the crime and conditions for the ICC's exercise of jurisdiction over it were later adopted in 2010 at the ICC Review Conference in Kampala, Uganda.[10] However, the ICC's jurisdiction over the crime is different than the ICC's jurisdiction over its other crimes, and it is at present quite limited.[11] The jurisdiction, for one thing, completely excludes crimes by the nationals of, or committed on the territory of, non-States Parties to the ICC's Rome Statute.[12] This excludes from the ICC's jurisdiction Russian nationals and aggression committed on Russian territory, as the Russian Federation is not an ICC State Party.[13] This gap in the ICC's jurisdiction is what has triggered discussions of how one might establish a freestanding, new tribunal to investigate and prosecute the crime of aggression in the instant situation.

The imperative of prosecuting the crime of aggression appears clear when one considers that without the initial act of aggression, one never reaches any of the war crimes, crimes against humanity, or other civilian injuries and fatalities. One also would not have soldiers on both sides (Russian or Ukrainian) killed[14]—targeting that is permissible under the laws of war (i.e., it is not a war crime during a state of armed conflict to target combatants).[15] Yet, under the crime of aggression, they too are victims. There is an extremely large "crime base" for the crime of aggression. Essentially, it includes all of the people of Ukraine who have suffered or died as a result of the war, as well as soldiers who have been killed and wounded on both sides, and potentially even those in other countries who have suffered from hunger from blocked grain shipments.[16] At another level, the crime is also an offense against the global order, as it is a violation of the core norm in the UN Charter, Article 2(4), that prohibits aggressive use of force.[17] When a powerful country—a permanent members of the UN Security Council, the very body charged under the UN Charter with the maintenance of international peace and security no less[18]—feels safe to brazenly invade its neighboring state, the borders of all countries are less secure. These broad ramifications of the crime of aggression explain why the crime was referred to in the Judgment of the IMT at Nuremberg as "the supreme international crime" because "it contains within itself the accumulated evil of the whole."[19]

While responsibility also exists at the state level—the Russian Federation has also committed an act of aggression[20] against the state of Ukraine—to only consider responsibility from that perspective seems vastly insufficient. As was eloquently explained in the Nuremberg Judgment: "Crimes against International Law are committed by men, not by abstract entities, and only by punishing individuals who commit such a crimes can the provisions of International Law be enforced."[21] This proposition is now well-established and forms the basis of the modern field of international justice—that, in addition to responsibility at the state level, there must be individual criminal responsibility for the most serious crimes of concern to the international community.[22]

Pooling the domestic jurisdictions of several countries

The first individual to prominently advocate for establishing a crime of aggression tribunal related to Russia's 2022 invasion was UK barrister and law professor Philippe Sands, with the idea subsequently endorsed by former UK Prime Minister Gordon Brown.[23] The proposal culminated in the issuance of a Declaration on a Special Tribunal for the Punishment of the Crime of Aggression against Ukraine.[24] The concept was that the tribunal would be established by pooling the domestic jurisdictions of several European countries.[25]

Precedent existed for such an approach in that the IMT at Nuremberg, formed through the London Charter,[26] was the result of the combined legislative powers of the four Allied Occupying Powers of Germany,[27] although the Charter was later endorsed by twenty additional states.[28] While the Nuremberg Tribunal was ground-breaking in 1945, and ultimately set extremely significant precedent that contributed to the formation of the modern field of international justice, tribunals have progressed considerably since then, with the development of a variety of subsequent international and hybrid criminal tribunals.[29] Moreover, one could easily imagine the Sands/Brown model being susceptible to potential future abuse, if, for example, other countries decided to pool their domestic jurisdictions in establishing a tribunal—consider the possibility of Russia and Belarus doing so (the Russian Federation has already acted in a seemingly retaliatory fashion by opening a case against the ICC Prosecutor and several ICC judges).[30] Furthermore, that the Sands and Brown proposal came from two UK nationals also struck some as hypocritical given the lack of accountability for the 2003 intervention by the US and UK into Iraq, one that lacked a clear legal theory or UN Security Council authorization.[31]

Notwithstanding, Philippe Sands and Gordon Brown made a significant contribution to putting the topic of establishing a crime of aggression tribunal for the situation of Ukraine on the table and galvanizing support for the proposition.

A regional tribunal

Once the issue came to the fore, a variety of other proposals started to surface, one being for some form of a regional tribunal. Various partnering institutions and organizations were suggested, such as the European Union ("EU") or Council of Europe.[32] In addition to the US, European states did seem the states most concerned with, and affected by, the war, so the suggestion appeared natural. There is also precedent for establishing such a hybrid regional tribunal. For example, the Extraordinary African Chambers in the Senegalese Courts was a hybrid tribunal formed by agreement between Senegal and the African Union (AU).[33]

Yet, these proposals for a regionally established aggression tribunal never received significant traction, and appear, as of this writing, to have fallen to the wayside. Indeed, the President of the European Commission,[34] the Parliamentary Assembly of the Council of Europe,[35] and the Parliamentary Assembly of NATO,[36] take the view that an international tribunal formed through the United Nations would be the preferable response.

The advantage of a regional tribunal could be in garnering the requisite level of political and financial support, as European states comprise a significant number of the Core Group of states committed to establishing a tribunal.[37] Yet, if one seeks to establish the precedent that the crime of aggression is an offence against the international legal order—as it is[38]—a regional tribunal could appear a weak response. It could inappropriately convey that the aggression was primarily only a problem for Ukraine and European states, and not a threat to international peace and security more broadly. As will be discussed below, a regional tribunal could also risk immunizing high-level leaders from prosecution.[39] A regional solution would not provide the strongest approach.

A Special Tribunal on the Crime of Aggression formed through the United Nations

Early in the spring of 2022, calls started to emerge for the establishment of a special international tribunal on the crime of aggression, to be formed by agreement between the United Nations and Ukraine, on the recommendation of the UN General Assembly.[40] The idea was formally presented to a number of UN Member States at the Yale Club in New York City on June 22, 2022, in a meeting sponsored by the Permanent Mission of Liechtenstein to the United Nations and the Permanent Mission of Latvia to the United Nations. The chair's summary of the meeting details the concept behind, and proposed structure of, the tribunal.[41] Some of the Yale Club speakers later expanded on their presentations in a series of blog posts on the website Just Security.[42]

While a full discussion of proposed features is beyond the scope of this article, the concept is for a narrowly tailored tribunal that would solely prosecute the crime of aggression, and solely in the situation of Ukraine.[43] It would have an internationally appointed prosecutor, utilize the definition of the crime of aggression found in Rome Statute article 8bis, and incorporate the full panoply of fair trial protections.[44] The tribunal would sit in The Hague in order to facilitate cooperation with the ICC,[45] which has been investigating war crimes and crimes against humanity in the situation of Ukraine, and has, at the time of writing, issued two arrest warrants.[46] The ICC has jurisdiction over the situation by virtue of Ukraine having executed two Article 12(3) declarations, thereby accepting the Court's jurisdiction,[47] although that jurisdiction, as explained above, does not encompass the crime of aggression.[48]

Some of the benefits of such a tribunal are that a tribunal created through the United Nations would represent a truly global response. As argued above, this is what is required to appropriately respond to a flagrant violation of the international legal order and breach of the core norm in the UN Charter against the aggressive use of force,[49] a breach that has been recognized, inter alia, by the UN General Assembly.[50] The STCoA could also benefit from having internationally appointed judges, which, in the present situation, could better ensure the appearance of impartiality than the appointment of members of the Ukrainian judiciary (as would be the case with various of the other proposals).[51] Moreover, as will be discussed in detail below,[52] it is an international tribunal that can avoid the application of personal immunities that could otherwise insulate high-level Russian leadership from prosecution. Concern about the potential application of immunities has proven a key issue. The crime of aggression is a "leadership crime" in that only leaders who are "in a position effectively to exercise control over or to direct the political or military action of a State" are covered by the current and internationally accepted definition of the crime.[53] It would be significantly problematic if the very same leaders most responsible for the crime would be immune from prosecution. The immunities problem is one that particularly exists with all proposals other than a tribunal formed through the United Nations—which would establish the tribunal as an international one.[54]

A closely related proposal exists to utilize the model of the Special Court for Sierra Leone.[55] The proponents of that proposal also envisioned going through the UN General Assembly, with the primary difference being the potential to have judges appointed by both the international community and ones selected by the Government of Ukraine.[56]

An internationalized chamber within the Ukrainian system

By the spring of 2023, a competing approach was proposed by US Ambassador-at-Large for Global Criminal Justice, Beth Van Schaack. Ambassador Van Schaack called for the establishment of "an internationalized court that is rooted in Ukraine's judicial system, but that also includes international elements . . . ."[57] She explained that such a court could have "significant international elements—in the form of substantive law, personnel, information sources, and structure," and might be located elsewhere in Europe than Ukraine.[58] The UK Government and Germany's Foreign Minister favor a similar approach. The UK has taken the view that the tribunal should not be an international one, but instead "integrated into Ukraine's national justice system with international elements."[59] The German Foreign Minister has endorsed a hybrid tribunal "deriving its jurisdiction from Ukrainian criminal law."[60] States in the G7 have aligned behind the hybrid/internationalized proposal.[61]

These approaches have sometimes been referred to as calling for a "hybrid tribunal"—but a hybrid within the Ukrainian system. Yet, at least what the United States and United Kingdom propose is perhaps better conceptualized as an "internationalized" domestic court in that they appear to call for a Ukrainian court with international backing. Significantly, the chamber would not be established through the United Nations, but within the Ukrainian court system. It has been suggested that the model of the Kosovo Specialist Chambers could be followed.[62] The Kosovo Specialist Chambers and Specialist Prosecutors Office were created within the legal system of Kosovo, with financial support from the EU and other contributing countries, and are located in The Hague.[63]

While details of the plan are not public, and while at one level it is rather extraordinary that the United States and United Kingdom take the view that the crime of aggression must be prosecuted,[64] at least two significant concerns with the approach quickly emerged. The first is that Ukraine's Constitution does not permit the formation of special or extraordinary chambers within the Ukrainian court system.[65] Thus, as Alexander Komarov and Oona A.

Hathaway, explain, if a special or extraordinary chamber is envisioned (as it is), or adding non-Ukrainian judges to a Ukrainian court (also sometimes suggested), an amendment of Ukraine's Constitution would be required.[66] Moreover, such amendments are not possible while Ukraine is under martial law or a state of emergency.[67] Accordingly, the approach could not be pursued until after the war is concluded.

A second problem is that, as a tribunal formed within the Ukrainian court system (even with internationalized elements and/or support), it would be a national court, meaning that high-level personal immunity for top leaders—the problem mentioned above[68]—would attach. This would render any head of state, head of government and minister of foreign affairs (referred to as "the troika") immune from prosecution.[69] The law mandating this is found in the 2002 *Yerodia* (Arrest Warrant) case before the International Court of Justice,[70] the Charles Taylor decision of the Special Court for Sierra Leone,[71] and the ICC's decision on Jordan's failure to arrest then Sudanese President Bashir.[72] These cases collectively established that the troika may not be prosecuted except by an international court or tribunal, created under international law, when adjudicating international crimes.[73] Thus, if one wants a tribunal to prosecute high-level leaders for the crime of aggression, an internationalized Ukrainian court would be unable to do so; it would only be able to prosecute leaders under the top tier. This raises the question of the utility of the whole endeavor, and whether, by insulating top level leadership one might not convey the very opposite impression than intended—that top level leaders, such as Russian President Putin, can escape accountability, pinning it on those below.

It is thought to be primarily for this reason—the need to avoid personal immunities (and consequent impunity)—that the Government of Ukraine has endorsed the establishment of an international tribunal established through the United Nations.[74]

Among the Core Group of states, there appears, as of this writing, to be a fairly even split between those states that support establishing the STCoA through the United Nations and those states that support establishing an "internationalized" Ukrainian tribunal.[75]

Utilizing the domestic jurisdiction of a third state

Perhaps suggested as a way of attempting to break the impasse within the Core Group, an idea that has recently emerged is to utilize the domestic jurisdiction of a third state.[76] While, at the time of writing, details of the idea are still vague,[77] one could imagine a court within, for example, The Netherlands being utilized. It might even receive financial and other backing from the EU, the Organization for Security and Co-operation in Europe ("OSCE"), the Council of Europe, and/or individual states. The author mentions The Netherlands in that the interim (misnamed) International Centre for the Prosecution of the

Crime of Aggression against Ukraine ("ICPA")—which has been established to compile evidence of the crime of aggression but has no prosecutorial capacity[78]—is located there. The ICC is also headquartered in The Hague, and any aggression-specific tribunal would need to work cooperatively with the ICC.[79] Thus, the suggestion of The Netherlands is plausible.[80] The court might have judges from Ukraine and additional states appointed to serve.[81]

Utilizing the domestic jurisdiction of a third state makes sense at one level. It avoids the problem of amending Ukraine's Constitution, since the court would no longer be established within Ukraine's legal system. This would obviate the need to delay establishing the tribunal until the end of the war (or when martial law or the state of emergency could be lifted).[82]

Notwithstanding, the proposal still contains obvious weaknesses. As a national court, even one that is "internationalized," it would suffer from the same immunity defects discussed above. High-level Russian—and Belorussian—leadership would have immunity (having permitted Russian forces to use its territory as a staging ground, the leaders of Belarus also face potential criminal responsibility for the crime of aggression).[83]

There is also the issue of jurisdiction. If the tribunal is formed by, or jointly with, Ukraine, the jurisdiction is obvious—territorial jurisdiction; at least part of the crime of aggression is clearly occurring within the territory of Ukraine.[84] Passive personality jurisdiction also exists due to the massive number of Ukrainian victims.[85] However, when one relies on the jurisdiction of a third state, such as The Netherlands, the jurisdictional basis is less obvious. The crime of aggression is a crime that can be prosecuted based on universal jurisdiction, so that a country that provides for universal jurisdiction in its domestic criminal code could prosecute the crime with no direct jurisdictional link.[86] However, whether states that would need to provide political and financial support to the tribunal would accept reliance on universal jurisdiction is quite unclear. It could create precedent for other states to rely on universal jurisdiction in prosecuting the crime of aggression domestically, a precedent that some states likely would be wary of furthering. Moreover, unlike, for example, the Malaysian Airlines MH-17 trial held in the Netherlands (given the substantial number of Dutch victims of the plane crash),[87] there are no significant Dutch fatalities in Ukraine; accordingly, there is no obvious passive personality jurisdiction. The suggestion has also been made that Ukraine could "transfer" its jurisdiction to The Netherlands, or transfer proceedings (i.e., Ukraine would retain jurisdiction but transfer high-level cases).[88]

The UN General Assembly's endorsement of a third state tribunal has also been suggested.[89] It is unclear what precisely this is intended to achieve—other than an additional imprimatur of international legitimacy, which it conceivable would provide. Yet, obtaining the votes for such a General Assembly endorsement of a national crime of aggression tribunal would seem to be even more difficult than obtaining the votes for an international tribunal (the

STCoA). One can easily imagine certain states being wary of setting the precedent of the General Assembly endorsing a national trial for the crime of aggression. The precedent of obtaining the General Assembly vote or any other international endorsement could also inadvertently risk leaving the mistaken impression of the need for such endorsement for a national prosecution of the crime of aggression.[90] One source suggests that the Council of Europe could alternatively provide the endorsement.[91]

Given the weaknesses of this proposal for a third state tribunal (including the potential reluctance of The Netherlands to utilize its courts), one wonders whether perhaps yet another model will be proposed to break the impasse that exists in designing a stand-alone aggression-specific tribunal.

Amending the Rome Statute to fix the ICC's jurisdiction over the crime of aggression

Regardless of whether a stand-alone aggression-specific tribunal is created for the situation of Ukraine, a parallel initiative has emerged. It is to amend the ICC's Rome Statute to bring the ICC's jurisdiction over the crime of aggression in line with the ICC's jurisdiction over its other crimes.[92]

As mentioned, the ICC's jurisdiction over the crime of aggression is hobbled by a restrictive jurisdictional regime.[93] If the crime of aggression is truly "the Supreme international crime" because "it contains within itself the accumulated evil of the whole,"[94] and one of "the most serious crimes of concern to the international community" as stated in the ICC's Rome Statute,[95] there is no reason to have this truncated jurisdictional regime.

If the ICC had the same jurisdiction over the crime of aggression as it has over the crimes of genocide, war crimes, and crimes against humanity, no standalone aggression-specific tribunal would be required, as the ICC would simply have jurisdiction over all four crimes if committed in the territory of Ukraine.[96]

How jurisdiction got to be so limited is a lengthy topic. Briefly summarized, the United States and other states insisted on the carve-out of the nationals of non-States Parties and crimes committed on their territories (Article 15bis(5)) during the 2010 Kampala Review Conference negotiations. Although the United States has never been a State Party, the US delegation had enough clout in the negotiations to prevail in this position.[97] States Parties then also wanted a carve-out from jurisdiction (an "opt out" process)—allowing them to "opt out" of crime of aggression jurisdiction, now found in Article 15bis(4) (only two states ever used the opt out).[98] Then, after a dispute arose as to the proper reading of the jurisdictional regime agreed to in Kampala (whether the default position for States Parties was "in" or "out" of the ICC's jurisdiction), States Parties, in a push led by the UK and France, further limited jurisdiction, or arguably did so;[99] they insisted that the default position was "out" of the regime. Thus, if that restrictive reading is valid, both the "aggressor state" and "victim state" would have had to have expressly ratified the crime of aggression amendment or accepted the Court's jurisdiction for there to be ICC jurisdiction over the crime. This was memorialized in operative paragraph 2 of the Activating Resolution that activated the crime of aggression's jurisdiction in 2017, effective July 17, 2018.[100] All of this—primarily the efforts led by the United States in 2010, and the United Kingdom and France in 2017—has resulted in the ICC having quite a limited jurisdictional regime over the crime.

Aware that this jurisdictional gap (specifically, the one negotiated by the US) is what is now preventing the ICC from investigating and prosecuting the crime of aggression in the situation of Ukraine, states such as Germany,[101] as well as NGOs such as the Global Institute for the Prevention of Aggression ("GIPA")[102] have called for amending the Rome Statute to bring the ICC's crime of aggression jurisdiction in line with the jurisdiction of the ICC's other three crimes.[103] Neither Germany (which backs one of the standalone proposals)[104] nor GIPA views the amendment as a substitute for an aggression-specific tribunal, but rather a way to fix the ICC's jurisdiction so that similar jurisdictional gaps do not occur in the future.[105] While a theoretical possibility exists that States will amend the Rome Statute while Russia's aggression is occurring, due to the complexity of the negotiations involved,[106] anticipated pushback from certain states about expanding the ICC's crime of aggression jurisdiction, and the likelihood that the amendment would not be retroactive, pursuing the amendment is not seen as a substitute for establishing a crime of aggression-specific tribunal. Rather, the two endeavors are seen as a two-step process of an aggression specific tribunal now, and amending the Rome Statute for the future.[107]

Conclusion and Analysis of Factors at Play

In the field of international justice, many variants of international and hybrid tribunals—as well as national institutions that have some degree of hybridity—have been established. Despite the ICTY and ICTR often being referred to as the "ad hoc" tribunals, most of the various international and hybrid tribunals have been "ad hoc" in that they are each unique, with different structures and features, and most formed in different ways. This variety of possibilities for structuring tribunals both provides the international community with many options (a benefit) and creates many choices (which can become a complicating factor).

In addition to the technical question of what would be the best model in terms of establishing the strongest deterrence against the commission of the crime of aggression, there is the fact that states may not always be looking to achieve the best model—at least when it comes to the crime of aggression.

One suspects that questions of self-interest come into play. A state may genuinely desire to create strong deterrence, whether to avoid future Russian aggression, or, for example, to create a check against other powerful states with clear territorial aspirations. At the same time, it is not inconceivable that some of the same states will consider the precedent that an aggression-specific tribunal for the situation of Ukraine might set for themselves. While those states are probably not contemplating a full-scale invasion of a neighboring state as brazen as that of Russia, there are times when military interventions have occurred supported by only a plausible (but not air-tight) legal theory, or even where the legal theory appears to be quite weak.[108]

One would like to think that designing a tribunal for the situation in Ukraine is all about what would be best for Ukraine (i.e., the strongest precedent)[109] and for setting precedent for the future. Yet, that would be too simplistic an assumption. What is best for Ukraine (and the global order) may align with the goals of states in creating the strongest precedent possible. This might be true, for example, for states such as Latvia, Lithuania, Estonia, or Poland, which likely view Russian aggression as a truly existential threat to their existence. But other states, not located as proximately to Ukraine, and/or with powerful militaries, may view the situation quite differently. These states are sometimes called upon (or feel impelled) to utilize force, and sometimes the law supporting their actions is unclear. An example would be interventions against forces of the so-called Islamic State ("IS") within Syria, which rested on the so-called "unable or unwilling" theory,[110] a theory other states do not accept.[111] It is for such situations that the "manifest" threshold was drafted into the crime of aggression's definition—that is, only a "manifest" UN Charter violation can become the basis of a crime of aggression prosecution at the international level.[112] Accordingly, in areas where the law is genuinely unclear, a "manifest" Charter violation will be lacking and the crime cannot be prosecuted.[113] This should provide enough comfort to states, but it is not clear that it does, and it did not help that the United States failed to attend the negotiations where the "manifest" threshold was negotiated and explained.[114]

Put differently, states making the calculation of whether to support an aggression-specific tribunal do not all view the rule of law from the perspective of Liechtenstein (which lacks an army), but may view it quite differently if they have a powerful military. While one can argue that even the most powerful militaries (or, especially the most powerful militaries) must adhere to the rule of law, there is unfortunately still wariness of international judicial institutions in some quarters.[115] Put more cynically, in some respects, brazen exceptionalism may still be at play—that the rule of law is "for others." Such calculations no doubt surface in many areas of international law, but they seem to particularly come to the fore when the crime of aggression is concerned. One saw such dynamics during the Princeton negotiations, the Kampala negotiations, and the 2017 decision to activate the crime's jurisdiction.[116] At each stage, it was countries with more powerful militaries that tried to limit the ICC's jurisdiction over the crime.[117] Unfortunately, this same dynamic now appears to be a factor in the negotiations for an aggression-specific tribunal for the situation of Ukraine—and could prove a similar factor as discussions advance for amending the Kampala crime of aggression amendments.

The author's view is that the strongest precedent in the situation of Ukraine would be creating an international tribunal through the UN, a STCoA. However, states such as the United States, the United Kingdom, and Germany are failing to support that proposal and instead support a weaker approach. It is weaker in that, as explained above, establishing a specialized chamber within the Ukrainian system would need to wait until the end of the war (which could cause significant delay), and would leave the highest level military and political leaders immune from prosecution.[118] The situation is particularly ironic when one considers that the United States, the United Kingdom, and France (which as a member of the G7 aligns with the United States and United Kingdom)[119] were three of the four Allies behind the establishment of the Nuremberg Tribunal—which centrally established the place of the crime of aggression in the pantheon of core international crimes. Another excuse one sometimes hears is that creating an international tribunal, a STCoA, would not attract enough votes within the General Assembly. This author suggests that enough votes could be mustered if all the countries in the Core Group of states were lobbying for it, including the United States, the United Kingdom, France, and Germany.

At the same time, it is concerning that there are few, if any, African or Central/South American states within the Core Group. States from other regions seem to be taking a back seat and waiting in the wings when it comes to an aggression-specific tribunal for the situation of Ukraine—an unfortunate stance when responding to a flagrant breach of the UN Charter. They may be doing so in part out of concern about double-standards—that not only aggression involving Ukraine should be prosecuted.[120] If that is the motivation, or part of it, these states should wholeheartedly support the Rome Statute amendment proposal, so that future aggression in other situations may be investigated and prosecuted before the ICC. States should not, however, let individual criminal responsibility for Russia's aggression off the hook in the meanwhile.

The international community stands at an existential moment in history. Do countries in fact believe that the crime of aggression must be prosecuted, or do they only support prosecutions when they know the rule of law can only be enforced against others (as it was at Nuremberg). If states stand for the rule of law and international institutions such as the United Nations, they cannot instrumentalize the law for use only against others. The US, UK, France, and Germany should be leading the way in establishing the strongest tribunal possible. States should also follow in the footsteps of Germany, as well as other states, which have called for amending the Kampala amendment to bring the ICC's jurisdiction over the crime of aggression in line with its jurisdiction over its other crimes.[121] Taking these steps can make the borders of all countries more secure. As a group of supportive states has written, "[e]nsuring accountability for the crime of aggression committed against Ukraine would signal that waging blatantly unlawful and colonizing wars will not go unpunished—whether in Ukraine or elsewhere."[122] It is high time for countries from all regions of the globe—many of which have suffered horrifically from the historical ravages of empire-building and colonialism[123]—to recognize this, and rally their support behind both initiatives.

Notes

1 *Thanks to Erin Lovall for formatting assistance. The Rome Statute of the International Criminal Court, July 17, 1998, 2187 UNTS 90 (as amended) [hereinafter, "Rome Statute"].

2 For the amendment proposal of the Global Institute for the Prevention of Aggression, see GIPA-model-amendment-proposal.pdf (crimeofaggression.info). The chapter does not discuss the proposal by the Public International Law and Policy Group to improve Ukrainian prosecutions and prosecute the crime of aggression, as well as the crimes of genocide, war crimes, and crimes against humanity, through Ukraine's ordinary courts. *See* PILPG, Draft Law for a Ukrainian High War Crimes Court (2022), *at* Draft Law for a Ukrainian High War Crimes Court — Public International Law & Policy Group (publicinternationallawandpolicygroup.org). That proposal is discussed in Chapter 7 with the draft legislation for the Ukrainian High War Crimes Court included in the Appendix.

3 Patryk Labuda, *Making Counter-Hegemonic International Law: Should a Special Tribunal for Aggression Be International or Hybrid?*, Just Security (Sept. 19, 2023), *at* Making Counter-Hegemonic International Law: Should A Special Tribunal for Aggression be International or Hybrid? (justsecurity.org) (listing 38 in the Core Group).

4 Council of Europe, *PACE Calls for an Ad Hoc International Criminal Tribunal to Hold to Account Perpetrators of the Crime of Aggression Against Ukraine*, *at* https://www.coe.int/en/web/portal/-/pace-calls-for-an-ad-hoc-international-criminal-tribunal-to-investigate-war-crimes-in-ukraine; European Commission, Statement by President Von der Leyen on Russian Accountability and the Use of Frozen Russian Assets (Nov. 30, 2022), *at* https://ec.europa.eu/commission/presscorner/detail/en/statement_22_7307; NATO Parliamentary Assembly, Res. 479, *at* https://www.nato-pa.int/download-file?filename=/sites/default/files/2022-11/RESOLUTION%20479%20-%20%20NATO%20POST%20MADRID%20.pdf.

5 Select statements by states are compiled on the website of the Global Institute for the Prevention of Aggression. *See* GIPA, *Situation in Ukraine, Documents: Reactions by the International Community*, *at* Documents: Reactions by the International Community | The Global Campaign for the Prevention of Aggression (crimeofaggression.info).

6 The General Assembly "emphasize[d] the need to ensure accountability for the most serious crimes under international law committed on the territory of

Ukraine through appropriate, fair and independent investigations and prosecutions at the national or international level, and ensure justice for all victims and the prevention of future crimes." GA Res. ES-11/6, paras. 1, 5, 9, passing by 141 votes.

7 Ukraine's Zelensky Urges "Special Tribunal" into Russian Invasion Following Latest Deadly Attack, Assoc. Press (July 15, 2022), at Ukraine's Zelensky urges 'special tribunal' into Russian invasion following latest deadly attack | South China Morning Post (scmp.com).

8 Charter of the International Military Tribunal, Art. 6(a), Aug. 8, 1945, 85 UNTS 251; International Military Tribunal for the Far East, Special Proclamation by the Supreme Commander for the Allied Powers at Tokyo, Art. 5(a), Jan. 19, 1946. For background on the negotiations to form the Nuremberg Tribunal, see Gary Bass, Stay the Hand of Vengeance: The Politics of International War Crimes Tribunals (Princeton U. Press 2000).

9 The Rome Statute of the International Criminal Court, Art. 5.1, July 17, 1998, 2187 UNTS 90 (as amended).

10 International Criminal Court, Assembly of States Parties, Review Conference, The Crime of Aggression, Annex I, ICC Doc. RC/Res.6 (June 11, 2010), *at* RC-11-ENG.16Dec1200 (un.org) [hereinafter, "Review Conference Resolution"].

11 The definition of the crime is found in the Rome Statute Article 8*bis* and the ICC's jurisdiction over the crime is governed by Articles 15*bis* and 15*ter*.

12 The Rome Statute of the International Criminal Court, Art. 15*bis*(5), July 17, 1998, 2187 UNTS 90 (as amended).

13 For a list of States Parties, see ICC, *The States Parties to the Rome Statute*, *at* The States Parties to the Rome Statute | International Criminal Court (icc-cpi.int).

14 Estimates of Ukrainian and Russian soldiers who have been killed or injured are nearly a half million. Helene Cooper, Thomas Gibbons-Neff, Eric Schmitt & Julian E. Barnes, *Troop Deaths and Injuries in Ukraine War Near 500,000, U.S. Officials Say*, N.Y. Times (Aug. 18, 2023), *at* Ukraine War Casualties Near Half a Million, U.S. Officials Say - The New York Times (nytimes.com).

15 The Rome Statute includes the war crime of attacks on the civilian population—not attacks on combatants. *See* The Rome Statute of the International Criminal Court, Arts. 8(2)(b)(i), 8(2)(e)(i), July 17, 1998, 2187 UNTS 90 (as amended).

16 Edward Wong & Ana Swanson, *How Russia's War on Ukraine is Worsening Global Starvation*, N.Y. Times (Jan. 2, 2023), *at* How Russia's War on Ukraine Is Worsening Global Starvation - The New York Times (nytimes.com).

17 Article 2(4) is complemented by the allowance of Security Council authorized interventions and the exercise by a state of individual and collective self-defense. *See* UN Charter, Ch. VII, Art. 51.

18 *Id.* Art. 24.1.

19 IMT, Judgment of 1 October 1946, in The Trial of German Major War Criminals. Proceedings of the International Military Tribunal Sitting at Nuremberg, Germany, Part 22, at 421 (Aug. 22, 1946–Oct. 1, 1946), *reprinted at* IMTJudgment.Endversion+Deckblatt (crimeofaggression.info) [hereinafter, "Nuremberg Judgment"].

20 For an early definition of what an "act of aggression" is, see GA Res. 3314 (1974).

21 IMT, Judgment of 1 October 1946, in The Trial of German Major War Criminals. Proceedings of the International Military Tribunal Sitting at Nuremberg, Germany, Part 22, at 447 (Aug. 22, 1946–Oct. 1, 1946), *reprinted at* IMTJudgment.Endversion+Deckblatt (crimeofaggression.info).

22 Under the Rome Statute, these are the crime of aggression, the crime of genocide, war crimes, and crimes against humanity. The Rome Statute of the International Criminal Court, Art. 5.1, July 17, 1998, 2187 UNTS 90 (as amended).

23 *See, e.g.*, Ruth Green, *Devastation Prompts Calls for Accountability in International Courts*, INT'L BAR ASS'N (Mar. 14, 2022), *at* Ukraine: devastation prompts calls for accountability in international courts | International Bar Association (ibanet.org).

24 Declaration on a Special Tribunal for the Punishment of the Crime of Aggression against Ukraine, *at* Combined-Statement-and-Declaration.pdf (gordonandsarahbrown.com).

25 *Id.* ("Countries should agree to grant jurisdiction arising under national criminal codes and general international law to a dedicated criminal tribunal…").

26 Charter of the International Military Tribunal, Annexed to the Agreement by the Government of the United Kingdom of Great Britain and Northern Ireland, the Government of the United States of America, the Provisional Government of the French Republic, and the Government of the Union of Soviet Socialist Republics for the Prosecution and Punishment of the Major War Criminals of the European Axis.

27 Matthew Lippman explains:

> The drafting and implementation of the Charter was the exercise of "sovereign legislative power by the countries to which the German Reich had unconditionally surrendered." According to the Tribunal, these countries had the undoubted legal right to legislate for the territory which they presently occupied. The Allies, in establishing the Tribunal, had "done together what any one of them might have done singly; for it is not to be doubted that any nation has the right thus to set up special courts to administer law."

Matthew Lippman, *Nuremberg: Forty Five Years Later*, 7 CONN. J. INT'L L. 1, 28 (1991), quoting Nuremberg Judgment, IMT, Judgment of 1 October 1946, in The Trial of German Major War Criminals. Proceedings of the International Military Tribunal Sitting at Nuremberg, Germany, Part 22, at 461 (Aug. 22, 1946–Oct. 1, 1946), *reprinted at* IMTJudgment.Endversion+Deckblatt (crimeofaggression.info). The IMT at Nuremberg "was composed of judges from the Allied Powers and was not, as its name suggests, an international court." Matthew Lippman, *Nuremberg: Forty Five Years Later*, 7 CONN. J. INT'L L. 1, 37 (1991).

28 UNTS, *at* UNTC.

29 The International Criminal Tribunal for the former Yugoslavia ("ICTY"), the International Criminal Tribunal for Rwanda ("ICTR"), and the ICC are examples of international tribunals. There have also been "hybrid" tribunals formed through the UN (internationally), such as the Special Court for Sierra Leone, as well as "hybrid" tribunals formed within the domestic court system of a single state, such as the Extraordinary Chambers in the Courts of Cambodia ("ECCC"). Some "hybrid" tribunals have also been formed by agreements with regional organizations, such as the Extraordinary African Chambers in the Courts of Senegal (formed jointly with the African Union). The Kosovo Specialist Chambers and Specialist Prosecutor's Office were established within Kosovo's legal system, with support from the European Union and other countries.

30 *See* Mark Trevelyan, *Russia Defies Putin Arrest Warrant by Opening Its Own Case Against ICC*, REUTERS (Mar. 20, 2023), *at* Russia defies Putin arrest warrant by opening its own case against ICC | Reuters.

31 The UK ultimately opened an inquiry into how it became embroiled in the war, known as the Chilcot Inquiry. *See* UK House of Commons Library, Briefing Paper, *Chilcot Inquiry*. For a way to help address double-standards in the future, see notes 92–107 *infra* (proposal to amend the Rome Statute's jurisdiction over the crime of aggression).

32 *See, e.g.*, *Owiso Owiso, An Aggression Chamber for Ukraine Supported by the Council of Europe*, OPINIO JURIS, *at* An Aggression Chamber for Ukraine

Supported by the Council of Europe - Opinio Juris ("The [Council of Europe] has—or can have—the legal competence to conclude a treaty with Ukraine for assistance in establishing and operating a tribunal on Russia's aggression."); Kevin Jon Heller, *The Best Option: An Extraordinary Ukrainian Chamber for Aggression*, Opinio Juris (Mar. 16, 2022), *at* The Best Option: An Extraordinary Ukrainian Chamber for Aggression - Opinio Juris (suggesting the Council of Europe and Ukraine form a regional tribunal).

33 Agreement between the Government of the Republic of Senegal and the African Union on the Creation of the Extraordinary African Chambers in the Senegalese Courts, *at* chambresafricaines.org (in French).

34 European Commission, Statement by President von der Leyen on Russian Accountability and the Use of Russian Frozen Assets, (Nov. 30, 2022), *at* President's statement on Russian accountability and (europa.eu).

35 Parliamentary Assembly, Res. 2463 Further Escalation in the Russian Federation's Aggression Against Ukraine, para. 13.6.1 (2002), *at* Res. 2463 - Resolution - Adopted text (coe.int) (calling for "the establishment of a Special (ad hoc) International Tribunal to prosecute the crime of aggression against Ukraine").

36 NATO Parliamentary Assembly, Doc. No. 111 SESP 22 E rev.1 fin, *at* NATO PA DECLARATION ON UKRAINE (nato-pa.int) (calling for "the establishment of a special ad hoc international criminal tribunal to investigate and prosecute the crime of aggression against Ukraine").

37 *See* U.S. Mission Geneva, Joint Statement of the Group of Friends of Accountability Following the Aggression Against Ukraine (Feb. 27, 2023), *at* Joint Statement of the Group of Friends of Accountability - U.S. Mission to International Organizations in Geneva (usmission.gov) (listing states in the core group).

38 The crime is predicated on a violation of Article 2(4) of the UN Charter. *See* The Rome Statute of the International Criminal Court, Art. 8*bis* (2), July 17, 1998, 2187 UNTS 90 (as amended). ("For the purpose of paragraph 1, 'act of aggression' means the use of armed force by a State against the sovereignty, territorial integrity or political independence of another State, or in any other manner inconsistent with the Charter of the United Nations."). That language in Article 8*bis* largely replicates language found in Article 2(4) of the UN Charter. *See* UN Charter, Ch. I, Art. 2(4) (also covering the threat of the use of force, but not including the word "sovereignty" that is found in Article 8*bis*).

39 *See* notes 52–54, 69–73 and accompanying text.

40 *See, e.g.*, Larry D. Johnson, *United Nations Response Options to Russia's Aggression: Opportunities and Rabbit Holes*, Just Security (Mar. 1, 2022), *at* United Nations Response Options to Russia's Aggression: Opportunities and Rabbit Holes (justsecurity.org); Jennifer Trahan, *U.N. General Assembly Should Recommend Creation of Crime of Aggression Tribunal: Nuremberg Is Not the Model*, Just Security (Mar. 7, 2022), *at* U.N. General Assembly Should Recommend Creation Of Crime Of Aggression Tribunal For Ukraine: Nuremberg Is Not The Model (justsecurity.org); Carrie McDougall, *Why Creating a Special Tribunal for Aggression Against Ukraine is the Best Available Option: A Reply to Kevin Jon Heller and Other Critics*, Opinio Juris (Mar. 15, 2022), *at* Why Creating a Special Tribunal for Aggression Against Ukraine is the Best Available Option: A Reply to Kevin Jon Heller and Other Critics - Opinio Juris.

41 Letter Dated August 12, 2022, from the Representatives of Latvia, Liechtenstein and Ukraine to the United Nations Addressed to the Secretary-General, UN Doc. A/ES-11/7-S/2022/616 (Aug. 17, 2022), *at* UNSC-Letter-12-August -2022.pdf (justsecurity.org).

42 *See Blog Series: The Case for Creating an International Tribunal to Prosecute the Crime of Aggression Against Ukraine (Parts I, II, III, IV)*, JUST SECURITY, *at* U.N. General Assembly and International Criminal Tribunal for the Crime of Aggression Against Ukraine Archives - Just Security (posts by Oona A. Hathaway, Astrid Reisinger Coracini, Jennifer Trahan, and David J. Scheffer).

43 *See* notes 41–42.

44 *Id.*

45 On the importance of such cooperation, see David J. Scheffer, *Forging a Cooperative Relationship Between International Criminal Court and a Special Tribunal for Aggression Against Ukraine*, JUST SECURITY (Oct 25, 2022), *at* Forging a Cooperative Relationship Between International Criminal Court and a Special Tribunal for Aggression Against Ukraine (justsecurity.org).

46 ICC Press Release, *Situation in Ukraine: ICC Judges Issue Arrest Warrants Against Vladimir Vladimirovich Putin and Maria Alekseyevna Lvova-Belova* (Mar. 17, 2023), *at* Situation in Ukraine: ICC judges issue arrest warrants against Vladimir Vladimirovich Putin and Maria Alekseyevna Lvova-Belova | International Criminal Court (icc-cpi.int). The ICC's investigation could also include the crime of genocide, if applicable.

47 International Criminal Court, Ukraine, Situation in Ukraine, *at* Ukraine | International Criminal Court (icc-cpi.int).

48 The Rome Statute of the International Criminal Court, Art. 15*bis*(5), July 17, 1998, 2187 UNTS 90 (as amended). For a list of States Parties, see ICC, *The States Parties to the Rome Statute*, *at* The States Parties to the Rome Statute | International Criminal Court (icc-cpi.int).

49 UN Charter, Ch. I, Art. 2(4).

50 GA Res. ES-11/1; GA Res. ES-11/2.

51 *See* Patryk Labuda, *Accountability for Russian Imperialism in the "Global East": A Special Tribunal for Aggression from a Post-Colonial, Eastern European Perspective*, JUST SECURITY (Aug. 21, 2023), *at* Accountability for Russian Imperialism in the "Global East" (justsecurity.org) (citing the concern that with Ukrainian judges, "Ukraine would be seen as a judge in its own case"). A regional or internationalized Ukrainian tribunal would presumably utilize Ukrainian judges, with the former potentially having mixed benches of international and Ukrainian judges.

52 *See* notes 69–73 *infra* and accompanying text.

53 Rome Statute, Ch. I, Art. 8*bis*.

54 For an explanation of what makes a tribunal an "international" one, see Astrid Reisinger Coracini & Jennifer Trahan, *The Case for Creating a Special Tribunal to Prosecute the Crime of Aggression Committed Against Ukraine (Part VI): On the Non-applicability of Personal Immunities*, JUST SECURITY (Nov. 8, 2022), *at* The Case for Creating a Special Tribunal to Prosecute the Crime of Aggression Committed Against Ukraine (Part VI): On the Non-Applicability of Personal Immunities (justsecurity.org). It might also be possible to utilize a treaty among a significantly large and representative enough number of states such that it might be said to represent the will of the international community and thereby obviate the application of personal immunities.

55 This model has been proposed by David Crane, Irwin Cotler, and Hans Corell. *See* The Ukraine Task Force of The Global Accountability Network, *Consideration for Setting up the Special Tribunal for Ukraine on the Crime of Aggression* (July 2022), *at* https://www.globalaccountabilitynetwork.org/_files/ugd/a982f0_6c35a85b089746a18a6334d2801e9c5d.pdf.

56 The Ukraine Task Force of The Global Accountability Network, *Proposal for a Resolution by the United Nations General Assembly and Accompanying Proposal for a Statute of a Special Tribunal for Ukraine on the Crime of Aggression* (Sept. 7,

2022), *at* a982f0_c9fb874d8cf14270b3c5fd0a1bfb4971.pdf (globalaccountabilitynetwork.org). A footnote, however, notes that one might alternatively utilize all internationally appointed judges. *Id.*, n. 31.

57 Jennifer Hansler, *US Announces It Supports Creation of Special Tribunal to Prosecute Russia for "Crime of Aggression" in Ukraine*, CNN (Mar. 28, 2023), *at* https://edition.cnn.com/2023/03/28/politics/us-support-special-tribunal-crime-of-aggression/index.html.

58 *Id.*

59 UK Government Press Release, *UK Joins Core Group Dedicated to Achieving Accountability for Russia's Aggression against Ukraine* (Jan. 20, 2023), *at* UK joins core group dedicated to achieving accountability for Russia's aggression against Ukraine - GOV.UK (www.gov.uk).

60 *Strengthening International Law in Times of Crisis – Rede von Außenministerin Annalena Baerbock in Den Haag* (Jan. 16, 2023), *at* Strengthening International Law in Times of Crisis - Rede von Außenministerin Annalena Baerbock in Den Haag - Auswärtiges Amt (auswaertiges-amt.de).

61 *See* Kuleba: *"Hybrid Tribunal: Does Not Give an Answer on How to Punish the Leaders of the Russian Federation* (Sept. 9, 2023), *at* Kuleba: "Hybrid tribunal" does not give an answer on how to punish the leaders of the Russian Federation | European Pravda (eurointegration.com.ua) (Ukrainian Minister of Foreign Affairs Dmytro Kuleba stating that "the position of the G7 is inclined towards a 'hybrid tribunal.'").The Group of Seven (G7) consists of Canada, France, Germany, Italy, Japan, the UK, and the United States.

62 Statement of Ambassador Van Schaack.

63 Kosovo Specialist Chamber, *Background*, *at* Background | Kosovo Specialist Chambers & Specialist Prosecutor's Office (scp-ks.org).

64 The UK ultimately opened an inquiry into how it became embroiled in the war, known as the Chilcot Inquiry. *See* UK House of Commons Library, Briefing Paper, *Chilcot Inquiry*. For a way to help address double-standards in the future, see notes 92–107 *infra* (proposal to amend the Rome Statute's jurisdiction over the crime of aggression).

(lack of clear legal support for the US and UK interventions in Iraq in 2003).

65 Article 125 of the Ukrainian Constitution states that the "[e]stablishment of extraordinary and special courts is not permitted." Constitution of Ukraine, Adopted at the Fifth Session of the Verkhovna Rada of Ukraine on June 28, 1996, as Amended, *at* CONSTITUTION OF UKRAINE (refworld.org).

66 Alexander Komarov & Oona A. Hathaway, *Ukraine's Constitutional Constraints: How to Achieve Accountability for the Crime of Aggression*, Just Security (Apr. 5, 2022), *at* Ukraine's Constitutional Constraints: How to Achieve Accountability for the Crime of Aggression (justsecurity.org).

67 Constitution of Ukraine, Constitution of Ukraine, Adopted at the Fifth Session of the Verkhovna Rada of Ukraine on June 28, 1996, as Amended, *at* CONSTITUTION OF UKRAINE (refworld.org), Art. 157 ("The Constitution of Ukraine shall not be amended in conditions of martial law or a state of emergency.").

68 *See* notes 69–73 *infra* and accompanying text. Rome Statute, Ch. I, Art. 8*bis*. For an explanation of what makes a tribunal an "international" one, see Astrid Reisinger Coracini & Jennifer.

69 In the case of Russia, they are President Vladimir Putin, Prime Minister Mishustin, and Foreign Minister Lavrov.

70 Arrest Warrant of 11 April 2000 (Dem. Rep. Congo v. Belg.), Judgment, 2002 ICJ Rep. 3 (Feb. 4).

71 Prosecutor v. Taylor, SCSL-2003-01-I, Decision on Immunity from Jurisdiction (May 31, 2004).

72 Prosecutor v. Al-Bashir, ICC-02/05-01/09 OA2, Judgment in the Jordan Referral re Al-Bashir Appeal (May 6, 2019).

73 For a detailed explanation of the rulings, see Astrid Reisinger Coracini & Jennifer Trahan, *The Case for Creating a Special Tribunal to Prosecute the Crime of Aggression Committed Against Ukraine (Part VI): On the Non-applicability of Personal Immunities*, Just Security (Nov. 8, 2022), *at* The Case for Creating a Special Tribunal to Prosecute the Crime of Aggression Committed Against Ukraine (Part VI): On the Non-Applicability of Personal Immunities (justsecurity.org).

74 President of Ukraine, Volodymyr Zelenskyy, Official website, *President: Ukraine Stands against Hybrid Formats of Tribunal for Russian Crime of Aggression* (May 4, 2023), *at* President: Ukraine stands against hybrid formats of tribunal for Russian crime of aggression — Official website of the President of Ukraine.

75 Observations of a Legal Adviser attending the Core Group meetings; *see also* Patryk Labuda, *Making Counter-Hegemonic International Law: Should a Special Tribunal for Aggression Be International or Hybrid?*, Just Security (Sept. 19, 2023), *at* Making Counter-Hegemonic International Law: Should A Special Tribunal for Aggression be International or Hybrid? (justsecurity.org) (note 3). [Counter-Hegemonic] ("Two main options have emerged: (1) a (purely) 'international' tribunal created through a bilateral treaty between Ukraine and the United Nations on the recommendation of the U.N. General Assembly, and (2) some form of 'hybrid' or 'internationalized' tribunal . . . .").

76 *See, e.g.*, Sergiy Sydorenko, *The "Hague Tribunal" Becomes a Reality: How Ukraine and the West Agree on a Special Court for Putin*, Eur. Pravda (Aug. 22, 2023), *at* "The Hague Tribunal" Becomes a Reality: How Ukraine and the West Agree on a Special Court for Putin | European Pravda (eurointegration.com.ua).

77 *See id.* for suggestions on how the court could be established.

78 "[T]here is no court that can currently prosecute the crime of aggression for the February 24, 2022, invasion"; "the new centre will collect evidence." Anthony Deutsch & Stephanie van den Berg, *Centre Opens to Build Cases Against Russian Leaders for Ukraine Aggression*, Reuters (July 3, 2023), *at* Centre opens to build cases against Russian leaders for Ukraine aggression | Reuters.

79 *See* David J. Scheffer, *Forging a Cooperative Relationship Between International Criminal Court and a Special Tribunal for Aggression Against Ukraine*, Just Security (Oct 25, 2022), *at* Forging a Cooperative Relationship Between International Criminal Court and a Special Tribunal for Aggression Against Ukraine (justsecurity.org).

80 Sergiy Sydorenko, *The "Hague Tribunal" Becomes a Reality: How Ukraine and the West Agree on a Special Court for Putin*, Eur. Pravda (Aug. 22, 2023), *at* "The Hague Tribunal" Becomes a Reality: How Ukraine and the West Agree on a Special Court for Putin | European Pravda (eurointegration.com.ua) (also discussing utilizing a Dutch court).

81 *Id.* (making the suggestion).

82 *See* notes Article 125 of the Ukrainian Constitution states that the "[e]stablishment of extraordinary and special courts is not permitted." Constitution of Ukraine, Adopted at the Fifth Session of the Verkhovna Rada of Ukraine on June 28, 1996, as Amended, *at* CONSTITUTION OF UKRAINE (refworld.org); Alexander Komarov & Oona A. Hathaway, *Ukraine's Constitutional Constraints: How to Achieve Accountability for the Crime of Aggression*, Just Security (Apr. 5, 2022), *at* Ukraine's Constitutional Constraints: How to Achieve Accountability for the Crime of Aggression (justsecurity.org); Constitution of Ukraine,

Constitution of Ukraine, Adopted at the Fifth Session of the Verkhovna Rada of Ukraine on June 28, 1996, as Amended, *at* CONSTITUTION OF UKRAINE (refworld.org), Art. 157 ("The Constitution of Ukraine shall not be amended in conditions of martial law or a state of emergency.") (timing).

83 *See* The Rome Statute of the International Criminal Court, July 17, 1998, 2187 UNTS 90 (as amended), Art. 8*bis*(2)(f). (including as an act of aggression, "[t]he action of a State in allowing its territory, which it has placed at the disposal of another State, to be used by that other State for perpetrating an act of aggression against a third State").

84 According to the ICC, only one element of a crime must occur in the territory of a state that has accepted the ICC's jurisdiction for the ICC to be able to prosecute. *See* Decision on the "Prosecution's Request for a Ruling on Jurisdiction Under Article 19(3) of the Statute," ICC-RoC46(3)-01/18 (Sept. 6, 2018) (situation of Myanmar/Bangladesh).

85 *See* Estimates of Ukrainian and Russian soldiers who have been killed or injured are nearly a half million. Helene Cooper, Thomas Gibbons-Neff, Eric Schmitt & Julian E. Barnes, *Troop Deaths and Injuries in Ukraine War Near 500,000, U.S. Officials Say*, N.Y. Times (Aug. 18, 2023), *at* Ukraine War Casualties Near Half a Million, U.S. Officials Say - The New York Times (nytimes.com) (fatality estimates).

86 Astrid Reisinger Coracini, *in* The Crime of Aggression: A Commentary, Ch. 31, at 1068–69 (Claus Kreβ & Stefan Barriga eds., 2016); *The Princeton Principles on Universal Jurisdiction* (2001), *at* Princeton-Principles-Universal-Jurisdiction-report-2001-eng.pdf (icj2.wpenginepowered.com). At least 18 states assert universal jurisdiction over the crime. Carrie McDougall, *Prosecuting Putin for His Crime of Aggression Against Ukraine: Part Two*, Oxford Human Rights Hub (Mar. 8, 2022), *at* Prosecuting Putin for his Crime of Aggression Against Ukraine: Part Two | OHRH (ox.ac.uk). *But see* Kevin Jon Heller, *The Best Option: An Extraordinary Ukrainian Chamber for Aggression*, Opinio Juris (Mar. 16, 2022), *at* The Best Option: An Extraordinary Ukrainian Chamber for Aggression - Opinio Juris (questioning whether states are entitled to exercise universal jurisdiction over the crime of aggression). Personal immunities, however, will prevent prosecution of the "troika" of top leaders if a Dutch or other national court is utilized. *See* In the case of Russia, they are President Vladimir Putin, Prime Minister Mishustin, and Foreign Minister Lavrov. *See* Arrest Warrant of 11 April 2000 (Dem. Rep. Congo v. Belg.), Judgment, 2002 ICJ Rep. 3 (Feb. 4); Prosecutor v. Taylor, SCSL-2003-01-I, Decision on Immunity from Jurisdiction (May 31, 2004); Prosecutor v. Al-Bashir, ICC-02/05-01/09 OA2, Judgment in the Jordan Referral re Al-Bashir Appeal (May 6, 2019); For a detailed explanation of the rulings, see Astrid Reisinger Coracini & Jennifer Trahan, *The Case for Creating a Special Tribunal to Prosecute the Crime of Aggression Committed Against Ukraine (Part VI): On the Non-applicability of Personal Immunities*, Just Security (Nov. 8, 2022), *at* The Case for Creating a Special Tribunal to Prosecute the Crime of Aggression Committed Against Ukraine (Part VI): On the Non-Applicability of Personal Immunities (justsecurity.org).

87 More than two-thirds of the victims were Dutch nationals. *MH17 Disaster: Dutch Take Russia to European Rights Court*, BBC News (July 10, 2020), *at* MH17 disaster: Dutch take Russia to European rights court - BBC News. As for the nationals of other countries, The Netherlands and Ukraine (where the crash occurred) entered into an agreement transferring Ukraine's territorial jurisdiction to The Netherlands. Agreement Between the Kingdom of the Netherlands and Ukraine on International Legal Cooperation Regarding Crimes Connected

with the Downing of Malaysia Airlines Flight MH17 on 17 July 2014, at https://wetten.overheid.nl/BWBV0006683/2018-08-28.

88 Observation of a delegate attending the negotiations. Concrete details of the proposal have not yet emerged. There is precedent for the transfer by one country of its jurisdiction to another country for trials in the second country. *See id.*

89 Sergiy Sydorenko, *The "Hague Tribunal" Becomes a Reality: How Ukraine and the West Agree on a Special Court for Putin*, EUR. PRAVDA (Aug. 22, 2023), *at* "The Hague Tribunal" Becomes a Reality: How Ukraine and the West Agree on a Special Court for Putin | European Pravda (eurointegration.com.ua).

90 Idea of Astrid Reisinger Coracini in email exchange with the author. The crime of aggression is criminalized under the domestic laws of numerous countries; such prosecutions need no General Assembly endorsement. For discussion of domestic crime of aggression statutes, see ANNEGRET HARTIG, MAKING AGGRESSION A CRIME UNDER DOMESTIC LAW, Ch. 6 (2023).

91 Sergiy Sydorenko, *The "Hague Tribunal" Becomes a Reality: How Ukraine and the West Agree on a Special Court for Putin*, EUR. PRAVDA (Aug. 22, 2023), *at* "The Hague Tribunal" Becomes a Reality: How Ukraine and the West Agree on a Special Court for Putin | European Pravda (eurointegration.com.ua).

92 *See* GIPA-model-amendment-proposal.pdf (crimeofaggression.info). *See also* GIPA's reasons for the proposed amendment, *at* GIPA-Proposal-Short.pdf (crimeofaggression.info).

93 *See* The Rome Statute of the International Criminal Court, Art. 15*bis*(5), July 17, 1998, 2187 UNTS 90 (as amended); For a list of States Parties, see ICC, *The States Parties to the Rome Statute*, *at* The States Parties to the Rome Statute | International Criminal Court (icc-cpi.int).

94 IMT, Judgment of 1 October 1946, in The Trial of German Major War Criminals. Proceedings of the International Military Tribunal Sitting at Nuremberg, Germany, Part 22, at 421 (Aug. 22, 1946–Oct. 1, 1946), *reprinted at* IMTJudgment.Endversion+Deckblatt (crimeofaggression.info).

95 The Rome Statute of the International Criminal Court, July 17, 1998, 2187 UNTS 90, Art. 5.1, (as amended).

96 Ukraine's acceptance of the ICC's jurisdiction, International Criminal Court, Ukraine, Situation in Ukraine, *at* Ukraine | International Criminal Court (icc-cpi.int), would cover the four crimes.

97 For details of the negotiations, see Jennifer Trahan, *Negotiating the Amendment on the Crime of Aggression: Proceedings at the Kampala Review Conference on the International Criminal Court*, 11 INT'L CRIM. L. REV. 49 (2011).

98 They are Kenya and Guatemala. *See* International Criminal Court, *Referrals and Declarations*, *at* Resource library | International Criminal Court (icc-cpi.int).

99 For an argument about the invalidity of the modification, made in the activating resolution, of the amendment text agreed on in Kampala, see Jennifer Trahan, *From Kampala to New York—The Final Negotiations to Activate the Jurisdiction of the International Criminal Court Over the Crime of Aggression*, 18 INT'L CRIM. L. REV. 197 (2018).

100 Activation of the Jurisdiction of the Court Over the Crime of Aggression, ICC-ASP/16/Res.5 (Dec. 14, 2017).

101 *See* Speech by Foreign Minister Annalena Baerbock at the Commemoration of the 25th Anniversary of the Adoption of the Rome Statute of the International Criminal Court, July 17, 2021, *at* Speech by Foreign Minister Annalena Baerbock at the commemoration of the 25th anniversary of the adoption of the Rome Statute of the International Criminal Court (long version) - Federal Foreign Office (auswaertiges-amt.de). A fair number of states present at the event

also agreed on the need to align the ICC's jurisdiction over its four crimes. Observations of the author who was present at the event.

102 *See* GIPA-model-amendment-proposal.pdf (crimeofaggression.info); *see also* Parliamentarians for Global Action, *Proposal to Amend Article 15*bis *of the Rome Statute on the Crime of Aggression*, *at* World Day for International Justice - News Center (pgaction.org).

103 *See* Jennifer Trahan, *Amending the Kampala Amendments: Proposal to Harmonize the ICC's Jurisdiction Over the Crime of Aggression with Its Jurisdiction Over Its Other Core Crimes*, Opinio Juris (Nov. 2, 2023), *at* Amending the Kampala Amendments: A Proposal to Harmonize the ICC's Jurisdiction - Opinio Juris.

104 *See Strengthening International Law in Times of Crisis – Rede von Außenministerin Annalena Baerbock in Den Haag* (Jan. 16, 2023), *at* Strengthening International Law in Times of Crisis - Rede von Außenministerin Annalena Baerbock in Den Haag - Auswärtiges Amt (auswaertiges-amt.de).

105 *See* GIPA, *Current Law and Existing Judicial Mechanisms are Insufficient to Adequately Secure Justice for the Crime of Aggression*, *at* The Global Campaign for the Prevention of Aggression | Page 3 (crimeofaggression.info) (calling for the establishment of an international tribunal); GIPA-model-amendment-proposal .pdf (crimeofaggression.info).

106 *See* Astrid Reisinger Coracini, *Is Amending the Rome Statute the Panacea Against Perceived Selectivity and Impunity for the Crime of Aggression Committed Against Ukraine?*, Just Security (Mar. 21, 2023), *at* Is Amending the Rome Statute the Panacea Against Perceived Selectivity and Impunity for the Crime of Aggression Committed Against Ukraine? (justsecurity.org). .

107 A third step would be Ukraine ratifying the Rome Statute rather than simply accepting ICC jurisdiction. *See* International Criminal Court, Ukraine, Situation in Ukraine, *at* Ukraine | International Criminal Court (icc-cpi.int), (Ukraine's Article 12(3) declarations).

108 The United States and United Kingdom *did* have a legal theory for the 2003 military intervention in Iraq; it was just not a strong one. It relied on an open-ended force authorization from Gulf War I that was still arguably in effect years later to the extent that Iraq continued to engage in "hostile or provocative" action. *See* Law Society of Scotland, *Iraq: A Basis in Law?* ("The primary legal justification for the invasion was predicated on what has become known as the 'revival argument'. The US and UK argued that the Security Council's resolutions 660, 678 and 687 in relation to the first Gulf War were revived by Iraq's alleged failure to comply with resolution 687.").

109 The author does not mean "strongest" in terms of ensuring convictions—that would be a foolhardy approach. It will be imperative that any tribunal established ensures fair trials.

110 "To surmount this hurdle [of lack of consent to use force in Syria], the Obama administration (and subsequent administrations) argued that Syria was 'unable or unwilling' to counter the threat posed by IS and [al-Qaeda]." Tess Bridgeman & Brianna Rosen, Still at War: The United States in Syria, Just Security (Apr. 29, 2022), at Still at War: The United States in Syria (justsecurity.org).

111 *See* Tess Bridgeman, *When Does the Legal Basis for U.S. Forces in Syria Expire?*, Just Security (Mar. 14, 2018), *at* When Does the Legal Basis for U.S. Forces in Syria Expire? - Just Security ("The scope and content of this . . . theory . . . remain deeply contested."). By contrast, intervention against the forces of the Islamic State within the territory of Iraq was based on the consent of the Government of Iraq. *See* Tess Bridgeman & Brianna Rosen, *Still at War: The United States in Syria*, Just Security (Apr. 29, 2022), *at* Still at War: The United

States in Syria (justsecurity.org), ("Iraqi consent was clearly a sufficient basis for the otherwise lawful use of force against IS within Iraq's borders.").

112 Article 8*bis* criminalizes individual conduct resulting from state action that rises to the level of a "manifest UN Charter violation," measured by the "character, gravity and scale" of the violation. The Rome Statute of the International Criminal Court, July 17, 1998, 2187 UNTS 90 (as amended), Art. 8*bis*(1). Absent a "manifest" Charter violation, there is no crime.

113 A June 2008 report of the Special Working Group on the Crime of Aggression ("SWGCA") explains: "Delegations supporting this threshold clause noted that it would appropriately limit the Court's jurisdiction to the most serious acts of aggression under customary international law, thus excluding cases of insufficient gravity and falling within a grey area [in terms of legality]." Report of the Special Working Group on the Crime of Aggression, ICC-ASP/6/20/Add.1, Annex II, para. 68 (June 2008). For more on the manifest requirement, see Astrid Reisinger Coracini, *in* THE CRIME OF AGGRESSION: A COMMENTARY, Ch. 31, at 1068–69 (Claus Kreβ & Stefan Barriga eds., 2016); CARRIE MCDOUGALL, THE CRIME OF AGGRESSION UNDER THE ROME STATUTE OF THE INTERNATIONAL CRIMINAL COURT (2d ed. 2021).

114 The United States did not attend the meetings of the SWGCA, held in Princeton, NJ, during the years when the George W. Bush Administration was in office. (The author attended the negotiations.) The United States re-engaged with the process during the Obama Administration and tried to shore up the "manifest threshold" through certain "Understandings" that were adopted at the Kampala Review Conference. *See* International Criminal Court, Assembly of States Parties, Review Conference, The Crime of Aggression, Annex I, ICC Doc. RC/Res.6 (June 11, 2010), *at* RC-11-ENG.16Dec1200 (un.org), Understandings 6–7.

115 The US Department of Defense ("DOD") had to be ordered by President Biden to cooperate with the ICC's Ukraine investigation; Congress's changing the law to allow such cooperation did not result in the DOD's cooperating. *See Pentagon Withholding Evidence in Russia War Crimes Case: Senators*, AL JAZEERA (May 11, 2023), *at* https://www.aljazeera.com/news/2023/5/11/pentagon-withholding-evidence-in-russia-war-crimes-case-senators; Charlie Savage, Biden Orders U.S. to Share Evidence of Russian War Crimes with Hague Court, N.Y. TIMES (July 26, 2023), *at* https://www.nytimes.com/2023/07/26/us/politics/biden-russia-war-crimes-hague.html.

116 During the Princeton negotiations, some of the four Security Council permanent members that attended took the view that only the Security Council should determine when an "act of aggression" had occurred; this would have effectively made the permanent members the "gatekeepers" of ICC crime of aggression prosecutions, in that the ICC would only have been able to investigate and/or prosecute the crime after Security Council referral. Recollection of the author. For pushback by the United States at Kampala, *see* For details of the negotiations, see Jennifer Trahan, *Negotiating the Amendment on the Crime of Aggression: Proceedings at the Kampala Review Conference on the International Criminal Court*, 11 INT'L CRIM. L. REV. 49 (2011); for pushback by the UK and France during the activating negotiations, see For an argument about the invalidity of the modification, made in the activating resolution, of the amendment text agreed on in Kampala, see Jennifer Trahan, *From Kampala to New York—The Final Negotiations to Activate the Jurisdiction of the International Criminal Court Over the Crime of Aggression*, 18 INT'L CRIM. L. REV. 197 (2018); Activation of the Jurisdiction of the Court Over the Crime of Aggression, ICC-ASP/16/Res.5 (Dec. 14, 2017).

117 *Id.*

118 *See* Constitution of Ukraine, Constitution of Ukraine, Adopted at the Fifth Session of the Verkhovna Rada of Ukraine on June 28, 1996, as Amended, *at* CONSTITUTION OF UKRAINE (refworld.org), Art. 157 ("The Constitution of Ukraine shall not be amended in conditions of martial law or a state of emergency."). *see also* Rome Statute, Ch. I, Art. 8*bis*. In the case of Russia, they are President Vladimir Putin, Prime Minister Mishustin, and Foreign Minister Lavrov. *see also* Arrest Warrant of 11 April 2000 (Dem. Rep. Congo v. Belg.), Judgment, 2002 ICJ Rep. 3 (Feb. 4); Prosecutor v. Taylor, SCSL-2003-01-I, Decision on Immunity from Jurisdiction (May 31, 2004); Prosecutor v. Al-Bashir, ICC-02/05-01/09 OA2, Judgment in the Jordan Referral re Al-Bashir Appeal (May 6, 2019). For a detailed explanation of what makes a tribunal an "international" one and of the rulings, see Astrid Reisinger Coracini & Jennifer Trahan, *The Case for Creating a Special Tribunal to Prosecute the Crime of Aggression Committed Against Ukraine (Part VI): On the Non-applicability of Personal Immunities*, Just Security (Nov. 8, 2022), *at* The Case for Creating a Special Tribunal to Prosecute the Crime of Aggression Committed Against Ukraine (Part VI): On the Non-Applicability of Personal Immunities (justsecurity.org).

119 *See* Kuleba: *"Hybrid Tribunal: Does Not Give an Answer on How to Punish the Leaders of the Russian Federation* (Sept. 9, 2023), *at* Kuleba: "Hybrid tribunal" does not give an answer on how to punish the leaders of the Russian Federation | European Pravda (eurointegration.com.ua) (Ukrainian Minister of Foreign Affairs Dmytro Kuleba stating that "the position of the G7 is inclined towards a 'hybrid tribunal.'").

120 *See, e.g.*, Sâ Benjamin Traoré, *Making Sense of Africa's Massive Abstentions During the Adoption of the UNGA Resolution on the Aggression Against Ukraine*, AfricLaw, *at* Making sense of Africa's massive abstentions during the adoption of the UNGA resolution on the Aggression Against Ukraine | AfricLaw ("The perception is that the western zealotry over Ukraine – and not for other situations of blatant violation of international law—is troubling, shocking and nothing short of hypocrisy and double standards in international politics."). It is true that aggression has occurred in the past, and in most situations—other than before the IMT at Nuremberg and the IMTFE (Tokyo)—there was no criminal accountability; yet, it is also true that law is not backwards-looking. The ICC's definition of the crime of aggression was adopted in 2010, and the ICC's jurisdiction was activated effective July, 17, 2018. It is therefore appropriate to look forward, not backward.

121 *See* Speech by Foreign Minister Annalena Baerbock at the Commemoration of the 25th Anniversary of the Adoption of the Rome Statute of the International Criminal Court, July 17, 2021, *at* Speech by Foreign Minister Annalena Baerbock at the commemoration of the 25th anniversary of the adoption of the Rome Statute of the International Criminal Court (long version) - Federal Foreign Office (auswaertiges-amt.de).

122 *Frequently Asked Questions (FAQ), Endorsed by Albania, Belgium, Estonia, Guatemala, Latvia, Liechtenstein, Lithuania, Luxembourg, Marshall Islands, North Macedonia, Poland and Ukraine, at* FAQ_Special-Tribunal-for-the-Crime-of-Aggression.pdf (justsecurity.org).

123 *See* Patryk Labuda, *Accountability for Russian Imperialism in the "Global East": A Special Tribunal for Aggression from a Post-Colonial, Eastern European Perspective*, Just Security (Aug. 21, 2023), *at* Accountability for Russian Imperialism in the "Global East" (justsecurity.org). (noting that "Ukraine is also a post-colonial society whose right to exist has been denied systematically by various empires").

7

UKRAINIAN WAR CRIMES CHAMBER

By Greg Noone and Kateryna Kyrychenko

Introduction

In numerous post-conflict settings, specialized war crimes chambers have been established within national legal systems to complement international tribunals in prosecuting atrocities such as war crimes, crimes against humanity, and genocide. These crimes, by their nature, are highly complex and require specialized legal expertise, particularly in adherence to international legal standards. By integrating international legal principles into national judicial frameworks, such chambers enable states to prosecute these crimes effectively while balancing domestic sovereignty with international obligations. The structure and design of war crimes tribunals are shaped by several factors, including the number of perpetrators to be tried, the varying degrees of their culpability, the perceived need for independence from the ordinary judicial system, and the expertise and capacity of the domestic judiciary. Additionally, the degree of international involvement in these chambers can range from limited foreign assistance to the establishment of hybrid models that closely resemble international tribunals, with significant international participation in key decisions related to prosecutions and convictions. Internationalization proves particularly valuable when domestic institutions lack the requisite resources or expertise, face questions of impartiality or independence, or require credibility with the international community.

This chapter examines the feasibility of establishing a specialized war crimes chamber in Ukraine to prosecute individuals responsible for the atrocities committed since Russia's full-scale invasion in February 2022. However, before outlining the rationale for such a chamber, the chapter provides an overview of previous instances in which specialized domestic war crimes

DOI: 10.4324/9781003458166-9

chambers have been created to support accountability for serious international crimes.

The first case explored is Bosnia's War Crimes Chamber (WCC), established in 2005 as a complement to the International Criminal Tribunal for the former Yugoslavia (ICTY). The ICTY's mandate was primarily focused on prosecuting high-level perpetrators deemed most responsible for the crimes committed during the Bosnian War (1992–1995), while the WCC addressed a broader range of lower- and mid-level perpetrators. The WCC operated as a hybrid tribunal, combining domestic jurisdiction with international support.

The second case involves the Iraqi High Tribunal (IHT), created in 2003 to prosecute individuals responsible for crimes under Saddam Hussein's regime. This tribunal, while domestically operated, was heavily influenced by the legal practices and procedures of international criminal courts, such as those established in the former Yugoslavia, Rwanda, and Sierra Leone. Additionally, we examine the special Piracy Chambers established in Seychelles and Mauritius in response to the surge in Somali piracy. These chambers, though addressing crimes on the high seas, relied heavily on international cooperation in evidence collection and ensured adherence to fair trial standards despite the extraterritorial nature of the crimes.

Through these case studies, this chapter delves into the legal challenges, prosecutorial issues, and judicial innovations that these specialized courts encountered, providing valuable insights into the role of domestic war crimes chambers in advancing post-conflict justice and accountability.

The chapter concludes by making the case for the establishment of a specialized war crimes chamber within Ukraine, arguing that such a chamber would be a critical complement to the international and domestic mechanisms currently being utilized to address the grave atrocities committed since Russia's invasion. As explored in other chapters of this book, the International Criminal Court (ICC) has already initiated prosecutions against high-level perpetrators of war crimes in Ukraine, including Russian President Vladimir Putin. One chapter specifically examines efforts to utilize universal jurisdiction to hold perpetrators accountable. Another chapter delves deeply into the proposals for addressing Russia's crime of aggression, over which the ICC currently lacks jurisdiction. Despite these various efforts to bring perpetrators of atrocity crimes committed in Ukraine to justice, accountability gaps remain. A specialized war crimes chamber in Ukraine can help to fill such gaps and will serve additional purposes, such as enhancing public engagement with the justice process and ensuring the creation of a historical record for the Ukrainian people.

The chapter not only explores and analyzes the reasons for creating a specialized war crimes chamber in Ukraine, but also details a proposal for a High War Crimes Court of Ukraine, based on a draft statute prepared by the Public International Law & Policy Group, the law firm of Weil, Gotshal & Manges LLP, and other consulted experts. Drawing from the Law on the

High Anti-Corruption Court of Ukraine and international best practices, the draft statute offers a comprehensive framework for prosecuting atrocity crimes committed in Ukraine since November 2013. This draft statute provides a concrete starting point for engaging in a much-needed discussion about whether and how to precisely constitute a war crimes chamber within Ukraine to ensure the broadest possible accountability for the many serious international crimes committed in the context of Russia's war with Ukraine.

The War Crimes Chamber in Bosnia and Herzegovina

One of the most illustrative examples of specialized chambers is the War Crimes Chamber of Bosnia and Herzegovina, established in March 2005 as part of significant domestic legal reforms. The WCC was created by the State Court of Bosnia and Herzegovina and the Special Department for War Crimes in the State Prosecutor's Office, with authorization from the Office of the High Representative for Bosnia and Herzegovina. Its establishment was supported by UN Security Council Resolutions 1503 (2003) and 1534 (2004), which endorsed the International Criminal Tribunal for the former Yugoslavia (ICTY)'s completion strategy.[1] This strategy aimed to transfer mid- and lower-level cases to national courts while allowing the ICTY to focus on high-level perpetrators.[2]

Located in Sarajevo, the WCC operates within the country's judicial system but received significant international support, particularly in terms of funding and capacity building, to ensure its adherence to international standards. The chamber was designed to address war crimes, crimes against humanity, and genocide committed during the Bosnian War (1992–1995). It complements the ICTY by prosecuting lower-level offenders who would not otherwise face trial at the international level. The Criminal Procedure Code of Bosnia and Herzegovina mandates the WCC to prosecute all war crimes cases referred to it, including cases transferred under ICTY Rule 11 bis.[3]

Notable cases handled by the WCC include that of Radovan Stanković, marking a significant step in the prosecution of war crimes within Bosnia and Herzegovina. Despite its challenges, the WCC represents an important mechanism for achieving accountability, strengthening the national judiciary, and advancing post-conflict reconciliation in Bosnia and Herzegovina. Its hybrid structure and operations have served as a model for similar efforts in other post-conflict societies, such as Sierra Leone's Special Court and Cambodia's Extraordinary Chambers in the Courts of Cambodia (ECCC), highlighting its broader significance in the field of transitional justice.[4]

Structurally, the WCC functions as a specialized division of the State Court, alongside the Organized Crime and General Crime Chambers, with jurisdiction over war crimes committed between 1992 and 1995. Its design integrates international standards within a domestic framework to strengthen national judicial capacity and foster public confidence in the rule of law. The early involvement of international judges and prosecutors was critical for ensuring impartiality, transparency, and mentorship for local judicial staff. The WCC applied both domestic and international laws, utilizing provisions from Bosnia and Herzegovina's Criminal Code (2003), which incorporated crimes such as war crimes, crimes against humanity, and genocide, in alignment with the ICC's Rome Statute. Earlier Yugoslavian criminal codes (SFRY) were also applied at lower courts, leading to legal distinctions in case handling that prompted some criticism, including protests from prisoners convicted under the newer code.

Regarding the issue of retroactivity, the Bosnia and Herzegovina's Criminal Code provided that no person could be punished for an act that was not criminalized at the time of its commission.[5] Nevertheless, it allowed for prosecution if the conduct was considered criminal under international law or general principles recognized by the international community. The Constitutional Court of Bosnia and Herzegovina upheld this principle in 2007, which ruled that the application of the 2003 Criminal Code for war crimes was lawful, as the conduct in question had already been defined as criminal under international law at the time it was committed. This ensured that prosecutions under the newer criminal code did not violate the principle of non-retroactivity.[6]

The WCC's establishment also aimed to address some of the societal challenges that arose from the ICTY's distance from affected communities. By holding trials in Sarajevo, the WCC increased accessibility for victims and witnesses, enabling a more localized and meaningful engagement with justice processes. However, the chamber has faced significant challenges, including financial constraints that occasionally hindered its operations and criticisms of perceived ethnic biases in its rulings. Moreover, while the WCC has been effective in prosecuting war crimes, it was not designed to serve as a truth and reconciliation commission, leaving gaps in addressing broader societal divisions and fostering a shared historical narrative.[7]

Despite being a domestic chamber, it received substantial international support, particularly in terms of funding and staffing, to help ensure that trials met international standards.[8] A key motivation for creating the Chamber was the ICTY's need to meet deadlines for completing its mandate, requiring it to finish all first-instance trials by 2008 and all appeals by 2010.[9] Rule 11 bis enabled the referral of cases from the ICTY to the WCC, which had no discretion to dismiss cases and was mandated to prosecute all referred cases. The hybrid nature of the Chamber, which involved the participation of both international and local judges and prosecutors, ensured that its operations were aligned with international legal standards, while also promoting local ownership of the justice process. This hybrid model was key to maintaining both credibility and independence, especially in a country still deeply divided along ethnic lines following the conflict.

The Chamber encountered significant prosecutorial and investigative challenges after its establishment to address the atrocities committed during the Bosnian War. One of the foremost difficulties was managing the immense volume of cases. With a large number of war crimes committed during the conflict, the Chamber had to prioritize cases to ensure efficiency, often focusing on high-ranking officials and those responsible for the most serious violations. This led to a stratified approach where lower-level cases were deferred to national courts, placing the Chamber's resources on prosecuting the most severe crimes under international and domestic law.[10]

Another key challenge was gathering evidence, particularly in a post-conflict setting where access to physical evidence was often compromised, and witnesses had been displaced. The passage of time, destruction of evidence, and manipulation of crime scenes made it difficult for investigators to collect reliable and corroborated evidence. In addition, the reluctance of many victims and witnesses to testify was a persistent obstacle due to ongoing security concerns and fear of retaliation. This required the development of sophisticated witness protection programs, offering measures like relocation, anonymity, and psychological support. These safeguards, while critical, strained the Chamber's resources and highlighted the difficulty in maintaining fair trials while ensuring the safety and cooperation of witnesses.[11]

Moreover, the Chamber had to navigate the politically charged environment of post-war Bosnia and Herzegovina, where ethnic divisions were still palpable. Prosecuting war crimes involving local actors—often viewed as either heroes or criminals depending on the ethnic group—presented significant challenges to maintaining judicial impartiality. The Chamber's hybrid nature, involving both international and domestic judges and prosecutors, was crucial in lending legitimacy to its operations. The presence of international actors helped to mitigate political pressures, foster judicial independence, and maintain compliance with international legal standards. This mix of international expertise and local involvement was intended to ensure that the international community and the local population saw the Chamber's work as credible and impartial.[12]

Further complicating the work of the Chamber was the task of ensuring fair trial standards in a divided society. The Chamber had to ensure that the rights of the accused were fully respected, even in cases involving highly contentious ethnic dynamics and historical grievances. This required a firm adherence to principles of due process, ensuring that all defendants received competent legal representation and were given a fair opportunity to challenge the evidence presented against them. In many cases, the defendants were high-ranking military or political leaders, necessitating a rigorous standard of proof, particularly in establishing command responsibility for war crimes committed by subordinates.[13]

One of the most significant legal challenges involved applying international legal principles within the domestic context. The Chamber had to integrate International Humanitarian Law (also known as the Law of Armed Conflict), such as the Geneva Conventions and customary international law, with the country's domestic legal system. This required a careful balancing act to ensure that international legal standards were upheld while remaining within the framework of national law. Moreover, the Chamber had to grapple with the concept of command responsibility, ensuring that military and political leaders who may not have directly participated in atrocities could be held accountable for their failure to prevent or punish war crimes committed by their subordinates.[14] The legal complexity of such cases required a detailed understanding of both international and domestic legal precedents, as well as an ability to handle the significant evidentiary challenges inherent in proving indirect responsibility for war crimes.

Lastly, international cooperation was essential for the Chamber's success. Much of the evidence and forensic support required to prosecute war crimes came from international sources, including the ICTY. The ICTY provided invaluable resources in terms of evidence collection, witness testimony, and legal precedents, particularly as many of the mid-level perpetrators tried by the Chamber had been involved in broader criminal enterprises prosecuted by the ICTY. This cooperation between the ICTY and the Chamber demonstrated the necessity of integrating international mechanisms with domestic systems to ensure comprehensive accountability for war crimes. The Chamber not only alleviated the workload of the ICTY but also helped the country build its judicial capacity to handle complex war crimes prosecutions independently. The establishment of the Chamber was a critical component of post-conflict justice, as it localized the accountability process, which was vital for building national ownership over the reconciliation and peacebuilding processes.

Post-2009, the Chamber underwent significant changes, particularly in terms of its composition. Although the Chamber was initially structured with a majority of international judges, prosecutors, and staff, who played a key role in ensuring the application of international standards in trials, the complete phase-out of international personnel was conducted by 2009, transitioning the Chamber to an entirely domestic system. After the phase-out, local judges and prosecutors assumed full control, which was intended to enhance the capacity of the local judiciary while maintaining continuity in war crimes prosecutions. While this transition marked a significant step towards full judicial independence, challenges remained. One key concern was the potential impact on the quality and consistency of war crimes prosecutions after the international personnel left. There were fears that without international oversight, political pressures and a lack of resources could undermine the Chamber's effectiveness in prosecuting complex war crimes cases. Nevertheless, the phase-out reflected the broader strategy to build Bosnia and Herzegovina's legal and institutional capacity for handling international crimes autonomously.[15]

In the years following the phase-out, the State Court of Bosnia and Herzegovina, including the War Crimes Chamber, continued to handle a large number of war crimes cases, albeit with increasing difficulty. Criticism emerged regarding delays in proceedings, inconsistencies in sentencing, and concerns about the politicization of cases. Despite these challenges, the Chamber remained a crucial part of the country's post-conflict justice system, dealing with cases transferred from the ICTY, as well as other war crimes that had not been prosecuted at the international level.[16]

The transition also led to an increased focus on capacity-building programs, funded by the European Union and other international donors, to strengthen the domestic judiciary's ability to manage complex international crimes without external support. However, the efficiency and quality of legal proceedings post-2009 remain subjects of ongoing debate, as the Chamber continues to confront the legacies of the war within a politically charged environment.[17]

The War Crimes Chamber of Bosnia and Herzegovina is widely regarded as a pioneering model in the field of transitional justice. It has been praised for localizing the prosecution of war crimes while adhering to international standards, facilitating accountability in a post-conflict society. By combining domestic and international expertise, the WCC successfully built judicial capacity, enhanced local ownership of justice processes, and fostered greater accessibility for victims and witnesses. The Chamber's hybrid structure, use of international legal principles, and ability to handle complex cases, such as those involving command responsibility, underscored its significance as a mechanism for achieving accountability and reconciliation.

Despite these successes, the WCC faced notable challenges. It operated in a politically charged environment, often strained by ethnic tensions, resource limitations, and the sheer volume of cases. Issues such as the reluctance of witnesses to testify, difficulty in evidence collection, and delays in proceedings post-2009 highlighted the obstacles of prosecuting war crimes in a domestic setting. Moreover, the transition to an entirely domestic system after the withdrawal of international personnel raised concerns about judicial independence and consistency in prosecutions.[18]

Nonetheless, the WCC is frequently commended for its contributions to post-conflict justice. Commentators have praised it as a critical mechanism for addressing the legacy of the Bosnian War, fostering the rule of law, and serving as a model for other post-conflict societies. Its integration of international legal standards within a domestic framework has demonstrated the potential for hybrid courts to bridge gaps between international justice and national reconciliation efforts.

The Chamber's initial hybrid nature and its reliance on international cooperation provided an important model for other post-conflict societies seeking to address mass atrocities while building domestic legal capacity. These lessons are particularly relevant for Ukraine, as it looks to potentially create its own specialized war crimes chambers to address the numerous crimes committed during the ongoing war with Russia.

The Iraqi High Tribunal

A different but equally significant example of specialized war crimes chambers is the creation of the Iraqi High Tribunal in 2003, which marked a significant effort to prosecute serious international crimes committed under Saddam Hussein's regime, including genocide, crimes against humanity, and war crimes.[19] Established by the Coalition Provisional Authority (CPA) in its capacity as the occupying power following the fall of Saddam Hussein, IHT was intended to serve as a hybrid model, applying both domestic Iraqi law and international legal standards to address the widespread atrocities committed over decades of the Ba'athist regime.[20] The IHT functioned similarly to a specialized war crimes chamber. Like other specialized war crimes chambers, it focused on complex cases involving mass atrocity crimes, though it also faced unique challenges due to the post-invasion political context and concerns over fair trial standards, which will be explored in detail further in this chapter. The IHT differed from other hybrid courts though – most notably in its establishment, as the CPA rather than an international body like the United Nations created it. While it had jurisdiction over serious crimes, it encountered criticisms over its legitimacy and perceptions of victor's justice, especially regarding its handling of high-profile cases like the prosecution of Saddam Hussein. Despite these differences, in terms of its function and focus, the IHT aligned closely with the concept of a specialized war crimes chamber.[21]

The IHT was formally established by CPA Order No. 48 on December 10, 2003, which created a national court empowered to try Iraqi nationals or residents accused of war crimes, crimes against humanity, and genocide between 1968 and 2003.[22] Upon its establishment in 2003 it was originally named the Iraqi Special Tribunal, but was renamed the Supreme Iraqi Criminal Tribunal (SICT) in 2005 to reflect its broader mandate to prosecute high-ranking officials for various international crimes. In 2006, the tribunal was renamed for the final time – the Iraqi High Tribunal. The final renaming to IHT was intended to assert the tribunal's permanence and sovereignty within the Iraqi legal system, emphasizing its role as a national court with jurisdiction over serious crimes committed by the former regime, while still maintaining adherence to international legal standards.

Similarly to the Bosnian War Crimes Chamber, the establishment of the IHT was also influenced by the UN Security Council's completion mandate for the ICTY. This requirement underscored the importance of having a strong national judiciary capable of conducting war crimes trials according to international standards.[23] The IHT was initially tasked with prosecuting high-ranking officials, including Saddam Hussein, for crimes committed during the regime's brutal campaigns, such as the Anfal Campaign against the Kurds in the 1980s and the chemical attacks on Halabja.

While the tribunal applied Iraqi criminal law, it incorporated principles from international law, such as the Convention on the Prevention and Punishment of the Crime of Genocide and the Geneva Conventions, to ensure that atrocity crimes were prosecuted according to the recognized global standards. Moreover, to ensure the tribunal operated efficiently and upheld a high standard of due process, lessons were drawn from the experiences of other international criminal tribunals, such as those for the former Yugoslavia and Rwanda, the Special Court for Sierra Leone, and the East Timor Serious Crimes Unit. These lessons informed the crafting of rules of procedure and evidence, detention rules, and sentencing guidelines. Additionally, practical matters such as the organization of the start-up phase, management structure design, and the creation of a defense counsel system were addressed.

The IHT's mandate was broad, covering crimes committed between July 17, 1968, and May 1, 2003, providing a wide temporal jurisdiction for prosecuting decades of atrocities. The time limitation is notable, and was the subject of significant debate, as other criminal tribunals established for the prosecution of international crimes, including the ICTY and the Special Court for Sierra Leone, provide for open-ended terms. The subject matter jurisdiction of IHT (i.e., war crimes, crimes against humanity, genocide, and certain specified Iraqi crimes) is generally in line with the types of criminal conduct prosecuted by other criminal tribunals, including those established in the former Yugoslavia and Sierra Leone. It is notable that the 2003 Statute limited the crime of genocide to acts committed against Kurds, and did not encompass acts against any other national, ethnical, racial or religious group. However, the 2005 revision to the Statute broadened the scope of genocide to include other groups. One criticism of the Statute is that it retroactively applied international criminal law norms to periods of time in which the international norm had not yet emerged. This practice, however, is consistent with other criminal tribunals, including the tribunals established in the former Yugoslavia and Rwanda.

In terms of particular prosecutorial and investigative challenges that the IHT has encountered, one of the principal challenges was ensuring judicial independence and impartiality in a deeply polarized post-invasion Iraq. Following Saddam Hussein's fall, Iraq was highly fragmented along sectarian lines, which created significant pressure on the tribunal to balance the demand for justice with concerns about victor's justice. The trial of Saddam Hussein, which began in 2005, became the focal point of the tribunal's work, but it was marred by allegations that the process lacked procedural fairness.

Saddam's defense team often argued that the tribunal was politically motivated and lacked proper safeguards for due process.[24]

In terms of investigation, gathering reliable and robust evidence proved to be a difficult task. Many of the crimes prosecuted by the IHT dated back to the 1980s and early 1990s, making evidence collection a logistical challenge. Forensic evidence from mass graves and chemical attacks was often incomplete or had been tampered with during the intervening years. Additionally, the political instability in post-invasion Iraq posed significant security challenges for investigators, lawyers, and witnesses involved in the proceedings.

The protection of witnesses was another critical issue in the IHT's proceedings. Many witnesses were reluctant to testify against former regime officials due to fear of reprisals from loyalist factions or insurgents.[25] Although the IHT attempted to establish witness protection programs, the security situation in Iraq made it difficult to offer full protection. This limited the willingness of key witnesses to come forward, weakening the prosecution's cases in some instances. Furthermore, the IHT operated in a society where many of the accused still had significant support within the Sunni community, creating a hostile environment for those seeking justice.[26]

Another legal challenge faced by the IHT was the application of command responsibility, particularly in cases involving Saddam Hussein and other top officials. The IHT had to establish that these individuals either committed or ordered crimes, or that they bore responsibility for failures to prevent or punish crimes committed by subordinates. This required the prosecution to link the actions of lower-level perpetrators to the decision-making processes of high-ranking officials, which was difficult given the secretive and authoritarian nature of the Ba'athist regime. Proving this level of complicity required the tribunal to rely heavily on documentary evidence, including records of government orders, policies, and directives, much of which was missing, destroyed, or classified.

One of the IHT's most challenging aspects was its approach to command responsibility in prosecutions of genocide. This was most evident in the prosecution of Saddam Hussein for the Anfal Campaign, during which Kurdish populations were systematically targeted. The IHT had to navigate complex legal doctrines to demonstrate that these actions were not only part of a broader ethnic cleansing campaign but also amounted to genocide under international law. The requirement to prove specific intent to destroy a particular group "in whole or in part," as outlined by the Genocide Convention, added legal complexity to the prosecution. The IHT's application of international law, combined with the challenges of attributing responsibility to senior officials, further complicated the process. This required the IHT to reconstruct the decision-making hierarchies within the Ba'ath Party and Iraq's military structure to show that high-level figures had direct involvement or culpability for these atrocities. Establishing the genocidal intent behind the Anfal Campaign relied on piecing together declassified documents, eyewitness accounts, and other indirect evidence, which were often difficult to locate and authenticate.

Fair trial standards were also a recurring concern in the IHT's proceedings. While the tribunal was designed to incorporate international legal principles, the execution of Saddam Hussein in 2006, following his conviction for crimes against humanity, attracted significant criticism. Many observers argued that the trial had been conducted too precipitously and without the rigorous procedural safeguards expected in trials of such magnitude. Concerns were raised about the competency of legal representation, the conduct of the trial judges, and the failure to provide adequate time for the defense to prepare its case. The execution itself was criticized for being carried out hastily, undermining perceptions of justice and reinforcing sectarian tensions within Iraq.

Overall, the IHT faced grave challenges in terms of international legitimacy. Unlike the International Criminal Tribunal for Rwanda (ICTR) or the ICTY, both established by the United Nations, the IHT was primarily set up by the United States, which drafted the tribunal's statute and provided $75 million in initial funding. This raised concerns regarding the IHT's independence and impartiality, as it was seen by many as a court imposed by occupation forces. Consequently, this perception undermined its credibility, with critics arguing that it was more a tool for political retribution than genuine transitional justice.

In conclusion, it may be a fair assessment that the creation and functioning of the IHT presented significant legal and practical challenges in addressing the atrocities committed under Saddam Hussein's regime. Despite its mandate to bring justice to the victims of decades of human rights abuses, the tribunal faced numerous practical obstacles related to political pressures, security concerns, evidentiary limitations, and fair trial guarantees. The IHT's reliance on both domestic and international legal standards allowed it to address a wide range of crimes but also exposed the difficulties of operating within a politically fragile environment. While it succeeded in holding high-ranking officials, including Saddam Hussein, accountable, its legacy is mixed, particularly in terms of perceptions of fairness and impartiality. Yet, the IHT's experience offers valuable lessons for future tribunals, including those being considered for ensuring accountability for crimes committed in Ukraine, where similar challenges of evidence collection, command responsibility, and ensuring legitimacy are highly likely to arise. By ensuring judicial independence, prioritizing security and witness protection, improving evidence collection and preservation procedures, emphasizing accountability at all levels of command, and upholding strict fair trial standards, Ukraine's specialized war crimes court can avoid many of the pitfalls faced by the IHT and offer a more effective mechanism for delivering justice for the atrocities committed during the war.

Unlike Iraq, Ukraine's specialized war crimes chamber would be built on a more nationally driven foundation with strong international support, enhancing both its legitimacy and impartiality. Additionally, Ukraine's greater institutional focus on the rule of law and democratic reform, coupled with international scrutiny, will help ensure that political pressures do not undermine the tribunal's work. With Ukraine's commitment to justice and accountability and a more unified national identity, the war crimes chamber can establish robust legal safeguards and ensure transparency and fairness in its proceedings, thus avoiding the legitimacy challenges that the IHT faced.

Piracy Chambers in Seychelles and Mauritius

Another example of specialized judicial mechanisms can be seen in the piracy chambers established in Seychelles and Mauritius to address the increasing threat of Somali piracy in the Indian Ocean, as part of a broader international effort to combat the surge in piracy off the coast of Somalia, particularly between 2008 and 2012, and given the legal and logistical barriers many countries faced in prosecuting crimes committed on the high seas. The surge in piracy originally triggered an unprecedented international response, with coalition naval forces, such as the United States-led Combined Task Force 151, patrolling the Gulf of Aden and wider Indian Ocean in an effort to intercept and apprehend suspected pirates.[27] Created with support from the United Nations Office on Drugs and Crime (UNODC) under its Counter Piracy Programme, and funded by international partners such as the European Union, the United States, and the United Kingdom, these chambers aimed to strengthen regional capacity for piracy trials while ensuring compliance with international legal standards. Their purpose was to provide fair trials, deter piracy, and alleviate the burden on other nations, as Seychelles and Mauritius were geographically well positioned for such efforts. By prosecuting suspected pirates transferred by international naval forces, the chambers contributed to enhancing maritime security, safeguarding shipping lanes, and stabilizing the region impacted by piracy. The Seychellois legal framework is a hybrid, incorporating elements of both common law and customary law, where the courts are empowered to administer these distinct sets of laws as appropriate.[28]

The issue of how to effectively prosecute and imprison those captured proved to be a uniquely significant challenge, especially regarding jurisdiction, as piracy-related crimes typically occur on the high seas, and often involve Somali nationals and foreign victims. Many nations have been reluctant to extradite suspected pirates to Somalia, where the judicial system was and remains in a state of disarray following years of civil conflict.[29] Other states only wanted to prosecute those who committed crimes against their own citizens on the high seas (or were alleged perpetrators) under their own domestic legislation, creating an accountability gap.[30] As a result, several countries in the region have taken steps to establish specialized courts and detention facilities to handle piracy cases. Recognizing this limitation, Seychelles and Mauritius stepped in to fill this gap.

Seychelles was the first country to set up a specialized piracy chamber within its existing legal framework, formally beginning operations in 2010. This initiative was not entirely voluntary but rather the result of encouragement and collaboration with the international community, particularly the United Nations and other stakeholders involved in combating piracy in the region. The legal foundation for the chamber was grounded in Seychellois domestic law, but it incorporated international maritime law, particularly the United Nations Convention on the Law of the Sea (UNCLOS) and the Suppression of Unlawful Acts Against the Safety of Maritime Navigation (SUA), to ensure that piracy could be prosecuted effectively as a crime of universal jurisdiction. The piracy chamber in Seychelles was empowered to prosecute not only acts of piracy but also the broader spectrum of maritime crimes. The legal and prosecutorial framework of the piracy chamber focused heavily on the principles of international cooperation, particularly given that international naval forces patrolling the region as part of the European Union Naval Force Somalia and other multinational naval missions captured most pirates.[31]

Following the success of Seychelles in prosecuting pirates, Mauritius also established a specialized piracy chamber in 2012 as part of the broader international effort to combat Somali piracy in the Indian Ocean. The legal framework for Mauritius' piracy chamber was grounded in international law, integrating provisions from UNCLOS, SUA, and other relevant international conventions addressing maritime crime. Like Seychelles, Mauritius faced challenges in prosecuting crimes that occurred outside its territorial waters, often involving pirates apprehended by foreign naval forces operating under multinational missions. To address these challenges, Mauritius implemented a legal regime that allowed for extraterritorial jurisdiction, enabling the prosecution of individuals for acts committed on the high seas even when those individuals had no direct connection to Mauritius. The UNODC supported Mauritius in developing the necessary legal infrastructure, reflecting the country's commitment to international cooperation in combating maritime crime.

In terms of specific prosecutorial and investigative challenges encountered by these piracy chambers, one of the primary challenges was related to the jurisdictional complexity of prosecuting crimes committed on the high seas. Although piracy is recognized as a crime of universal jurisdiction, applying this concept within a domestic legal framework required legislative reforms in both Seychelles and Mauritius. The countries had to amend their criminal codes to permit the prosecution of piracy under domestic law while simultaneously adhering to international legal standards. For instance, both countries incorporated international definitions of piracy from UNCLOS, which defined piracy as acts of violence or detention committed for private ends on the high seas, ensuring that their domestic laws reflected internationally recognized definitions.[32]

Similarly to specialized war crimes chambers, the issue of evidence collection was another significant hurdle in the piracy chambers proceedings. Piracy cases often involved pirates captured by foreign navies, meaning that non-Seychellois or non-Mauritian officials frequently collected evidence on the high seas. This introduced issues of chain of custody and the admissibility of evidence in domestic courts, especially when international actors gathered forensic evidence and witness testimonies. The piracy chambers relied heavily on international cooperation, with the UNODC playing a pivotal role in ensuring that evidence was properly documented and transmitted in a manner consistent with both international evidentiary standards and domestic admissibility rules.[33]

Witness availability also posed a considerable challenge for the proceedings. Many witnesses were crewmembers of international ships that had been attacked or hijacked by pirates. Ensuring the presence of these witnesses, sometimes years after the incidents occurred, required intricate coordination. Some witnesses were unwilling or unable to return to Seychelles or Mauritius for the trials, necessitating the use of video conferencing and other methods of remote testimony.[34] The chambers had to develop innovative methods of ensuring witness testimony was obtained securely and in accordance with fair trial standards, while safeguarding the rights of the accused to cross-examination.

Ensuring fair trial standards and human rights compliance was quite challenging in the piracy chambers proceedings. Both Seychelles and Mauritius faced the delicate task of ensuring that the rights of accused pirates were protected throughout the judicial process. This involved adherence to international human rights obligations, including the International Covenant on Civil and Political Rights (ICCPR), to which both Seychelles and Mauritius are state parties. Fair trial standards, including the presumption of innocence, the right to legal representation, and the right to appeal, were paramount in ensuring the legitimacy of the prosecutions. Moreover, the piracy chambers faced the logistical challenge of securing legal representation for the pirates, many of whom were Somali nationals with limited or no access to legal resources. Both Seychelles and Mauritius, in coordination with international partners, worked to provide defense counsel for accused pirates, ensuring compliance with the right to legal representation and fair trial standards as outlined under both domestic law and international human rights conventions. Legal representation was provided through locally trained attorneys and sometimes by attorneys with expertise in international maritime law.[35]

The presence of international observers, including from the UNODC, was instrumental in maintaining the transparency and fairness of the proceedings, particularly given the high level of international interest in the outcomes of these trials. The courts were also conscious of the conditions of detention for convicted pirates, who were often held in Seychelles or Mauritius after their trials. Both countries worked closely with international partners to ensure that detention conditions met international standards, despite the challenges posed by overcrowding and limited resources in local detention facilities. In some instances, pirates were repatriated to Somalia under transfer agreements, provided that Somalia could guarantee their humane treatment in accordance with international law.

The prosecution of piracy in these chambers also raised questions about the applicability of the doctrine of command responsibility in cases where pirates were part of larger organized criminal enterprises. Establishing the criminal liability of pirate leaders—who often operated from within Somalia, directing operations on the high seas but never setting foot on board the ships they attacked—was a significant challenge. Prosecutors had to navigate complex issues of indirect responsibility and joint criminal enterprise, using a combination of forensic evidence, intercepted communications, and testimonies from captured pirates to build cases against those higher up in the piracy networks.[36]

In conclusion, the foregoing analysis illustrates that the piracy chambers in Seychelles and Mauritius represent an important legal innovation in addressing a modern maritime crime that posed significant jurisdictional and logistical challenges. Through careful legal reform, international cooperation, and a commitment to upholding human rights and fair trial standards, these chambers became regional hubs for the prosecution of piracy, setting a precedent for the prosecution of transnational crimes. The success of these piracy chambers demonstrates the potential of specialized courts to handle complex international crimes while balancing the need for effective prosecution with the protection of the rights of the accused. This model of specialized judicial mechanisms provides valuable lessons for the prosecution of other international crimes, such as war crimes and crimes against humanity, where cross-border cooperation, legal innovation, and adherence to international standards are similarly critical.

Incorporating the lessons from the piracy chambers in Seychelles and Mauritius could be incredibly valuable when proposing a specialized war crimes chamber in Ukraine. The piracy chambers in Seychelles and Mauritius addressed significant accountability gaps by prosecuting crimes that occurred in international waters, where jurisdiction was often unclear. Similarly, a hybrid war crimes chamber in Ukraine could fill the accountability gap for atrocities committed by foreign nationals or separatists within the context of an ongoing conflict. The piracy chambers also integrated international law with domestic legal frameworks, offering a flexible approach to prosecuting crimes that would be beneficial in Ukraine, where complex jurisdictional issues exist. Furthermore, the chambers benefited from international cooperation, particularly through the support of the UNODC and other partners, which would be essential for Ukraine's war crimes chamber to operate effectively. Ensuring fair trials and human rights protections in the face of complex prosecutions, as seen in the piracy chambers, would also be crucial in Ukraine's context, especially given the international attention on ensuring justice for war crimes. Lastly, just as the piracy chambers in Seychelles and Mauritius tackled the challenge of prosecuting both low-level offenders and those higher up in criminal networks, Ukraine's chamber could address accountability at multiple levels, including command responsibility and joint criminal enterprise. By drawing on the experience of these chambers, Ukraine could develop a model that balances effective prosecution with respect for both domestic sovereignty and international legal standards.

Ukraine: Possibility of Creating a Specialized War Crimes Chamber

The lessons learned from the case studies discussed above are highly relevant for Ukraine, which is currently dealing with significant atrocities stemming from the ongoing Russian invasion. As previously discussed, the establishment of a specialized war crimes chamber would address the significant accountability gap for crimes perpetrated in Ukraine since the commencement of the Russian invasion. As noted in other chapters, the ICC, by its very design, functions as a court of last resort, mandated to prosecute only those individuals deemed most responsible for the gravest offenses. Its jurisdictional and operational limitations, including constrained financial and institutional resources, restrict its capacity to pursue more than a limited number of cases arising from any given situation[37]. Several states, including Lithuania[38], Spain[39], Sweden[40], Germany[41], and Poland[42], are exploring or conducting prosecutions under universal jurisdiction. However, as outlined in Chapter 8, such efforts remain limited in scope, often constrained to a small number of perpetrators who are present within the prosecuting state's territory. This underscores the necessity of establishing additional mechanisms, such as a specialized war crimes chamber within Ukraine's judicial system, to effectively address the existing accountability gap.[43] Moreover, the ICC presently lacks jurisdiction over the crime of aggression in this context, though proposals to address this gap, as detailed in Chapter 6, remain under discussion. Whether these initiatives will ultimately materialize into concrete mechanisms is, at this stage, uncertain.

In addition to bridging the accountability gap, the establishment of a specialized war crimes chamber would ensure fairness of the prosecutions[44] for several reasons. First, while the chamber would operate domestically, it could incorporate international legal standards and practices through technical assistance, training, and monitoring by international advisors, enhancing its credibility and adherence to global norms. Second, operating as a fully domestic court ensures local ownership of the accountability process, fostering trust among the Ukrainian population and avoiding perceptions of external interference. Third, the chamber would be uniquely tailored to Ukraine's specific legal, cultural, and historical context, enabling a more nuanced and context-sensitive approach to atrocity crimes. Fourth, it would contribute to strengthening Ukraine's judicial capacity by building expertise among domestic legal professionals and creating a framework for handling complex atrocity crimes in the future. Finally, international oversight or monitoring could play a supplementary role, ensuring that the chamber adheres to international standards of fairness, impartiality, and due process while maintaining Ukraine's judicial autonomy.

On March 2, 2022, the International Criminal Court officially opened an investigation into possible war crimes and crimes against humanity committed in Ukraine, following the referral by 39 State Parties under Article 14 of the Rome Statute.[45] While this offers an excellent step towards accountability, the scale of Russian crimes and the limited capacity of the ICC mean that Ukraine cannot rely solely on the ICC to prosecute all instances of international crimes committed on its territory since 2014.

In line with its principle of complementarity, the ICC would most likely focus on prosecuting a limited number of high-level perpetrators responsible for the most serious atrocities, meaning it would be narrowly focused. As mentioned in previous chapters, while the ICC has jurisdiction over crimes against humanity and war crimes committed in Ukraine since 2013 due to Ukraine's declaration accepting the Court's jurisdiction from November 2013 onward, this does not mean that the ICC can or will prosecute all perpetrators of every crime committed in Ukraine since 2013 – or even since February 2022. This approach reflects the Court's mandate and capacity constraints, which prioritize targeting individuals who played central roles in orchestrating or authorizing widespread violence. As a result, lower-level offenders or cases involving less severe crimes may be left to national courts or other mechanisms, if pursued at all. Consequently, while the ICC's efforts are crucial for setting precedents and delivering justice in key cases, they may address only a fraction of the overall violations committed. The ICC is not intended to be the world's court – not only is it not designed to be so – it simply does not have the funding, resources, or capacity to litigate all public international crimes.[46] For Ukraine, this means that the majority of atrocities committed by Russians on Ukrainian soil will likely be handled by domestic courts in Ukraine. A specialized domestic war crimes tribunal would assist with this caseload.

Next, a specialized war crimes chamber is necessary because the crimes being committed in Ukraine are so numerous that the existing accountability mechanisms are unlikely to have sufficient capacity and expertise to fairly and effectively try many of the perpetrators of atrocity crimes.[47] There is no doubt

Ukraine has general expertise and experience in investigating and adjudicating crimes of this nature. However, the strain that would be placed on the domestic prosecution service to investigate and prosecute crimes of this scope and gravity is apparent and will necessarily give rise to concerns over the sufficiency of personnel, resources, and breadth of expertise in international criminal law.[48]

Further, the prosecution of foreign nationals in ordinary Ukrainian courts in the context of an ongoing war will undoubtedly raise international concerns about fairness, impartiality, and objectivity of such trials. Ordinary courts may be perceived as lacking the necessary specialization and distance from political and public pressures inherent to wartime conditions, potentially casting doubt on the credibility and legitimacy of their proceedings. A specialized war crimes chamber, by contrast, would offer a focused, transparent, and internationally recognized mechanism specifically designed to adjudicate such complex and sensitive cases by incorporating international legal expertise, robust procedural safeguards, and oversight mechanisms tailored to address war crimes, thereby bolstering confidence among the international community that justice in Ukraine is being pursued impartially and effectively. The chamber would also demonstrate Ukraine's commitment to upholding international legal standards and protecting the rights of all accused, mitigating potential claims of bias and strengthening the legitimacy of prosecutions on the global stage.

In 2022, the Public International Law and Policy Group (PILPG) prepared a draft law and proposed the adoption of a specialized war crimes chamber for Ukraine, offering a model that could effectively address the prosecution of atrocity crimes committed within the country since November 2013.[49] The proposal is reproduced in the Appendix at the end of this book. Drawn from the Law "On the High Anti-Corruption Court of Ukraine" of 2018 and best practices of internationalized domestic war crimes courts around the globe, the proposal provided the template for a Ukrainian High War Crimes Court to prosecute atrocity crimes committed in Ukraine since November 2013.[50] This proposal envisions a hybrid court model, where both domestic and international legal frameworks are integrated, reflecting best practices from similar tribunals established in post-conflict settings. Thus far, history has shown that without international assistance and involvement it is inherently difficult to fairly and effectively prosecute foreign nationals and separatists in ordinary domestic courts during and in the aftermath of an armed conflict.

Drawing on the experiences of Bosnia and Herzegovina, Iraq, Seychelles, Mauritius, and other states that have established specialized chambers, Ukraine might consider a hybrid model that integrates international legal expertise while maintaining jurisdiction within its national courts, which would allow the country to retain control over the prosecution of atrocity crimes committed within its borders while ensuring that international standards of justice are met.

According to PILPG's proposal, such a High War Crimes Court could have broad jurisdiction over both the core international crimes, as well as relevant domestic crimes to cover the kinds of crimes being perpetrated in Ukraine. While it is intended to be a court to assist in the prosecution of mid-level offenders, it is not prohibited from prosecuting crimes of aggression, criminalized by Ukrainian criminal law (though it would be precluded by the doctrine of head of state immunity from prosecuting Vladimir Putin). Thus, the court would be able to focus on the prosecution of serious crimes such as war crimes, crimes against humanity, genocide, and, as mentioned, crimes of aggression, ensuring adherence to international humanitarian law and human rights law, while maintaining Ukrainian sovereignty. The court's jurisdiction over war crimes, crimes against humanity, and genocide would be grounded in both Ukrainian law and international legal frameworks, such as the Geneva Conventions and the Rome Statute of the ICC. By adopting this hybrid model, Ukraine can bridge the gap in accountability, ensure a fair prosecution of atrocity crimes, and guarantee that justice is served in a manner that respects Ukrainian judicial autonomy and international legal standards.

A core aspect of this approach is the structure and jurisdiction of the war crimes chamber, which would be positioned within Ukraine's existing judicial system but operate with specialized procedures to handle the complexity of international crimes. The court would have jurisdiction over crimes committed throughout Ukrainian territory, including in the occupied areas, and would focus on individuals most responsible for orchestrating and committing these crimes. The inclusion of command responsibility in the court's mandate is particularly significant, as it allows for the prosecution of military commanders and political leaders who may not have directly committed war crimes but who bear responsibility for ordering or failing to prevent such crimes. This doctrine is a cornerstone of international criminal law and is essential for addressing the hierarchical nature of war crimes, where the most culpable individuals are often far removed from the battlefield. Such a structure of the model tribunal allows for the prosecution of both military and civilian leaders, including those in high-ranking positions, who may not otherwise be subject to prosecution by domestic courts. It also enables the chamber to focus on systematic violations, which may involve widespread or organized attacks on civilian populations, thus capturing the scope of war crimes in a more comprehensive manner.

Including both international and domestic personnel in key positions at the High War Crimes Court could help to close the capacity gap. While the chamber would not include international judges or prosecutors, the proposal emphasizes the integration of international legal standards and practices as an integral part of the chamber's functioning. International advisors and organizations could provide technical assistance, training, and monitoring, which would strengthen the fairness and credibility of the domestic judicial process. International personnel can assist by providing international criminal law expertise, while domestic personnel would add local knowledge about local laws and culture for a robust tribunal. International involvement is a key feature of this model, though, and can be informed by lessons from the piracy court in Seychelles and Mauritius.

A key lesson from the piracy chambers for a potential creation of a specialized war crimes chamber in Ukraine would be the importance of such international cooperation and shared expertise. As discussed in previous sections, the piracy chambers not only successfully integrated international legal standards with national legal frameworks, addressing jurisdictional issues and ensuring fair trials, but also highlighted the value of specialized expertise from international personnel in addressing crimes involving multiple jurisdictions and cross-border elements, which would be critical for prosecuting high-ranking Russian officials and complex war crimes in Ukraine. Therefore, a specialized tribunal in Ukraine would benefit from the expertise of international legal professionals, including prosecutors, judges, and investigators, to ensure that the prosecution of war crimes meets the highest standards of international law. This approach was also adopted in the Special Court for Sierra Leone, where international judges and prosecutors worked alongside national counterparts to prosecute serious crimes. The incorporation of international legal advisors and expert witnesses would be vital in addressing the challenges of interpreting complex areas of international law, such as the elements of genocide or the principle of command responsibility, which are critical in high-level prosecutions.

Another significant feature of PILPG's proposed specialized court model is its witness protection program. Given the sensitive nature of war crimes prosecutions, many witnesses may face intimidation or retribution for their testimony, particularly if they are testifying against high-ranking officials or military leaders. The court would establish comprehensive protection measures to safeguard witnesses, ensuring their safety before, during, and after their involvement in proceedings. This includes measures such as anonymity, relocation, and psychosocial support, modeled after witness protection programs used in other international and hybrid tribunals. Protecting witnesses is not only vital for ensuring their cooperation but also for maintaining the integrity of the judicial process.

The proposed tribunal's design includes multiple levels of review, including trial chambers and an appeals chamber, ensuring that defendants have access to appellate review and that legal questions are thoroughly examined. Such a design reflects international standards for fair trial procedures, mirroring structures seen in international tribunals like the ICC and other specialized chambers established in Bosnia and Herzegovina and Rwanda. The emphasis on due process rights—including the right to counsel, the right to cross-examination of witnesses, and the protection of defendants' rights—would ensure that the court's decisions are both legitimate and grounded in legal rigor.

The court's political, judicial, and administrative independence of any improper influence is a core component of its design, ensuring that it operates without interference from any political actors or external pressures. This independence and integrity is critical in maintaining the legitimacy of the court's proceedings, as war crimes prosecutions are often politically charged and can be subject to attempts at manipulation or obstruction. The court's financial and administrative autonomy, coupled with international support mechanisms, would protect it from undue influence, ensuring that its judgments are based solely on the law and the evidence presented.

Creating a specialized war crimes chamber in Ukraine would undoubtedly require substantial resources. To alleviate the burden on the national system, the chamber's establishment could draw on both international and local funding sources to enhance its legitimacy. Distributing the financial responsibility among various stakeholders, including those directly impacted by and invested in addressing Russia's aggression and the resulting atrocity crimes, presents a viable solution. Importantly, securing international funding contributes to maintaining a political distance between financial supporters and judicial decision makers, thereby minimizing any potential bias or pressure to favor a particular funder and reinforcing judicial integrity. This model has proven effective in other international tribunals such as the ICTY, ICTR, Special Court for Sierra Leone, Extraordinary Chambers in the Courts of Cambodia, and Special Tribunal for Lebanon, where voluntary contributions successfully supported judicial operations while maintaining judicial independence. Although some may perceive a funding system involving voluntary contributions as potentially subject to external influence, access to funding beyond domestic bureaucratic constraints offers greater financial flexibility and stability. Fixed budget allocations from the Ukrainian government underscore national ownership and commitment to the tribunal, balancing external contributions with a strong domestic anchor. The establishment of an oversight board to govern external funding would ensure transparency and accountability, further safeguarding judicial independence. Given the international community's demonstrated willingness to support Ukraine in its efforts to hold perpetrators accountable for atrocity crimes, this blended funding model appears both practical and realistic for the effective functioning of a specialized war crimes chamber.

In conclusion, the establishment of a specialized war crimes chamber in Ukraine offers a viable solution to the challenges of prosecuting the numerous war crimes, crimes against humanity, and potentially genocide that have been committed during the ongoing Russian invasion. By integrating international legal standards into its domestic legal system, Ukraine can ensure that justice is delivered in a fair, transparent, and effective manner. The court's reliance on international expertise, its comprehensive approach to witness protection, and its emphasis on independent and fair trial standards, as the PILPG's proposal suggests, make it a strong option for addressing the legal complexities of war crimes prosecutions in the country.

As Ukraine continues to grapple with the legal challenges posed by the ongoing Russian invasion, the creation of a specialized war crimes chamber could play a critical role in guaranteeing that justice is delivered efficiently and fairly, both for the victims of atrocities and for the broader international community, ensuring that impunity for atrocity crimes is not tolerated. This hybrid approach would also strengthen Ukraine's legal infrastructure for future prosecutions, creating a lasting legacy within the judicial system, likely serving as a model for future accountability processes regarding serious violations of international law even beyond Ukraine.

Notes

1 United Nations Security Council, *Resolution 1503 (2003)*, UN Doc. S/RES/1503, August 28, 2003; *Resolution 1534 (2004)*, UN Doc. S/RES/1534, March 26, 2004.

2 International Crimes Database (ICD), "Domestic War Crimes Chambers," T.M.C. Asser Institute, https://www.internationalcrimesdatabase.org/Courts/Domestic

3 Hybrid Justice Project, "The War Crimes Chamber in Bosnia and Herzegovina," https://hybridjustice.com/the-war-crimes-chamber-in-bosnia-and-herzegovina/.

4 Rachel Kerr and Eirin Mobekk, *Peace and Justice: Seeking Accountability After War.* Cambridge: Polity, 2007.

5 Council of Europe, *Criminal Code of Bosnia and Herzegovina (Consolidated Text)*, 2003, https://rm.coe.int/bih-criminal-code-consolidated-text/16806415c8.

6 Organization for Security and Co-operation in Europe (OSCE), *War Crimes Trials Before the Court of Bosnia and Herzegovina: Progress and Obstacles*, 2017, pp. 5, 9, https://www.osce.org/files/f/documents/4/d/314846.pdf

7 Clark, Janine Natalya. International Trials and Reconciliation: Assessing the Impact of the International Criminal Tribunal for the Former Yugoslavia. Routledge, 2012.

8 International Criminal Tribunal for the former Yugoslavia (ICTY), Press Release, "Donors Raise 15.6 Million Euros for the War Crimes Chamber in BiH Court," The Hague, 2004, https://www.icty.org/en/press/donors-raise-156-million-euros-war-crimes-chamber-bih-court

9 International Criminal Tribunal for the former Yugoslavia (ICTY), *Completion Strategy of the ICTY*, https://www.icty.org/en/about/tribunal/completion-strategy.

10 International Center for Transitional Justice (ICTJ), *Bosnia and Herzegovina: Domestic Court for War Crimes – ICTJ Briefing Paper*, 2008, p. 8, https://www.ictj.org/sites/default/files/ICTJ-FormerYugoslavia-Domestic-Court-2008-English.pdf.

11 International Center for Transitional Justice (ICTJ), *Bosnia and Herzegovina: Domestic Court for War Crimes – ICTJ Briefing Paper*, 2008, p. 17, https://

www.ictj.org/sites/default/files/ICTJ-FormerYugoslavia-Domestic-Court-2008-English.pdf.

12 International Center for Transitional Justice (ICTJ), *Bosnia and Herzegovina: Domestic Court for War Crimes – ICTJ Briefing Paper*, 2008, p. 34, https://www.ictj.org/sites/default/files/ICTJ-FormerYugoslavia-Domestic-Court-2008-English.pdf.

13 Human Rights Watch, *Narrowing the Impunity Gap: Trials Before Bosnia's War Crimes Chamber*, February 2007, https://www.hrw.org/reports/2007/ij0207/ij0207.htm.

14 International Center for Transitional Justice (ICTJ), *Bosnia and Herzegovina: Domestic Court for War Crimes – ICTJ Briefing Paper*, 2008, p. 30, https://www.ictj.org/sites/default/files/ICTJ-FormerYugoslavia-Domestic-Court-2008-English.pdf.

15 International Center for Transitional Justice (ICTJ), *Bosnia and Herzegovina: Domestic Court for War Crimes – ICTJ Briefing Paper*, 2008, pp. 22, 49, https://www.ictj.org/sites/default/files/ICTJ-FormerYugoslavia-Domestic-Court-2008-English.pdf.

16 Hybrid Justice Project, "The War Crimes Chamber in Bosnia and Herzegovina," https://hybridjustice.com/the-war-crimes-chamber-in-bosnia-and-herzegovina.

17 International Criminal Tribunal for the former Yugoslavia (ICTY), Outreach Programme, "Capacity Building," https://www.icty.org/en/outreach/capacity-building

18 International Center for Transitional Justice (ICTJ), *Bosnia and Herzegovina: Domestic Court for War Crimes – ICTJ Briefing Paper*, 2008, p. 39, https://www.ictj.org/sites/default/files/ICTJ-FormerYugoslavia-Domestic-Court-2008-English.pdf.

19 Raid Juhi al Saedi, Regime Change and the Restoration of the Rule of Law in Iraq. Available at https://digital-commons.usnwc.edu/cgi/viewcontent.cgi?article=1094&context=ils.

20 United States Department of State, The Future of Iraq Project, (2005). Available at https://nsarchive2.gwu.edu/NSAEBB/NSAEBB198/FOI%20Transitional%20Justice.pdf.

21 United States Institute of Peace, *Special Report 122: The Iraq Special Tribunal: A Statutory Analysis*, 2004, https://www.usip.org/sites/default/files/sr122.pdf.

22 United States Institute of Peace Special Report, Building the Iraqi Special Tribunal: Lessons from Experiences in International Criminal Justice, Special Report 122 (June 2022). Available at https://www.usip.org/sites/default/files/sr122.pdf.

23 United States Institute of Peace, *Special Report 122: The Iraq Special Tribunal: A Statutory Analysis*, 2004, https://www.usip.org/sites/default/files/sr122.pdf

24 Chatham House, The Iraqi Tribunal: The Post-Saddam Cases, A Summary of the Chatham House International Law Discussion Group meeting held on 4 December 2008, (2008). Available at https://www.chathamhouse.org/sites/default/files/public/Research/International%20Law/il041208.pdf; Mark A. Drumbl, The Iraqi High Tribunal and Rule of Law: Challenges, Proceedings of the Annual Meeting (American Society of International Law) Vol. 100 (MARCH 29–APRIL 1, 2006), pp. 79–83. Available at https://www.jstor.org/stable/25660065?typeAccessWorkflow=login.

25 United States Commission on International Religious Freedom (USCIRF), "Sectarian Violence in Iraq," https://www.uscirf.gov/publications/did-you-knowsectarian-violence-iraq.

26 Human Rights Watch, Iraq: A Broken Justice System Ten Years after Invasion, Opponents Punished, Trial Rights Ignored, (Jan 31, 2013). Available at https://

www.hrw.org/news/2013/01/31/iraq-broken-justice-system; Interview with Batool Aldaghir, Manager of the Women's Rights Center in Samawa; Executive Board Iraqi Civil Action Network.

27 Chalk, P. (2012). Assessing the Utility of Current Counterpiracy Initiatives Off the Horn of Africa. Studies in Conflict & Terrorism, 35(7–8), 553–561. https://doi.org/10.1080/1057610X.2012.684653; Onuoha, F. (2009). Sea piracy and maritime security in the Horn of Africa: The Somali coast and Gulf of Aden in perspective. African Security Review, 18(3), 31–44. https://doi.org/10.1080/10246029.2009.9627540; Bueger, C. Drops in the bucket? A review of onshore responses to Somali piracy. WMU J Marit Affairs 11, 15–31 (2012). https://doi.org/10.1007/s13437-012-0022-5; Chalk, P. (2012). Assessing the Utility of Current Counterpiracy Initiatives Off the Horn of Africa. Studies in Conflict & Terrorism, 35(7–8), 553–561. https://doi.org/10.1080/1057610X.2012.684653; Onuoha, F. (2009). Sea piracy and maritime security in the Horn of Africa: The Somali coast and Gulf of Aden in perspective. African Security Review, 18(3), 31–44. https://doi.org/10.1080/10246029.2009.9627540.

28 J. N. D. Anderson, Judicial and Legal Systems in Africa, African Affairs, Volume 61, Issue 244, July 1962, Page 255, https://doi.org/10.1093/oxfordjournals.afraf.a095005.

29 Bueger, C. Drops in the bucket? A review of onshore responses to Somali piracy. *WMU J Marit Affairs* **11**, 15–31 (2012). https://doi.org/10.1007/s13437-012-0022-5; Onuoha, F. (2009). Sea piracy and maritime security in the Horn of Africa: The Somali coast and Gulf of Aden in perspective. African Security Review, 18(3), 31–44. https://doi.org/10.1080/10246029.2009.9627540.

30 Douglas Guilfoyle, "Prosecuting Pirates in National Courts: A Comparative Survey," *SSRN Working Paper*, 2011, https://papers.ssrn.com/sol3/papers.cfm?abstract_id=1931870.

31 Case Western Reserve University, *War Crimes Research Office Memorandum on Terrorism Conventions*, https://scholarlycommons.law.case.edu/cgi/viewcontent.cgi?article=1033&context=war_crimes_memos; United Nations, *International Convention for the Suppression of the Financing of Terrorism*, 1999, https://treaties.un.org/doc/db/terrorism/conv8-english.pdf.

32 Michael Bahar, "Prosecution of Apprehended Pirates: Lessons Learned from the Major Jurisdictions," *Journal of International Humanitarian Legal Studies* 11, no. 1 (2020), https://www.tandfonline.com/doi/full/10.1080/25725084.2020.1788200.

33 Nova Southeastern University, *ILSA Journal of International & Comparative Law*, Vol. 16, Issue 2 (2010), https://nsuworks.nova.edu/cgi/viewcontent.cgi?article=1793&context=ilsajournal

34 Roger O'Keefe, "Universal Jurisdiction: Clarifying the Basic Concept," *Notre Dame Journal of International & Comparative Law*, Vol. 2, Issue 1 (2012), p. 125, https://scholarship.law.nd.edu/cgi/viewcontent.cgi?article=1169&context=ndjicl.

35 Harmen van der Wilt, "Piracy Trials in The Hague: The Justice Cascade Meets the Fight against Impunity," *Amsterdam Law School Research Paper*, University of Amsterdam, 2012, pp. 149–150, https://pure.uva.nl/ws/files/774918/60244_09.pdf.

36 Douglas Guilfoyle, *Prosecuting Maritime Piracy: Domestic Solutions to International Crimes*, Cambridge University Press, 2013, ch. 9, "Piracy and the Problem of Command Responsibility," https://www.cambridge.org/core/books/abs/prosecuting-maritime-piracy/piracy-and-the-problem-of-command-responsibility/5F12F5AA93C2628B8DC33DE512D338BF.

37 *American University Law Review*, "The War in Ukraine and the Legitimacy of the International Criminal Court," March 2022, https://aulawreview.org/blog/the-war-in-ukraine-and-the-legitimacy-of-the-international-criminal-court/.
38 Reuters, "Lithuania Prosecutors Launch Ukraine War Crimes Investigation," March 3, 2022, https://www.reuters.com/world/europe/lithuania-prosecutors-launch-ukraine-war-crimes-investigation-2022-03-03/.
39 The Local (Spain), "Spain Opens Probe into 'Serious Violations' by Russia in Ukraine," March 8, 2022, https://www.thelocal.es/20220308/spain-opens-probe-into-serious-violations-by-russia-in-ukraine.
40 The Local (Sweden), "Sweden Launches Investigation into Ukraine War Crimes," April 5, 2022, https://www.thelocal.se/20220405/sweden-launches-investigation-into-ukraine-war-crimes.
41 Andrii Kozik, "Ukrainian Prosecution of ICC Statute Crimes: Fair, Independent and Impartial?" *EJIL: Talk!* (Blog of the European Journal of International Law), 2022, https://www.ejiltalk.org/ukrainian-prosecution-of-icc-statute-crimes-fair-independent-and-impartial/.
42 Rebecca Hamilton and Tom Dannenbaum, "Mechanisms for Criminal Prosecution of Russia's Aggression against Ukraine," *Just Security*, July 2022, https://www.justsecurity.org/80626/mechanisms-for-criminal-prosecution-of-russias-aggression-against-ukraine/.
43 Case Western Reserve Journal of International Law, Vol. 53, Issue 2 (2021), https://scholarlycommons.law.case.edu/cgi/viewcontent.cgi?article=2658&context=jil.
44 Opinio Juris, "High War Crimes Court of Ukraine for Atrocity Crimes in Ukraine," July 29, 2022, https://opiniojuris.org/2022/07/29/high-war-crimes-court-of-ukraine-for-atrocity-crimes-in-ukraine/.
45 International Criminal Court (ICC), *Statement of ICC Prosecutor Karim A.A. Khan QC on the Situation in Ukraine: Receipt of Referrals from 39 States Parties*, March 2, 2022, https://www.icc-cpi.int/news/statement-icc-prosecutor-karim-aa-khan-qc-situation-ukraine-receipt-referrals-39-states.
46 *Washington University Global Studies Law Review*, "Hybrid Tribunals and the Rule of Law," Vol. 3, Issue 3 (2004), https://journals.library.wustl.edu/globalstudies/article/id/65/.
47 tAlexander Clapp, "Ukraine's Nuremberg Moment Amid Flood of Alleged Russian War Crimes," *Foreign Policy*, June 10, 2022, https://foreignpolicy.com/2022/06/10/ukraines-nuremberg-moment-amid-flood-of-alleged-russian-war-crimes/.
48 BBC News, "Ukraine Prosecutors Tackle First Russian War Crimes Trial," June 10, 2022, https://www.bbc.com/news/world-europe-61749877.
49 Public International Law & Policy Group (PILPG), *Draft Statute for a Ukrainian High War Crimes Court*, July 2022, https://static1.squarespace.com/static/5900b58e1b631bffa367167e/t/62d6c27baae10b6ca51cadb7/1658241661209/DRAFT+Ukraine+High+War+Crimes+Court.pdf.
50 Verkhovna Rada of Ukraine, Law of Ukraine No. 2447-19, "On the High Anti-Corruption Court," adopted June 7, 2018, https://zakon.rada.gov.ua/laws/show/2447-19?lang=en#Text.

8

ACCOUNTABILITY FOR CRIMES COMMITTED IN UKRAINE

Universal Jurisdiction Proceedings in National Jurisdictions

By Yvonne Dutton

Introduction

This chapter continues exploring the possibility of accountability for the many atrocities that have been committed in Ukraine since Russia's invasion of the country in February 2022.[1] It specifically considers whether and in what circumstances states might invoke universal jurisdiction prosecutions in their domestic courts to provide justice for victims of the many serious international crimes that have been well-documented since the conflict commenced.

The chapter begins by explaining the concept of universal jurisdiction, discussing some of the main challenges that have historically caused states to invoke it infrequently or only against lower-level suspects—especially those found in their country. It follows by considering the potential role that universal jurisdiction cases will play in the context of the crimes being committed in Ukraine since Russia's February 2022 invasion. The chapter notes that states have cooperated extensively to gather and preserve evidence of the crimes committed in Ukraine. These efforts certainly may increase the likelihood that states will be willing to mount universal jurisdiction prosecutions because the cooperative efforts help to ensure that sufficient evidence to convict is more readily available than it otherwise might be. The commitment to documenting atrocities while the conflict is ongoing also contributes to building a deep historical narrative of the crimes being committed and of the victims of these crimes to these crimes—a narrative which is useful for those advocating support for Ukraine as it fights against its aggressor. Finally, the fact that states have signaled they are investigating crimes committed in Ukraine and are willing to prosecute them sends a message to perpetrators

DOI: 10.4324/9781003458166-10

that they likely may not be able to travel freely and find safe haven outside of Russia.

The chapter, however, concludes on a cautious note. It commends those states that have already announced their willingness to investigate and prosecute crimes committed in Ukraine. Such efforts contribute to closing the accountability gap and ensure that at least some perpetrators do not escape justice. Nevertheless, considering the historical precedents, the chapter suggests that even if states commence universal jurisdiction prosecutions to address the situation in Ukraine, the number of cases will be relatively small, and the great majority will include some nexus to the offense or be against lower-level perpetrators who are found present in the foreign state.

Universal Jurisdiction and its Challenges

Universal Jurisdiction in Theory

Universal jurisdiction is an exception to the general jurisdictional rule that requires states to show some connection to their territory, nationality, or national security interests before exercising jurisdiction.[2] To exercise universal jurisdiction, states need not show any nexus to the offense committed and can prosecute certain crimes even where they did not occur on the state's territory and where neither the perpetrator nor the victim is a national of the state. States, though, may only exercise this extraordinary power over certain serious international crimes that are considered *jus cogens* crimes; crimes that violate norms the international community accepts and recognizes as those from which no derogation is permitted.[3] Included within this list are genocide, crimes against, humanity, and war crimes, the very crimes over which the International Criminal Court (ICC) also has jurisdiction and which many have alleged are being committed in Ukraine.[4] Even though they need not have a jurisdictional hook for states to exercise universal jurisdiction over any of these crimes, they must nevertheless incorporate them into their domestic legislation.[5]

According to Maximo Langer, there are two main rationales for permitting—and indeed, encouraging—states to exercise universal jurisdiction over *jus cogens* crimes. One rationale focuses on the heinousness of the crimes committed and conceives of states as "global enforcers" of peremptory norms empowered to step in to prosecute offenders even without a jurisdictional link. The second rationale is grounded in ensuring that states do not become "safe havens" for those who have committed serious international crimes. The possibility of universal jurisdiction prosecutions should reduce the ability of perpetrators of atrocity crimes to find safe havens, allowing them to settle and escape justice.[6]

Universal Jurisdiction: Historical State Practice

Although some commentators argue that universal jurisdiction is an essential tool of international justice to help close an impunity gap that would otherwise exist, historically, states have only invoked it infrequently. For example, in a study conducted by Maximo Langer, the evidence showed that only twenty-six people were convicted under universal jurisdiction in the twenty-five years preceding 2010.[7] Human Rights Watch also found little evidence that states were embracing universal jurisdiction; their study revealed that in the 15 years before 2009, states had tried fewer than 20 universal jurisdiction cases worldwide.[8] Evidence since 2010 suggests that states may be invoking universal jurisdiction more regularly than in the past. Langer and Eason found that between 2010 and 2017, states worldwide had completed 29 universal jurisdiction cases.[9] Other studies have reached similar conclusions: namely, that states rarely invoke universal jurisdiction to prosecute international crimes without any nexus to the offense, despite the gravity of the alleged conduct.[10] In short, the evidence demonstrates that historically states have not invoked universal jurisdiction in its pure form—with no nexus to the offense—frequently enough to close any impunity gap that exists for perpetrators of serious international crimes.

In fact, many states have not incorporated into their domestic legislation all the relevant international crimes—aggression, genocide, crimes against humanity, and war crimes—or incorporated them to allow the state to exercise jurisdiction with no nexus to the offense.[11] For example, the United States has no statute specifically criminalizing crimes against humanity.[12] Only recently, in response to the war in Ukraine, did the United States finally amend its war crimes statute to allow for the exercise of jurisdiction over perpetrators found on its soil, "regardless of the perpetrator or victim's nationality or where the crime took place."[13] Even so, the new statute requires that, to exercise universal jurisdiction, the perpetrator must be located within US territory.[14] Other states also add presence requirements, thus helping to ensure that their states do not become safe havens for perpetrators of atrocity crimes. For instance, although France has incorporated war crimes, crimes against humanity, and genocide into domestic legislation, when those crimes occur on foreign soil, prosecutors can only exercise jurisdiction where the accused is a "habitual resident" of France.[15] These presence requirements, however, mean that the state will not be acting pursuant to the global enforcer rationale for the exercise of universal jurisdiction; it will act pursuant to the safe haven rationale and commence a trial if and when the perpetrator appears on its territory.

The Main Challenges to States' Invocation of Universal Jurisdiction

The literature has suggested several explanations for states' apparent reluctance to invoke universal jurisdiction in its pure form where the state has no nexus to the offense—for example, where the victim is not a state national. Several of those explanations are discussed below: (1) the political costs states may experience if they pursue universal jurisdiction cases; (2) the inability to obtain custody over perpetrators; (3) difficulties obtaining evidence sufficient to convict; and (4) limited domestic prosecutorial resources.

Political Costs

Particularly if the state seeks to prosecute high-level, powerful offenders, the historical evidence has shown that it may be exposed to political costs and unwillingly drawn into foreign relations conflicts. One frequently noted example of political costs imposed in response to the exercise of universal jurisdiction over high-level leaders concerns Palestine and Israel. In 2001, a group of Palestinians brought a universal jurisdiction action in Belgian courts accusing Israeli Prime Minister Ariel Sharon of playing a key role in the massacre of Palestinian refugees in Lebanon in 1982.[16] Israel initially retaliated against Belgium, with the Israeli Prime Minister refusing to visit European Union headquarters in Brussels.[17] Thereafter, a group of Israelis filed a universal jurisdiction complaint in Belgium against Palestinian leader Yasser Arafat seeking to hold him responsible for a series of bomb attacks and murders that occurred some decades before.[18] Though the complainants in that case denied acting in retaliation for the suit against Sharon,[19] the timing of the suit suggests otherwise as it was filed a day before a Brussels court was due to consider whether to proceed with the lawsuit against the Israeli Prime Minister.[20]

Another oft-cited example of political costs associated with pursuing universal jurisdiction cases involves a Belgian prosecutor's decision to initiate actions against a range of high-level leaders, including former President and Vice President of the United States, George Bush and Dick Cheney.[21] The United States promptly responded to these actions, threatening Belgium that it may lose its status as an international meeting place and the NATO headquarters if it did not rescind its law permitting the broad use of universal jurisdiction in its courts.[22] Belgium succumbed to these and other diplomatic pressures, amending its laws so that, at present, it can only exercise universal jurisdiction in cases where a treaty such as the Convention against Torture requires it to do so.[23]

Spain was likewise pressured into changing its expansive laws when, in 2013, a Spanish judge issued arrest warrants against five high-ranking Chinese officials charging them with committing human rights abuses in Tibet.[24] China responded with a statement warning Spain that it would face consequences if the charges were not withdrawn.[25] Concerned about economic reprisals, the Spanish government thereafter sought to amend Spain's law to restrict the use of universal jurisdiction.[26] Spain now requires that for the country to have jurisdiction over crimes such as those charged in the cases against the Chinese officials, the victims must be Spanish nationals.[27]

One way for states to avoid these types of political costs is to pursue low-cost defendants—those who hail from a weak state or who are not leaders or considered important enough for the home state to use its diplomatic or other resources to intervene to fight against the prosecution.[28] In fact, studies have shown that most universal jurisdiction cases have been brought against low- to mid-level offenders. In one study, Langer examined all universal jurisdiction complaints presented around the world charging defendants with war crimes, genocide, crimes against humanity, or torture since the 1961 case Israel brought against Adolf Eichmann and before 2010.[29] He found that of the thirty-two cases brought to trial, twenty-four were "Rwandans, former Yugoslavs, and Nazis," all of whom he classified as "low-cost" defendants because the international community had generally agreed they must be prosecuted and because their home states did not intervene on their behalf.[30] Langer's later work with Eason reached a comparable conclusion with respect to universal jurisdiction cases brought to trial between July 2010 and 2017, finding that the twenty-nine universal jurisdiction cases brought during that time tended to involve "low-cost" defendants—as opposed to the kinds of defendants who would tend to make "noise" in international legal circles.[31]

Obtaining Custody over Perpetrators

States may also fail to pursue universal jurisdiction prosecutions because of difficulties related to obtaining custody over perpetrators of atrocity crimes committed by foreign nationals on foreign soil. The saga of Spain's case against former Chilean dictator Augusto Pinochet illustrates this point well. Pinochet was arrested in London on a warrant issued by Judge Baltazar Garzon of Spain charging Pinochet with serious international crimes committed in Chile.[32] Subsequently, the United Kingdom found that it had the authority to extradite Pinochet to Spain to stand trial, but it declined to do so, citing Pinochet's poor health.[33] Because Spain requires the accused to be present for the oral phase of the trial, the case against Pinochet in Spain did not proceed.[34]

The potential difficulties incident to obtaining custody over foreign perpetrators may help to explain why many states require the presence of the accused in their territory before they will proceed to trial. As noted above, the United States' newly amended war crimes statute requires the perpetrator to be located within the country to prosecute. France goes further and requires the perpetrator of alleged atrocity crimes to be a "habitual resident."

The Netherlands' laws permit it to exercise jurisdiction without any territorial nexus to the offense if either (1) the perpetrator or victim is a Dutch citizen or (2) the perpetrator is present on Dutch soil (or expected to be present shortly).[35] To exercise universal jurisdiction over war crimes, crimes against humanity, or genocide, Switzerland requires the crime be committed by a person present in Switzerland who has not been extradited to another state or delivered to an international criminal court whose jurisdiction is recognized by Switzerland.[36]

Indeed, studies have shown that states are more likely to mount universal jurisdiction cases against those perpetrators who are residing in or found on their territory.[37] From a practical standpoint, ensuring the accused's presence allows the state to avoid expenses required to locate and ensure the capture and transfer of the accused. The presence requirement also prioritizes the state's interest in not becoming a safe haven for serious international criminals.

Obtaining Sufficient Evidence

States may also conclude that because of their unique evidentiary challenges, universal jurisdiction cases are too burdensome to pursue. Human Rights Watch explains this challenge as follows:

> From the initial complaint to the conclusion of the trial and any appeal, cases involving universal jurisdiction present special demands on police, prosecutors, defense counsel and courts. Because the acts in question will have occurred in a foreign country, and often many years earlier, cases rarely arise in the manner to which local authorities are accustomed-such as through a victim simply reporting to a police station. Investigators and prosecutors may lack familiarity with both the historical and political context of the alleged crime, and the applicable international law.
>
> Witnesses may be dispersed across several countries, or the state in which the crime was committed may decline to cooperate with investigative requests. For similar reasons, a defendant may also face considerable problems gaining access to witnesses or evidence that exculpates him or her.[38]

If the state can obtain evidence documenting the accused's role in committing atrocity crimes, it still must consider whether that evidence will be admissible in domestic proceedings. Even within the European Union, countries have different rules and procedures regulating the admissibility of evidence in criminal proceedings,[39] meaning that there are limits on whether and how the evidence collected by the various mechanisms, bodies, organizations, or individuals will be used.[40] In addition, while much evidence on which the prosecuting state may wish to rely may have been collected using proper methods and according to criminal justice standards, at least some of the evidence collected by civilians, such as photos or videos from mobile devices, likely will not be sufficiently authenticated to permit its introduction.

Regarding witnesses, should the prosecuting state succeed in persuading foreign witnesses to travel to provide trial testimony, it may have to be prepared to protect the safety of witnesses and their families both before and after any trial. This is no small matter if the witness resides in a place where the atrocity occurred and where they might be subjected to threats of harm to them and their families.[41]

Limited Prosecutorial Resources

Finally, domestic audiences may not tolerate a state's decision to devote its limited prosecutorial resources to cases that have no direct relationship with the state. As Maximo Langer states, although domestic constituencies may value human rights in foreign countries, they may also require the state to devote most of its resources to domestic matters that can benefit the domestic populace. In short, although the populace may be committed to international justice, they may prefer closing the impunity gap through mechanisms that do not deplete resources needed to hold accountable those who harm their own nationals.[42] International courts such as the ICC can aid in this regard, and they have the advantage of being a venue where even high-level defendants cannot claim an immunity defense.[43]

Considering the Role of Universal Jurisdiction Prosecutions in the Ukraine Context

What role might we expect universal jurisdiction cases to play in the Ukraine context? To answer this question, this section considers the various challenges to invoking universal jurisdiction above using the historical evidence of state practice, as well as some of the evidence surrounding efforts underway to ensure accountability for atrocity crimes committed since Russia's February 2022 invasion.

Political Costs and Obtaining Custody over Suspects

The discussion above reveals that historically, one strategy that states might employ to avoid political costs and the difficulty of obtaining custody over suspects when invoking universal jurisdiction is to pursue lower-cost defendants and defendants who are otherwise found on their territory. There are several reasons to believe that states may behave similarly in the context of the Ukraine situation.

First, to the extent that Putin or someone aligned with him remains in power, states may conclude that pursuing high-level Russian officials, such as Putin or his inner circle of advisors and collaborators, may pose significant political costs and present problems in terms of obtaining custody over suspects. Since the start of the war in Ukraine, Putin has made numerous threats against those aiding Ukraine. In September 2022, Putin threatened to halt all energy supplies to Europe if Brussels imposed a cap on the price of Russian gas.[44] In that same month, he threatened to restrict grain exports to Europe, presumably to detract from arguments that it was his invasion of Ukraine that has caused a grain shortage.[45] According to news reports, Putin has frequently threatened to use nuclear weapons or to refuse to abide by protocols associated with their maintenance and control in order to boost his chances for defeating Ukraine.[46] One might expect that Putin would similarly issue significant threats to any country seeking to assert universal jurisdiction over himself or any of his allies. Many states might want to avoid being put into such a situation.

Second, as the historical evidence shows, obtaining custody over high-level suspects can be difficult—not only in terms of locating suspects or convincing them to appear, but also in terms of causing the state to incur political costs. To the extent that Putin or his allies remain in power, they are unlikely to comply with arrest warrants issued against their nationals. To avoid prosecution in foreign jurisdictions, many Russian accused may choose not to travel to states that are not allied with Russia. Indeed, Russian perpetrators may wish to remain in Russia where they can expect that Putin to continue labeling them "heroes."[47] This situation thus differs from that following the Rwandan genocide where the genocidaires knew that if they remained in Rwanda, the new Rwandan government would seek to hold them accountable.[48] Some of those Rwandan defendants were evidently willing to risk the possibility of a universal jurisdiction prosecution to avoid the likelihood of prosecution in Rwanda. It also differs from the situation in Syria where accused and others fled the country to escape ongoing violent conflict raging within.[49] Here, the conflict is being waged in Ukraine, not in Russia.

Finally, as to high-level defendants, even if one puts aside potential political costs and the potential difficulty of obtaining custody over the defendant, states may not want to pursue prosecutions where the defendant may be able to successfully advance an immunity defense. According to the International Court of Justice's *Yerodia* decision, heads of state and those occupying similarly high-level positions enjoy immunity from prosecution in national courts, even for serious international crimes while they remain in such positions.[50] Because of this decision, some states have declined to prosecute foreign nationals. French prosecutors, for example, dismissed a complaint filed by civil society organizations charging former US Secretary of Defense Donald Rumsfeld with torture in Guantanamo and Iraq, citing the likelihood of a successful immunity defense.[51] Furthermore, research conducted by Human Rights Watch shows that national authorities have in some instances relied on the *Yerodia* decision to decline to pursue universal jurisdiction cases against former high-level officials.[52] In fact, in 2005 German authorities declined to pursue charges against former Chinese President Jiang Zemin, concluding that he may be entitled to assert the immunity defense.[53] Although one may not agree with these decisions in that they allow a potentially guilty accused to escape justice, one can also understand the state's position. In such cases, it may face significant political costs by pursuing powerful persons or those who enjoy the support of powerful leaders. States may also wish to save resources to pursue cases that have a greater likelihood of being adjudicated on the merits.

Some Russian perpetrators of atrocities in Ukraine may nonetheless travel, and if they are found within a foreign territory possessing the necessary universal jurisdiction laws, states may be willing to mount an action against them—particularly if they are low-cost defendants. This is likely true of both the countries that require the presence of the accused to proceed and those that have not written that restriction into their universal jurisdiction legislation. The reason is simple: in such cases, the prosecuting state will not have to expend resources to track down the suspects. Furthermore, to the extent that the prosecution is against an ordinary accused without ties to powerful protectors, the Russian leadership may not be inclined to use political capital to intervene.

Evidence from Germany and Sweden helps to illustrate this point. Neither requires the presence or residence of the suspect for their courts to exercise jurisdiction over serious international crimes, nor to open an investigation.[54] Indeed, both countries had mounted structural investigations regarding crimes committed in Syria, meaning that they were already collecting "evidence in relation to the crimes committed during the armed conflict, in order to enable investigators to pro-actively build cases for the benefit of future criminal proceedings."[55] Nevertheless, Germany has a procedural rule permitting prosecutors to refrain from pursuing universal jurisdiction cases where the suspect is not present in Germany and such presence is not expected.[56] Sweden similarly provides that prosecutors should commence a case against an individual if "there is no reasonable chance of apprehending the suspect in Sweden."[57] Nor does either country permit a trial to be held without the presence of the accused, thus eliminating the possibility of providing justice to victims in an in absentia proceeding.[58]

Although both Germany and Sweden have some of the broadest universal jurisdiction laws[59] and were proactive in mounting structural investigations concerning the Syria situation, the evidence reveals that most of their universal jurisdiction cases have been brought against lower-level suspects who have been found in their territories.[60] In other words, their practice is consistent with the historical evidence concerning states' invocation of universal jurisdiction. While one cannot know exactly why Germany and Sweden proceeded as they did, political costs, the difficulty and expense of obtaining custody over suspects, and evidentiary difficulties all likely influenced their decisions. Not only do cases against higher-level accused impose greater political costs, but they are also harder to prove because they require strong linkage evidence connecting the leaders to the crimes committed by those on the ground.[61] As to custody over defendants, apparently fewer high-level accused left Syria to relocate.[62]

Evidentiary Difficulties

Evidentiary difficulties associated with prosecuting universal jurisdiction cases should pose less of a problem than they otherwise might because states, international and civil society organizations, and individuals have been cooperating to gather and preserve evidence of atrocity crimes committed in Ukraine since Russia's February 2022 invasion. As a result, some commentators have suggested that states might be more willing than they otherwise would to invoke universal jurisdiction to provide accountability for the crimes committed in Ukraine.[63] However, as discussed below, despite the many coordinated efforts to collect and preserve evidence of serious international crimes committed in Ukraine, at least some evidentiary difficulties will remain.

The Coordinated Efforts to Collect and Preserve Evidence of Atrocities Committed in Ukraine

The international community has devoted significant resources to ensure that evidence from Ukraine will be available for future accountability proceedings, including by domestic prosecutors willing to invoke universal jurisdiction. For example, almost immediately after Russia's invasion, the United Nations Human Rights Council created an independent international commission of inquiry for Ukraine (Ukraine COI).[64] The Ukraine COI's mandate is to among other things, investigate alleged crimes committed in the context of Russia's invasion of Ukraine, to collect and analyze evidence of such crimes, and to record and preserve such evidence, including tangible and witness evidence, "in view of any future legal proceedings."[65] Within months, the team investigating in furtherance of the mandate had traveled numerous times to Ukraine, visiting dozens of cities and towns, where they conducted hundreds of interviews, and "inspected sites of destruction, graves, places of detention and torture, as well as weapon remnants; and consulted documents, photographs, satellite imagery and videos."[66] Based on that investigation, the Commission concluded that "[t]he body of evidence collected shows that Russian authorities have committed a wide range of violations of international human rights law and international humanitarian law in many regions of Ukraine and in the Russian Federation," many of which "amount to war crimes and include wilful killings, attacks on civilians, unlawful confinement, torture, rape, and forced transfers and deportations of children."[67]

Also shortly after Russia's invasion of Ukraine, the Organization for Security and Cooperation in Europe (OSCE) invoked the Moscow Mechanism in consultation with Ukraine and at the request of 45 states to establish an ad hoc mission of independent experts to investigate "the humanitarian and human rights impacts on the people of Ukraine caused by Russia's further invasion with the support of Belarus."[68] The experts' mandate required them to gather evidence concerning any "violations and abuses of international human rights law and international humanitarian law by Russia's forces" and to prepare a report that would be shared with OSCE states and any relevant accountability mechanisms, including national courts invoking universal jurisdiction.[69] States invoked that same Moscow Mechanism in March 2023,[70] where the mandate explicitly called upon the experts to collect and analyze evidence, as well as provide information to relevant accountability mechanisms, including national courts that may in the future have jurisdiction over perpetrators of atrocity crimes in Ukraine.[71] Like the Ukraine COI, the OSCE has released reports of its experts' findings, detailing numerous violations of international humanitarian law committed by Russian forces since the February 2022 invasion.[72]

The European Union and individual states have also sought to gather and preserve evidence of crimes committed in Ukraine so that it is available for future accountability efforts, including by states invoking universal jurisdiction. The European Union is playing a significant role in these efforts, with Eurojust[73] providing operational, legal, and financial support to a Joint Investigative Team (JIT) created by Ukraine, Poland, and Lithuania, with the participation of other states, as well as the ICC Office of the Prosecutor (OTP). Comprised of prosecutors and law enforcement authorities as well as judges,[74] the JIT works to gather and share evidence to support accountability efforts within Ukraine, at the ICC, and that may be pursued by various domestic jurisdictions invoking universal jurisdiction.[75] In March 2023, the United States signed a Memorandum of Understanding, enabling "practical arrangements for cooperation, information exchange and the participation of the United States' authorities in coordination meetings organised with Eurojust's support."[76] To support the JIT, Eurojust has also created a Core International Crimes Database (CICED), which is a secure data storage tool to preserve, store, and analyze evidence of genocide, crimes against humanity and war crimes—with the idea that such evidence will be made available to the ICC, as well as interested national authorities.[77]

Civil society organizations, such as the Ukrainian organization Truth Hounds, are also gathering evidence for use in future criminal proceedings.

They are conducting witness interviews, but also assembling, evaluating, and storing open source digital intelligence[78]—namely data that is collected from public sources and that can be used in criminal investigations.[79] Such open source digital intelligence might include social media posts and newspapers, geospatial information, as well as photos and videos recorded by private individuals.[80] The amount of such evidence gathered about alleged crimes committed in Ukraine, in fact, is massive. For instance, just one NGO in Berlin (Mnemonic) has collected approximately 3 million records of potential serious international crimes or human rights violations committed in Ukraine since the Russia's February 2022 invasion, much of which comes from Telegram, YouTube, Twitter, and Facebook posts.[81]

These many efforts to collect and preserve evidence of crimes committed in Ukraine certainly should make prosecuting perpetrators at the ICC and in domestic jurisdictions less burdensome than such prosecutions would have been without these efforts. They should also encourage some states to be more willing than they otherwise might have been to invoke universal jurisdiction—as other commentators have suggested.

Evidentiary Difficulties Remain Despite Those Coordinated Efforts

Some evidentiary difficulties associated with mounting universal jurisdiction cases in domestic courts may remain despite these coordinated efforts. First, not all the evidence gathered and preserved will be admissible in all countries since states have different standards that govern whether and how evidence will be admitted in criminal trials. Indeed, some commentators have mentioned that many states following the inquisitorial model "seek to and are often even obliged to conduct investigations themselves."[82] Another concern mentioned above is whether some of the evidence gathered—particularly by civilians—has been authenticated sufficiently to permit it to be introduced in a criminal trial. Thus, states may not be able to use some of the evidence that these various bodies have collected and preserved.

Regarding witness testimony, the fact that witnesses have already been identified and provided statements or recorded testimony is not without its negative aspects. On the one hand, states invoking universal jurisdiction may be able to access those witnesses or obtain useful information from the statements or testimony already collected. On the other hand, because witnesses have once chosen to speak does not necessarily mean that they will be willing to testify at a trial. Witnesses, for instance, may be afraid to testify against some defendants, and if the witness is a foreign national residing outside the prosecuting state, obtaining their presence may be impossible or at least very difficult. Also noted by some commentators are the risks associated with "over-documentation" as concerns witness statements: namely, situations where victims are repeatedly asked to recount their experiences to different individuals, often without fully understanding who is recording their story or what it will be used for.[83] One concern is that for victims and witnesses, the repeated telling of their stories may repeatedly re-traumatize them. In addition, the repeated retelling can make individuals less reliable as trial witnesses to the extent that their many statements may contain inconsistencies that will have to be explained at trial.[84]

Limited Resources

Limited prosecutorial resources may also cause states to be cautious when deciding whether and in which instances to invoke universal jurisdiction in order to provide accountability for crimes committed in Ukraine. Concerns that the populace may wish to see resources focused on cases where the domestic populace has suffered injury makes it more likely that states will be reluctant to pursue pure universal jurisdiction cases where there is no nexus to the offense. This prediction is not without factual support. Amongst states that have announced investigations into international crimes being committed in Ukraine, at least some are pursuing cases where the victim is a state national. Lithuania's Prosecutor General's office has confirmed that as part of its investigation into crimes committed in Ukraine, it is seeking accountability for the death of Lithuanian filmmaker Mantas Kvedarvicius, who was killed during an attack by Russian forces near Mariupol.[85] The cases being pursued by France involve French citizens as victims,[86] including a journalist killed by rocket fire in Eastern Ukraine.[87] Spain has announced that it is investigating crimes committed in Ukraine,[88] but restrictions in its universal jurisdiction law discussed above mean that its courts can only adjudicate international crimes occurring on foreign soil if the victim is a Spanish citizen. The United States, too, has announced that it is pursuing war crimes charges for crimes committed in Ukraine—against four Russian soldiers accused of torturing an American citizen.[89]

Further, history suggests that states can sometimes tire of funding accountability for international crimes. For instance, states eventually complained about the costs associated with maintaining the ad hoc international criminal tribunals for Rwanda and the former Yugoslavia.[90] States have frequently complained about, and sought to limit, the budget of the ICC.[91] In the case of Ukraine, states have obviously committed significant resources developing the mechanisms discussed above designed to secure and preserve evidence of atrocities. States have also committed significant resources to aid Ukraine in the effort to defeat Russia militarily. But one can also see some evidence, at least in the United States, that the once widespread enthusiasm for supporting Ukraine's war efforts is waning. According to a Reuters survey, as of October 2023 only 41% of American want Congress to provide additional weaponry to Ukraine—down from 65% in only June 2023.[92] As late as February 2024, the US Congress was still fighting over the possibility of providing Ukraine another $US 60 billion in aid. Even if the aid package does pass, the evidence still suggests that states will focus on their limited resources when deciding what funds they are willing to invest in international justice.

Conclusion

The many cooperative efforts that states and others have engaged in to gather and preserve evidence of crimes committed in Ukraine are a welcome development and one that should encourage some states to invoke universal jurisdiction to bring perpetrators of atrocity crimes to justice. Nonetheless, based on the historical precedent and the various obstacles that make invoking universal jurisdiction costly and burdensome for states, states will likely continue to invoke universal jurisdiction sparingly. Furthermore, to the extent that states are willing to mount universal jurisdiction cases, for all the reasons discussed above, they will probably proceed more regularly against lower-level perpetrators found within their territory, as well as in cases where the state has some nexus to the offense. Many states, in fact, have a presence requirement, and even those states that do not may want to avoid expending the resources necessary to locate a foreign national residing (or hiding) outside the state's borders. Proceeding against lower-level suspects is also less burdensome, as it avoids political costs and involves cases that are easier to prove. Finally, the domestic state obviously has a great interest in ensuring accountability where its own nationals have been the victims of an offense, and in such cases obtaining the support of the domestic populace for the expenditure of resources should pose few difficulties.

This chapter applauds those states that have already commenced universal jurisdiction cases to provide accountability for crimes committed in Ukraine. Many more states will hopefully follow that lead and take advantage of the evidence that is being gathered and made available for domestic prosecutions. The good news is that the cooperative documentation efforts in Ukraine are useful beyond their ability to assist with prosecutorial efforts. As one commentator has suggested in connection with the Syrian documentation efforts, documentation is a method of "non-violent resistance to ongoing, violent conflict" that "resists the hijacking of narratives and the destruction of evidence, history, and memory."[93] This is true in the Ukraine situation as well. The evidence gathered can provide a historical narrative and institutional memory of the crimes that have been committed against innocent Ukrainians. That narrative is useful for advocacy purposes—to support Ukraine in its efforts to fight off Russian aggression. It can also be used during a later transitional justice phase within Ukraine to inform accountability decisions, as well as to support community building, reparations, and reconciliation.[94]

Notes

1 This chapter draws on material in two articles written by the author to which the reader is directed if they wish to delve further into this subject. *See* Yvonne M. Dutton, *Investigative Mechanisms and Tools for Ukraine: Exploring the Consequences for Universal Jurisdiction,* OHIO ST. L. J. (2024); Yvonne M. Dutton, *Prosecuting Atrocities Committed in Ukraine: A New Era for Universal Jurisdiction?*, 55 CASE WESTERN RESERVE J. INT'L L. 391 (2023).

2 *Universal Jurisdiction*, CTR. FOR JUST. AND ACCOUNTABILITY, https://cja.org/what-we-do/litigation/legal-strategy/universal-jurisdiction/.

3 *See* Vienna Convention on the Law of Treaties art. 53, May 23, 1969, 1155 U.N.T.S. 331 (defining *jus cogens*).

4 *See, e.g.*, *Basic Facts on Universal Jurisdiction*, HUM. RTS. WATCH (Oct. 19, 2009), https://www.hrw.org/news/2009/10/19/basic-facts-universal-jurisdiction [https://perma.cc/9GLV-CVUF] [hereinafter HRW Basic Facts UJ].

5 Leila Nadya Sadat, *Redefining Universal Jurisdiction*, 35 NEW ENG. L. REV. 241, 256 (2001).

6 Maximo Langer, *Universal Jurisdiction is not Disappearing: The Shift from 'Global Enforcer' to 'No Safe Haven' Universal Jurisdiction*, 13 J. INT'L CRIM. JUST. 245, 247 (2015).

7 Maximo Langer, *The Diplomacy of Universal Jurisdiction: The Political Branches and the Transnational Prosecution of International Crimes*, 105 AM. J. INT'L L. 1, 45 (2011).

8 *Basic Facts on Universal Jurisdiction*, Hum. Rts. Watch (Oct. 19, 2009), https://www.hrw.org/news/2009/10/19/basic-facts-universal-jurisdiction [https://perma.cc/9GLV-CVUF].

9 *See* Maximo Langer & Mackenzie Eason, *The Quiet Expansion of Universal Jurisdiction*, 30 EUR. J. INT'L L. 779, 788 (2019). Like Langer and Eason, this chapter focuses on completed trials as the best indicator of states' commitment to the exercise of universal jurisdiction. As those scholars explain: "[g]iven the relatively low cost of receiving and reviewing criminal complaints, an increase in the number of complaints gives us little insight into the level of support for universal jurisdiction among state officials in the venue state. Indeed, since private individuals and organizations may file criminal complaints, any attempt to use this rate as a measure of state support would need to account for the confounding effects of the preferences and choices of private complainants and advocacy organizations. By contrast, seeing such cases through the process of formal investigation, indictment and trial is an expensive and difficult task for prosecuting states and the decision to do so rests more squarely in the hands of state officials." *Id.* at 790.

10 *See, e.g.*, Eugene Kontorovich, *The Inefficiency of Universal Jurisdiction*, UNIV. ILL. L. REV. 389, 395 (referencing a study by Luc Reydams indicating that few states have ever exercised universal jurisdiction and only "over a miniscule fraction of cases that might be subject to it"); STEPHEN MULLIGAN, CONGR. RSCH. SERV., LSB10747, INTERNATIONAL ATROCITY CRIMES AND THEIR DOMESTIC COUNTERPARTS 1–3 (2005) [hereinafter CRS 2022 Report] (explaining that the US had never exercised a universal jurisdiction prosecution for genocide or war crimes, and that the US has no domestic law criminalizing crimes against humanity).

11 *See, e.g.*, Amnesty Int'l, *Universal Jurisdiction: A Preliminary Survey of Legislation Around the World – 2012 Updated,* AI Index IOR 53/019/2012, at 12 (Oct. 2012) [hereinafter Amnesty Int'l UJ Report] at 1–2 (showing that although approximately 75% of states provide for universal jurisdiction over at least one of the crimes of genocide, crimes against humanity, war crimes, or torture, they have not all provided for jurisdiction over all the relevant international crimes).

12 STEPHEN MULLIGAN, CONGR. RSCH. SERV., LSB10747, INTERNATIONAL ATROCITY CRIMES AND THEIR DOMESTIC COUNTERPARTS 3 (2005) [hereinafter CRS 2022 Report].
13 Elise Baker, *Closing the Impunity Gap for War Crimes*, JUST SEC. (Jan. 12, 2023), https://www.justsecurity.org/84737/closing-the-impunity-gap-for-war-crimes/ [https://perma.cc/2WZC-MZYF].
14 Grace Lin, *Expanding U.S. Prosecutorial Power Over International War Crimes*, COLUM. J. TRANSNAT'L L. ONLINE (Feb. 14, 2023), https://www.jtl.columbia.edu/bulletin-blog/expanding-us-prosecutorial-power-over-international-war-crimes#:~:text=Passed%20following%20an%20address%20by%20Ukraine%E2%80%99s%20leader%20and,not%20Americans%2C%20or%20the%20crimes%20were%20committed%20abroad [https://perma.cc/4MAQ-TTM9].
15 *See* Roger Lu Phillips, *2nd Time's the Charm: France's Cour de Cassation Broadens Universal Jurisdiction Law*, JUST SEC. (May 24, 2023), https://www.justsecurity.org/86689/2nd-times-the-charm-frances-cour-de-cassation-broadens-universal-jurisdiction-law/ [https://perma.cc/TL5S-26JH].
16 *Belgium to Amend Controversial War Crimes Law*, DW.COM (June 23, 2006), https://learngerman.dw.com/en/belgium-to-amend-controversial-war-crimes-law/a-899778 [https://perma.cc/Y85W-D67L].
17 *See* Brian Kenety, *RIGHTS: Israelis File Complaint Against Arafat, Palestinians in Belgium*, INTER PRESS SERV.
(Nov. 28, 2001), http://www.ipsnews.net/2001/11/rights-israelis-file-complaint-against-arafat-palestinians-in-belgium/ [https://perma.cc/PCF4-CGPU].
18 *Id.*
19 *Id.*
20 *Id.*
21 Richard Bernstein, *Belgium Rethinks Its Prosecutorial Zeal*, N.Y. TIMES (Apr. 1, 2003), https://www.nytimes.com/2003/04/01/world/belgium-rethinks-its-prosecutorial-zeal.html?pagewanted=all [https://perma.cc/7SNW-XT72].
22 *Belgium: Universal Jurisdiction Law Repealed*, HUM. RTS. WATCH (Aug. 1, 2003, 8:00 PM), https://www.hrw.org/news/2003/08/02/belgium-universal-jurisdiction-law-repealed [https://perma.cc/5B6Q-2AFX].
23 *See, e.g.*, Malvina Halberstam, *Belgium's Universal Jurisdiction Law: Vindication of International Justice or Pursuit of Politics?*, 25 CARDOZO L. REV. 247, 251 (2003).
24 *China dismisses as Absurd Spanish Arrest Warrants over Tibet*, REUTERS, https://www.reuters.com/article/uk-china-tibet-spain/china-dismisses-as-absurd-spanish-arrest-warrants-over-tibet-idUKBRE9AJ06420131120 (Nov. 19, 2013, 10:46 PM) [https://perma.cc/565R-UK6M].
25 *Id.*
26 Soeren Kern, *Spain Rethinks Universal Jurisdiction*, GATESTONE INST. (Jan. 31, 2014, 5:00 AM), https://www.gatestoneinstitute.org/4149/spain-universal-jurisdiction [https://perma.cc/3CXB-HERW].
27 *Spain Amends Law to Abolish Court's Universal Justice Power*, TIBETAN REV. (May 21, 2014), https://www.tibetanreview.net/spain-amends-law-to-abolish-courts-universal-justice-power/ [https://perma.cc/95P9-TZAX].
28 *See, e.g.*, Maximo Langer, *Universal Jurisdiction is not Disappearing: The Shift from 'Global Enforcer' to 'No Safe Haven' Universal Jurisdiction*, 13 J. INT'L CRIM. JUST. 245, 247 (2015) at 5 (defining "low-cost" defendants).
29 Maximo Langer, *Universal Jurisdiction is not Disappearing: The Shift from 'Global Enforcer' to 'No Safe Haven' Universal Jurisdiction*, 13 J. INT'L CRIM. JUST. 245, 247 (2015) at 7 (defining "low-cost" defendants).
30 *Id.* at 7, 28.

31 Maximo Langer & Mackenzie Eason, *The Quiet Expansion of Universal Jurisdiction*, 30 EUR. J. INT'L L. 779, 782 – 788 (2019).
32 David Connett et al., *Pinochet Arrested in London*, THE GUARDIAN (Oct. 17, 1998, 8:29 PM), https://www.theguardian.com/world/1998/oct/18/pinochet.chile [https://perma.cc/UL8U-D24B].
33 *See Belgium Begins Pinochet Challenge*, BBC NEWS (Jan. 25, 2000, 2:27 PM), http://news.bbc.co.uk/2/hi/uk_news/politics/618166.stm [https://perma.cc/8VQ5-288Q].
34 *See* Maximo Langer, *Universal Jurisdiction is not Disappearing: The Shift from 'Global Enforcer' to 'No Safe Haven' Universal Jurisdiction*, 13 J. INT'L CRIM. JUST. 245, 247 (2015) at 36 (defining "low-cost" defendants).
35 SYRIA JUST. AND ACCOUNTABILITY CTR., A GUIDE TO NATIONAL PROSECUTIONS IN THE NETHERLANDS FOR CRIMES COMMITTED IN SYRIA 2 (2020).
36 *See* Amnesty Int'l, *Universal Jurisdiction: A Preliminary Survey of Legislation Around the World – 2012 Updated*, AI Index IOR 53/019/2012, at 110 (Oct. 2012) (detailing Switzerland's universal jurisdiction provisions over serious international crimes).
37 *See, e.g.*, Maximo Langer & Mackenzie Eason, *The Quiet Expansion of Universal Jurisdiction*, 30 EUR. J. INT'L L. 779, 782 (2019); David Mandel-Anthony, *Hardwiring Accountability for Mass Atrocities*, 11 DREXEL L. REV. 903, 940 (2019).
38 *Universal Jurisdiction in Europe: The State of the Art*, HUM. RTS. WATCH 5 (June 27, 2006), https://www.hrw.org/report/2006/06/27/universal-jurisdiction-europe/state-art [hereinafter HRW UJ in Europe].
39 *See, e.g.*, Katalin Ligeti, Balázs Garamvölgyi, Anna Ondrejová, and Margarete von Galen, *Admissibility of Evidence in Criminal Proceedings in the EU*, in The European Criminal Law Associations' Forum, *The Future of EU Criminal Justice – Expert Perspectives* at 201 (2020).
40 *See* Lauren Baillee, *How to Achieve Accountability for Atrocities in Ukraine*, U.S. INST. PEACE (Apr. 21, 2022), https://www.usip.org/publications/2022/04/how-achieve-accountability-atrocities-ukraine [https://perma.cc/QRZ5-RR56].
41 *Universal Jurisdiction in Europe: The State of the Art*, HUM. RTS. WATCH 5 (June 27, 2006), at 19–20, https://www.hrw.org/report/2006/06/27/universal-jurisdiction-europe/state-art (explaining problems Belgian authorities faced in protecting Rwandan witnesses who traveled to Belgium to testify against alleged Rwandan genocidaires).
42 *Id.* at 6.
43 Leila Nadya Sadat, *Heads of State and Other Government Officials Before the International Criminal Court: The Uneasy Revolution Continues*, *in* THE ELGAR COMPANION TO THE INTERNATIONAL CRIMINAL COURT 96, 96–127 (Margaret DeGuzman & Valerie Oosterveld, eds., 2020).
44 Reuters, *Russia Threatens to Stop Exporting Energy to Europe; Ukraine Claims Advances in the East*, THE ECON. TIMES, https://economictimes.indiatimes.com/news/international/business/russia-threatens-to-stop-exporting-energy-to-europe-ukraine-claims-advances-in-the-east/articleshow/94067762.cms (Sept. 8, 2022, 11:57 AM) [https://perma.cc/RW2W-G4A3].
45 Teele Rebane et al., *Putin Threatens to Restrict Ukrainian Grain Exports for European Countries, Accusing Them of Acting 'Like Colonial Powers'*, CNN, https://www.cnn.com/2022/09/07/europe/russia-ukraine-grain-ports-intl (Sept. 18, 2022, 10:18 PM) [https://perma.cc/248P-GHTP].
46 *See, e.g.*, Jacob Geanous, *Putin threatens preemptive nuclear strike as war drags on*, The New York Post (May 17, 2023), https://nypost.com/2022/12/10/putin-threatens-preemptive-nuclear-strike-as-war-drags-on/; Guy Faulconbridge,

Russia's Putin issues new nuclear warnings to West over Ukraine, Reuters (Feb. 21, 2023), https://www.reuters.com/world/putin-update-russias-elite-ukraine-war-major-speech-2023-02-21/.

47 *See* Ali Abbas Ahmadi, *Putin vows to 'intensify' attacks against Ukraine military targets*, BBC (Jan. 1, 2024), https://www.bbc.com/news/world-67858038.

48 *See* Helena Cobban, *The Legacies of Collective Violence*, Bos. Rev. (Apr. 1, 2002), https://www.bostonreview.net/articles/helena-cobban-legacies-collective-violence/ [https://perma.cc/CEB8-MAHA].

49 *See, e.g.*, Cathrin Schaer, Germany's ongoing identity crisis on Syria, DW, (March 14, 2021), https://www.dw.com/en/germany-identity-crisis-syria/a-56805301.

50 Arrest Warrant of 11 April 2000 (Dem. Rep. Congo v. Belg.), Judgment, 2002 I.C.J. 3, ¶¶ 13, 17 (Feb. 14, 2002).

51 *See* Maximo Langer, *Universal Jurisdiction is not Disappearing: The Shift from 'Global Enforcer' to 'No Safe Haven' Universal Jurisdiction*, 13 J. Int'l Crim. Just. 245, 247 (2015) at 25 (defining "low-cost" defendants). The Court distinguished the application of the immunity defense in national and international courts, recognizing that the defense of head of state immunity would not likely be available in international courts. *Id.* ¶¶ 52, 54, 70, 76–77.

52 *See Universal Jurisdiction in Europe: The State of the Art*, Hum. Rts. Watch (June 27, 2006), https://www.hrw.org/report/2006/06/27/universal-jurisdiction-europe/state-art.

53 *Id.*

54 Open Society Justice Initiative and Trial International, Briefing Paper, *Universal Jurisdiction Law and Practice in Sweden*, at 12 (Apr. 2020) [hereinafter Sweden UJ Briefing Paper]; Open Society Justice Initiative and Trial International, Briefing Paper, *Universal Jurisdiction Law and Practice in Germany*, at 17 (Apr. 2019) [hereinafter Germany UJ Briefing Paper].

55 *See* Wolfgang Kaleck & Patrick Kroker, *Syrian Torture Investigations in Germany and Beyond*, 16 J. Int'l Crim. Just. 165, 179 (2018).

56 *See* Open Society Justice Initiative and Trial International, Briefing Paper, *Universal Jurisdiction Law and Practice in Germany*, at 17 (Apr. 2019).

57 Open Society Justice Initiative and Trial International, Briefing Paper, *Universal Jurisdiction Law and Practice in Sweden*, at 13 (Apr. 2020).

58 *See* Open Society Justice Initiative and Trial International, Briefing Paper, *Universal Jurisdiction Law and Practice in Germany*, at 16 (Apr. 2019); Open Society Justice Initiative and Trial International, Briefing Paper, *Universal Jurisdiction Law and Practice in Sweden*, at 13 (Apr. 2020).

59 *Id.* (explaining the competence of German and Swedish authorities to prosecute serious international crimes committed in Syria).

60 Human Rights Watch, *"These are the Crimes We are Fleeing": Justice for Syria in Swedish and German Courts*, Human Rts. Watch (Oct. 3, 2017), https://www.hrw.org/report/2017/10/04/these-are-crimes-we-are-fleeing/justice-syria-swedish-and-german-courts [https://perma.cc/93SU-6RAU] [hereinafter HRW Justice for Syria].

61 *See* Brianne McGonigle Leyh, *Ukraine Symposium-Documentation and Investigation Responses to Serious International Crimes*, Lieber Inst. W. Point (July 13, 2022), https://lieber.westpoint.edu/documentation-investigation-responses-serious-international-crimes [https://perma.cc/W5UZ-P547] [hereinafter McGonigle Leyh Ukraine Symposium].

62 *See* Human Rights Watch, *"These are the Crimes We are Fleeing": Justice for Syria in Swedish and German Courts*, Human Rts. Watch (Oct. 3, 2017), https://www.hrw.org/report/2017/10/04/these-are-crimes-we-are-fleeing/justice-syria-swedish-and-german-courts [https://perma.cc/93SU-6RAU].

63 *See, e.g.*, Mark Kersten, *Universal Jurisdiction in Ukraine: States Should Commit to Using Their Own Courts to Address Russian Atrocities*, JUST. CONFLICT (Oct. 17, 2022), https://justiceinconflict.org/2022/10/17/universal-jurisdiction-in-ukraine-states-should-commit-to-using-their-own-courts-to-address-russian-atrocities/ [https://perma.cc/A8MJ-WE7S]; Anya Neistat, *Victims of War Crimes in Ukraine Have an Unprecedented Chance to Seek Justice*, THE GUARDIAN (July 24, 2022), https://www.theguardian.com/commentisfree/2022/jul/24/war-crimes-ukraine-investigations-justice [https://perma.cc/Z6WC-5DVZ].

64 *See Independent International Commission of Inquiry on Ukraine*, U.N. HUM. RTS. COUNCIL, https://www.ohchr.org/en/hr-bodies/hrc/iicihr-ukraine/index [https://perma.cc/DU3Y-WX3U].

65 *See* Human Rights Council Res. 49/1, U.N. Doc A/HRC/RES/49/1, at para. 11.

66 *See* Hum. Rts. Council, Indep. Int'l Comm'n on Ukraine, Rep. of the Independent International Commission of Inquiry on Ukraine, U.N. Doc. A/HRC/52/62 (2023) [hereinafter March 2023 Ukraine COI Report].

67 *See* Hum. Rts. Council, Indep. Int'l Comm'n on Ukraine, Rep. of the Independent International Commission of Inquiry on Ukraine, U.N. Doc. A/HRC/52/62 (2023).

68 *See* Press Release, U.S. Dep't of State, *Moscow Mechanism Invoked by 45 OSCE States To Review Reported Abuses by Russia* (Mar. 3, 2022), https://www.state.gov/moscow-mechanism-invoked-by-45-osce-states-to-review-reported-abuses-by-russia/ [https://perma.cc/3G7M-H66V] [hereinafter US Moscow Mechanism March 2022 Press Release]. Adopted in 1991, the Moscow Mechanism "provides the option of sending missions of experts to assist participating States in the resolution of a particular question or problem relating to the human dimension." *See Moscow Mechanism*, OSCE. (Dec. 1, 1991), https://www.osce.org/odihr/20066 [https://perma.cc/B2AT-D38W].

69 *See* Press Release, U.S. Dep't of State, *Moscow Mechanism Invoked by 45 OSCE States To Review Reported Abuses by Russia* (Mar. 3, 2022), https://www.state.gov/moscow-mechanism-invoked-by-45-osce-states-to-review-reported-abuses-by-russia/ [https://perma.cc/3G7M-H66V].

70 Press Release, Joint Statement on the Invocation of the Moscow Mechanism to Address the Forced Transfer and Deportation of Children by the Russian Federation, U.S. Mission to the OSCE (March 30, 2023), https://osce.usmission.gov/joint-statement-on-the-invocation-of-the-moscow-mechanism-to-address-the-forced-transfer-and-deportation-of-children-by-the-russian-federation/ [https://perma.cc/54C5-6VYG] [hereinafter US Mission March 2023 Press Release].

71 *See id.*

72 *See, e.g.*, WOLFGANG BENEDEK, VERONIKA BÍLKOVÁ, & MARCO SASSÒLI, OSCE, REPORT ON VIOLATIONS OF INTERNATIONAL HUMANITARIAN AND HUMAN RIGHTS LAW, WAR CRIMES AND CRIMES AGAINST HUMANITY COMMITTED IN UKRAINE SINCE 24 FEBRUARY 2022, OSCE (2022); VERONIKA BÍLKOVÁ, LAURA GUERCIO, & VASILKA SANCIN, OSCE, REPORT ON VIOLATIONS OF INTERNATIONAL HUMANITARIAN AND HUMAN RIGHTS LAW, WAR CRIMES AND CRIMES AGAINST HUMANITY COMMITTED IN UKRAINE (1 APRIL – 25 JUNE 2022); VERONIKA BILKOVA, CECILIE HELLESTVEIT & ELĪNA ŠTEINERTE, OSCE, REPORT ON VIOLATIONS AND ABUSES OF INTERNATIONAL HUMANITARIAN AND HUMAN RIGHTS LAW, WAR CRIMES AND CRIMES AGAINST HUMANITY, RELATED TO THE FORCIBLE TRANSFER AND/OR DEPORTATION OF UKRAINIAN CHILDREN TO THE RUSSIAN FEDERATION (2023).

73 Based in The Hague, Eurojust is the European Union Agency for Criminal Justice Cooperation.

74 *See Joint Investigation Teams*, EUROJUST, https://www.eurojust.europa.eu/judicial-cooperation/instruments/joint-investigation-teams [https://perma.cc/MW4R-YRUF].

75 *See, e.g.*, Michele Caianiello, *The Role of the EU in the Investigation of Serious International Crimes Committed in Ukraine. Towards a New Model of Cooperation?*, 30 EUR. J. CRIME, CRIM. L. & CRIM. JUST. 219, 228–29 (2022).

76 *Id.*

77 *See* EUROJUST, CORE INTERNATIONAL CRIMES EVIDENCE DATABASE (CICED) (2023), https://www.eurojust.europa.eu/publication/core-international-crimes-evidence-database-ciced [https://perma.cc/4QVL-L8Y4].

78 *See, e.g.*, Balkan Insight, *As War Grinds On In Ukraine, Investigators Doggedly Track Crimes — Analysis*, EURASIAREVIEW (Jan. 4, 2023), https://www.eurasiareview.com/04012023-as-war-grinds-on-in-ukraine-investigators-doggedly-track-crimes-analysis/ [https://perma.cc/MXR5-7CUL].

79 *See* HUM. RTS. CENTER, U.C. BERKELEY SCH. L., BERKELEY PROTOCOL ON DIGITAL OPEN SOURCE INVESTIGATIONS (2022), https://www.ohchr.org/sites/default/files/2022-04/OHCHR_BerkeleyProtocol.pdf, at 3 (describing open source digital information).

80 *See* Office of the Prosecutor, Press Release: ICC Prosecutor and Eurojust launch practical guidelines for documenting and preserving information on international crimes, Sept. 21, 2022, at 5–6, https://www.icc-cpi.int/news/icc-prosecutor-and-eurojust-launch-practical-guidelines-documenting-and-preserving-information.; *see also* HUM. RTS. CENTER, U.C. BERKELEY SCH. L., BERKELEY PROTOCOL ON DIGITAL OPEN SOURCE INVESTIGATIONS (2022), https://www.ohchr.org/sites/default/files/2022-04/OHCHR_BerkeleyProtocol.pdf, at 3 (explaining that open source digital information "comprises both user generated and machine-generated data, and may include, for example: content posted on social media; documents, images, videos and audio recordings on websites and information sharing platforms; satellite imagery; and government-published data").

81 *See* Joanna York, *'Accountability and Justice': Gathering Digital Evidence of War Crimes in Ukraine*, FRANCE 24 (Feb. 28, 2023), https://www.france24.com/en/europe/20230228-accountability-and-justice-gathering-digital-evidence-of-war-crimes-in-ukraine [https://perma.cc/R9VN-6Y4L]. Mnemonic also archives digital information relevant to human rights abuses committed in Syria, Sudan, and Yemen.

82 Wolfgang Kaleck & Patrick Kroker, *Syrian Torture Investigations in Germany and Beyond*, 16 J. INT'L CRIM. JUST. 165, 170 (2018).

83 Brianne McGonigle Leyh, *Ukraine Symposium – Documentation and Investigation Responses to Serious International Crimes*, LIEBER INST. W. POINT (July 13, 2022), https://lieber.westpoint.edu/documentation-investigation-responses-serious-international-crimes [https://perma.cc/W5UZ-P547].

84 *See, e.g.*, Lauren Wolfe, *Ukraine's True Detectives: The Investigators Closing in on Russian War Criminals*, GUARDIAN (Oct. 20, 2022), https://www.theguardian.com/world/2022/oct/20/ukraine-true-detectives-investigators-closing-in-on-russian-war-crimes [https://perma.cc/62AA-433H].

85 *See Lithuanian Prosecutors to Probe Filmmaker's Killing in Ukraine as War Crime*, LRT (Apr. 5, 2022), https://www.lrt.lt/en/news-in-english/19/1662906/lithuanian-prosecutors-to-probe-filmmaker-s-killing-in-ukraine-as-war-crime [https://perma.cc/64D3-9MXL].

86 *France Launches War Crime Investigation After Reporter Arman Soldin Killed in Ukraine*, CBS NEWS (May 10, 2023), https://www.cbsnews.com/news/arman

-soldin-reporter-killed-ukraine-france-war-crime-investigation/ [https://perma.cc/GW2X-65SE].

87 *See* Tassilo Hummel, *France Opens War Crime Investigation After AFP Journalist Died in Ukraine*, REUTERS (May 10, 2023), https://www.reuters.com/world/europe/france-opens-war-crime-investigation-after-afp-journalist-died-ukraine-2023-05-10/ [https://perma.cc/KJ57-L4LL].

88 *How Universal Jurisdiction Can Punish Putin and His Minions for War Crimes in Ukraine*, EUR. PRAVDA (June 6, 2022), https://www.eurointegration.com.ua/eng/news/2022/06/6/7140690/ [https://perma.cc/98BF-X9BW].

89 Devlin Barrett and Perry Stein, *U.S. files its first war-crimes charges related to Russia-Ukraine war*, Washington Post (Dec. 6, 2023).

90 *See Dominic Raab, Evaluating the ICTY and its Completion Strategy, 3* J. INT'L CRIM. JUSTICE 82, 88 (2005).

91 *See* Yvonne Dutton and Milena Sterio, *The War in Ukraine and the Legitimacy of the International Criminal Court*, 72 AMERICAN U. L. REV. 779, 789–794 (2023).

92 *See* Simon Shuster, *'Nobody Believes in Our Victory Like I Do.' Inside Volodymyr Zelensky's Struggle to Keep Ukraine in the Fight*, TIME (Nov. 1, 2023).

93 NOHA ABOUELDAHAB, Writing Atrocities: Syrian Civil Society and Transitional Justice, BROOKINGS INST. (MAY 2018) AT 1, HTTPS://WWW.BROOKINGS.EDU/WP-CONTENT/UPLOADS/2018/04/TRANSITIONAL-JUSTICE-ENGLISH _ WEB.PDF.

94 *See* Brianne McGonigle Leyh, *Ukraine Symposium – Documentation and Investigation Responses to Serious International Crimes*, LIEBER INST. W. POINT (July 13, 2022), at 369, https://lieber.westpoint.edu/documentation-investigation-responses-serious-international-crimes [https://perma.cc/W5UZ-P547].

9

PROSECUTING ENVIRONMENTAL CRIMES IN UKRAINE AS EITHER WAR CRIMES OR ECOCIDE

By Michael J. Kelly

Introduction

Environmental crime is emerging as a distinct focus of accountability simultaneously in The Hague, at the International Criminal Court (ICC), and in Kyiv as Ukrainian prosecutors seek to hold Russian perpetrators accountable for the environmental devastation they have wrought in their aggressive war on Ukraine—from blowing up the Kakhovka Dam to burning forests, polluting river ways, and killing Black Sea dolphins. In February 2024, the ICC issued a call for commentary on the Court's ability to define, investigate, and prosecute environmental crimes as crimes within its jurisdiction under the Rome Statute. Prosecutor Karim Khan stated, "Damage to the environment poses an existential threat to all life on the planet. For that reason, I am firmly committed to ensuring that my Office systematically addresses environmental crimes in all stages of its work, from preliminary examinations to prosecutions."[1] In 2023, Ukrainian prosecutors began training in Washington D.C. with the U.S. Department of Justice to learn how to investigate environmental crimes committed during the war.[2]

In October 2024, as these investigations began to coalesce into triable evidence, I joined a Public International Law and Policy Group (PILPG) team, consisting of Paul R. Williams, Michael P. Scharf, Milena Sterio, and Meg deGuzman, on the Polish border with Ukraine training Ukrainian regional and national prosecutors as well as Supreme Court judges on how to bring those cases to trial at the national level in Ukraine. Internationally, such crimes could be identified as modalities of commission for crimes against humanity[3] or war crimes, or possibly aggression.[4] The Rome Statute does not have a separate provision for ecocide, although an effort to amend it in this

DOI: 10.4324/9781003458166-11

way was proffered at the 2024 Assembly of States Parties.[5] Ecocide has been defined at the international level as "unlawful or wanton acts committed with knowledge that there is substantial likelihood of severe and either widespread or long-term damage to the environment."[6]

Consequently, there is both broad and growing agreement internationally and within Ukraine that environmental crime should be prosecuted. The next question is how to do so. In Ukraine, environmental crime can be prosecuted either as a form of war crime or as ecocide. This is not a "Hobson's choice." Either path is open, albeit with attendant pros and cons. Chiefly, on the war crimes side, very strong defenses grounded in military necessity must be overcome. On the ecocide side, inexperience with this type of prosecution coupled with high hurdles under Ukrainian law to prove causation must be overcome. Either way, however, Ukraine stands poised to make a lasting contribution to this important legal conversation.

This chapter focuses on domestic accountability before Ukrainian courts. However, because of certain provisions within the Ukrainian constitution and within the Criminal Code itself, one cannot adequately discuss prosecution under Ukrainian law without also discussing international law because the former specifically implicates the latter. The Ukrainian Constitution provides:

> Article 9: International treaties that are in force, agreed to be binding by the Verkhovna Rada of Ukraine, are part of the national legislation of Ukraine.
>
> Article 18: The foreign political activity of Ukraine is aimed at ensuring its national interests and security by maintaining peaceful and mutually beneficial cooperation with members of the international community, according to generally acknowledged principles and norms of international law.[7]

Thus, Article 9 makes international law part of Ukrainian law, and Article 18 mandates that Ukraine adhere to internationally recognized principles and norms, which include obligations under international humanitarian law. International treaties that have been ratified have a higher status than ordinary national laws. However, they are still subject to the Constitution of Ukraine. If a treaty conflicts with national legislation, the provisions of the Constitution will prevail, unless the treaty provides for a higher level of protection of human rights (hierarchy of norms). This is enshrined in Article 8 of the Ukrainian Constitution:

> Article 8: In Ukraine, the principle of the rule of law is recognized and effective. The Constitution of Ukraine has the highest legal force. Laws and other normative legal acts are adopted on the basis of the Constitution of Ukraine and shall conform to it. The norms of the Constitution of

> Ukraine are norms of direct effect. Appeals to the court in defense of the constitutional rights and freedoms of the individual and citizen directly on the grounds of the Constitution of Ukraine are guaranteed.[8]

Consequently, as the two are intertwined for the purposes of Ukraine deciding between prosecuting Russian defendants on the basis of environmental crime as a species of war crime or prosecuting them on the basis of ecocide, the discussion must include international legal touchpoints. Importantly, however, either path Ukraine elects will be precedent-setting. Environmental crime has not been prosecuted as such on the international level and only very rarely in domestic jurisdictions. Ecocide has not been prosecuted at all. Although the *in absentia* nature of many of the prosecutions Ukraine is planning to undertake could be seen to dampen the impact of what Ukraine can contribute to the legal conversation, it must be recalled that such proceedings are far more widely accepted in civil law jurisdictions and also echo historically on the international level. After the Second World War, France prosecuted Klaus Barbie in absentia for his role as the "Butcher of Lyon" killing, rounding up, and deporting French Jews during the Holocaust,[9] and Martin Borman was prosecuted *in absentia* before the International Military Tribunal for Nuremberg for his role during the war in the Nazi high command.[10]

Environmental Destruction as a War Crime

With respect to utilizing the war crimes provision, the Ukrainian Criminal Code provides for prosecution under Article 438:

> Article 438. Violation of the Laws and Customs of War
>
> 1. Cruel treatment of prisoners of war or civilians, expulsion of civilians for forced labour, looting of national property in the occupied territory, use of means of warfare prohibited by international law, other violations of the laws and customs of war stipulated by international treaties ratified by the Verkhovna Rada of Ukraine, as well as ordering such actions shall be punishable by imprisonment for a term of eight to twelve years.
>
> 2. The same acts, if combined with premeditated murder shall be punishable by imprisonment for a term of ten to fifteen years or life imprisonment.[11]

Article 438 thus incorporates treaties by reference. In 2024, Ukraine became a State Party to the Rome Statute, thereby triggering those provisions and incorporating them into Article 438. Why are these international instruments important for domestic prosecution? A key problem with the judicial interpretation and application of Article 438 of the Ukrainian Criminal Code is the blanket nature of the provision, which creates difficulties and might have negative consequences when put in practice.[12] For example, Article 438 refers to the use of means of warfare prohibited by international law but does not contain the list of such means. Therefore, it is necessary to refer to international acts ratified by the Parliament of Ukraine to understand which means of warfare are prohibited by international law and to cross reference these with international law.[13] Additionally, it is also necessary to determine which violations of these international treaties can be considered criminal offenses within the meaning of Article 438 of the CCU and identify auxiliary sources for the systematic interpretation of the provisions of the article, namely the practice of international courts.

Following is a list of treaties to which Ukraine is a party that the ICC Prosecutor could use as a basis for establishing a rule that was violated by a perpetrator in the commission of an environmental crime that renders such perpetrator criminally liable if direct intent and causation can be established. Such an interpretation could then be transposed into Ukraine by a Ukrainian judge for use within Ukraine's judicial system.

Rome Statute of the International Criminal Court (ICC)

- Article 8(2)(b)(iv) of the Rome Statute: "Intentionally launching an attack in the knowledge that such attack will cause incidental loss of life or injury to civilians or damage to civilian objects or widespread, long-term and severe damage to the natural environment which would be clearly excessive in relation to the concrete and direct overall military advantage anticipated."
- Article 8(2)(b)(ii) of the Rome Statute: "Intentionally directing attacks against civilian objects, that is, objects which are not military objectives."
- Ukraine ratified the Rome Statute in August 2024.

1949 Geneva Conventions

- These conventions form the core of international humanitarian law (IHL), setting out the legal standards for the humanitarian treatment of individuals during armed conflicts.
- Article 35 (3) Additional Protocol I to the Geneva Conventions: In any armed conflict, the right of the Parties to the conflict to choose methods or means of warfare is not unlimited. It is prohibited to employ weapons, projectiles, and material and methods of warfare of a nature to cause superfluous injury or unnecessary suffering. It is prohibited to employ methods or means of warfare which are intended, or may be expected, to cause widespread, long-term and severe damage to the natural environment.

- Article 55 Additional Protocol I to the Geneva Conventions: Care shall be taken in warfare to protect the natural environment against widespread, long-term and severe damage. This protection includes a prohibition of the use of methods or means of warfare which are intended or may be expected to cause such damage to the natural environment and thereby to prejudice the health or survival of the population. Attacks against the natural environment by way of reprisals are prohibited.
- Ukraine is a state party to all four Geneva Conventions of 1949.

1977 Additional Protocols to the Geneva Conventions

- These additional protocols reinforce and add protection to victims in international armed conflict (AP I) and non-international armed conflict (AP II).
- Ukraine is a state party to both Additional Protocols.

Hague Regulations

- The Hague Regulations refer to the Regulations concerning the Laws and Customs of War on Land, which are annexed to the Hague Conventions of 1899 and 1907. These regulations form a key part of international humanitarian law (IHL), establishing rules on the conduct of hostilities, the protection of civilians, and the treatment of property during armed conflicts.
- Ukraine is bound by the Hague Regulations as part of the Hague Conventions of 1907, which are considered part of customary international law.

Convention on the Prohibition of Military or Any Other Hostile Use of Environmental Modification Techniques (ENMOD)

- The purpose of the ENMOD Convention is to prevent the use of environmental modification techniques for hostile purposes that could cause widespread, long-lasting, or severe damage to the environment as a means of warfare.
- Ukraine (when part of the USSR) ratified the ENMOD in 1978.

Convention on Biological Diversity (CBD)

- While not primarily a criminal law instrument, the CBD obligates states to protect biodiversity, and violations could potentially be interpreted as criminal in nature, particularly in the context of state responsibility.
- Ukraine ratified the CBD in 1995.

United Nations Framework Convention on Climate Change (UNFCCC) and Paris Agreement

- These treaties aim to combat climate change and could inform obligations regarding the prevention of environmental harm. While they do not directly create criminal liabilities, they establish standards and responsibilities that could be enforced through domestic legal frameworks.
- Ukraine ratified the UNFCCC and Paris Agreement in 2016.

Military Necessity Defense

One of the main drawbacks to mounting a prosecution for environmental crimes as a form of war crime is that the defendant may raise a military necessity defense. This is a potent defense that can stymie a successful prosecution if well grounded in particular battlefield facts and if the decision of the commander to undertake the attack that resulted in the environmental destruction is deemed reasonable. ICC jurisprudence considers that the destruction of an enemy's property to be justified if "it was required for the attainment of a military purpose and otherwise in conformity with IHL."[14] The destruction and seizure of an enemy's property are allowed so long as such measures are necessary to accomplish a legitimate military purpose, which can only be "to weaken the military capacity of the adversary."[15] The standard of necessity required is considered as "quite high."[16] For example, the measure consisting of clearing a section of trees to set up a camp on the only safe location—which would be on top of a forested hill—could be considered as necessary.[17] Necessity is often regarded as what the commander in the field assessed the case to be—which is a much more subjective determination than, say, what the commander back at headquarters might more objectively consider to be necessary.

One way to blunt this defense is to demonstrate that the Russian commander, when ordering direct or foreseeing indirect disproportionate environmental destruction in furtherance of achieving a valid military objective, knew that the destruction would occur in an environmentally protected area.

Elemental Analysis of Rome Statute Article 8(2)(b)(iv)

This provision requires that the conduct took place in the context of and was associated with an international armed conflict and the perpetrator was aware of the factual circumstances that established the existence of an armed conflict. The perpetrator then launched an attack, and the attack was such that it would cause widespread, long-term, and severe damage to the natural environment. The damage would be of such an extent as to be clearly excessive in relation to the concrete and direct overall military advantage anticipated, and the perpetrator knew that the attack would cause widespread, long-term, and severe damage to the natural environment.

How do these elements work together?

Nexus with international armed conflict

"Armed conflict" and "international armed conflict" are not defined in the Rome Statute or the ICC's Elements of Crimes. Consequently, the principles and rules of international law apply. According to conventional and customary international humanitarian law, international armed conflict relates to any armed conflict between two or more states, cases of military occupation of all or part of the territory of the state, as well as wars of national liberation.[18] The acts that destroy the environment must be in connection with the armed conflict—a purely private act unrelated to an armed conflict cannot be prosecuted even if an armed conflict is going on at the same time, unless there is some connection.

The perpetrator "launched an attack"

The Rome Statute and Elements do not define the term "attack." The International Committee of the Red Cross (ICRC) definition,[19] adopted in the Additional Protocol I,[20] by *ad hoc* tribunals, and by the ICC is that "attacks" are acts of violence against the adversary, whether in offense or in defense.[21] Again, this element should be relatively easy to meet in most cases, assuming the acts that cause destruction of the environment can be viewed as "violence." A defendant, however, may concede on the one hand that an attack occurred, but may contest that the attack was directed at the aspect of the environment which was damaged and which gave rise to the environmental crime charge. Such a defendant could claim unintentionality or unforeseeability to try to dampen this charge. In such a scenario, even the "violence" could be conceded without undermining a defendant's position.

The "attack" must cause . . . "widespread, long-term and severe damage to the natural environment."

The act of causing damage to the natural environment constitutes a war crime even if such environmental damage does not directly harm other human interests.[22] Second, the environment need not be the object of attack—the primary object could be anything (e.g. civilian objects, civilian population, enemy's forces etc.). What matters is that the actions cause collateral damage to the natural environment.

All three elements, widespread, long-term, and severe, are required if the damage assessment is going to form the basis of the charge. But there is some conceptual overlap. For example, the idea of "severe" may include aspects of the spread of harm and the long-term consequences. Again, the Rome Statute and the ICC's Elements of Crimes do not define these concepts. Under article 21 of the Rome Statute, recourse must be had to applicable treaties and the principles and rules of international law, including the established principles of the international law of armed conflict. According to the *travaux preparatoires* of the Additional Protocol I, for instance, the concept of long term seems to have meant lasting decades. This is quite a high standard. In a 1993 Report to the UN General Assembly the ICRC noted:

The question as to what constitutes "widespread, long-term and severe" damage and what is acceptable damage to the environment is open to interpretation. There are substantial grounds, including from the *travaux preparatoires* of Protocol I, for interpreting "long-term" to refer to decades rather than months. On the other hand, it is not easy to know in advance exactly what the scope and duration of some environmentally damaging acts will be.[23]

Under the Convention on the Prohibition of Military or Any Other Hostile Use of Environmental Modification Techniques (ENMOD), the term is long-lasting rather than long-term and it is interpreted to mean lasting for a period of months, or approximately a season. So (i) "widespread" could be encompassing an area on the scale of several hundred square kilometers and (iii) "severe" could involve serious or significant disruption or harm to human life, natural, and economic resources or other assets.[24]

In sum, there is no settled understanding of these terms, so the precedents of Ukraine's courts will be important in the world's understanding of what constitutes widespread, long-term, and severe damage to the natural environment. Consequently, Ukrainian judges should frame their judgments, accordingly, taking into account at least the following:

(1) Terms should be interpreted taking into account how environmental damage affects a particular area, for instance, due to its unique biological environment and community; courts should consider both direct and indirect damage (effects beyond the concrete geographical area where the attack took place). For example, during the Vietnam war, millions of displaced people fled their villages into jungles when American military attacks came. They then cut down surrounding jungles to make new villages, impacting the environment and the biodiversity therein that they were forced into habitating.
(2) Consider the interdependency of the natural environment, as damage to one component (or "part") can have immediate, lasting or deferred effects on other components.

(3) Separate events of damage (series of events) of the same kind (taking place in parallel or during some period of time within the same armed conflict) may be considered as one "continuous" war crime.

Damage must be clearly excessive in relation to the concrete and direct overall military advantage anticipated

"Clearly excessive" is not defined in the Rome Statute or the Elements of Crimes. Inclusion of the descriptor "clearly" suggests an intention to set a high threshold.[25] In 2000, a committee established by the ICTY prosecutor to examine NATO's bombing of Serbian military positions as it was protecting Kosovar refugees fleeing from Serb destruction decided that "clearly" ensures that criminal responsibility only applies in cases where the excessiveness of the incidental damage was obvious.[26]

Clearly excessive in relation to the concrete and direct overall military advantage anticipated

One way to measure "clearly" is to set it off against the military advantage to be gained by taking the destructive action. The Elements of Crimes in footnote 36 sets forth that the expression "concrete and direct overall military advantage" refers to a military advantage that is foreseeable by the perpetrator at the relevant time. This analysis includes a proportionality context.[27] There is considerable debate about how to understand what is excessive (disproportionate). There is also no agreed understanding about what "military advantage" includes. Commentators disagree about whether this concept should be understood in a narrow or expansive way.[28] Another debate relates to how "military advantage" differs from "military necessity."[29] Rulings by international tribunals or Ukrainian courts in hearing environmental crimes cases will most certainly inform future judges, prosecutors, and commentators.

Concreteness and directness are elements that are in somewhat less dispute. The ICRC states that the term "concrete and direct" was used "to indicate that the advantage must be substantial and relatively close, and that advantages which are hardly perceptible and those which would only appear in the long term should be disregarded."[30] Some might consider this interpretation too narrow.

The perpetrator launches an attack "intentionally" and "in the knowledge" that such attack will cause damage to the natural environment

The ICC's Elements of Crimes states that, unless otherwise provided, a person shall be criminally responsible and liable for punishment for a crime only if the material elements are committed with intent and knowledge. A person has intent where: (i) in relation to conduct, that person means to engage in the conduct; (ii) in relation to a consequence, that person means to cause that consequence or is aware that it will occur in the ordinary course of events. Footnote 37 of the Elements of Crimes clarifies that the knowledge element requires that the perpetrator make the value judgment as described therein (as to the consequences of the attack launched). An evaluation of that value judgment must be based on the requisite information available to the perpetrator at the time.[31]

This means the perpetrator should possess the actual or constructive knowledge as to the gravity of the damage to the environment resulting from the attack. A mistake that the conduct is warranted by military necessity could be a defense.[32] In light of this high *mens rea* (which is even higher in your national law) it seems most feasible to prove the mental elements of this war crime in the conduct of a superiors/commander(s) who gave the instructions to his/her subordinates to launch a particular attack. Superiors will generally be more conscious and have more knowledge as to the harmful effects of the specific attack. The Rome Statute states that it applies equally to all persons without any distinction based on official capacity. Thus, from the practical standpoint, it would be reasonable to investigate the conduct of both direct executors of the attack and their superiors who execute the effective control/supervision and/or give the instructions to the respective subordinates to act in the respective manner.

Other Relevant Rome Statute Provisions

The Natural Environment is Protected as a Civilian Object

Intentionally directing attacks against civilian objects, that is, objects which are not military objectives (Article 8(2)(b)(ii))

The definition of civilian objects may be interpreted broadly to encompass natural environment. Military objectives are "limited to those objects which by their nature, location, purpose or use make an effective contribution to military action and whose total or partial destruction, capture or neutralization, in the circumstances ruling at the time, offers a definite military advantage," which will be analyzed below. There is no exhaustive list of civilian objects, or list of military objectives. Given the absence of any additional categories in international humanitarian law, and the "negative" construction used in Article 8(2)(b)(ii) unless the objects are military objectives, they should be regarded as civilian objects. Thus, it appears reasonable to treat the natural environment by default as a civilian object.

Consequently, all components of the natural environment not considered military objectives could fall under the protection of general principles and rules of international humanitarian law, including prohibition of deliberate and/or wanton attacks on civilian objects, principles of distinction, proportionality and precautions. Where the natural environment does not qualify as military objective and therefore qualifies as a civilian object, including for the purposes of Article 8(2)(b)(ii) of the Rome Statute, the general rules affording protection to civilian objects, including any part of the natural environment that is not a military objective, would apply and may, depending on the circumstances, cover damage to the natural environment that has failed to pass the requirements of Article 8(2)(b)(iv).

Therefore, it is reasonable to consider the environment and all its components in its broadest interpretation by default as protected by the international humanitarian law as the civilian object(s) (including, under 1949 Geneva Conventions, Additional Protocols thereto, and customary international humanitarian law) unless they qualify as military objectives.

The Natural Environment is Protected as an Enemy Property

Destroying or seizing the enemy's property unless such destruction or seizure be imperatively demanded by the necessities of war (Article 8(2)(b)(xiii) (international armed conflict);
or Destroying or seizing the property of an adversary unless such destruction or seizure be imperatively demanded by the necessities of the conflict (Article 8(2)(e)(xii)) (non-international armed conflict).

Environmental objects should be protected by the prohibition of destruction or seizure if they are considered as property.[33] Private or public owned environmental property can be either moveable (natural resources, natural goods, such as agricultural goods), or immoveable (forests or fields belonging to individuals or communities). Secondly, the Elements of Crimes provide two conditions related to the property: (i) the property must belong to a hostile party and (ii) the property must be protected from that destruction or seizure under the international law of armed conflict.

On the second condition, the ICC usually considers that international law protects properties that are not "military objectives," i.e. "objects which by their nature, location, purpose or use make an effective contribution to military action and whose total or partial destruction, capture or neutralization, in the circumstances ruling at the time, offers a definite military advantage."[34] The "military advantage" must be definite and cannot be potential or indeterminate.[35] It is assessed from the attacker's perspective.[36]

For example, the following are considered military objectives: "establishments, buildings and positions where enemy combatants, their materiel and armaments are located, and military means of transportation and communication" or "economic targets that effectively support military operations."[37] On the contrary, the following are considered civilian objects, which are therefore not military objectives, "civilian areas (...), dwelling (...), and the natural environment as prima facie civilian objects, provided in the final analysis, they have not become military objectives."[38]

ICC jurisprudence considers that the destruction of an enemy's property to be justified if "it was required for the attainment of a military purpose and otherwise in conformity with IHL."[39] The destruction and seizure of an enemy's property are allowed so long as such measures are necessary to accomplish a legitimate military purpose, which can only be "to weaken the military capacity of the adversary."[40] The standard of necessity required is considered to be "quite high"[41] For example, clearing a section of trees to set up a military camp on the only safe location—which would be on top of a forested hill—could be considered as necessary, but is also environmentally destructive.[42]

The Natural Environment is Protected by the Prohibition of Pillaging

Pillaging a town or place, even when taken by assault (Article 8 (2)(b)(xvi)).

Damage to the environment may qualify as pillaging if there is an appropriation intended for "private or personal use," which can be difficult to demonstrate in practice (except for the case of private exploitation of the environment, including for the benefit of a public authority acting as a private entity).

Pursuant to the Rome Statute, the Court has jurisdiction with respect to war crimes, which include "serious violations of the laws and customs applicable in international armed conflict, within the established framework of international law, namely, any of the following acts: (...) (xvi) pillaging a town or place, even taken by assault."[43] The Elements of Crimes provide for a list of points to be considered for the qualifying acts of pillage as war crimes. These include the following:

- The perpetrator appropriated certain property;
- The perpetrator intended to deprive the owner of the property and to appropriate it for private or personal use;
- The appropriation was without the consent of the owner;
- The conduct took place in the context of, and was associated with, an armed conflict (international and non-international);
- The perpetrator was aware of factual circumstances that established the existence of an armed conflict.

Neither the Rome Statute nor the Elements of Crimes provide any specification regarding the property protected by the prohibition of pillaging. The ICC has ruled that the prohibition of pillaging encompasses (i) private or public goods and (ii) moveable or immoveable goods. The qualification of pillaging has been applied for goods owned by individuals, such as agricultural items (food, livestock, and animals). Considering the broad scope of the notion of "property," the war crime of pillaging could also concern the pillaging of at least the following:

- Privately-owned natural goods: moveable goods, such as resources, agricultural goods, or other natural resources; immovable goods such as fields or forests;
- Moveable or Immovable goods owned by communities;
- Publicly-owned immovable goods: public-owned infrastructures or public-owned natural goods (e.g. national protected areas, national parks).

The property can be determined based on the national rules of the country where alleged pillaging occurs or on "the customary law of the community (i.e. practices on possession, titles and registration)." On the action prohibited as pillaging, first, pillaging must be understood as the "appropriation" of a property. The ICC explained that the term "appropriation" implies that "the enemy's property has come under the control of the perpetrator." The theft of objects belonging to civilians is a classic example of "appropriation." As for immovable goods, the occupation and control of a natural space could be considered as an appropriation. "Appropriation" can take various forms, whether perpetrated by individuals or as "acts of organized or systematic appropriation."

Secondly, "pillaging" also implies the appropriation of a good without the consent of its owner. This lack of consent can be deduced from the fact that the owner has fled or by acts of coercion, which can be established in the event of armed conflict, for example, using force or through threats, intimidation or pressure by the perpetrator.[44] Pursuant to the Elements of Crimes, the perpetrator must have appropriated goods for a "private or personal use." If the Elements of Crimes do not define what should be considered as a "private or personal use," they indicate that appropriation justified by military necessity cannot be qualified as pillaging. The ICC did not provide any clear definition or exhaustive elements regarding the scope of the "private or personal use." In the Bosco Ntaganda case, the ICC analyzed in particular whether the seized goods could be used for military purposes: since vehicles and medical equipment could be used for military purpose, the ICC could not establish the "private or personal use." For other goods (chairs, mattresses, etc.), the ICC considered the fact that such goods did not "serve an inherently military purpose" and that some goods "considered of high quality or value were usually given to the commanders" or could be found at Ntaganda's residence.[45]

In the *Ongwen* case, the ICC considered that the special intent condition ("private or personal use") was met considering that Ongwen gave the instruction to pillage goods and that "the circumstances of the appropriation do not allow for consideration of military necessity as a justification."[46] Regarding "military necessity," explanatory elements have been provided by the ICC with regard to the war crime of destruction of enemy property: the ICC referred to the definition set by Article 14 of the Lieber Code of 24 April 1863: "Military necessity . . . consists in the necessity of those measures which are indispensable for securing the ends of the war, and which are lawful according to the modern law and usages of war." In the light of the above, "private or personal use" may be assessed on the basis of the type of goods involved, as well their potential use as military items or for a military purpose.[47] In addition, the criterion of "private or personal use" is not required by other international norms applicable to pillaging and could therefore be considered as excessively restrictive.

As a result, to determine whether the appropriation or occupation of natural or environmental property was intended for private or personal use, the assessment should focus on whether such environmental properties may be used as military items or for a military purpose (for instance by applying the grid of analysis applicable to "military objectives"). If this is not the case, it is a serious indication that the environmental property may have been used for private or personal interest, especially if the exploitation of the natural resources appropriated offers "the potential of substantial enrichment."

In addition, reference to "private use" corresponds to the case where an individual or a group would appropriate a property for the "private use" of another individual or another entity. Therefore, the appropriation by individuals of natural resources or areas for the benefit of private corporate entities (for example, if the exploitation of such properties would support the activity of these entities or increase their revenues) may also be qualified as pillaging. Similarly, appropriation by individuals of natural resources or areas for the benefit of public authority acting as a private corporate entity may also be qualified as pillaging.

Environmental Crime as Ecocide

With respect to utilizing the ecocide provision, the Ukrainian Criminal Code provides for prosecution under Article 441:

> Mass destruction of flora or fauna, poisoning of the atmosphere or water resources, as well as committing other actions that may cause an ecological disaster shall be punishable by imprisonment for a term of eight to fifteen years.[48]

As is the case with Article 438, noted earlier, one of the drawbacks of this language in Article 441 is its generality. The crime of ecocide, as described in Article 441 of the CCU, contains too many evaluative concepts that are not reflected either in the current CCU or in the legal positions of the Supreme Court of Ukraine. This applies to the concepts of 'mass destruction of flora or fauna.' Since it is not clear at what stage of damage flora or fauna can be considered destroyed, and there is no quantitative criterion that would constitute mass destruction, this requirement is challenging to prove. This also applies to the concept of 'poisoning of the atmosphere or water resources.'

In addition, for charges to be upheld according to Article 441, the environmental harm must be significant enough to meet the criteria of an "environmental disaster." The criticism is that Article 441 criminalizes ecocide but lacks a precise legal definition of what actually constitutes an "environmental disaster," making it difficult for law enforcement to substantiate these charges in court. This legal ambiguity prevents the prosecution from meeting the evidentiary burden needed to bring cases to trial, as courts require a more specific framework for determining when environmental damage rises to the level of environmental disaster and thus ecocide. Without a clear definition of what environmental harm meets this threshold, the law cannot be applied consistently, leaving room for interpretation and making successful prosecution difficult. Therefore, a well-defined standard for environmental disaster is essential for Article 441 to function effectively in practice.

As with war crimes, international activity on ecocide will be brought in to inform the Ukrainian position through the previously cited constitutional provisions. One of the major steps towards the adoption of adequate legislation to address environmental crimes is the proposed definition of ecocide: "unlawful or wanton acts committed with knowledge that there is substantial likelihood of severe and either widespread or long-term damage to the environment."[49] This definition was developed by a panel of international legal experts and presented in June 2021 as a new crime to be added to the Rome Statute of the ICC.[50] This definition is part of an initiative to make ecocide the fifth international crime under the ICC's jurisdiction,[51] alongside genocide, crimes against humanity, war crimes, and the crime of aggression. Proposing such an amendment to the Rome Statute serves several purposes:

- **Filling a Legal Gap:** Ecocide, as a crime, fills a gap in international criminal law where large-scale environmental destruction could be prosecuted in cases where it doesn't necessarily fall under existing categories like war crimes or crimes against humanity. It also adequately captures the gravity of this crime, which does not affect only a group of individuals but the entire humanity and next generations.

- **Strengthening Environmental Protection:** Adding ecocide to the ICC's jurisdiction would elevate the global importance of environmental protection. It would create international accountability for governments, corporations, and individuals responsible for environmental destruction that crosses national borders and causes severe harm, as other courts will follow the lead of the ICC.
- **Climate Justice:** Some nations see the recognition of ecocide as part of the broader fight for climate justice, against discrimination and oppression. By making ecocide a prosecutable offense, it creates a pathway to hold those responsible for large-scale environmental harm caused by exploitation of natural resources accountable, potentially addressing both corporate and state actions that contribute to climate change and ecological destruction.

This definition is accompanied by several clarifications to explain the key terms. "Unlawful or wanton" refers to actions that either violate international law (unlawful) or are reckless, carried out with disregard for potential environmental harm (wanton). In the context of "wanton" acts, the damage is considered clearly excessive in relation to the anticipated social or economic benefits. "Severe" refers to serious adverse changes, disruption, or harm to any element of the environment, including significant impacts on human life, natural resources, cultural heritage, or economic stability. "Widespread" describes damage that affects a large geographic area, crosses state boundaries, or harms entire ecosystems, species, or large numbers of people. "Long-term" means damage that is irreversible or cannot be rectified through natural recovery in a reasonable period of time. Finally, "environment" is broadly defined to encompass the Earth's biosphere, cryosphere (ice systems), lithosphere (land), hydrosphere (water), atmosphere, and outer space.[52]

To be prosecuted as ecocide under the proposed definition, the acts at issue must meet the following requirements: (1) unlawful or wanton acts; (2) committed with knowledge that there is a substantial likelihood of severe damage; and (3) either widespread or long-term damage to the environment being caused by those acts. With respect to the *actus reus* element: The actions must involve either unlawful conduct (violating international or domestic environmental law) or reckless conduct (where the perpetrator knowingly disregards the risk of causing environmental damage). The *mens rea* element requires the perpetrator to have knowledge of a substantial likelihood that their actions will cause severe, widespread, or long-term damage to the environment. This is akin to the notion of recklessness. The term "unlawful" refers to actions that violate international law, including IHL. If such actions are found to be in violation of IHL, they would meet the "unlawful" requirement.

Even if such attacks do not qualify as unlawful actions, they may still be prosecuted as ecocide if they qualify as wanton acts. "Wanton" acts, according to the proposed definition, involve reckless disregard for environmental damage where such damage is excessive compared to the anticipated social and economic benefits. If the environmental destruction outweighs any tangible social or economic benefit to the local population, the relevant acts committed would be considered "wanton." Moreover, the acts must be committed "with knowledge of substantial likelihood of severe and either widespread OR long-term damage." In other words, it must be shown that the perpetrators were aware of the environmental risk and the extent of gravity of their actions considering the consequences on the environment and despite that they committed such acts (e.g. recklessness). The knowledge requirement must be assessed in conjunction with the severe damage and either widespread or long-term damage requirements. In other words, it is not sufficient that the perpetrators had some knowledge of the consequences of their actions on the environment: they must be aware that their actions carried a substantial likelihood of causing severe and widespread or long-term damage. It is important to note that "severe" is a cumulative requirement (AND) whereas widespread and long-term damage are alternative requirements (OR).[53]

The proposed definition of "severe damage" includes "very serious adverse changes, disruption or harm to any element of the environment, including grave impacts on human life or natural, cultural, or economic resources." The displacement of ecosystems, destruction of agricultural land, and contamination of water supplies could qualify as severe under this definition, especially if they have led to long-lasting harm to the environment and local communities.[54] There is already evidence that Russian actions in Ukraine may be causing such severe damage. In addition to proving that the damage is severe, prosecutors must prove that it is either widespread or long-term. Widespread damage is defined as damage extending beyond a limited geographic area, affecting an entire ecosystem, species, or large numbers of people. Russian actions have already caused environmental harm not just to Crimea but potentially to surrounding regions as well. This harm affects the broader ecosystem, disrupts agricultural production, and alters the natural water balance across a significant area. If these actions result in cross-border environmental harm, they could be classified as widespread. Long-term damage refers to environmental harm that is irreversible or cannot be naturally redressed in a reasonable period of time. Many of the environmental changes caused by resource extraction—such as groundwater depletion, soil degradation, and destruction of wetlands—are long-lasting and may be impossible to fully reverse, particularly if natural recovery would take decades or longer. These characteristics would qualify the environmental harm as long-term under the proposed definition of ecocide. There is already evidence to suggest that Russian actions in Ukraine are causing long-term damage to the environment.

The definition of the term "environment" in the proposed amendment is quite broad as it encompasses the biosphere, cryosphere, lithosphere, hydrosphere, and atmosphere, as well as outer space. Under this definition, any harm caused to the ecosystems in these territories, such as the destruction of biodiversity or critical habitats, would be directly relevant under this broad understanding of the environment.[55] Considering that Ukraine has ratified the Rome Statute and therefore, pursuant to Article 9, the Rome Statute has become national law, Ukraine may greatly benefit from the adoption of an ecocide amendment for the prosecution of environmental crimes in several ways, not least of which includes Ukraine utilizing it to interpret its own Article 438 in a more concrete way. Additionally, recognition of ecocide as a distinct crime would make it the fifth international crime under the Rome Statute, alongside genocide, war crimes, crimes against humanity, and crimes of aggression. In this way, the Rome Statute would mirror Ukraine's criminal code with ecocide lodged in its own provision. That would elevate the legal status of environmental destruction as ecocide, giving it international visibility and enforceability.[56]

Moreover, once the amendment is in place, Ukraine could refer cases of ecocide to the ICC. This would allow Ukrainian prosecutors to work with the ICC in investigating and prosecuting individuals responsible for significant environmental harm, particularly during the war, such as the destruction of ecosystems, contamination of water sources, or widespread deforestation.[57] The amendment would also facilitate global cooperation in prosecuting ecocide, making it easier to gather evidence and bring perpetrators to justice. Since Ukraine is now a party to the Rome Statute, it would benefit from increased international support and resources in prosecuting crimes committed during the conflict.

Finally, the amendment could provide the basis for holding Russia or other actors accountable for large-scale environmental degradation resulting from military operations, such as chemical pollution, habitat destruction, and other long-term ecological harm. This would ensure that environmental damage inflicted as part of war crimes does not go unpunished; however, that would only be the case for environmental crimes committed after the amendment was adopted, as there is little prospect of retroactive enforcement of new provisions in the Rome Statute.

Comparing War Crimes to Ecocide in Ukraine

Direct intent is a key aspect of Ukrainian law with which prosecutors must deal to successfully bring a case. In Ukrainian criminal law, direct intent (прямий умисел) refers to a situation where a person is aware of their actions and consciously aims to bring about a specific illegal result. This is one of two types of intent, the other being indirect (or eventual) intent (н е п р я м и й у м и с е л). Indirect intent occurs when a person foresees the possibility of harmful consequences but does not actively seek them yet allows them to happen. Direct intent requires two main elements: (1) Awareness of the consequences: the person understands that their actions will cause a specific harmful result; and (2) Desire to achieve the result: the person wants or seeks to bring about that harmful outcome.

For example, if a person sets fire to a building knowing that people are inside, and their goal is to cause death or destruction, this would be classified as direct intent under Ukrainian law. The Criminal Code of Ukraine codifies this in Article 24, which distinguishes between direct and indirect intent. Direct intent is essential in prosecuting serious offenses where the perpetrator deliberately aims to achieve the criminal outcome, such as in cases of premeditated murder (Criminal Code). Other key aspects that prosecutors must lock down are: (1) the perpetrator – generally, in the first five forms, there is no specific requirement. The subject of the crime when the act is "giving an order to commit such actions" is special: it is an official who, by virtue of his/her authority, can give orders relating to the law of war (*see* Article 438 (1) "as well as ordering such actions"); (2) victim – the object may be the environment. If not specified in Article 438, applicable and relevant treaties like the Geneva Conventions or customary law identify the object of war crimes; (3) to trigger the application of Article 438, the actions at issue must take place in armed conflict. In international criminal law, the Tadic Test provides a legal framework for determining whether a situation qualifies as an armed conflict.

Conclusion

Ukraine's efforts to hold Russians accountable for the environmental destruction they have wrought since the aggressive war they commenced in February 2022 tracks international legal efforts to define and prosecute environmental crimes as such. Whether environmental crime is prosecuted as a form of war crime or as ecocide, the choices Ukraine makes, the arguments its prosecutors present, and the reasoning its courts employ will hold incredibly valuable legal weight not only for Ukraine but also for the international community. The lessons learned from Ukraine's new efforts in this direction are bound to be instructive. Even though many of the defendants Ukraine's prosecutors will pursue are not in Ukrainian custody, which will force those Ukrainian trials to be undertaken *in absentia*, the evidence collected, curated, and proffered will build up a public record from which Russia will not be able to escape and which other authoritarian states also thinking about invading their neighbors will have to consider. The international tide has turned against perpetrators of environmental crimes. The more accountability for environmental destruction that can be achieved by both international and domestic courts, whether as a war crime or as ecocide, the better for our world.

Notes

1 *How the ICC Is Using International Criminal Law to Prosecute Suspects of Eco Crimes*, LEGAL PLANET, May 1, 2021, https://legal-planet.org/2024/05/01/how-the-icc-is-using-international-criminal-law-to-prosecute-suspects-of-eco-crimes/.
2 Office of Public Affairs, U.S. Dept. of Justice, Press Release, *Justice Department Hosts Ukrainian Prosecutors for Training on Investigating and Prosecuting Environmental Crimes*, May 19, 2023, https://www.justice.gov/opa/pr/justice-department-hosts-ukrainian-prosecutors-training-investigating-and-prosecuting.
3 Jessica Durney, *Crafting a Standard: Environmental Crimes as Crimes Against Humanity under the International Criminal Court*, 24 HASTINGS ENV'T L. J. 413, 415 (2018).
4 MATTHEW GILLET, PROSECUTING ENVIRONMENTAL HARM BEFORE THE INTERNATIONAL CRIMINAL COURT 53 (2022).
5 Rebecca Root, *Climate Crisis: Push for Ecocide to be Added to Rome Statute*, IBA, Oct. 14, 2024, https://www.ibanet.org/ecocide-rome-statute.
6 Philippe Sands & Dior Fall Sow, et al, *Independent Expert Panel for the Definition of Ecocide: Commentary & Context*, STOP ECOCIDE FOUNDATION (June 2021), https://static1.squarespace.com/static/5ca2608ab914493c64ef1f6d/t/60d7479cf8e7e5461534dd07/1624721314430/SE+Foundation+Commentary+and+core+text+revised+(1).pdf.
7 Constitution of Ukraine, Articles 9 & 18.
8 Constitution of Ukraine, Article 8.
9 Christian Delage, *The Klaus Barbie Trial: Traces and Temporalities*, 48 COMP. LIT. STUDIES 320, 320–321 (2011).
10 Jason Greenglass, *What Does International Human Rights/International Criminal Tribunal Jurisprudence Say about Trials In Absentia?*, CASE WESTERN RESERVE UNIVERSITY SCHOOL OF LAW SCHOLARLY COMMONS, at 13, 2009, https://scholarlycommons.law.case.edu/cgi/viewcontent.cgi?article=1087&context=war_crimes_memos.
11 Criminal Code of Ukraine, Article 438.
12 Nataliya Marchuk, *Violation of the Laws and Customs of War: Features of the Qualification of Article 438 of the Criminal Code of Ukraine Analyzed by Supreme Court Judge Nataliya Marchuk*, Supreme Court of Ukraine, Nov. 11, 2022, https://supreme.court.gov.ua/supreme/pres-centr/news/1345046/.
13 *Id.*
14 *Le Procureur c. Bosco Ntaganda*, Case No. ICC-01/04-02/06-2359, Judgement, para. 1164 (July 8, 2019), https://www.icc-cpi.int/sites/default/files/CourtRecords/CR2019_03568.PDF.
15 Vanessa Murphy, Helen Obregón Gieseken and Laurent Gisel, *Guidelines on the Protection of the Natural Environment in Armed Conflict*, ICRC (2020), https://www.icrc.org/sites/default/files/document_new/file_list/guidelines_on_the_protection_of_the_natural_environment_in_armed_conflict_advance-copy.pdf.
16 *Id.*
17 *Id.*
18 Geneva Conventions 1949, Art. 2; Protocol Additional to the Geneva Conventions of 12 August 1949, and relating to the Protection of Victims of International Armed Conflicts (Protocol 1), Art. 1(3), 4, June 8, 1977, 1125 U.N.T.S. 3, 16 I.L.M. 1391 (1977), https://treaties.un.org/doc/publication/unts/volume%201125/volume-1125-i-17512-english.pdf; *Prosecutor v. Thomas Lubanga Dyilo*, Case No. ICC-01/04-01/06, Judgment, para. 541 (Mar. 14, 2012), https://www.icc-cpi.int/sites/default/files/CourtRecords/CR2012_03942.PDF; *Prosecutor*

v. Germain Katanga, Case No. ICC-01/04-01/07, Judgment, para. 1177 (Mar. 7, 2014), https://www.icc-cpi.int/sites/default/files/CourtRecords/CR2015_04025.PDF.

19 Draft Rules for the Limitation of the Dangers Incurred by the Civilian Population in Time of War, ICRC at Art. 3 (1956), https://ihl-databases.icrc.org/en/ihl-treaties/icrc-draft-rules-1956.

20 Protocol Additional to the Geneva Conventions of 12 August 1949, and relating to the Protection of Victims of International Armed Conflicts (Protocol 1), Art. 49, June 8, 1977, 1125 U.N.T.S. 3, 16 I.L.M. 1391 (1977), https://treaties.un.org/doc/publication/unts/volume%201125/volume-1125-i-17512-english.pdf.

21 *Prosecutor v. Pavle Strugar*, Case No. IT-01-42-T, Judgment, para. 282 (Jan. 31, 2005), https://ucr.irmct.org/LegalRef/CMSDocStore/Public/English/Judgement/NotIndexable/IT-01-42/JUD133R2000184306.pdf.

22 Kevin Jon Heller & Jessica C. Lawrence, *The Limits of Article 8(2)(b)(iv) of the Rome Statute, the First Ecocentric Environmental War Crime*, 20 Georgetown Int'l Env't L. Rev. 1, 2 (2007).

23 Knut Dörmann, Elements of War Crimes under the Rome Statute of the International Criminal Court: Sources and Commentary 175 (2004).

24 1976 CCD Understanding Relating to Article I of ENMOD, 31 United Nations General Assembly Official Records Supp. No. 27 (A/31/27), Annex I.

25 Steven Freeland, Addressing the Intentional Destruction of The Environment During Warfare Under the Rome Statute of the International Criminal Court 207 (2015).

26 International Criminal Tribunal for the former Yugoslavia, *Final Report to the Prosecutor by the Committee Established to Review the NATO Bombing Campaign Against the Federal Republic of Yugoslavia*, para. 21, https://www.icty.org/x/file/Press/nato061300.pdf.

27 ICC, *Elements of Crimes*, 13, fn. 36 (2013), https://www.icc-cpi.int/sites/default/files/Publications/Elements-of-Crimes.pdf.

28 Steven Freeland, Addressing the Intentional Destruction of The Environment During Warfare Under the Rome Statute of the International Criminal Court141 (2015).

29 Knut Dörmann, Elements of War Crimes under the Rome Statute of the International Criminal Court: Sources and Commentary 173 (2004).

30 ICRC, *Commentary on Article 57 of Additional Protocol I*, para. 2209 (1987).

31 ICC, *Elements of Crimes*, 13, fn. 37 (2013), https://www.icc-cpi.int/sites/default/files/Publications/Elements-of-Crimes.pdf.

32 International Criminal Tribunal for the former Yugoslavia, *Final Report to the Prosecutor by the Committee Established to Review the NATO Bombing Campaign Against the Federal Republic of Yugoslavia*, para. 23, *available at* https://www.icty.org/x/file/Press/nato061300.pdf.

33 Matthew Gillet, Prosecuting Environmental Harm before the International Criminal Court (2022). *See also*, ICRC, *Guidelines on the Protection of the Environment*.

34 *Ongwen*, Case No. ICC-02/04-01/15, February 4th, 2021, para. 2777.

35 *Le Procureur c. Bosco Ntaganda*, Case No. ICC-01/04-02/06-2359, Judgement, n. 3182 (July 8, 2019), https://www.icc-cpi.int/sites/default/files/CourtRecords/CR2019_03568.PDF.

36 *Prosecutor v. Germain Katanga*, Case No. ICC-01/04-01/07, Judgment, para. 893 (Mar. 7, 2014), https://www.icc-cpi.int/sites/default/files/CourtRecords/CR2015_04025.PDF.

37 Jean-Marie Henckaerts & Louise Doswald-Beck, Customary International Humanitarian Law, Vol. 1, Rules, Rule 8 (2009).

38 Jean-Marie Henckaerts & Louise Doswald-Beck, Customary International Humanitarian Law, Vol. 1, Rules, Rule 9 (2009).
39 *Le Procureur c. Bosco Ntaganda*, Case No. ICC-01/04-02/06-2359, Judgement, para. 1164 (July 8, 2019), https://www.icc-cpi.int/sites/default/files/CourtRecords/CR2019_03568.PDF.
40 ICRC, *Guidelines on the Protection of the Environment.*
41 *Id.*
42 *Id.*
43 Rome Statute, Article 8 (2) (b) (xvi). Similar provisions apply to non-international conflicts, *see* Article 8 (2) (e) (v). The analysis presented in this comment applies for both articles.
44 Yulia Nuzban, *"For Private or Personal Use": The Meaning of the Special Intent Requirement in the War Crime of Pillage under the Rome Statute*, 102 Int'l Rev. of the Red Cross 1249, 1251–54 (2021), https://international-review.icrc.org/sites/default/files/reviews-pdf/2022-01/for-private-or-personal-use-special-intent-requirement-pillage-rome-statute-icc-915.pdf.
45 *Id.* at 1263 (*citing Ntaganda*, Judgment, ICC-01/04-02/06-2359, 8 July 2019, paras 1041–2).
46 *Id.* at 1264 (*quoting Ongwen*, Trial Judgment, ICC-02/04-01/15-1762-Red, 4 February 2021, paras 2873, 2926, 2972 and 3019).
47 *Id.* at 1267.
48 Criminal Code of Ukraine, article 441.
49 Sands & Fall Sow, et al, *International Panel of Experts (Ecocide)* at 5.
50 *Id.*
51 *Id.* at 2.
52 *Id.* at 5.
53 *Id.* at 6–12.
54 *Id.*
55 *Id.*
56 Iryana Marchuk & Aloka Wanigasuriya, *Ukraine's Perspective on the Long-Awaited Ratification of the Rome Statute and What Comes Next*, OpinioJuris, Aug. 29, 2024, https://opiniojuris.org/2024/08/29/ukraines-perspective-on-the-long-awaited-ratification-of-the-rome-statute-and-what-comes-next/.
57 Mission of the President of Ukraine in the Autonomous Republic of Crimea, *Verkhovna Rada of Ukraine Ratified the Rome Statute of the International Criminal Court*, Press Release, Aug. 21, 2024, https://ppu.gov.ua/en/press-center/verkhovna-rada-ukrainy-ratyfikuvala-rymskyy-statut-mizhnarodnoho-kryminalnoho-sudu/; Daryna Vialko, *What Ukraine Gains from Ratifying the Rome Statute: Expert Explanation*, RBC-Ukraine, Aug. 21, 2024, https://newsukraine.rbc.ua/news/what-ukraine-gains-from-ratifying-rome-statute-1724260389.html

PART III

Accountability and Related Issues

10

HOW TO MAKE RUSSIA PAY REPARATIONS

By Oona A. Hathaway and Maggie M. Mills

Introduction

War destroys lives, property, infrastructure, and entire communities. Historically, victors would seize the land and property of defeated nations as compensation for the costs they suffered in the war. Conquest and booty were the reward for victory; destitution and loss the price of defeat.[1] In the modern era, however, war is illegal, and conquest and booty have been outlawed along with it.[2] Yet even under this new paradigm, wars still occur. When they do, who pays for the terrible costs they inflict?

Russia's manifestly illegal assault on Ukraine has thrown this perennial problem into sharp relief. After nearly two years of war, Ukraine will need—at least—an estimated $486 billion to recover and rebuild.[3] In a September 2022 speech to the United Nations General Assembly, President Zelenskyy declared that "Russia should pay for this war with its assets."[4] In November 2022, the United Nations General Assembly took up this charge, passing a resolution stating that Russia "must be held to account for any violations of international law in or against Ukraine, including its aggression," and that Russia must "mak[e] reparation for the injury, including any damage" that its unlawful acts have caused.[5] The Council of Europe has since established a Register of Damage designed to support a future compensation mechanism.[6]

In the modern era, large-scale reparations mechanisms have been established in four ways: (1) imposed by victors after total defeat and unconditional surrender, (2) mandated by a United Nations Security Council resolution, (3) formed through the responsible state's consent to a negotiated resolution, or (4) created pursuant to an international court judgment.[7] For Ukraine, as for

DOI: 10.4324/9781003458166-13

most victims of war, these four options are unlikely to satisfy the full balance of reparations: Russia has made clear that it will veto any Security Council resolution and has indicated no intent to halt the war or pay reparations. While modest reparations may be awarded in the context of ongoing International Court of Justice (ICJ), International Criminal Court (ICC), and European Court of Human Rights (ECHR) proceedings,[8] those awards are not likely to address most of the damage.

Of course, other victim states have also suffered due to the serious shortcomings of the reparations status quo. And yet the degree of global support for reparations for the war in Ukraine, while by no means universal, appears to have reached a level not seen since World War II. As a result, there are many proposals aimed at effecting reparations through the outright unilateral seizure of Russian assets. Unfortunately, these proposals risk running afoul of well-established rules of international law, including the doctrine of sovereign immunity. Put simply, they would attempt to cure one international legal violation by engaging in another.

There is another way forward for Ukraine and for other states that might find themselves in a similar situation in the future—a path toward reparations that would not require violating international law. The international law doctrine of countermeasures permits the continued freezing of an aggressor's assets until the reparations obligation is met. Moreover, where the collective prohibition on the use of force is violated, states other than the immediate victim may put in place collective countermeasures (sometimes called "third-party" countermeasures).[9] Ukraine's plight has forced renewed consideration of the question of collective countermeasures, on which the International Law Commission's Draft Articles on State Responsibility remain agnostic. Recognizing such countermeasures' legitimacy under certain conditions could have beneficial implications beyond the current conflict, extending not only to future war reparations but also to international responses to cyber operations, human rights violations, or violations of environmental law obligations.

Unilateral Seizures Are Not the Answer

Proposals to seize Russia's sovereign assets outright promise a quick fix to the reparations challenge. Before discussing collective countermeasures in depth, it is important to understand the fundamental legal shortcomings that render these simpler approaches inadequate. Ukraine has benefited greatly from its ability to demonstrate time and again that it is on the right side of the law, in contrast to an opponent bent on breaking every rule on the books.[10] In seeking reparations, neither Ukraine nor its allies stand to benefit from abandoning that legal high ground.

Proposals for Unilateral Seizures

Russian central bank assets are the primary target of proposals to confiscate or seize (and subsequently transfer to Ukraine) Russian assets.[11] Rather than aiming to persuade or induce Russia to make reparation, proposals to seize these assets seek directly to obtain what might be termed "unilateral reparations."[12]

Some have floated alternatives that purport to stop short of the outright unilateral seizure of Russian central bank assets while still extracting value from those assets. For example, in late 2022, the European Commission (EC) proposed transferring proceeds from the investment of frozen Russian assets, as distinct from the principal assets themselves, to Ukraine, to be "offset against" Ukraine's reparations claims against Russia.[13] That proposal, however, remains fundamentally confiscatory, especially given the risk of negative returns that would diminish the value of the principal. US and European policymakers have also entertained proposals to collateralize frozen Russian central bank assets to help finance loans to Ukraine.[14] This approach, too, is a unilateral seizure by another name. Its implementation would necessarily rest on the prospect that the "collateral" Russian central bank assets could eventually be confiscated to satisfy debts issued against them.

In no small part because of the legal hurdles facing unilateral seizures, Europe has gravitated instead toward an alternative plan that would involve leaving the central bank assets in place but taxing their earnings and transferring the proceeds (an expected three billion euros annually) to Ukraine.[15] Unlike plans to confiscate the assets or invest them in ways that pose a risk of loss, this approach would preserve the underlying assets pending Russia's compliance with its international law obligations and thus would not confront the legal impediments to unilateral seizures.

The Legal Barrier to Unilateral Sanctions: Sovereign Immunity

The prime international legal barrier to confiscatory proposals is the customary international legal principle of Sovereign Immunity, according to which states and their assets enjoy immunity from other states' jurisdiction and acts of execution or enforcement.[16] Virtually all states "accept sovereign immunity as something which is legally binding under international law," rather than as a matter of mere comity.[17] The protection of this principle is widely understood to extend with particular force to foreign central bank assets.[18]

None of the exceptions to state immunity enumerated in the UN Convention on Jurisdictional Immunities of States and Their Property, which the ICJ has understood to "shed light on the content of customary international law" regarding sovereign immunity,[19] apply to the Russian central bank assets in question here.[20] Nor would linking the assets to Russia's violations of either jus ad bellum or jus in bello necessarily dissolve their sovereign-immunity protection, since—as the law currently stands—even jus cogens violations do not preclude "the applicability of the customary international law on State immunity."[21] Some claim that the Convention on Jurisdictional Immunities applies only to actions taken in connection with a judicial proceeding or judgment and not to legislative or executive actions.[22] To be sure, the Convention's stated focus is on "the immunity of a State and its property from the jurisdiction of the courts of another State."[23] But the treaty defines "court" broadly, to encompass "any organ of a State, however named, entitled to exercise judicial functions."[24] If sovereign equality is the animating principle of sovereign immunity, as the ICJ stated in Jurisdictional Immunities of the State, a seizure of central bank assets based on a decision by the executive branch poses the same fundamental problem as would a seizure of those assets based on a decision by a court.[25] Seizures and related measures are are functionally adjudicative; they are premised on the decisive disapprobation of the target state's conduct, informed by a finding of unlawfulness, however institutionally veiled. Executive actors, just like "national judges," "are generally ill-suited to administer justice in an impartial and objective way" with respect to foreign sovereigns.[26]

Distinguishing executive from judicial actors demands a functional rather than strictly formal analysis given the diversity of "internal organizational structure[s]" found within states.[27] Indeed, in most states, the operation of each branch necessarily implicates powers or authorities held and exercised by the others.[28] This might explain the International Law Commission's commentary on the Convention on Jurisdictional Immunities, that "the scope of judicial functions . . . should be understood to cover such functions whether exercised by courts or by administrative organs."[29] Those functions likely include "changing title to property."[30]

For these reasons, sovereign immunity cannot be circumvented by simply prohibiting subsequent judicial review of "executive" exercises of judicial or adjudicative authority, which would in any case raise serious due process concerns.[31] The contrary view would effectively eliminate sovereign immunity, as states could simply evade immunities by performing all acts potentially covered by immunities through nominally executive organs.

In short, sovereign immunity likely protects sovereigns from measures of constraint—including seizures of sovereign assets—whether undertaken by a judicial, legislative, or executive-administrative actor.[32]

(Failed) Arguments for Overcoming Sovereign Immunity

To seize sovereign assets without incurring state responsibility would require the invocation of one of what the Draft Articles on State Responsibility term "circumstances precluding wrongfulness."[33] However, attempts to preclude the wrongfulness of sovereign asset seizures on either self-defense or countermeasures fall short on doctrinal grounds, at least in the case of Ukraine's allies with respect to the seizure of Russia's central bank assets. Nor can a recommendation by the UN General Assembly legitimize such seizures, though an authoritative international judgment arguably would. In addition to their legal inadequacy, strategic and diplomatic considerations weigh heavily against these proposals and the asset seizures they endeavor to legitimize.

Some have proposed the invocation of self-defense to justify the seizure of assets in order "to force a wrongdoing sovereign to make compensatory reparations."[34] Following the principle of collective self-defense incorporated in the UN Charter,[35] "it is arguable that states adopting economic sanctions in support of a third party that fell victim to aggressive war should be entitled to go as far as they could if their own security was affected."[36]

Accordingly, it might seem that Ukraine's supporters could couch asset seizures as acts of collective self-defense, especially while hostilities are ongoing, without purporting to be belligerents themselves. Indeed, the International Law Commission's Draft Articles might be read to suggest that states "formally at peace" may still invoke self-defense as a circumstance precluding wrongfulness if other conditions are met.[37] However, even if so, states cannot reasonably invoke self-defense as a justification of asset seizures once the threat or use of force (whether against them or against Ukraine alone) is no longer operative. A race to seize as many assets as possible in the meantime would not materially affect Russia's ability to finance the invasion, since asset freezes have already deprived Russia of the ability to use them for that purpose. Moreover, seizures justified by self-defense are properly used for self-defense, not reparation.[38]

Practically, although some states considering the seizure of Russia's assets may have responded to the war in Ukraine in ways that blur the line between war and peace,[39] Ukraine's allies appear largely to have refrained from suggesting that they have entered, in their own capacity, into a state of belligerency with Russia. An explicit invocation of self-defense or collective self-defense to justify coercive seizures would be in tension with this delicately delineated abstention.

Legal scholars have yet another argument to justify unilateral seizures: They argue that countermeasures doctrine can be used to permit the seizure of frozen Russian central bank assets.[40] But this is wrong for two key reasons.

First, "[c]ountermeasures may only be taken by an injured State in order to induce the responsible State to comply with its obligations . . . namely, to cease the internationally wrongful conduct, if it is continuing, and to provide reparation to the injured state."[41] Yet seizures for reparations—including seizures framed as a "down payment" credited to Russia's ultimate obligation[42]—are not designed to induce compliance, but rather to enjoin or force it. This puts seizures "in fundamental tension with the basic structure of countermeasures."[43] Countermeasures are to be taken "with a view to procuring cessation of and reparation for the internationally wrongful act" through persuasion, "not by way of punishment."[44] In emplacing countermeasures, states must not create "new situations which cannot be rectified whatever the response of the latter State to the claims against it."[45] Countermeasures doctrine thus cannot be bent to justify asset confiscation or quasi-seizures, which force rather than induce compliance and thereby contradict the doctrine's raison d'être.[46]

Second, proposals for asset seizures violate the reversibility requirement, which limits countermeasures "to the non-performance for the time being of international obligations of the State taking the measures" and must, "as far as possible, be taken in such a way as to permit the resumption of performance."[47] As the commentary to the Draft Articles explains, "as far as possible" does not create a loophole that third-party states could exploit to justify irreversible measures, but rather obliges states faced with several possible measures to select one that is reversible.[48]

The reversibility requirement cannot be satisfied, as some argue,[49] by suspending and then later reinstating respect for sovereign immunity, without regard to actions taken while immunity was suspended. The correct focus of the reversability analysis is the suspension of performance of an obligation—not the extension of immunity per se, but the protection of the assets that immunity provides. It is the seizure that must be reversible, not merely the suspension of the sovereign immunity obligation.[50]

In short, countermeasures must be "temporary in character" and "as far as possible reversible in their effects in terms of future legal relations between the two states,"[51] and they must not inflict "irreparable damage on the responsible State" while in operation.[52] Moreover, when presented with a number of options for countermeasures, a state's choice must be informed by the reversibility requirement.[53] The seizure of hundreds of billions of dollars of state assets, unlikely ever to be restored once transferred, does not meet these requirements.

A group of leading international lawyers have argued that seizing Russian sovereign assets can be justified by countermeasures doctrine so long as the assets are transferred "to an international compensation mechanism,"[54] which would, they argue, "serve as an inducement or incentive to Russia to cease its wrongful conduct and bring itself into compliance with the peremptory norms it has been violating."[55] So long as the assets are transferred to an international body that will preserve them, this argument can be sustained, but it fails if assets are transferred to Ukraine. For as soon as assets are depleted, the power of the countermeasure to induce compliance, as well as its reversibility, evaporate. Unfortunately, the proposal contemplates just such transfers, claiming, puzzlingly, that "there is no material difference between a measure freezing another State's assets, and one which transfers them to the victim of the wrongful conduct as reparations for the injuries it has suffered."[56] Granted, money is fungible—what is owed could be theoretically repaid. And yet for the countermeasures to be reversible, there must be some realistic prospect that money, once dispersed, could be recovered or replaced. Here, given the amount of money at issue and the financial straits in which Ukraine finds itself, that is beyond unlikely. Transferring states are, moreover, highly unlikely to make up the shortfall if Ukraine fails to repay the transferred funds.

Adopting the argument that seizures can be justified by countermeasures doctrine would set a dangerous precedent for sovereign immunity, making state assets extraordinarily vulnerable the world over. It should not be forgotten that countermeasures are measures that are otherwise illegal, and they are only permissible if they are exercised in limited circumstances and in accordance with key conditions, including reversibility and proportionality. Aggressive invocation of countermeasures doctrine where these conditions do not hold—as in the case of seizures or confiscations—risks the very proliferation of unlawful conduct that the Draft Articles carefully sought to constrain.[57]

Why Following the Law is in Ukraine's Best Interests

Though legal theories purporting to justify asset seizures are inconsistent with existing international law, some still urge these steps in the interests of reparations, or even simply to fund the war.[58] For Ukraine and its allies, however, illegal seizures risk compromising the legal and moral narrative around which a large part of the international community has coalesced against Russian aggression.[59] Unilateral seizures of Russian assets also threaten to undercut Russia's incentive to negotiate and eventually return to compliance with its international obligations to cease aggression and provide reparations.[60]

In contrast, the approach we propose below reflects a commitment to upholding both of these obligations without spurning other prevailing and vitally important norms. The extended asset freezes we advocate, rooted in collective countermeasures, would manifest states' moral and legal condemnation of Russia's aggression without risking further erosion of international law.

The Way Forward for Reparations

That seizure proposals are flawed does not imply that states must acquiesce in Russia's violation of its obligation to make reparations for its unlawful use of force. Indeed, inaction risks further eroding this obligation's authority, leaving Russia and other aggressors with little incentive to eventually comply. If the international community is committed to upholding and giving effect to the reparations obligation, it must devise a new path forward.

Countermeasures doctrine can mark that path. While countermeasures doctrine does not support the seizure of Russian funds for the immediate rebuilding of Ukraine, it does allow states to continue to hold assets frozen unless and until Russia provides reparations.

Though few states have offered a clear international legal rationale for their asset freezes, those freezes can be justified as countermeasures, specifically "collective" countermeasures. These countermeasures are "collective" in the sense that they are premised on violations of collective obligations, or obligations *erga omnes*. They need not end with the war; as long as Russia has failed to meet its obligation to provide adequate reparations, the asset freezes may remain in place. The novelty of this countermeasures-based approach is thus twofold. First, it justifies asset freezes after the end of the illegal war; second, it justifies asset freezes by third states.

Countermeasures and Asset Freezes

Although it is not uncommon for states to impose asset freezes as sanctions in response to internationally wrongful acts, states rarely label their sanctions as "countermeasures" because doing so might be seen to concede that the sanctions would otherwise be wrongful. Nevertheless, like seizures of sovereign assets, asset freezes may also be prima facie unlawful and thus require countermeasures doctrine to avoid liability for their use.

Most critically, sovereign immunity and its underlying sovereign-equality rationale apply to both seizures and freezes.[61] Freezes, like seizures, are measures of constraint that pose serious obstacles to target states' exercise of their sovereignty.[62] The notion that "immunity rules do not apply" to freezes would put state assets in the "absurdly paradoxical position of being inviolable and immune from judicial measures, but at the mercy of administrative or executive actions."[63]

Unlike seizures, however, freezes are substantially reversible and can reasonably be construed as designed to induce compliance.[64] True, even an asset freeze may not be entirely reversible—a frozen asset might depreciate over time, for example. But the Draft Articles require reversibility only "as far as possible," and in this case, asset freezes appear to be the one effective measure "which permits the resumption of performance of the obligations suspended" to the greatest extent.[65] Thus, countermeasures doctrine can be invoked to preclude any international wrongfulness that might otherwise attach to asset freezes, even if imposed indefinitely pending Russia's payment of reparations.

To be clear, countermeasures need not take the form of asset freezes or other economic sanctions. A countermeasure can involve suspending any of the thousands of international legal obligations that most states owe to other states, if the measure meets the constraints on countermeasures, including proportionality and reversibility. We focus here on asset freezes only because of their exceptional salience in the Russia-Ukraine context.

Countermeasures and Reparations

Countermeasures may only be taken "against a State which is responsible for an internationally wrongful act in order to induce that State to comply with its obligations."[66] Crucially, a state that refuses to pay reparations it owes has failed to comply with its international obligations. Countermeasures designed to induce payment are a suitable response to that failure.

It is "a well-established rule of international law that an injured State is entitled to obtain compensation from the State which has committed an internationally wrongful act for the damage caused by it."[67] Indeed, the "obligation to make reparation" is the "indispensable complement" of an internationally wrongful act.[68] The Draft Articles make clear that a "responsible State is under an obligation to make full reparation," necessarily implying that the failure to pay reparations—insofar as it violates that obligation—is itself an internationally wrongful act. It follows that countermeasures may extend to "the pursuit by the injured State . . . of naturalis restitutio, pecuniary compensation, and the various forms of satisfaction."[69] In other words, countermeasures "may also be taken to ensure reparation."[70]

This logic applies equally to reparations obligations arising from violations of the UN Charter's prohibition on the use of force.[71] Since World War II, absent bilateral agreement or a reparations mandate issuing from the UN Security Council, states have rarely paid reparations for wrongfully waged wars. Countermeasures to compel war reparations could help fill this compliance gap, giving greater effect to the right of injured states—including Ukraine, following Russia's aggression against it—to obtain reparations.

Furthermore, a state commits an internationally wrongful act for so long as it engages in attributable "conduct consisting of an action or omission" that "constitutes a breach of an international obligation,"[72] such as refusing to pay reparations duly owed. Accordingly, states may sustain countermeasures responsive to the failure to repair even after the initial injury-causing conduct—in this case, Russia's unlawful use of force—has ceased.

Collective Countermeasures After Violations of Obligations Erga Omnes

Ukraine has already begun a domestic effort to repurpose roughly $500 million in confiscated Russian assets to fund reconstruction.[73] However, Ukraine has jurisdiction over only a small fraction of the total Russian assets frozen worldwide. That global total includes Russian central bank assets worth an estimated $300 billion.[74] Herein lies the crucial importance of collective countermeasures, which allow third states to respond to a violation of an obligation *erga omnes*—that is, an obligation arising "towards the international community as a whole," in the protection of which all states have a "legal interest."[75] The obligation to abstain from acts of aggression is a seminal obligation *erga omnes*, which Russia's ongoing war of aggression against Ukraine clearly violates.[76]

The Draft Articles disclaim any attempt "to regulate the taking of countermeasures by States other than the injured State."[77] Yet they suggest that non-injured states may invoke state responsibility—a necessary condition for the taking of countermeasures—when *erga omnes* obligations are at stake. Article 48(1), reflecting Barcelona Traction's influence,[78] establishes that "[a]ny State other than an injured State is entitled to invoke the responsibility of another State" if "the obligation breached is owed to the international community as a whole."[79] In addition to "cessation of the internationally wrongful act, and assurances and guarantees of non-repetition," a state other than the injured state "may claim from the responsible State . . . performance of the obligation of reparation . . . in the interest of the injured State."[80]

The ICJ's decisions concerning breaches of obligations *erga omnes* partes support by analogy the limited resort to collective countermeasures for violations *erga omnes*. In The Gambia v. Myanmar, the ICJ found that The Gambia had "standing to invoke the responsibility of Myanmar for the alleged breaches of its obligations."[81] It rejected Myanmar's argument that "the opposite conclusion would lead to a proliferation of disputes and raise questions concerning the entitlement of 'non-injured' states to claim reparation on behalf of alleged victims who are not their nationals."[82] Even in its much earlier South West Africa judgment, "perhaps the purest embodiment of the bilateralist view,"[83] the ICJ allowed that "states may have a legal interest in vindicating a principle of international law, even though they have, in the given case, suffered no material prejudice," provided "that such rights or interests" are "clearly vested in those who claim them, by some text or instrument, or rule of law. . . ."[84]

The Draft Articles themselves offer little guidance on collective countermeasures, even for violations of obligations *erga omnes*. While the final version of Article 54 "recognizes the right of states . . . to resort to lawful measures to ensure cessation of the wrongful act and reparation," it notably "avoids the use of the term 'countermeasures' . . . while at the same time not ruling out future developments in this respect."[85] That "leaves open the question whether any State may take measures to ensure compliance with certain international obligations in the general interest as distinct from its own individual interest as an injured State."[86]

The evolution of customary international law since the Articles' adoption suggests growing support for collective countermeasures. States have increasingly pursued a "widespread and representative affirmative" practice of adopting or supporting collective countermeasures, with only rare diplomatic protests.[87]

Some evidence of corresponding *opino juris* is also available, including the Group of 77's 1982 declaration "affirm[ing] the legitimacy of . . . economic sanctions and other measures in the struggle against apartheid," which "emphasized the rights of developing countries, individually and collectively, to adopt such sanctions and other measures," even absent a Security Council mandate.[88]

More recently, a decidedly "collectivist" approach has emerged in the cyber context, "broaden[ing] the notion of injured states, and therefore the availability of countermeasures."[89] Within this debate, countermeasures taken "in response to violations of *erga omnes* obligations (as in the case of Ukraine)" are already seen as relatively uncontroversial, compared to the bolder position, advanced by states like Estonia and New Zealand, that collective countermeasures may be "taken at the request of an injured state even absent breaches of obligations *erga omnes*."[90] The latter, more permissive view has been criticized as an invitation to "international vigilantism."[91] But a total prohibition on collective countermeasures imposes its own costs, "depriv[ing] states of opportunities to engage together on their shared governance project" in order "to rally behind the violated norms and to insist that these norms apply equally to all states."[92] Standard "bilateral countermeasures strongly favour states that are more powerful."[93] Without resort to collective countermeasures, then, the "conditions of de facto inequality prevailing in the international community" are likely to "effectively leave many of the most serious breaches without redress."[94]

Requiring a violation of an obligation *erga omnes* sets a "sensible guardrail" on the use of collective countermeasures, helping to prevent a spiral of reprisal.[95] Moreover, even before the adoption of the Draft Articles, some members of the UN General Assembly already viewed "a serious breach of an essential obligation owed to the international community" as "the only exception" allowing "any State to take countermeasures at the request of any injured State."[96] That view enjoyed "overwhelming support" among commentators and governments in the years following the Draft Articles' adoption.[97]

This "guardrail," then, is neither a radical doctrinal innovation nor an unduly restrictive one. It leaves space for collective countermeasures to address the most serious violations of shared international norms, whether they occur in the context of an aggressive invasion, a cyber operation, severe environmental damage, or some other internationally wrongful act justifying a collective response. Furthermore, when the *erga omnes* condition is met, collective countermeasures may properly aim to induce appropriate reparations.

Collective Countermeasures to Compel Reparations

Collective countermeasures may be used to compel reparations provided that the "ongoing failure to meet the obligation to make reparations" arises from a violation of an obligation *erga omnes*.[98]

Whether or not the reparations obligation passes the heightened *jus cogens* threshold is not dispositive of its *erga omnes* status.[99] Nor is it relevant that a state's failure to pay reparations only materially injures the state to which the reparations are owed; the ICJ has recognized obligations *erga omnes* the violation of which may cause no direct injury to any state at all, but rather to individual persons.[100] Ultimately, qualification of an obligation as *erga omnes* rests on "the importance of the rights involved"[101] and the interest of every state in upholding those rights and the values they embody. Because the reparations obligation is the "immediate corollary"[102] of injurious wrongful conduct, the importance of the "right to demand reparation"[103] must also be intimately linked thereto. Failure to pay reparations owed in relation to an *erga omnes* violation is therefore a wrongful act susceptible, like the initial *erga omnes* violation, to collective countermeasures.

Consider the 2019 Advisory Opinion on the Legal Consequences of the Separation of the Chagos Archipelago from Mauritius in 1965. There, the ICJ reiterated that, because "respect for the right to self-determination is an obligation *erga omnes*, all states have a legal interest in protecting that right."[104] The Court emphasized both the United Kingdom's "obligation to bring to an end its administration of the Chagos Archipelago" and the obligation of all states to "co-operate with the United Nations to complete the decolonization of Mauritius."[105] The distinction drawn between these two obligations seems incongruous with the view that the international community's legal interests and the responsible state's original *erga omnes* violation (in this case, the act of colonization) are precisely coextensive, such that the former is entirely extinguished when the latter ceases. Indeed, in addition to the United Kingdom's obligation to decolonize, the ICJ also noted in Chagos that the General Assembly (not the United Kingdom alone) ought to address "the resettlement on the Chagos Archipelago of Mauritian nationals."[106] By analogy, one might recognize the international community's ongoing, collective interest not only in Russia's cessation of aggression (comparable to the ending of colonial administration in Chagos) but also in Russia's payment to Ukraine of reparations (akin to the complete decolonization, including resettlement, recognized in Chagos as a matter of concern for the entire UN General Assembly).[107]

Considerations for the Application of Collective Countermeasures

States may only take countermeasures to compel reparations if there is a sufficient causal nexus between the target state's wrongful act and the injured state's compensable damage."[108] Various international tribunals have observed that some injuries may be too "uncertain to be appraised" and proven, or simply "too indirect and remote to become the basis, in law, for an award of indemnity."[109] However, as the ICJ has observed, "[i]n a situation of a long-standing and large-scale armed conflict . . . the causal nexus between the wrongful conduct and certain injuries . . . may be readily established."[110] Certain harmful but indirect consequences of aggression, such as inflated global prices of energy and agricultural goods, may not add to the reparations balance. But the potentially compensable harms resulting directly from unlawful armed attacks are nonetheless vast, including not only damage to human life and property but also, for example, "damage to the environment."[111]

The use of collective countermeasures to induce reparations also remains subject to the standard conditions for the lawful application of countermeasures, including proportionality.[112] Here, collective countermeasures introduce a new wrinkle: if numerous states join in deploying collective countermeasures, the cumulative impact may be disproportionate to the severity of the violation *erga omnes* to which they respond, even if each individual state's countermeasures are individually proportional. The Draft Articles make clear that the "obligation to compensate is limited by the damage" caused by the responsible state's wrongful act.[113] That material damages are at least conceptually quantifiable suggests that they might serve as a relatively objective metric by which to assess the proportionality of collective countermeasures taken to compel reparation. Still, states will need to coordinate not only how much reparation is due but also what countermeasures each participating state will take to induce compliance. Such coordination is best achieved through a international mechanism established for that purpose.

Realizing Reparations in Ukraine and Beyond

Collective countermeasures do not legally require the imprimatur of any multilateral institution or international tribunal. Even a single state can take "collective" countermeasures to induce reparations on behalf of another, materially injured state.[114] However, some form of multilateral institutionalization could help to imbue collective countermeasures with greater moral force by plausibly linking the measures to a broader coalition of states. In particular, the involvement of the UN General Assembly could increase the legitimacy and efficacy of collective countermeasures, in turn facilitating the replicability of collective countermeasures as a means of realizing reparations in future circumstances involving violations of obligations *erga omnes.*

A Proposal for Institutionalizing Collective Countermeasures

The General Assembly could lay the groundwork for a reparations system by establishing an international registry of frozen assets. Article 14 of the UN Charter empowers the Assembly to "recommend measures for the peaceful adjustment of any situation . . . which it deems likely to impair the general welfare . . . including situations resulting from a violation of the provision of the present Charter . . . ."[115] Using this authority, the General Assembly could recommend the creation of a registry documenting the value, status, and location of frozen assets.[116] The registry could serve to gather and organize funds, clarifying the value, status, and location of frozen assets. That information could inform future negotiations and create additional pressure on Russia to comply with its international obligations.

While the General Assembly does not have the authority to establish an international claims commission that binds non-consenting states, nothing bars it from cooperating in this way with states that volunteer to participate.[117] The UN General Assembly could pass a resolution requesting that the Secretary-General negotiate an agreement with those states.[118] The United Nations could then enter into a binding international agreement with participating states specifying that states registering frozen assets agree to either transfer those assets to a future UN-approved authority to fund a reparations mechanism, or to unfreeze the assets following a UN determination that Russia has otherwise satisfied its reparations obligation. The agreement could also provide for cooperation with the ICC and other international justice mechanisms, should compensation be awarded through the prosecution of crimes committed during the war.

This UN frozen asset registry would exist alongside the new Register of Damage already established by the Council of Europe after a General Assembly resolution supported its creation in late 2022.[119] Once established, the UN registry would better position the United Nations to structure the details of a compensation mechanism, having a view of not only the scale of the damages, but also the potential funding available to redress them. Because funds would not be disbursed until a lawful settlement (likely involving Russia's cooperation) is reached, this arrangement would respect the reversibility requirement of countermeasures doctrine. The institutional structure would also address the proportionality concerns raised by collective countermeasures; centralizing asset freezes in a visible registry, measured against the quantum set by the damage registry, would assuage concerns (however unrealistic) that countermeasures against Russia could become disproportionate to the harms Russia has inflicted on Ukraine.

The Advantages of Institutionalizing Collective Countermeasures

Aggregating frozen assets resulting from collective countermeasures under the auspices of the United Nations would improve the chances of success by organizing and aligning the individual efforts of many nations, lowering the transaction costs for Russia to engage in negotiations for reparations by making the United Nations the central locus of the process, and improving the legitimacy of the process by reducing politicization.

Introducing the organizing force of the General Assembly into the countermeasures effort against Russia would transform what promises to be a long and high-pressure period of holding assets from an individual state effort into a collective one. Considering the dizzying array of legal theories and approaches to the freeze-to-seize problem, it appears unlikely that nations will reach a consensus regarding how long to extend the freezes and whether, or under what circumstances, they should either conclude the freezes or seize the assets for Ukraine's benefit. Aggregating information regarding frozen assets in a registry would strengthen the global commitment to a particular theory of collective countermeasures and relieve internal political pressures to either end the freezes before Russia complies or violate international law and seize the assets—thereby mitigating an otherwise potentially intractable collective action problem.

This approach would also clarify the stakes for Russia and increase its incentives to cooperate. Negotiating with a central institution would reduce transaction costs and assure Russia that it would not have to negotiate individually with each state that holds frozen assets. A collective, moreover, would wield more bargaining power than individual nations would. A central institution can promise a unified end to the full range of sanctioning freezes, creating a significant incentive to arrive at a negotiated agreement.[120] Establishing a registry of frozen assets and monitoring their eventual disbursement through a central international authority would also make the misappropriation of those assets through corruption more difficult,[121] offering participating states greater assurance that funds intended as reparations will actually reach those to whom they are owed.

Importantly, institutionalizing collective countermeasures would strengthen the legitimacy of the continued freezing of Russian state assets. Particularly because collective countermeasures against Russia were taken largely by its geopolitical opponents, some may criticize them as merely pretextual attempts to strike a blow against Russia, rather than as a legal response to Russia's violation of obligations *erga omnes*. Aggregating assets under a General Assembly registry with agreed conditions that no expropriations or seizures would be made against the assets without Russian consent would lend legitimacy to the countermeasures effort, taking it out of the realm of political or national security-motivated decisions of the few and instead vesting in them the judgment of a broad coalition.[122]

Relatedly, institutionalizing collective countermeasures would have a democratizing effect. The status quo grants outsized power to the wealthy states that control the frozen Russian assets, sidelining the views and interests of less economically powerful nations. With the proliferation of economic sanctions in recent decades, a handful of financial powers have wielded independent enforcement powers to the exclusion of economically weaker plenary members.[123] Shifting that authority to the United Nations would democratize control and strengthen the legitimacy of asset freezes. Of course, the decision of whether to take independent countermeasures in the first instance would remain with the states that control the assets. Looking forward, however, those states' participation in the registry would shift some authority to a collective institution designed to represent a broader range of states. A more egalitarian distribution of agency in enforcement would strengthen newly empowered states' stake in the pursuit of justice and reinforce the collective nature of the obligations *erga omnes* at stake.[124]

Some degree of democratization of the enforcement of reparations obligations would be critical to extending the precedent of Ukraine to the pursuit of accountability in other contexts. If only a small number of powerful states have the power to decide when reparations are to be enforced, the obligation will suffer from uneven enforcement—and its legitimacy will suffer as a result.[125] Though the institutionalization of reparations through a recommendation of the General Assembly would rest firmly on that body's well-established authorities, accomplishing it in practice would add a novel option to the menu of reparations mechanisms available in future conflicts.[126] Particularly given the historically uneven enforcement of reparations obligations, developing a tangible and replicable precedent could facilitate better outcomes for future victims of aggression and other violations of obligations *erga omnes*.

A Path Toward Reparations Beyond Ukraine

After decades of global indifference to uncompensated suffering elsewhere, some states are understandably critical of the double standard apparently at play in the race to aid a European victim of aggression.[127] However, reckoning with the historical injustice of reparations obligations left unfulfilled does not require repeating these moral failures with respect to Ukraine. On the contrary, justice demands an assertive yet lawful approach to securing reparations in the present conflict. Harnessing the exceptional support Ukraine enjoys could revive the reparations obligation to the benefit of all states.

The intervention of the Saudi-led coalition in the ongoing armed conflict in Yemen, for example, underscores the broader potential of collective countermeasures to compel reparations. The coalition, which has at times benefited from US support, has been accused of repeated, severe violations of international humanitarian obligations[128]—obligations "essentially of an *erga omnes* character."[129] As in Ukraine's case, the UN Security Council is unlikely to act. Instead, states could consider collective countermeasures to induce reparations.

Collective countermeasures become more powerful as more states participate in them; this is a source of both strength and constraint. Action by a broad coalition of states can impose significant costs on even economically and militarily powerful wrongdoers, but that kind of coalition is likely to emerge only when states are persuaded of the unlawfulness of the target state's behavior. Ukraine has succeeded in the current war because it has made a compelling case that it is the subject of an unlawful invasion. For other states to take advantage of this approach, they, too, would need to persuade others that the target state has acted unlawfully. In such cases, countermeasures could concretize international disapprobation while reinforcing the compulsory character of the obligation to pay reparations.

As the process of reparations for Ukraine moves forward, some states may favor a narrow approach to avoid ramifications for their own future behavior. However, forging an effective and legitimate solution to the problem of reparations in Ukraine requires recognizing that broader reparative efforts for violations committed during war are long overdue. Such a solution has the potential not only to address current and future injuries but also, perhaps most importantly, to create incentives to deter violations in the first place. A more predictable reparations mechanism would reaffirm and strengthen the fundamental prohibition of illegal uses of force—a legal principle at the heart of the international legal order.

Conclusion

While collective countermeasures provide an invaluable tool enabling states to support Ukraine's demands for accountability for Russia's violations of *erga omnes* obligations, they do not deliver Ukrainians the immediate support they want and need. Under our proposal, Russia's assets would be indefinitely frozen, but Ukraine would not receive reparations until Russia finally agrees to a reparations scheme (with the possible exception of a modest annual sum that could be obtained through taxing the earnings on the assets). Yet a system of collective countermeasures, institutionalized through the United Nations, would create pressure to bring Russia to the table. The proposal offered in this chapter would give Ukraine a valuable bargaining chip as it seeks to negotiate peace. It thus offers a path for repairing the harms suffered by Ukraine. Moreover, by developing a doctrine that could be employed by other states in the future, this proposal charts a path for repairing the losses suffered by any other state subjected to an unlawful war in the future.

Notes

1 †This chapter is adapted from "War Reparations: The Case for Countermeasures," with the permission of *Stanford Law Review*. Oona A. Hathaway, Maggie M. Mills & Thomas M. Poston, *War Reparations: The Case for Countermeasures*, 76 STANFORD L. REV. 971-1050 (2024).

See Oona A. Hathaway & Scott J. Shapiro, The Internationalists: How a Radical Plan to Outlaw War Remade the World 31–55, 93–98 (2017).

2 *Id*. at 302.

3 Press Release: Updated Ukraine Recovery and Reconstruction Needs Assessment Released, World Bank (Feb. 15, 2024).
4 U.N. GAOR, 77th Sess., 7th plen. mtg. at 52, U.N. Doc. A/77/PV.7 (Sept. 21, 2022).
5 G.A. Res. ES-11/5, at 2 (Nov. 14, 2022).
6 *See* Council of Europe Comm. of Ministers, Resolution CM/Res(2023)3. Establishing the Enlarged Partial Agreement on the Register of Damage Caused by the Aggression of the Russian Federation Against Ukraine (May 12, 2023), https://rm.coe.int/0900001680ab2595.
7 *See* Luke Moffett, Reparations and War: Finding Balance in Repairing the Past 101–02 (2023).
8 *See* Michael J. Kelly, *The Role of International Law in the Russia-Ukraine War*, 55 Case W. Res. J. Int'l L. 61, 77–85 (2023) (collecting cases).
9 These terms are often used interchangeably. *See* Martin Dawidowicz, *Public Law Enforcement Without Public Law Safeguards? An Analysis of State Practice on Third-Party Countermeasures and Their Relationship to the UN Security Council*, 77 British Yearbook Int'l L. 333, 333 n.1 (2007).
10 Oona A. Hathaway, *International Law Goes to War in Ukraine: The Legal Pushback to Russia's Invasion*, Foreign Affs. (Mar. 15, 2022).
11 *See, e.g.*, S. 2003, 118th Cong. § 104(b) (2024) (authorizing the president to "seize, confiscate, transfer, or vest any Russian sovereign assets . . . subject to the jurisdiction of the United States").
12 *See* Pierre d'Argent, Les Réparations de Guerre en Droit International Public: La Responsabilité Internationale des États à l'Épreuve de la Guerre 808–13 (2002).
13 *See* Directorate-General for Neighbourhood and Enlargement Negotiations, *Ukraine: Commission Presents Options to Make Sure That Russia Pays for Its Crimes*, Eur. Comm'n (Nov. 30, 2022), https://neighbourhood-enlargement.ec.europa.eu/news/ukraine-commission-presents-options-make-sure-russia-pays-its-crimes-2022-11-30_en.
14 *Advancing National Security and Foreign Policy Through Sanctions, Export Controls, and Other Economic Tools: Hearing Before the S. Comm on Banking, Housing, and Urban Affairs*, 118th Cong. (2023) (statement of Daleep Singh, Former Deputy National Security Advisor for International Economics), https://www.banking.senate.gov/hearings/advancing-national-security-and-foreign-policy-through-sanctions-export-controls-and-other-economic-tools; Timothy Ash, *Who Can Pay for Putin's War? Step Forward Vladimir*, Ctr. Euro. Pol. Analysis (Mar. 7, 2023), https://cepa.org/article/who-can-pay-for-putins-war-step-forward-vladimir.
15 Monika Pronczuk & Eshe Nelson, *E.U. Moves to Tap Frozen Russian Assets to Help Ukraine*, N.Y. Times (Dec. 12, 2023), https://www.nytimes.com/2023/12/12/business/eu-russia-frozen-assets-ukraine.html.
16 *See* Jurisdictional Immunities of the State (Ger. v. It.), 2012 I.C.J. 99, ¶¶ 113, 116–18 (Feb. 3); *see also* U.N. Convention on Jurisdictional Immunities of States and Their Property, art. 21(1)(c), *opened for signature* Dec. 2, 2004, G.A. Res. 59/38 (not in force) [hereinafter Convention on Jurisdictional Immunities].
17 Jasper Finke, *Sovereign Immunity: Rule, Comity or Something Else?*, 21 Eur. J. Int'l L. 853, 874 (2010).
18 *See* Ingrid (Brunk) Wuerth, *Immunity from Execution of Central Bank Assets*, *in* The Cambridge Handbook of Immunities and International Law 266 (Tom Ruys, Nicolas Angelet & Luca Ferro eds., 2019).
19 Jurisdictional Immunities of the State (Ger. v. It.), Judgment, 2012 I.C.J. Rep. 99, ¶ 66 (Feb. 3).

20 U.N. Convention on Jurisdictional Immunities of States and Their Property, art. 21(1)(c), *opened for signature* Dec. 2, 2004, G.A. Res. 59/38 (not in force) at 5; *id.* at 9 (permitting "post-judgment measures of constraint" where "it has been established that the property is specifically in use or intended for use by the State for other than government non-commercial purposes").
21 Jurisdictional Immunities of the State (Ger. v. It.), Judgment, 2012 I.C.J. Rep. 99, ¶¶ 92–93, 97 (Feb. 3).
22 *See* Philip Zelikow & Simon Johnson, How Ukraine Can Build Back Better: Use the Kremlin's Seized Assets to Pay for Reconstruction, FOREIGN AFFS. (Apr. 19, 2022), https://perma.cc/2PW3-KBU3; Anton Moiseinko, *Trading with a Friend's Enemy*, 116 AM. J. INT'L L. 720, 726 (2022); *see also* Laurence H. Tribe & Jeremy Lewin, $100 Billion. Russia's Treasure in the U.S. Should Be Turned Against Putin., N.Y. TIMES (Apr. 15, 2022), https://perma.cc/NR3B-QG4L.
23 U.N. Convention on Jurisdictional Immunities of States and Their Property, art. 21(1)(c), *opened for signature* Dec. 2, 2004, G.A. Res. 59/38 (not in force) at 1.
24 *Id.* at 1 (emphasis added).
25 2012 I.C.J. Rep. 99 at ¶ 57. The Court explicitly recognizes an "immunity from enforcement enjoyed by States in regard to their property situated on foreign territory" that is broader than the strictly "jurisdictional immunity enjoyed by those same States before foreign courts." *Id.* ¶ 113.
26 Christian Tomuschat, *The International Law of State Immunity and Its Development by National Institutions*, 44 VAND. J. TRANSNAT'L L. 1105, 1131 (2011).
27 *See Report of the Commission to the General Assembly on the Work of its Forty-Third Session*, [1991] 2 Y.B. Int'l L. Comm'n, U.N. Doc. A/CN.4/SER.A/1991/Add.l, art. 2 cmt. (3).
28 *See* Bernard H. Oxman, *Jurisdiction of States*, *in* MAX PLANCK ENCYCLOPEDIAS OF INTERNATIONAL LAW ¶ 6 (Rüdiger Wolfrum ed., 2007), https://opil.ouplaw.com/display/10.1093/law:epil/9780199231690/law-9780199231690-e1436; RESTATEMENT (FOURTH) OF THE FOREIGN RELATIONS LAW OF THE UNITED STATES, Part IV Introductory Note (AM. L. INST. 2017).
29 *Id.*; Ingrid Brunk, Central Bank Immunity, Sanctions, and Sovereign Wealth Funds, 91 GEO. WASH. L. REV. 1616, 1642 (2023).
30 *Id.* at 1642–43.
31 *See* Ingrid Wuerth [Brunk], *The Due Process and Other Constitutional Rights of Foreign Nations*, 88 FORDHAM L. REV. 633, 690 (2019).
32 Jean-Marc Thouvenin & Victor Grandaubert, *The Material Scope of State Immunity from Execution*, *in* THE CAMBRIDGE HANDBOOK OF IMMUNITIES AND INTERNATIONAL LAW 245, 247 (Tom Ruys, Nicolas Angelet & Lucas Ferro eds., 2019).
33 Int'l L. Comm'n, Draft Articles on Responsibility of States for Internationally Wrongful Acts, with Commentaries, U.N. Doc. A/56/10, art. 49 (2001), ch. 5, comment (1).
34 Gabriella Blum, *The Crime and Punishment of States*, 38 YALE J. INT'L L. 57, 63 (2013).
35 U.N. Charter art. 51, ¶ 1.
36 Anton Moiseinko, Trading with a Friend's Enemy, 116 AM. J. INT'L L. 720, 729 (2022).
37 Int'l L. Comm'n, Draft Articles on Responsibility of States for Internationally Wrongful Acts, with Commentaries, U.N. Doc. A/56/10, art. 21, cmt (2) (2001). However, Article 21 does not reference *collective* self-defense and is silent on "all issues of the effect of action in self-defence *vis-à-vis* third States." *Id.*

38 *Cf.* Int'l L. Comm'n, Draft Articles on Responsibility of States for Internationally Wrongful Acts, with Commentaries, U.N. Doc. A/56/10, art. 21, cmt (2) (2001) ("The essential effect . . . is to preclude the wrongfulness of conduct of a State acting in self-defence *vis-à-vis* an attacking State.").

39 Ingrid (Wuerth) Brunk & Monica Hakimi, *Russia, Ukraine, and the Future World Order*, 116 Am. J. Int'l L. 687, 695 (2022).

40 *See* Laurence H. Tribe, Raymond P. Tolentino, Kate M. Harris, Jackson Erpenbach, & Jeremy Lewin, Renew Democracy Initiative, The Legal, Practical, and Moral Case for Transferring Russian Sovereign Assets to Ukraine 58 (Sept. 17, 2023), https://rdi.org/wp-content/uploads/2023/10/RDI-Making-Putin-Pay-Report-September-2023_compressed-1.pdf; Dapo Akande, Shotaro Hamamoto, Pierre Klein, Paul Reichler, Philippe Sands, Nico Schrijver, Christian Tams, & Philip Zelikow, Legal Memorandum on Proposed Countermeasures Against Russia to Compensate Injured States for Losses Caused by Russia's War of Aggression Against Ukraine 13 (Nov. 20, 2023), https://united4ukraine.network/wp-content/uploads/2023/12/legal-memo-on-countermeasures.pdf.

41 *See* Int'l L. Comm'n, Draft Articles on Responsibility of States for Internationally Wrongful Acts, with Commentaries, U.N. Doc. A/56/10, art. 49, cmt (1) (2001).

42 Laurence H. Tribe, Raymond P. Tolentino, Kate M. Harris, Jackson Erpenbach & Jermey Lewin, Renew Democracy Initiative, The Legal, Practical, and Moral Case for Transferring Russian Sovereign Assests to Ukraine 59 (2023), https://perma.cc/46QU-JC2A.

43 Ingrid Brunk, Central Bank Immunity, Sanctions, and Sovereign Wealth Funds, 91 GEO. WASH. L. REV. 1616, at 34 (2023); Int'l L. Comm'n, Draft Articles on Responsibility of States for Internationally Wrongful Acts, with Commentaries, U.N. Doc. A/56/10, art. 49(1) (2001). ("An injured State may only take countermeasures against a State . . . in order to induce that State to comply with its obligations."); *see also* Gabčikovo-Nagymaros Project (Hungary/Slovakia), Judgment, 1997 I.C.J. Rep. 7, ¶ 87 (Sept. 25).

44 Int'l L. Comm'n, Draft Articles on Responsibility of States for Internationally Wrongful Acts, with Commentaries, U.N. Doc. A/56/10, art. 48, cmt. (6) (2001).

45 *Id.*, art. 49, cmt. (7).

46 The inducement logic that undergirds the reversibility requirement as the ICJ articulated it in *Gabč íkovo-Nagymaros Project*, *see* Int'l L. Comm'n, Draft Articles on Responsibility of States for Internationally Wrongful Acts, with Commentaries, U.N. Doc. A/56/10, art. 49, cmt. (9) (2001), helps explain why seizures that short-circuit (rather than induce) compliance likely do not qualify as countermeasures even if the assets are perfectly fungible, as some have argued. *See* Dapo Akande et al., On Proposed Countermeasures Against Russia to Compensate Injured States for Losses Caused by Russia's War of Aggression Against Ukraine 13 (2023), https://perma.cc/GK9J-VAF7.

47 *See* Int'l L. Comm'n, Draft Articles on Responsibility of States for Internationally Wrongful Acts, with Commentaries, U.N. Doc. A/56/10, art. 49(2)–(3) (2001).

48 *Id.* at art. 49, cmt. (9).

49 *See* Laurence H. Tribe, Raymond P. Tolentino, Kate M. Harris, Jackson Erpenbach & Jermey Lewin, Renew Democracy Initiative, The Legal, Practical, and Moral Case for Transferring Russian Sovereign Assests to Ukraine 58–59 (2023), https://perma.cc/46QU-JC2A.

50 The Draft Articles explicitly clarify that "[w]here countermeasures are taken . . . *the underlying obligation is not suspended,* still less terminated; the wrongfulness

of the conduct in question is precluded for the time being by reason of its character as a countermeasure." Int'l L. Comm'n, Draft Articles on Responsibility of States for Internationally Wrongful Acts, with Commentaries, U.N. Doc. A/56/10, art. 22, cmt (4) (2001) (emphasis added). Some seizure proponents' reliance on a so-called "legal-relations conception of reversibility" is therefore misplaced. *Contra* Laurence H. Tribe, Raymond P. Tolentino, Kate M. Harris, Jackson Erpenbach & Jermey Lewin, Renew Democracy Initiative, The Legal, Practical, and Moral Case for Transferring Russian Sovereign Assests to Ukraine 58–59 (2023), https://perma.cc/46QU-JC2A.

51 Int'l L. Comm'n, Draft Articles on Responsibility of States for Internationally Wrongful Acts, with Commentaries, U.N. Doc. A/56/10, at ch. 2, cmt (6) (2001).

52 *Id.* at art. 49, cmt. (9). *Contra* Laurence H. Tribe, Raymond P. Tolentino, Kate M. Harris, Jackson Erpenbach & Jermey Lewin, Renew Democracy Initiative, The Legal, Practical, and Moral Case for Transferring Russian Sovereign Assests to Ukraine 59 (2023), https://perma.cc/46QU-JC2A.

53 Even if, *arguendo*, seizures were "lawful and effective countermeasures," an "injured State" would still "ha[ve] a choice" of alternatives, including extended asset freezes, and thus the Draft Articles would still require the selection of "one which permits the resumption of performance of the obligations suspended," again consistent with "the duty" (not merely a "preference," *see* Laurence H. Tribe, Raymond P. Tolentino, Kate M. Harris, Jackson Erpenbach & Jermey Lewin, Renew Democracy Initiative, The Legal, Practical, and Moral Case for Transferring Russian Sovereign Assests to Ukraine 59 (2023), https://perma.cc/46QU-JC2A) "to choose measures that are reversible" "as far as possible." Int'l L. Comm'n, Draft Articles on Responsibility of States for Internationally Wrongful Acts, with Commentaries, U.N. Doc. A/56/10, art. 49, cmt (9) (2001).

54 *See* Dapo Akande et al., On Proposed Countermeasures Against Russia to Compensate Injured States for Losses Caused by Russia's War of Aggression Against Ukraine 11 (2023), https://perma.cc/GK9J-VAF7.

55 *Id.*

56 *Id.* at 22.

57 Int'l L. Comm'n, Draft Articles on Responsibility of States for Internationally Wrongful Acts, with Commentaries, U.N. Doc. A/56/10, at ch. 2, cmt (2) (2001).

58 David E. Sanger & Alan Rappeport, *U.S. and Europe Eye Russian Assets to Aid Ukraine as Funding Dries Up*, N.Y. Times (Dec. 21, 2023), https://www.nytimes.com/2023/12/21/us/politics/russian-assets-ukraine.html.

59 Oona A. Hathaway, *International Law Goes to War in Ukraine: The Legal Pushback to Russia's Invasion*, Foreign Affs. (Mar. 15, 2022).

60 *Cf.* Nicolas Véron & Joshua Kirschenbaum, *Now Is Not the Time to Confiscate Russia's Central Bank Reserves*, Bruegel Blog (May 16, 2022), https://www.bruegel.org/blog-post/now-not-time-confiscate-russias-central-bank-reserves.

61 Jean-Marc Thouvenin, *Gel des fonds des banques centrales et immunité d'exécution*, *in* Immunities in the Age of Global Constitutionalism 209, 215 (Anne Peters, Evelyne Lagrange, Stefan Oeter & Christian Tomuschat eds., 2015).

62 *Id.*

63 Tom Ruys, *Non-UN Financial Sanctions Against Central Banks and Heads of State: In Breach of International Immunity Law?*, EJIL: Talk! (May 12, 2017), https://www.ejiltalk.org/non-un-financial-sanctions-against-central-banks-and-heads-of-state-in-breach-of-international-immunity-law.

64 *See* Int'l L. Comm'n, Draft Articles on Responsibility of States for Internationally Wrongful Acts, with Commentaries, U.N. Doc. A/56/10, at ch. 2, cmt (6) (2001).
65 *Id.* at art. 49, cmt. (9).
66 Int'l L. Comm'n, Draft Articles on Responsibility of States for Internationally Wrongful Acts, with Commentaries, U.N. Doc. A/56/10, art. 49(1) (2001).
67 Gabč íkovo-Nagymaros Project (Hungary/Slovakia), Judgment, 1997 I.C.J. Rep. 7, ¶ 152 (Sept. 25).
68 Int'l L. Comm'n, Draft Articles on Responsibility of States for Internationally Wrongful Acts, with Commentaries, U.N. Doc. A/56/10, art. 31, cmt (1) (2001). (quoting Factory at Chorzów (Ger. v. Pol.), Jurisdiction, 1927 P.C.I.J. (ser. A) No. 9, at 21 (July 26)).
69 Gaetano Arangio-Ruiz (Special Rapporteur), *Fourth Rep. on State Responsibility*, U.N. Doc. A/CN.4/444, ¶ 3 (1992).
70 Int'l L. Comm'n, Draft Articles on Responsibility of States for Internationally Wrongful Acts, with Commentaries, U.N. Doc. A/56/10, art. 49, cmt (8) (2001). ("[C]ountermeasures . . . may also be taken to ensure reparation . . . .").
71 U.N. Charter art. 2, ¶ 4.
72 Int'l L. Comm'n, Draft Articles on Responsibility of States for Internationally Wrongful Acts, with Commentaries, U.N. Doc. A/56/10, art. 2 (2001).
73 *See* Commc'ns Dep't of the Secretariat of the CMU, *Statement by Prime Minister of Ukraine Denys Shmyhal at a Government Session*, Gov'T Ukr. (Jan. 10, 2023), https://www.kmu.gov.ua/en/news/promova-premier-ministra-ukrainy-denysa-shmyhalia-na-zasidanni-uriadu-10-1-23.
74 *See* Anton Moiseinko, Trading with a Friend's Enemy, 116 AM. J. INT'L L. 720, 721 (2022).
75 The Barcelona Traction, Light and Power Company, Ltd. (Belg. v. Spain), Judgment, 1970 I.CJ. Rep. 3, ¶ 33 (Feb 5.).
76 *Id.* at ¶¶ 33–34.
77 Int'l L. Comm'n, Draft Articles on Responsibility of States for Internationally Wrongful Acts, with Commentaries, U.N. Doc. A/56/10, at Part III, ch. 2, cmt. (8) (2001) (emphasis added).
78 *Barcelona Traction* at ¶¶ 33–34.
79 Int'l L. Comm'n, Draft Articles on Responsibility of States for Internationally Wrongful Acts, with Commentaries, U.N. Doc. A/56/10, art. 48(1) (2001).
80 *Id.* art. 48(2)(a)–(b).
81 Application of the Convention on the Prevention and Punishment of the Crime of Genocide (The Gambia v. Myanmar), Preliminary Objections, 2022 I.C.J. Rep. 477, ¶ 114 (July 22).
82 *Id.* at ¶ 99.
83 Michael N. Schmitt & Sean Watts, *Collective Cyber Countermeasures?*, 12 Harv. Nat'l Sec. J. 373, 391 (2021).
84 South West Africa (Eth v. S. Afr; Liber. v. S. Afr.), Second Phase, Judgment, 1966 I.C.J. Rep. 6, ¶ 44 (July 18).
85 *See* Elena Katselli Proukaki, The Problem of Enforcement in International Law: Countermeasures, the Non-Injured State and the Idea of International Community 85 (2010).
86 Int'l L. Comm'n, Draft Articles on Responsibility of States for Internationally Wrongful Acts, with Commentaries, U.N. Doc. A/56/10, art. 22, cmt (6) (2001).
87 Martin Dawidowicz, THIRD-PARTY COUNTERMEASURERS IN INTERNATIONAL LAW 242–43 (2017).

88 Ministerial Declaration Adopted at the Sixth Annual Meeting of Ministers for Foreign Affairs of the Member States of the Group of 77, para. 8 (Oct. 6–8, 1982, New York), *reprinted in* VI THE COLLECTED DOCUMENTS OF THE GROUP OF 77, at 525 (Mourad Ahmia ed., 2015).
89 Michael N. Schmitt & Sean Watts, Collective Cyber Countermeasures?, 12 HARV. NAT'L SEC.J. 373, 386 (2021).
90 *Countermeasures in Cyberspace,* in THE OXFORD PROCESS ON INTERNATIONAL LAW PROTECTIONS IN CYBERSPACE: A COMPENDIUM 488, 491 (2022*)*, https://perma.cc/27DXNLCF; *see also* Miles Jackson & Federica Paddeu, *The Countermeasures of Others: When Can States Collaborate in the Taking of Countermeasures?* 3–4 (2023) (unpublished manuscript) (available at https://papers.ssrn.com/sol3/papers.cfm?abstract_id =4603233).
91 *See* D.N. Hutchinson, *Solidarity and Breaches of Multilateral Treaties*, 59 BRIT. Y.B. INT'L L. 151, 201–02 (1988).
92 Monica Hakimi, *Constructing an International Community*, 111 AM. J. INT'L L. 317, 349 (2017).
93 Martin Dawidowicz, *Public Law Enforcement Without Public Law Safeguards? An Analysis of State Practice on Third-Party Countermeasures and Their Relationship to the UN Security Council*, 77 BRITISH Y.B. INT'L L. 336–7 n.17 (2007). (collecting citations).
94 *Id.* at 337. *But see* Federica Paddeu, 77 CAMBRIDGE L.J. 427, 429 (2018) (reviewing MARTIN DAWIDOWICZ, THIRD-PARTY COUNTERMEASURES IN INTERNATIONAL LAW (2017)) (suggesting that collective countermeasures may be "used as political tools by the powerful to oppress, and bend the will of, the weak").
95 *Countermeasures in Cyberspace,* in THE OXFORD PROCESS ON INTERNATIONAL LAW PROTECTIONS IN CYBERSPACE: A COMPENDIUM 488, 501 (2022), https://perma.cc/27DXNLCF.
96 U.N. Secretariat, *Report of the International Law Commission on the Work of its Fifty-Second Session (2000): Topical Summary of the Discussion Held in the Sixth Committee of the General Assembly During its Fifty-Fifth Session*, ¶¶ 179–81 U.N. Doc. A/CN.4/513, (Feb. 2001), https://documents-dds-ny.un.org/doc/UNDOC/GEN/N01/251/22/PDF/N0125122.pdf.
97 *See* MARTIN DAWIDOWICZ, THIRD-PARTY COUNTERMEASURERS IN INTERNATIONAL LAW 269 & n.191 (2017).
98 Christian Dominicé, *The International Responsibility of States for Breach of Multilateral Obligations*, 10 EUR. J. INT'L L. 353, 363 (1999).
99 Pierre-Marie Dupuy, *Back to the Future of a Multilateral Dimension of the Law of State Responsibility for Breaches of 'Obligations Owed to the International Community as a Whole'*, 23 EUR. J. INT'L L. 1059, 1063 n.13 (2012).
100 Barcelona Traction, Light and Power Co., Ltd. (Belg. v. Spain), Judgment, 1970 I.C.J. Rep. 3, ¶ 34 (Feb. 5).
101 *Id.* at ¶ 33.
102 Int'l L. Comm'n, *Draft Articles on Responsibility of States for Internationally Wrongful Acts, with Commentaries*, U.N. Doc. A/56/10, art. 31, cmt. (4), (2001). For a succinct overview of the "conditions and limitations" international law imposes on the use of countermeasures, see David E. Pozen, Self-Help and the Separation of Powers, 124 YALE L.J. 2, 57–58 (2014).
103 ANDRÉ DE HOOGH, OBLIGATIONS ERGA OMNES AND INTERNATIONAL CRIMES: A THEORETICAL INQUIRY INTO THE IMPLEMENTATION AND ENFORCEMENT OF THE INTERNATIONAL RESPONSIBILITY OF STATES 148 (1996).
104 Legal Consequences of the Separation of the Chagos Archipelago from Mauritius in 1965, Advisory Opinion, 2019 I.C.J. Rep. 140, ¶ 180 (Feb. 25).

105 *Id.* at ¶ 182.
106 *Id.* at ¶ 181.
107 *See* Yoshifumi Tanaka, *The Legal Consequences of Obligations* Erga Omnes *in International Law*, 68 NETHERLANDS INT'L L. REV. 1, 28 (2021).
108 Int'l L. Comm'n, *Draft Articles on Responsibility of States for Internationally Wrongful Acts, with Commentaries*, U.N. Doc. A/56/10, art. 31, cmt. (10), (2001). For a succinct overview of the "conditions and limitations" international law imposes on the use of countermeasures, see David E. Pozen, Self-Help and the Separation of Powers, 124 YALE L.J. 2, 57–58 (2014).
109 Trail Smelter (U.S. v. Can.), 3 R.I.A.A. 1905, 1931 (1941); *see also* Mixed Claims Commission (U.S./Germ.), Administrative Decision No. II, 7 R.I.A.A. 23, 30 (1923); Application of the Convention on the Prevention and Punishment of the Crime of Genocide (Bosn. & Herz. v. Serb. & Montenegro), Judgment, 2007 I.C.J. Rep. 43, ¶ 462 (Feb. 26).
110 Armed Activities on the Territory of the Congo (Dem. Rep. Congo v. Uganda), Judgment, 2022 I.C.J. Rep. 13, ¶ 94 (Feb. 9).
111 *See* Certain Activities Carried Out by Nicaragua in the Border Area (Costa Rica v. Nicar.), Judgment, 2018 I.C.J. Rep., ¶ 42 (Feb. 2).
112 Int'l L. Comm'n, *Draft Articles on Responsibility of States for Internationally Wrongful Acts, with Commentaries*, U.N. Doc. A/56/10, art. 51, (2001). For a succinct overview of the "conditions and limitations" international law imposes on the use of countermeasures, see David E. Pozen, Self-Help and the Separation of Powers, 124 YALE L.J. 2, 57–58 (2014).
113 Int'l L. Comm'n, *Draft Articles on Responsibility of States for Internationally Wrongful Acts, with Commentaries*, U.N. Doc. A/56/10, art. 47, cmt. (9), (2001). For a succinct overview of the "conditions and limitations" international law imposes on the use of countermeasures, see David E. Pozen, Self-Help and the Separation of Powers, 124 YALE L.J. 2, 57–58 (2014).
114 Int'l L. Comm'n, *Draft Articles on Responsibility of States for Internationally Wrongful Acts, with Commentaries*, U.N. Doc. A/56/10, art. 48, cmt (12), (2001). For a succinct overview of the "conditions and limitations" international law imposes on the use of countermeasures, see David E. Pozen, Self-Help and the Separation of Powers, 124 YALE L.J. 2, 57–58 (2014).
115 U.N. Charter art. 14 (emphasis added).
116 Under the Charter, the General Assembly has the authority to establish "[s]uch subsidiary organs as may be found necessary." U.N. Charter art. 7(2). Article 22 provides a more tailored version of this authority. *Id.* art. 22. The ICJ has upheld significant exercises of these authorities. *See, e.g.*, Effects of Awards of Compensation by the United Nations Administrative Tribunal, 1954 I.C.J. at 53.
117 *See* U.N. Charter arts. 10, 11.
118 The vote would require a two-thirds majority of the members present and voting. U.N. GEN. ASSEMBLY, RULES OF PROCEDURE OF THE GENERAL ASSEMBLY, at 23, U.N. Doc. A/520/Rev.17, U.N. Sales No. E.08.I.9 (2008). Such resolutions are not subject to a Security Council veto.
119 *See* G.A. Res. ES-11/5, Furtherance of Remedy and Reparation for Aggression Against Ukraine, ¶ 4 (Nov. 14, 2022).
120 *See, e.g.*, Lee C. Buchheit & Paul Stephan, *The REPO Act: Confiscating Russian State Assets and Ukrainian Reparations*, LAWFARE (July 7, 2023), https://www.lawfaremedia.org/article/the-repo-act-confiscating-russian-state-assets-and-ukrainian-reparations. (noting that Russia may prefer to hold out in negotiations until the fate of its assets has been determined in each jurisdiction, but that "[t]his dispute could not take place, however, if the assets were to pass to

an entity that could spend the money only on reparations. . . . [That condition] would be satisfied if the recipient of the funds were a body or facility created by an international agreement that clearly limits what the body could do with the funds.").

121 *Cf.* Thomas de Waal, *Fighting a Culture of Corruption in Ukraine*, CARNEGIE EUR. (Apr. 18, 2016), https://carnegieeurope.eu/2016/04/18/fighting-culture-of-corruption-in-ukraine-pub-63364.

122 *See* David D. Caron, *The Legitimacy of the Collective Authority of the Security Council*, 87 AM. J. INT'L L. 552, 560 (1993).

123 Simon Caney, *Cosmopolitan Justice and Institutional Design: An Egalitarian Liberal Conception of Global Governance*, 32 SOC. THEORY & PRAC. 737, 745–47 (2006). (critiquing the institutional design of the WTO for producing the same dynamic).

124 *See id.* at 736, 745.

125 *See infra* Part IV.C.

126 *See* Thomas Gehring, Christian Dorsch & Thomas Doerfler, *Precedent and Doctrine in Organisational Decision-Making: The Power of Informal Institutional Rules in the United Nations Security Council's Activities on Terrorism*, 22 J. INT'L RELS. & DEV. 107, 116 (2019).

127 *See* Sarah Cliffe, *The West Is Fully Behind Ukraine. Developing Countries See a Double Standard.*, BARRON'S (May 20, 2022, 3:45 AM ET), https://www.barrons.com/articles/the-west-is-fully-behind-ukraine-developing-countries-see-a-double-standard-51652998228.

128 *See* Oona A. Hathaway, Aaron Haviland, Srinath Reddy Kethireddy, & Alyssa T. Yamamoto, *Yemen: Is the U.S. Breaking the Law?*, 10 HARV. NAT'L SEC. J. 1, 4 (2019).

129 Legal Consequences of the Construction of a Wall in the Occupied Palestinian Territory, Advisory Opinion, 2004 I.C.J. 136, ¶ 157 (Jul. 9) (characterizing violations of international humanitarian law as "essentially of an *erga omnes* character").

11

INVESTIGATING AND DOCUMENTING WAR CRIMES IN UKRAINE

*By Mark S. Ellis**

Introduction

In the ever-evolving landscape of international justice, the past two decades have witnessed a remarkable departure from the previous era, which was characterized by impunity. This transformation, which continues to unfold before us, signifies a historic shift toward justice and accountability — an evolution once deemed unimaginable as the world grappled with unchecked atrocities.

In this transformative period, Ukraine emerged as a beacon for accountability. Since the Russian Federation's full-scale invasion on February 24, 2022, Ukraine's Office of the Prosecutor General has meticulously documented over 183,000 crimes of aggression and war crimes.[1] Tragically, these acts have exacted a heavy toll, claiming the lives of over 500 children and inflicting life-altering wounds on well over 1,200 more. These numbers will only increase.

Ukraine's unwavering commitment to justice positions it as the driving force behind the international community's push for accountability. In a world fraught with challenges, the country's steadfast dedication to justice illuminates a path toward a future where impunity recedes into history and accountability stands as the cornerstone of international justice.

Moreover, technological advancements have transformed the way we capture and disseminate information over the last two decades. Social media and smartphones have led to an unprecedented surge in online audio files, photos, and videos, which can raise awareness and knowledge of atrocities being committed. However, a persistent challenge remains in conflict-ridden regions — verifying pictorial evidence depicting mass killings and atrocities. These digital records often hover on the periphery when they fail to meet the

DOI: 10.4324/9781003458166-14

stringent admissibility criteria of legal proceedings. To address this challenge, emerging technologies have been developed to overcome obstacles in documenting grave human rights violations.

Russia's invasion of Ukraine is not merely a theoretical concern but a stark reality. In this context, the intersection of cutting-edge technology and the imperative of justice raises complex and pressing questions regarding the role of digital evidence in documenting and prosecuting war crimes. It underscores Ukraine's unparalleled role in championing justice and accountability and emphasizes the critical importance of the international community's role in holding Russia accountable for its actions. In an era where global cooperation and shared values are paramount, the collective response to such crises has never been more crucial.

Ukraine's Role in Documenting War Crimes

Ukraine has been actively prosecuting Russian war crimes domestically, demonstrating a solid commitment to upholding justice in the face of conflict and aggression. The Office of the Prosecutor General, under the leadership of Andriy Kostin, has been at the forefront of this effort. In an interview on September 26, 2023, Kostin emphasized that Ukraine's focus extends beyond the international law aspect of justice and accountability; it prioritizes the humanitarian element and the war's profound impact on the Ukrainian people.[2]

Kostin took immediate action when the war broke out to enhance the efficiency of the justice system by reorganizing key departments within the Office of the Prosecutor General.[3] He also increased the number of prosecutors in the War Crimes Department, underscoring the importance of effectively investigating and prosecuting war crimes. Additionally, he bolstered the department responsible for handling cases involving national security and established a dedicated unit to address conflict-related sexual violence.[4]

In its pursuit of justice, Ukraine has collaborated with an international council of experts comprising more than forty-five non-governmental organizations (NGOs); they are divided into six groups to prioritize cases of war crimes where civilians are physically harmed.[5] Additionally, Ukraine has established nine prosecuting units in regions close to the war, providing specialization in war crime prosecution to ensure a unified practice across the nation.

Ukraine has made history by prosecuting environmental crimes and cyberattacks as war crimes, a groundbreaking move unprecedented in the annals of warfare.[6] In a concerted effort to address environmental crimes and prosecute those responsible, Ukraine has taken significant steps with international support. Recently, in Krakow, Poland, Ukrainian prosecutors and environmental enforcement investigators joined forces with the United States Justice Department's Environment and Natural Resources Division's (ENRD)

Environmental Crimes Section and the Environmental Protection Agency's Office of Criminal Enforcement, Forensics, and Training (OCEFT), alongside the Justice Department's War Crimes Accountability Team.[7] This collaborative initiative aims to equip Ukrainian authorities with essential skills, knowledge, and techniques to amass evidence of environmental harm resulting from the Russian Federation's invasion and to facilitate the prosecution of potential war crimes and related legal violations.[8] The urgency of addressing environmental damage became evident following the catastrophic explosion of the Nova Kakhovka dam on June 6, 2023. This incident led to immediate investigations into war crimes and ecocide. Ukraine's dedicated team of more than 150 prosecutors and over 250 regional and national investigators are diligently working on this extensive inquiry, encompassing areas significantly affected by the flooding, including Kherson, Mykolaiv, and Zaporizhzhia.

Recognizing the potential international implications, Ukrainian prosecutors have undergone training by the International Criminal Court (ICC). This training ensures that the evidence gathered meets international standards, whether it is dealt with domestically or referred to the ICC.[9]

Ukraine's commitment to justice and accountability is further demonstrated by its collaboration with giants of information technology, such as Palantir and Microsoft, to manage the vast amount of evidence, which amounts to over 500 terabytes, making this the most thoroughly documented war in history.[10] This collaboration helps establish patterns and store evidence, including documenting property damage.

There are also other new tools, such as the Core International Crimes Evidence Database (CICED).[11] It is a recently established, highly secure database designed for collaborative investigations, which was invested in by the European Union's Agency for Criminal Justice Cooperation.[12] Thousands of Ukrainians have already submitted reports from various countries. The development of this database spanned over a year. Now, if one person in Germany, Poland, or the Czech Republic comes to a police officer and reports an incident that occurred in Bucha, for example, they will carefully document it in the file.

Furthermore, Ukraine's domestic efforts extend to innovative digital initiatives, such as the mobile application known as DIIA (meaning "action"). Developed by a dedicated team of twenty-five developers at Ukraine's Digital Ministry to transform the country into one of the world's most digitally advanced societies, this app has played a vital role in keeping the country running during wartime.[13] Within eight hours of its launch in September 2019, the app garnered an astounding 2 million users.[14] Initially designed for peacetime tasks like birth or marriage registration and passport renewal, the app's usage skyrocketed after Russia's invasion. Now, the app enables victims of Russian bombings to apply for funds to repair damaged buildings, provides access to vital information like radio broadcasts during blackouts, and offers a digital "evacuation document" for faster identification at checkpoints, "e-aid" financial support for small businesses, state-backed mortgages for military and key workers, and even an "e-enemy" chatbot to report the location of Russian troops.[15]

These various domestic applications represent several digital instruments the government has established for soliciting and validating evidence concerning alleged war crimes. In response to the military invasion, Ukrainian authorities, legal practitioners, and human rights organizations have been devising novel methodologies for the systematic categorization and authentication of substantial volumes of visual, photographic, and first-hand testimonial records depicting illicit conduct attributed to Russian military forces. To this end, Ukraine has repurposed widely used governmental applications, enabling citizens to document the destruction sustained by their residences. Additionally, the country has employed facial recognition software to identify Russian military personnel within photographic materials. It has introduced fresh resources designed to guide users in geo-tagging and time-stamping their multimedia content.

The applications, chatbots, and websites developed under the auspices of the Ukrainian authorities serve to categorize various forms of war crimes and human rights violations. These tools collectively contribute data to a centralized database established by the Office of the Prosecutor General. This database encompasses a spectrum of offenses, including civilian fatalities or injuries attributed to Russian forces, physical abuse or unlawful detainment, withholding of medical assistance, and the appropriation of property by occupying military units. Verified users are prompted to report acts of violence targeting medical personnel or religious figures, damage incurred by civilian infrastructure, and the utilization of military equipment within residential areas.

The Ukrainian population has exhibited remarkable unity in support of these endeavors. Notably, the website "warcrimes.gov.ua," established by the Prosecutor General's Office, has garnered over 10,000 submissions of comprehensive evidence from citizens. The government's initiatives are bolstered by an extensive network of external human rights organizations, citizen investigators, cyber-volunteers, retired military personnel, journalists, and open-source analysts with experience documenting evidentiary materials during conflicts.

Several Ukrainian NGOs have played a crucial role alongside the Office of the Prosecutor General. Their dedicated efforts complement the broader mission to hold the Russian Federation accountable for its actions. Ukraine's civil society is more active in conflict than that of other countries.

Collectively, these Ukrainian NGOs, in collaboration with international partners, are playing a pivotal role in bringing those responsible for war crimes to justice and ensuring that the suffering of victims is acknowledged on the global stage. Their dedication underscores Ukraine's unwavering commitment to justice and accountability in the face of ongoing conflict and adversity.

Founded by democracy and human rights activists in 2007, the Center for Civil Liberties (CCL) emerged as a beacon of hope in Kyiv, Ukraine, working tirelessly to advance democracy and the rule of law.[16] Initially, it focused on pushing for Ukraine's accession to the ICC. However, when Russia annexed Crimea in 2014 and supported separatist movements in Donetsk and Luhansk, the CCL shifted its mission to document human rights abuses in these regions.[17] In 2022, amidst Russia's full-scale attack, the CCL concentrated on meticulously documenting war crimes and the forced relocations of civilians, collaborating closely with international bodies like the ICC.[18] The center's remarkable efforts earned it the Nobel Peace Prize, a testament to its unwavering commitment to justice and human rights.[19] Today, the CCL remains a steadfast advocate for democracy and human rights.

The 5 AM Coalition is a notable initiative of thirty-one nonprofit organizations and four international law and human rights experts. Named after the early morning hour when Ukrainians awoke to the sounds of Russian aggression on February 24, 2022, this coalition has been tireless in documenting Russian war crimes.[20] Its members have identified priority areas, tools, and protocols for joint advocacy efforts aimed at the ICC and domestic prosecutions.

The Ukrainian Helsinki Human Rights Union (UHHRU) has also played a significant role as a partner organization within the 5 AM Coalition. As the largest association of human rights organizations in Ukraine, it unites twenty-six human rights NGOs that provide legal assistance, monitor human rights violations, conduct research on human rights issues, offer training, and host educational events.[21]

The Reckoning Project: Ukraine Testifies is another vital effort in Ukraine's quest for justice. This project addresses the need for legally admissible testimonies from conflict journalists and researchers to ensure that the voices of victims can be heard within the courts of law. The Reckoning Project seeks to provide essential evidence in pursuing justice by training high-performing individuals in this field.[22] The initiative recognizes that Russia's invasion of Ukraine threatens the country's security and sovereignty and assaults Ukrainians' identity, memory, and ability to determine their future.

Finally, in addition to these domestic efforts, Ukraine has been actively engaged in public diplomacy and information campaigns to raise awareness about the conflict and its impact on Ukrainian society. President Volodymyr Zelenskyy's address to the United Nations General Assembly on September 19, 2023, is a notable example of Ukraine's efforts to shed light on the situation and garner international support.[23] He also addressed the ongoing Russian invasion of Ukraine at the 2022 International Bar Association's conference in Miami, Florida. Zelenskyy stressed the importance of international cooperation but, most importantly, highlighted that along with politicians and the military, lawyers will be the ones to truly end this war.[24] He emphasized that lawyers must work together to ensure that all those guilty are brought to justice and all damages caused by Russia are compensated for at the expense of the assets of the aggressor state itself.[25] Concluding the opening ceremony, Zelenskyy declared that those aiding in the fight against Russia would be remembered in world history for the protection of freedom and law and order for all people, all countries and all times.[26] He concluded with a resolute statement, affirming that "[t]ogether, we can demonstrate the efficacy of the law, assuring that each war crime is thoroughly investigated and every war criminal is brought to justice."[27]

The International Community's Role in Investigating and Documenting Atrocities

Despite the jurisdictional technicalities and enforcement challenges, the Ukrainian conflict has attracted international attention to the principle of accountability. Not since the Nuremberg Principles emerged after World War II has the call for upholding this principle been so strong and widespread. The world's attention has been focused on the social media phenomenon, which rapidly broadcasts the ongoing fighting.

As early as 2012, the ICC's Office of the Prosecutor (OTP) recognized the significance of technology in gathering pictorial evidence.[28] Digital evidence from smartphones and tablets prompted the office to prioritize "expanding its capabilities to collect different forms of scientific evidence."[29] Furthermore, the ICC has taken immediate steps to assist Ukraine, including dispatching an investigative team to Ukraine and establishing a partnership with the UK Metropolitan Police War Crimes Team.[30] These actions are driven by growing concerns about accountability in armed conflicts and the challenges in collecting evidence during and after such conflicts.

On September 14, 2023, the ICC opened a field office in Kyiv, Ukraine, marking the largest ICC office outside The Hague. As previously mentioned, Prosecutor General Kostin stated that more than 104,000 war crimes have been registered during Russia's aggression against Ukraine, and the number of such crimes continues to rise. Ukraine has been transparent and open in providing access to all the necessary materials, crime scenes, evidence, and testimony necessary for the ICC experts to see the aftermath of the aggressor's crimes with their own eyes and draw their independent conclusions.[31]

It is worth noting that evidence gathering is not just aimed at atrocity crimes. Addressing the crime of aggression is also essential to the fight against impunity. Aggressive actions undertaken by Russia against Ukraine catalyzed the commission of other serious international offenses. Consequently, the consensus within the international community suggests that the most appropriate course of action is establishing a specialized international tribunal dedicated to adjudicating the crime of aggression concerning Ukraine.

The ICC possesses the jurisdiction to prosecute the most grave international crimes, including genocide, crimes against humanity, war crimes, and the crime of aggression. The latter involves using armed force by one state against another state's sovereignty, integrity, or independence.[32] The comprehensive definition of the crime of aggression was adopted by amending the Rome Statute during the first review conference held in Kampala, Uganda, in 2010.[33] Nevertheless, it is crucial to note that the ICC can only exercise its jurisdiction over the crime of aggression in relation to those countries that are States Parties to the Rome Statute and have accepted its jurisdiction concerning this specific offense. Regrettably, at the time of the Russian invasion, neither Ukraine nor Russia was a party to the Rome Statute. Consequently, the ICC cannot apply this jurisdiction in the context of prosecuting Russia for the crime of aggression against Ukraine. Although in a positive step, Ukraine ratified the Rome Statute, and the treaty entered into force for Ukraine on January 1, 2025. However, Russia remains outside the Court's jurisdiction for the crime of aggression; the only way to prosecute Russia for such crimes is if the UN Security Council refers such cases to the ICC under Article 13 of the Rome Statute.[34] Russia's status as a permanent member of the Security Council would ensure a veto on any such referral.

As a result, the International Centre for the Prosecution of the Crime of Aggression against Ukraine (ICPA) started its operations in The Hague, hosted by the European Union Agency for Criminal Justice Cooperation (Eurojust). The creation of the ICPA was the first step toward introducing the special tribunal for the crime of aggression against Ukraine. Prosecutors from different countries will be able to cooperate in a consolidated manner, quickly and efficiently exchanging evidence and developing joint strategies for investigation and prosecution.

The ICPA will facilitate the efficient preparation of cases and participate in any future prosecution for the crime of aggression, regardless of the jurisdiction in which the case is brought. Its main tasks include ensuring the collection, preservation, and analysis of evidence of aggression against Ukraine, ensuring proper cooperation between members of the Joint Investigative Group (JIG) and other international partners in the investigation of the crime of aggression and other international crimes, and subsequently sending indictments to national courts and the ICC.

Eurojust also established a Joint Investigative Team (JIT) into alleged core international crimes committed in Ukraine. The speed at which the JIT was set up between Ukraine, Lithuania, and Poland, followed by the prompt membership of four additional countries (Estonia, Latvia, Slovakia, and Romania), the participation of the ICC, and a memorandum of understanding with the United States, sent a clear message that no effort would be spared in gathering evidence and bringing to justice those responsible for the atrocities.[35] The JIT facilitates close cooperation among all parties involved, enabling an effective and swift exchange of information and evidence.

In January 2023, a Core Group of approximately 40 countries was established to spearhead the creation of the special tribunal. This initiative ran from March 19 to 21 of 2025, the Core Group convened in Strasbourg, France, to finalise the Tribunal's Statute – it was the 14th and most consequential of the Group's meetings. The process then moved to the political stage. On May 9th, European foreign ministers met in Lviv, Ukraine, to approve the establishment of the Special Tribunal. The author attended the event.

The planned mechanism for the Tribunal is an "Enlarged Partial Agreement," where Ukraine confers jurisdiction on the Tribunal through a treaty under the Council of Europe, and states, including non-European states, can join to establish and finance the Tribunal.

Current Technologies Being Used to Document and Investigate Atrocities

Social Media and Its Challenges

The advent of digital information sharing has brought about a profound transformation in how we both learn about and document human rights abuses. The internet has effectively eliminated barriers to access and proximity, ushering in an era where evidence of events that would once have stayed hidden can be disseminated instantaneously and globally. Notably, social media platforms such as YouTube, Facebook, Google, Instagram, and Twitter (X) have emerged as prominent tools for the real-time dissemination of news and firsthand accounts, especially in conflict-ridden scenarios. They also allow ordinary citizens to become journalists. This seismic shift in our news consumption habits has significantly heightened our awareness of places and occurrences that might otherwise have remained obscure. To put it into perspective, over 300 million photos are uploaded daily on Facebook, while on YouTube, an astonishing 300 hours of video content are uploaded every minute.[36]

The ongoing conflict in Ukraine is a striking example of this phenomenon, as it stands out as one of the most extensively documented conflicts in history.[37] In both social media feeds and conventional news outlets, a plethora of evidence highlights the perpetration of war crimes during the Russian invasion of Ukraine, drawing even more attention than recent conflicts in Syria and Iraq.[38] This phenomenon is assisted by the fact that more than 75% of Ukrainians have access to the internet, with over 80% enjoying high-speed connectivity.[39]

Instagram features Ukrainians sharing stories containing videos depicting bombed-out buildings and plumes of smoke rising from residential neighborhoods. At the same time, Telegram, an encrypted multipurpose application similar to WhatsApp, showcases a Kharkiv news feed that bravely shares images of slain civilians in the heart of the city, their blood staining the streets, alongside depictions of razed apartment buildings.[40] Meanwhile, Twitter is awash with videos portraying the aftermath of bombings in Kyiv. This widespread circulation of harrowing content mirrors the nature of contemporary warfare and underscores how international efforts to hold perpetrators of mass atrocities accountable have evolved from the Nuremberg trials.

Notably, technological advances and the assistance of artificial intelligence have significantly reshaped the landscape of retributive justice, amplifying the importance of photographic evidence.[41] The ability to monitor the invasion's progress, document alleged misconduct by Russian soldiers, and record the events preceding and following attacks on civilians and civilian infrastructure, as well as military operations in general, is unparalleled.

Still, for investigation and documentation, social media has significant drawbacks. Photographs and videos uploaded to sites such as YouTube are rarely attributed and verifiable and do not carry information about the videos' dates, times, geographical coordinates, or "authors." They can also be easily manipulated and misrepresented. Thus, mainstream media (e.g., CNN, BBC) often report that information "cannot be verified or confirmed," which weakens a story's credibility. The documentation of evidence in a court of law requires the authentication of each link in the chain of custody. Without that, pictorial evidence is of little or no use to authorities. In the event of a criminal prosecution, video footage is likely to be rejected or given little weight.

This problem is currently being exploited by the very countries committing atrocities. When the images from Bucha were published showing atrocities, Russia immediately launched a "targeted disinformation blitz," calling the footage a "stage production."[42] The Russian foreign minister, Sergey Lavrov, called the massacre a "fake attack," and Russia's Defense Ministry said the photos were "fake."[43]

While witness documentation distributed on social media raises awareness of atrocities, there are difficulties in using it to prosecute individuals who commit such crimes, as retrieving social media evidence that meets the legal standard is time-consuming and resource-intensive. In addition, social media platforms often remove posts of interest to investigators for breaching policies on depictions of violence.[44] Valuable evidence that isn't collected in time can effectively be lost forever.[45] Eagerness to rebuild, which is common in wartime, can lead to the destruction of evidence. During my first visit to Ukraine after the war started, I witnessed how communities hurried to rebuild after the initial bombings. This is where the eyeWitness to Atrocities mobile app and other emerging technologies come into play.

eyeWitness to Atrocities and Other Emerging Documentative Technologies

War crime prosecutions require reliable evidence, typically involving witness testimony, documents, and conventional forensic evidence. However, as indicated, evidence from social media is rarely featured in such cases because of concerns about its reliability and susceptibility to manipulation. Several initiatives have been developed to address this issue, incorporating more rigorous protocols and technology for archiving evidence.

The Justice & Accountability Project and others

In response to Russia's invasion of Ukraine, the Global Legal Action Network (GLAN) and Bellingcat launched the Justice & Accountability Project to investigate alleged atrocity crimes in Ukraine. Bellingcat, a pioneer in open-source investigative techniques, employs social media analysis and geolocation to investigate and document international incidents, including war crimes. Their work identifying the Buk missile launcher responsible for downing Malaysia Airlines Flight MH17 in Ukraine on July 17, 2014, showcased the power of open-source information.[46]

The Justice & Accountability Project conducts open-source investigations into incidents causing civilian harm in Ukraine, adhering to rigorous legal standards. The methodology used is based on the experience gained from collaborating on the Yemen Project,[47] aiming to ensure the use of vital open-source information as evidence in legal proceedings.[48]

This methodology, specifically tailored to the Ukrainian context, incorporates legal principles and international guidelines, including the Berkeley Protocol on Digital Open Source Investigations.[49] That protocol requires investigators to use a clean and unused computer login and web browser, free from cookies, and to carefully note every step taken, including the search terms entered and the reasons for doing so.[50]

Furthermore, the evidence gathered through the Justice & Accountability Project is organized in an analysis database, allowing for legal assessments of compliance with international humanitarian law and international criminal law.[51] Last year, Bellingcat's founder, Eliot Higgins, took part in a mock trial jointly organized with GLAN, in which opposing barristers sparred over the reliability of material gathered by the group before a British judge, who now serves on the ICC.[52] The judge ultimately decided that open-source evidence was valid.[53]

In 2014, the Syrian Archive was established as a rapid response project, collaborating with Syrian reporters and documentation groups. Its primary goal was to preserve digital information related to the Syrian conflict, including images, videos, and other postings.[54] Subsequently, the Berlin-based organization Mnemonic was formed, recognizing the potential to adapt the Syrian Archive's workflows to regions where the documentation of human rights violations was underdeveloped. Mnemonic operates globally, aiding human rights defenders in effectively utilizing digital documentation of human rights violations and international crimes. The organization focuses on developing and supporting tools for discovering, archiving, annotating, and categorizing large-scale digital content.[55] It also preserves the open-source content collected during Bellingcat's investigations on Ukraine, as it has done for Syria, Yemen, and Sudan.[56]

Amnesty International's Digital Verification Corps (DVC) is a volunteer-driven initiative that focuses on authenticating and validating digital content, particularly concerning human rights abuses in conflict zones. The DVC relies on a global network of about 100 volunteers, including students and researchers, who undergo training in digital verification methodologies.[57] These techniques encompass reverse image searches, geolocation, metadata analysis, and source credibility assessments, all aimed at verifying the authenticity of digital assets, such as photos, videos, and social media posts. Collaborative partnerships with other organizations and experts further enhance the DVC's capabilities. During crises and conflicts, the DVC provides swift verification and validation of digital materials, thereby contributing valuable information to enhance public awareness, promote accountability, and mitigate misinformation.[58]

The United Nations Investigative Team to Promote Accountability for Crimes Committed by Da'esh/Islamic State in Iraq and the Levant (UNITAD) has developed user-friendly online platforms allowing affected communities to come forward with their accounts. Through collaboration with Microsoft, it has strengthened its facial recognition and machine translation capabilities, along with automatic detection and labeling of videos with graphic content.[59] UNITAD has developed a system that efficiently handles large amounts of evidence. The system enables secure uploading and preparation of raw data for analysis. Subsequently, Microsoft's cloud computing platform, Azure, employs cognitive services to examine the recovered files, retrieving relevant information and labeling them with insights. This enables investigative teams to process evidence more efficiently and quickly.[60]

Conflict Armament Research (CAR) specializes in tracing the flow of weapons and ammunition in conflict zones, offering insights into weaponry sources and supply chains. It is a UK-based investigative organization that tracks the supply of conventional weapons, ammunition, and related military material (such as IEDs) in conflict-affected areas. By documenting the presence of advanced weaponry in conflict regions, CAR contributes to efforts aimed at arms control and accountability.[61] Established in 2011, CAR specializes in working with governments to discover how weapons end up in war zones and the hands of terrorists and insurgent groups.[62] The group maintains the public-access iTrace Global Weapon Reporting System, which the European Union and the German government fund.[63]

The Sentinel Project is a Canadian nonprofit organization that assists communities threatened by mass atrocities through innovative technology. It specializes in using technology and data analysis to help prevent and respond to mass atrocities and genocides. The organization primarily focuses on early warning and response in areas with a risk of violence and mass killings.[64]

The project develops and deploys early warning systems that utilize a variety of data sources, including social media, satellite imagery, and on-the-ground reports. It uses advanced data analytics and machine learning to monitor and analyze these sources for signs of potential conflict or violence. It aims to provide timely alerts to relevant authorities and organizations. The organization collects and analyzes data related to human rights abuses, conflict dynamics, and risk factors in areas at risk of mass atrocities. It aggregates and processes large volumes of data, which helps it identify patterns and trends that can indicate escalating tensions or threats to vulnerable populations.[65]

Closing the Gap of Impunity: eyeWitness to Atrocities

To close the authenticity gap, the author conceived the eyeWitness project through the IBA, with the support of LexisNexis Legal & Professional.[66] The app offers a breakthrough method for ensuring that real-time documentation of abuses is secure and verifiable and can be used as evidence in a court of law. The app solves the evidentiary challenges of mobile phone footage by authenticating information and establishing a reliable chain of custody. The app has received numerous awards, including the UK App Design Award for Best App of the Year (2015)[67] and the Geneva Centre for Security Policy Prize for Innovation in Global Security, which was established to "recognize deserving individuals or organizations that have an innovation approach to addressing international security challenges" and demonstrate excellence in new ideas.[68] Most recently, eyeWitness was selected by the United Nations Sustainable Development Goal (SDG) Digital Acceleration Agenda as a technological game changer.

How It Works

While mobile devices can collect the information needed for verification, such as the date, time, or geographic coordinates, this information, as stated above, can be manipulated. Photos captured with a regular phone camera can be altered. The eyeWitness app collects and embeds metadata: GPS coordinates, date, time, and information about nearby cell towers and Wi-Fi networks. These independent sources help ensure the accuracy of the data received from the app.[69] The app records the GPS time-stamp, which cannot be altered. Footage is stored and encrypted on the recording device so it cannot be edited. In addition, the app embeds a unique identifying code (known as a hash value), which is used to verify that the footage has not been edited or altered in any way. The code is the "digital footprint."

A user submits images directly from the app to a storage database maintained by eyeWitness, creating a trusted chain of custody. Only footage captured with and sent from the app is stored, ensuring its originality. The encrypted footage is securely stored until needed for an investigation or trial. Users can separately upload the newly verifiable footage to social media or other outlets. The collection and embedding are thus done to meet the legal standard for chain of custody and authentication in court. Because the app does not require significant memory, it can be used on an affordable Android phone.[70]

The eyeWitness app also guards against barriers of "digital access, digital literacy and trust." Although the risk of taking and uploading evidence can be high, the app protects its users as it requires no more than taking a photo on one's phone. The app's safety and security protocols help in this regard. These features encompass a hidden gallery secured with a password, an app icon disguise to maintain a low profile, robust encryption to safeguard sensitive data, and even an emergency uninstall option for added security.[71] These measures help mitigate the inherent dangers of gathering evidence in life-threatening situations. Additionally, as footage is automatically uploaded to the storage database once captured with the app, digital evidence would not be lost if one's devices were seized or stolen.

The Use and Impact of eyeWitness in Ukraine

Between February 24 and September 27, 2022, following Russia's full-scale invasion, eyeWitness to Atrocities app users uploaded almost 20,000 photos, videos, and audio recordings relating to Ukraine's deteriorating human rights situation.[72] Almost 2,000 were captured in and around Chernihiv, a city 70% destroyed in less than five weeks.[73] The footage exposed the vast destruction of residential areas, educational facilities, cultural heritage sites, and commercial properties. The media had not widely reported some of the incidents. To date, users in Ukraine have uploaded nearly 80,000 images and videos.

The eyeWitness app is crucial in supporting citizens and independent journalists who brave dangerous situations to report on international atrocity crimes. These journalists often confront significant obstacles when capturing trustworthy photographic evidence that the public and legal authorities can rely upon. Moreover, delivering such evidence to accountability mechanisms can be complex and risky, particularly for those needing more resources and access to major news organizations.

An illustrative example of the app's efficacy can be found in the work of the photojournalist Anastasia Taylor-Lind. She utilized the eyeWitness app to collect critical evidence of attacks on civilian housing in Ukraine while concurrently documenting the daily lives of civilians during wartime.[74] Her professional photographs from this mission were featured prominently in TIME magazine in 2018, and her eyeWitness footage served as crucial evidence submitted to the United Nations in 2020.[75]

In one of the most important documentary efforts, the eyeWitness to Atrocities app played a pivotal role in contributing to a collaborative investigative report that exposed deliberate attacks by Russia on Ukraine's healthcare system. The report was published on February 21, 2023, by eyeWitness, in collaboration with Insecurity Insight (II), Media Initiative for Human Rights (MIHR), Physicians for Human Rights (PHR), and the Ukrainian Healthcare Center (UHC).

Drawing on 10 detailed case studies and a joint dataset of 707 reported attacks, the report paints a disturbing picture of Russia's apparent violations of international humanitarian law.[76] It uncovers a deliberate assault on Ukraine's healthcare system as part of a broader campaign targeting the civilian population and critical infrastructure.[77]

The case studies were based on UHC and MIHR's visits to hospitals across Ukraine to inspect attack sites, assess damage, take photographs, and interview survivors and witnesses. Fueled by the eyeWitness app, the report found a reasonable basis to believe that attacks on Ukraine's healthcare system constitute war crimes and could potentially constitute crimes against humanity.

The report documents, in detail, the targeting of the healthcare system carried out in several ways: (1) attacks on healthcare facilities, (2) attacks on ambulances, (3) destruction of critical health infrastructure and theft of supplies, and (4) assaults, torture, and ill-treatment of health workers, including doctors, nurses, and paramedics.[78] Ukraine's healthcare infrastructure was damaged every day for thirty-five days, and in the first two weeks of the invasion, an average of four to five hospitals and clinics were attacked daily.[79] A total of 235 attacks occurred in March, and 47 occurred each month from April through December 2022.[80] From February 24 to December 31, 2022, there was an average of more than two attacks on healthcare facilities daily.

The power of technology and comprehensive documentation showed that the attacks on the healthcare infrastructure of Ukraine were targeted attacks against workers and civilian infrastructure and carried out indiscriminately.[81] The attacks likely constitute crimes against humanity, as they were committed as part of a state policy on a widespread and systematic basis.[82] As a result, the creation of the Register, which will be discussed below, has been crucial to seeking justice for Ukraine and holding Russia accountable.

Domestic Challenges to the Use of Accountability Technology

Even with technologies like eyeWitness, it is important to note limitations. For instance, senior legal advisor with TRIAL International Chiara Gabriele argues that while mobile documentation apps can increase the reliability of photos and videos, there is a gap between the evidence that prosecutors need to prove a crime and the knowledge that some of the groups on the frontlines have in terms of capturing information that can be relevant to an investigation.[83] Local documentation teams and legal actors can build the knowledge to incorporate technology in their investigations, develop evidence collection plans, analyze photo and video evidence, identify the most suitable legal strategy, and present the material in court. However, as this collaboration shows, these partnerships are resource-intensive and rare in international criminal justice.[84]

Lastly, in their study on new technologies in international justice, Federica D'Alessandra and Kirsty Sutherland argue that an over-reliance on "the observable" may omit less visible violations such as gender-based violence, starvation, or crimes against children.[85] Online disinformation campaigns and good-faith reporting also shape understanding of events and influence witnesses' perceptions of what is worth documenting.[86] These potential vulnerabilities could be remedied by more comprehensive documentation and more attention to the "less visible" crimes.[87] Having witnesses on the ground would also bring to light the violations that might otherwise be overlooked.

Unsurprisingly, there remains a gap in utilizing technology like eyeWitness in Ukraine's domestic criminal trials. Although the Ukrainian Office of the Prosecutor has encouraged the use of such technology, it has expressed reluctance to employ it in domestic proceedings.

Article 91 of the Criminal Procedural Code (CPC) of Ukraine requires proof in criminal proceedings of the "occurrence of [the] Criminal offence (when, where, how [the] criminal offence has been committed and under what circumstance)." Although the CPC (Art. 99) provides for "documents" to be admissible, including: "materials of photography, sound recording, video recording and other data media (including electronic ones)," some scholars have questioned how digital evidence should be regarded, as it appears to fall somewhere between "physical evidence" (i.e., tangible objects) and "documentary evidence" (i.e., material objects to save information like photos).[88] However, it is reasonable to assume that digital evidence can be submitted pursuant to CPC Articles 98(1) and 99 as physical or documentary evidence.

One of the significant concerns expressed by the Office of the Prosecutor is that technologies like eyeWitness do not allow for the capture of information about the individual taking the photos and videos, such as their name, contact information, and other identifying details. The office has expressed the need to identify the "authors" of the photo and video materials to interrogate them. For the office, the anonymity of the author of the pictorial evidence "negatively affects the court's further assessment of such evidence in criminal proceedings regarding its sufficiency.[89] This position confirms that "verifying the reliability of digital evidence is the most difficult and problematic issue."[90] However, despite these apparent limitations, since 2022, four cases in Ukraine have relied on footage captured using the eyeWitness app, demonstrating the app's growing role in domestic legal proceedings. In each of the four cases, domestic courts admitted the eyeWitness footage as valid evidence, reflecting that the app meets the standards required for use in court. [91]

As Russia's war against Ukraine continues, along with the accompanying atrocity crimes, Ukraine's domestic court procedures must adapt more to admitting digital evidence. Particularly, Ukraine must abandon the notion that digital proof can only be used if the author's identification is known. In the current age of technology, given the data provided by other registered apps and investigation methods, it is no longer viable or necessary to identify such data.

Dangers and Challenges of Artificial Intelligence and 'Deepfakes' in Using Pictorial Evidence to Prosecute War Crimes

Deepfakes are fabricated audiovisual content created or altered to appear authentic.[92] In the prosecution of war crimes, as in other legal proceedings, the advent of AI-driven deepfake technology poses a challenge to the established norms of evidence presentation and the pursuit of truth.

There are two main ways in which deepfakes can harm. When introduced as evidence, they can be very hard to prove fake because the verification technology has not kept pace with their creation. Also, the very existence of deepfakes and the public's awareness of them create a cloud of skepticism over all audiovisual evidence. This is sometimes called the Liar's Dividend.[93] Lawyers may sow seeds of doubt about authenticity even when the evidence is genuine.[94]

A notable example vividly illustrates the problem. In March 2022, a deepfake video of Zelenskyy surfaced online, claiming that Ukraine had surrendered to Russia.[95] In the video, Zelenskyy was seen asking his soldiers to lay down their weapons and go back to their families.[96] "There is no need to die in this war. I advise you to live," he was seen as saying.[97] The video was massively circulated on social media and briefly ran on Ukrainian television, suggesting that Zelenskyy had fled Kyiv.[98] Additionally, on October 11, 2023, in the wake of the Hamas attack on Israel on October 7, a video that appeared to be a BBC News report claimed that the Ukrainian government had supplied weapons to Hamas.[99] The widely shared video, which includes the BBC's distinctive block-text logo, had been fabricated, as officials with the BBC and Bellingcat, an investigative news website cited in the video as the source, confirmed.[100] Bellingcat: Ukrainian military offensive failure and HAMAS attack linked," reads the text over the video, which has more than 2,500 comments and 110,000 views on the messaging service Telegram.[101] "The Palestinians purchased firearms, ammunition, drones and other weapons."[102]

Fakes such as this have spurred organizations like Facebook and McAfee to develop software that can automatically detect signs of manipulation and provide explainable AI reports to assist reviewers in assessing the credibility of digital content.[103] Simultaneously, the advancement of deepfake technology and its growing sophistication have given rise to various detection technologies. These include innovative methods like biological signals, which focus on detecting imperfections in skin color changes resulting from facial blood flow, and phoneme-viseme mismatches, which target discrepancies between pronunciation and mouth movements.[104] Additionally, correlations can be drawn between facial and head movements, allowing for the distinction between authentic and manipulated content.[105] Recurrent convolutional models inspect inconsistencies between video frames, treating them as a sequence of images for deep learning-based analysis.[106]

This dynamic landscape of synthetic-media creation and detection can be likened to an arms race. As computer scientists continually develop more effective algorithms for generating various forms of synthetic content, they simultaneously create counter-algorithms to detect such content.[107] This perpetual back-and-forth between generation and detection methods exemplifies the evolving nature of the challenge; vigilance is needed to ensure rapid adaptation to emerging technologies. Intel, for instance, recently unveiled its real-time deepfake detector, named FakeCatcher, which is set to launch soon. Synthetic-media creation and detection remain closely intertwined, with new detection methods often prompting the development of improved generation algorithms. Intel's FakeCatcher offers a key advantage as it is not easily reverse-engineered.

To confront the challenges presented by deepfakes, it is imperative to underscore the pivotal role of the eyeWitness to Atrocities app. By authenticating pictorial evidence and eradicating doubt, this app can bolster confidence in the evidence presented to a court.

Evidence Collected, What's Next?

When reviewing the prominent role that innovative technologies play in documenting the war atrocities committed in Ukraine, it is also important to keep in mind the extensive property damage inflicted upon the country. To document this damage, on May 12, 2023, the Council of Europe, through an enlarged partial agreement, announced the establishment of the Register of Damage Caused by the Aggression of the Russian Federation Against Ukraine, inspired by the success of the UN Register of Damage Caused by the Construction of the Wall in the Occupied Palestinian Territory (UNRoD).[108]

Through the Register, evidence gathering would create a comprehensive record of damage, loss, or injury caused by Russia's internationally wrongful acts in or against Ukraine while promoting and coordinating evidence-gathering efforts.

Since the first meeting of the Conference of Participants in June, a Host State Agreement with the Netherlands as the seat of the Register in The Hague was signed and has come into force.[109] A second meeting was devoted to financial issues and the procedure for appointing the Board.[110] The Register's budget is funded by annual assessed contributions of participant states, as well as voluntary contributions; the Netherlands and the European Union have made substantial voluntary contributions to the startup costs of the Register.[111]

As of September 2023, the ministers of Justice of Council of Europe member and observer states have adopted a declaration outlining a series of principles ("Riga principles") to achieve comprehensive accountability for the Russian Federation's aggression against Ukraine. A strong workforce, an excellent Board, and the digital platform being developed will enable the Register to become fully operational and in a position to start accepting claims.[112] The Council has set the ambitious goal of that happening in the first quarter of 2024.[113]

The creation and maintenance of the Register are crucial steps toward achieving a potential future compensation mechanism. The dimensions of such a mechanism will depend on various factors, including the outcome of the current conflict, Russia's role in future negotiations, and the ability of participating states in the Register to agree on the adjudication processs and funding sources for registered claims.[114] It is important to note that, at this juncture, the outcome of these negotiations remains uncertain.[115] Nonetheless, the Register represents a significant step toward justice and accountability for the damage inflicted upon Ukraine by Russia.

Conclusion

In the quest to document and investigate war crimes in Ukraine, it is crucial to recognize the important role that Ukraine itself has played. Numerous Ukrainian NGOs have been instrumental in collecting evidence, ensuring that those responsible for these atrocities face justice.

Simultaneously, the international community is responsible for investigating and documenting these heinous acts. Initiatives like eyeWitness to Atrocities and projects such as Justice & Accountability by GLAN play a critical role in this global effort. These projects leverage cutting-edge technology and the expertise of legal professionals to empower courageous individuals who document and photograph the gravest of crimes.

However, documenting and investigating war crimes is a challenging endeavor in the era of social media. The proliferation of digital content presents difficulties in authenticating evidence for legal proceedings. eyeWitness to Atrocities has addressed this challenge head-on. Nevertheless, as technology advances, the dangers and challenges posed by AI and deepfakes in using pictorial evidence to prosecute war crimes become increasingly evident. These emerging technologies require vigilant scrutiny to maintain the integrity of evidence and the pursuit of justice.

In addition to documenting and investigating war crimes, establishing the Register and developing a compensation method and fund for the crimes committed by Russia are paramount. The victims of these heinous acts must receive the support and reparations they deserve.

In conclusion, the efforts to document and investigate war crimes in Ukraine involve a multifaceted approach encompassing Ukraine's tireless pursuit of justice, the global community's collective responsibility, and the use of advanced technologies like eyeWitness to Atrocities. While challenges persist, these endeavors represent a steadfast commitment to holding perpetrators accountable and achieving a more just and stable Ukraine.

Notes

1 *Dr. Ellis would like to thank Caroline Massias for her superb assistance in researching and drafting this chapter. https://www.reuters.com/world/europe/zelenskiy-says-russia-has-committed-over-183000-war-crimes-ukraine-2025-03-31/

2 *Ukraine's Quest for Justice: A Conversation with Prosecutor General Andriy Kostin*, YOUTUBE (Sept. 26, 2023), https://www.youtube.com/watch?v=2Yfj70ANE7g&ab_channel=CarnegieEndowment.

3 Ruth Green, *The IBA interview: Andriy Kostin, Prosecutor General of Ukraine*, INTERNATIONAL BAR ASSOCIATION (Oct. 4, 2022), https://www.ibanet.org/interview-Andriy-Kostin-Prosecutor-General-of-Ukraine.

4 *Id.*

5 *Ukraine's Quest for Justice: A Conversation with Prosecutor General Andriy Kostin*, YOUTUBE (Sept. 26, 2023), https://www.youtube.com/watch?v=2Yfj70ANE7g&ab_channel=CarnegieEndowment.

6 *Id.*

7 *Justice Department Helping Train Ukrainians in Gathering Evidence of Environmental Harm from Russian Invasion*, United States Department of Justice (July 28, 2023), https://www.justice.gov/opa/blog/justice-department-helping-train-ukrainians-gathering-evidence-environmental-harm-russian. See also Full text: Franck Petit, Kakhovka Dam: *Ukraine Pioneers Prosecution for Ecocide*, JUSTICE INFO, https://www.justiceinfo.net/en/119148-kakhovka-dam-ukraine-pioneers-prosecution-ecocide.html.

8 *Id.*

9 *Ukraine's Quest for Justice: A Conversation with Prosecutor General Andriy Kostin*, YOUTUBE (Sept. 26, 2023), https://www.youtube.com/watch?v=2Yfj70ANE7g&ab_channel=CarnegieEndowment.

10 *Id.*

11 Vera Bergengruen, *How Ukraine is Pioneering New Ways to Prosecute Crimes*, TIME MAGAZINE, (Nov. 6, 2023), https://time.com/6331902/ukraine-war-crimes-prosecutor/.
12 *Id.*
13 Lisa O'Carroll, *Meet Diia: the Ukrainian app used to do taxes and report Russian soldiers*, THE GUARDIAN (May 26, 2023), https://www.theguardian.com/world/2023/may/26/meet-diia-the-ukrainian-app-used-to-do-taxes-and-report-russian-soldiers.
14 *Id.*
15 *Id.*
16 *History of the Center for Civil Liberties*, CENTER FOR CIVIL LIBERTIES, https://ccl.org.ua/en/19301-2/. *See also full text: The Fight for Human Rights and Democracy*, THE NOBEL PRIZE, https://www.nobelprize.org/prizes/peace/2022/center-for-civil-liberties/facts/.
17 *Id.*
18 *Id.*
19 *Id.*
20 *Welcoming the 5 AM Coalition from Ukraine,* CEELI INSTITUTE, https://ceeliinstitute.org/welcoming-the-5am-coalition-from-ukraine/.
21 *Our Mission and History of the Union*, UKRAINIAN HELSINKI HUMAN RIGHTS UNION (Apr. 4, 2016), https://www.helsinki.org.ua/informatsiya/.
22 *Our Mission*, THE RECKONING PROJECT, https://www.thereckoningproject.com/ (last visited Oct. 9, 2023).
23 @AndriyKostinUa, TWITTER (Sept. 19, 2023, 4:42 PM), https://twitter.com/AndriyKostinUa/status/1704234727903735996. *See also full text: Zelenskyy's speech to the UN General Assembly*, AL JAZEERA (Sept. 20, 2023), https://www.aljazeera.com/news/2023/9/20/full-text-zelenskyys-speech-to-the-un-general-assembly.
24 *Miami 2022 Opening Ceremony - President Volodymyr Zelensky,* INTERNATIONAL BAR ASSOCIATION (Oct. 30, 2022), https://www.ibanet.org/Miami2022/Opening-Ceremony-Volodymyr-Zelenskyy.
25 *Id.*
26 *Id.*
27 *Id.*
28 *Strategic plan June 2012–2015*, International Criminal Court, The Office of the Prosecutor (Oct. 11, 2013), https://www.icc-cpi.int/sites/default/files/iccdocs/otp/OTP-Strategic-Plan-2013.pdf.
29 *Id.*
30 United Kingdom Government, *International coalition to support ICC Russian war crimes investigation* (March 24, 2022), https://www.gov.uk/government/news/international-coalition-to-support-icc-russian-war-crimes-investigation.
31 @AndriyKostinUa, TWITTER (Sept. 14, 2023, 8:23 AM), https://twitter.com/AndriyKostinUa/status/1702297006671003752.
32 *How the Court Works*, THE INTERNATIONAL CRIMINAL COURT, https://www.icc-cpi.int/about/how-thecourtworks#:~:text=Finally%2C%20the%20fourth%20crime%20falling,or%20independence%20of%20another%20State.
33 *Id.*
34 *The International Centre for Prosecution for the Crime of Aggression Against Ukraine*, INSTITUTE FOR WAR AND PEACE REPORTING (Aug. 8, 2023), https://iwpr.net/global-voices/international-centre-prosecution-crime-aggression-against-ukraine#:~:text=Its%20purpose%20is%20to%20facilitate,Russian%20Federation's%20invasion%20of%20Ukraine.

35 *Joint Investigation Team Alleged Crimes Committed*, EUROJUST, https://www.eurojust.europa.eu/joint-investigation-team-alleged-crimes-committed-ukraine.
36 Dustin W. Stout, *Social Media Statistic 2020: Top Networks By the Numbers* (last visited Oct. 9, 2023, 2:28 PM), https://dustinstout.com/social-media-statistics/.
37 Roger Cohen, *A Surge of Unifying Moral Outrage Over Russia's War*, NEW YORK TIMES (March 1, 2022; March 3, 2022), https://www.nytimes.com/2022/03/01/world/europe/zelensky-ukraine-war-outrage.html.
38 Emerson T. Brooking and P. W. Singer, *WAR GOES VIRAL: How social media is being weaponized across the world*, THE ATLANTIC (Nov. 2016), https://www.theatlantic.com/magazine/archive/2016/11/war-goes-viral/501125/.
39 *Putin's War*, THE ECONOMIST 55 (Apr. 2, 2022).
40 Kate Linthicum, *TikTok and Twitter capture Ukraine war in frighteningly real time*, LOS ANGELES TIMES (March 31, 2022), https://www.latimes.com/world-nation/story/2022-03-31/ukraine-war-social-media-tik-tok.
41 Linda Kinstler, *What Russia Is Doing to Ukraine Must Be Preserved – Not Just Seen. Images of crimes against humanity are in danger of being lost. Fortunately, best practices exist, and the international community needs to implement them*, WIRED (March 3, 2022), https://www.wired.com/story/russia-ukraine-war-crimes-evidence-digital-media/.
42 Flynn Coleman, *To Prosecute Putin for War Crimes, Safeguard the Digital Proof*, FOREIGN POLICY (Apr. 10, 2022), https://foreignpolicy.com/2022/04/10/prosecute-putin-war-crimes-evidence-bucha-safeguard-digital-proof/
43 *Id.*
44 Tim Simonite, *The Race to Archive Social Posts That May Prove Russian War Crimes*, WIRED (Apr. 11, 2022, 7:00 AM), https://www.wired.com/story/open-source-russia-war-crimes-ukraine/.
45 *Id.*
46 Will Croxton, *How Bellingcat tracked a Russian missile system in Ukraine*, CBS News (February 23, 2020), https://www.cbsnews.com/news/how-bellingcat-tracked-a-russian-missile-system-in-ukraine-60-minutes-2020-02-23/.
47 See *Yemen: A humanitarian crisis*, GLOBAL LEGAL ACTION NETWORK, YEMEN, https://www.glanlaw.org/yemen.
48 See *Ukraine Investigations*, GLOBAL LEGAL ACTION NETWORK, UKRAINE INVESTIGATIONS, https://www.glanlaw.org/ukraine-investigations.
49 *Id.* See also *Berkeley Protocol on Digital Open Source Investigation*, HUMAN RIGHTS CENTER UC BERKELEY SCHOOL OF LAW AND UNITED NATIONS HUMAN RIGHTS OFFICE OF THE HIGH COMMISSIONER (2022), https://www.ohchr.org/sites/default/files/2022-04/OHCHR_BerkeleyProtocol.pdf ("Although open-source evidence has not been well tested as evidence of war crimes, there are signs that the idea is becoming more mainstream. In December, the UN Human Rights Office and lawyers at UC Berkeley released legal guidelines, called the Berkeley Protocol, for gathering, verifying, and using open source and social media evidence of human rights violations.").
50 Tim Simonite, *The Race to Archive Social Posts That May Prove Russian War Crimes*, WIRED (Apr. 11, 2022, 7:00 AM), https://www.wired.com/story/open-source-russia-war-crimes-ukraine/.
51 *Id.*
52 *Id.*
53 *Id.*
54 *The Syrian Archive*, https://syrianarchive.org/ (last visited October 11, 2023).
55 *Mnemonic*, https://mnemonic.org/ (last visited October 11, 2023).

56 Will Croxton, *How Bellingcat tracked a Russian missile system in Ukraine,* CBS News (February 23, 2020), https://www.cbsnews.com/news/how-bellingcat-tracked-a-russian-missile-system-in-ukraine-60-minutes-2020-02-23/.
57 Sam Dubberley, *The Digital Verification Corps: Amnesty International's Volunteers for the Age of Social Media*, Amnesty International (Dec. 6, 2019), https://citizenevidence.org/2019/12/06/the-digital-verification-corps-amnesty-internationals-volunteers-for-the-age-of-social-media/.
58 *Id.*
59 *Harnessing Advanced Technology in International Criminal Investigations,* UNITAD, https://www.unitad.un.org/sites/www.unitad.un.org/files/general/2105390-harnessing_advanced_technology_in_international_criminal_investigations_web10may_0.pdf.
60 *AI for Humanitarian Action projects, MICROSOFT, https://www.microsoft.com/en-gb/ai/ai-for-humanitarian-action-projects?activetab=pivot1%3aprimaryr5.*
61 *Latest Publications*, Conflict Armament Research, https://www.conflictarm.com/.
62 *About Us*, Conflict Armament Research, https://www.conflictarm.com/about-us/.
63 *Id.*, See also *itrace*, Conflict Armament RESEARCH, HTTPS://WWW.CONFLICTARM.COM/ITRACE/.
64 *Who We Are*, The Sentinel Project, https://thesentinelproject.org/who-we-are/. See also Full text Ryan Flanagan, *This Canadian group wants to stop genocides before they happen*, CTV News (Feb. 12, 2020), https://www.ctvnews.ca/world/this-canadian-group-wants-to-stop-genocides-before-they-happen-1.4808558.
65 *The Role of Technology*, The Sentinel Project, https://thesentinelproject.org/what-we-do/the-role-of-technology/, See also full text Valerie Hill, *Sentinel Project Saving Lives, One Algorithm At a Time*, Waterloo Region Special (Nov. 7, 2019), https://www.therecord.com/life/sentinel-project-saving-lives-one-algorithm-at-a-time/article_4110c4d5-c143-5fc6-9a16-143b8684b3ef.html.
66 *International Bar Association Launches Mobile App that Captures Verifiable Images to Aid Prosecution for Human Rights Atrocities,* International Bar Association (June 8, 2015), https://www.ibanet.org/Article/NewDetail.aspx?ArticleUid=F8FF99F9-43E4-4301-B1A4-9935A25F0FDD.
67 *A Silver Winner of the UK App Deserve Award for Best App of the Year* (2015) Who we are – eyeWitness to Atrocities, eyeWitness to Atrocities, https://www.eyewitness.global/documents/who-we-are.pdf.
68 *eyeWitness to Atrocities app Wins 2016 Innovation in Global Security Prize*, Human Rights at Sea (Nov. 28, 2016), https://www.humanrightsatsea.org/eyewitness-atrocities-app-wins-2016-innovation-global-security-prize.
69 Chiara Gabriele et al., *The Role of Mobile Technology in Documenting International Crimes*, 19 J. Int'l Crim. L. 108 (2021).
70 Chiara Gabriele et al., *The Role of Mobile Technology in Documenting International Crimes*, 19 J. Int'l Crim. L. 108 (2021).
71 *Destruction and Devastation in Ukraine*, eyeWitness to Atrocities et al. (Feb. 2023), https://www.eyewitness.global/documents/Destruction-and-Devastation-Ukraine-Feb2023.pdf
72 *eyeWitness Submitted Evidence of Human Rights Violations Committed in Chernihiv to UN Commission of Inquiry*, eyeWitness to Atrocities (Oct. 20, 2022), https://www.eyewitness.global/eyewitness-submitted-evidence-of-human-rights-violations-committed-in-Chernihiv-to-UN.
73 *Id.*
74 *Id.*

75 *Id.*
76 *eyeWitness and Partners Launch New Report on Attacks on Ukraine's Healthcare System*, EYEWITNESS TO ATROCITIES (Feb. 21, 2023), https://www.eyewitness.global/eyewitness-and-partners-launch-new-report-on-attacks-on-ukraines-health-care-system.
77 *Id.*
78 *Destruction and Devastation*, EYEWITNESS TO ATROCITIES ET AL. (Feb. 2023), https://www.eyewitness.global/documents/Destruction-and-Devastation-Ukraine-Feb2023.pdf.
79 *Id.*
80 *Id.*
81 *Id.*
82 *Interview with Dymtro Gladky* (Oct. 21, 2023).
83 Chiara Gabriele, *The Role of Mobile Technology in Documenting International Crimes: The Affaire Castro et Kizito in the Democratic Republic of Congo*, 19 J. OF INT'L CRIM. JUST. 107-130 (2021).
84 *Id.*
85 Federica D'Alessandra and Kirsty Sutherland, *The Promise and Challenges of New Actors and New Technologies in International Justice*, 19 J. INT'L CRIM. JUSTICE 22, n. 1 (March 2021).
86 *Id.*
87 *Id.*
88 Dr. Iryna Marchuk, *Mass Atrocities and Admissibility of Evidence in Criminal Proceedings in Ukraine* (2023) (on file with author).
89 *Interview with Dmytro Gladky* (Oct. 1, 2023).
90 *Id.*
91 https://www.eyewitness.global/eyeWitness-footage-used-in-Ukraine-Cases
92 Delfino, Rebecca, *The Deepfake Defense—Exploring the Limits of the Law and Ethical Norms in Protecting Legal Proceedings from Lying Lawyers*, (Feb. 12, 2023), LOYOLA LAW SCHOOL, https://ssrn.com/abstract=4355140.
93 Robert Chesney & Danielle Keats Citron, *Deep Fakes: A Looming Challenge for Privacy, Democracy, and National Security*, 107 Cali. L. REV. 1753, 1758 (2019).
94 Delfino, Rebecca, *Interview with Dmytro Gladky* (Oct. 1, 2023).
95 Jane Wakefield, *Deepfake Presidents Used in Russia-Ukraine War*, BBC NEWS (March 22, 2023), https://www.bbc.co.uk/news/technology-60780142.
96 *Id.* See also Full text: Bobby Allyn, *Deepfake video of Zelenskyy could be 'tip of the iceberg' in info war, experts warn*, NPR NEWS (March 16, 2022), https://www.npr.org/2022/03/16/1087062648/deepfake-video-zelenskyy-experts-war-manipulation-ukraine-russia.
97 *Id.*
98 *Id.*
99 Eduardo Suarez, *BBC expert on debunking Israel-Hamas war visuals: "The volume of misinformation on Twitter was beyond anything I've ever seen,"* REUTERS INSTITUTE (Oct. 13, 2023), https://reutersinstitute.politics.ox.ac.uk/news/bbc-expert-debunking-israel-hamas-war-visuals-volume-misinformation-twitter-was-beyond.
100 *Israel Hamas Gaza Misinformation Fact Check*, ASSOCIATED PRESS NEWS (Oct. 13, 2023), https://apnews.com/article/israel-hamas-gaza-misinformation-fact-check-e58f9ab8696309305c3ea2bfb269258e.
101 *Israel Hamas Gaza Misinformation Fact Check*, ASSOCIATED PRESS NEWS (Oct. 13, 2023), https://apnews.com/article/israel-hamas-gaza-misinformation-fact-check-e58f9ab8696309305c3ea2bfb269258e.
102 *Id.*

103 *Facing reality? Law enforcement and the challenge of deepfakes, an observatory report from the Europol Innovation Lab*, Europol (2022), https://www.europol.europa.eu/cms/sites/default/files/documents/Europol_Innovation_Lab_Facing_Reality_Law_Enforcement_And_The_Challenge_Of_Deepfakes.pdf. See also Full Text: Caroline Brooks, *MSU, Facebook develop research model to fight deepfakes*, Michigan State University (June 16, 2021), https://msutoday.msu.edu/news/2021/deepfake-detection.

104 Id. See also Full text: *The Deepfakes Lab: Detecting & Defending Against Deepfakes with Advanced AI*, McAfee (2020), https://www.mcafee.com/blogs/enterprise/securityoperations/the-deepfakes-lab-detecting-defending-against-deepfakes-with-advanced-ai.

105 Id. See also Full Text: *Top AI Based Tools & Techniques for Deepfake Detection*, AIM (2020), https://analyticsindiamag.com/top-ai-based-tools-techniques-for-deepfake-detection.

106 Id.

107 Matthew Hutson, *Detection Stays One Step Ahead of Deepfakes*, IEEE Spectrum (March 6, 2023), https://spectrum.ieee.org/deepfake.

108 *Collecting Claims and Evidence of Damage by Russia's Invasion of Ukraine*, Am. Society Int'l L., https://www.asil.org/insights/volume/27/issue/7. (The Register was established through an agreement among members of the Council of Europe and the European Union, signed during the Council of Europe Summit in Reykjavik, Iceland, on May 12, 2023. It entered into force on May 16, 2023, with the United States expressing its intention to join the enlarged partial agreement on May 15, 2023. On May 17, 2023, the 44 participating countries and the Council of Europe publicly announced the establishment of the Register.).

109 *The Conference of Participants of the Register of damage for Ukraine holds its second meeting*, Council of Europe, (Sept. 23, 2023), https://www.coe.int/hr/web/portal/-/the-conference-of-participants-of-the-register-of-damage-for-ukraine-holds-its-second-meeting.

110 *Id.*

111 *Id.*

112 *Id.*

113 *Id.*

114 *Top AI Based Tools & Techniques for Deepfake Detection*, AIM (2020), https://analyticsindiamag.com/top-ai-based-tools-techniques-fordeepfake-detection.

115 *Id.*

PART IV

New Global Order?

12

NEGOTIATING JUSTICE IN UKRAINE[1]

Paul R. Williams and Sindija Beta

Introduction

The Russian war of aggression against Ukraine manifests not only through conventional acts of war but also extends to a wide spectrum of atrocity crimes,[2] amplifying the humanitarian crisis and violating a series of international laws and norms.[3] Russia's war in Ukraine represents a grave violation of the post-World War II global order founded upon principles of state sovereignty, equality, and territorial integrity, and amounts to a rare 21st-century case of a blatant commission of an act of aggression.[4]

Prior to the full-scale invasion in 2022, many in the West continued to believe that normalization of relations with Russia would increase European and global stability and that the world had moved past the 20th-century phenomenon of spheres of influence. Following Russia's military engagements in Moldova in the 1990s, Georgia in 2008, and Ukraine in 2014, relatively few repercussions were imposed on Russia from the international community. Preliminary examinations were launched by the International Criminal Court (ICC) in Ukraine and Georgia.[5] Ukrainian domestic courts were successful in the prosecution of several perpetrators of the post-2014 crimes, most notably its former president Viktor Yanukovych for the crime of aggression in violation of Ukraine's criminal code Article 437(2).[6] A prominent case on the downing of the Malaysia Airlines flight MH17 en route from Amsterdam to Kuala Lumpur was also launched in Dutch courts, addressing the responsibility of four pro-Russian separatists for the death of 298 people during the crash.[7] Despite these efforts, Russia largely enjoyed unfettered impunity for its acts in Ukraine and in other post-Soviet territories.

DOI: 10.4324/9781003458166-16

With this context in mind and a belief that the West will again appease Russia's demands for an unimpeded sphere of influence in Europe's East, Russia's President Vladimir Putin authorized a full-scale invasion of Ukraine on February 24, 2022. Much to Mr. Putin's surprise, this 2022 invasion caused an outcry not just in the West but across the globe and has led to unprecedented initiatives launched across a variety of platforms and in many areas of the world to seek and hold Russia accountable for its crimes.

Ukraine itself has been a leading force in this comprehensive effort to hold Russia accountable for the full range of atrocity crimes.[8] Ukraine's initiative leverages domestic prosecutions,[9] embraces the jurisdiction of the ICC,[10] and champions international efforts to form a tribunal specifically tasked with addressing the crime of aggression.[11]

If and when Ukraine and Russia find themselves on a path to peace, accountability will be one of the core issues, along with sovereignty, territory, NATO security guarantees, and human rights protections, that will need to be addressed. At this point, all those engaged in this process will be "negotiating justice."[12] While the peace proposals from China[13] and certain key African states[14] may rationalize Russia's goal of impunity, the global order is no longer favorable to peace with amnesty and impunity. In contrast, the expectation of accountability has become woven into post-conflict societies[15] and Ukraine is on a straight path towards it.

This chapter begins by defining what we mean by "negotiating justice." It then turns to describing how international law has developed to not just encourage accountability for conflict-related crimes but has even prohibited impunity for atrocity crimes. Next, the chapter examines how the global order has drifted towards accountability through a consistent demand for engaging or developing justice mechanisms to address crimes during conflict. Lastly, it discusses how the justice efforts launched by Ukraine and the international community have bypassed the stage at which Russia or other international actors may try to reverse Ukraine's path to peace with justice.

Negotiating Justice

"Negotiating justice" refers to the process where the parties to peace talks negotiate the extent to which those responsible for atrocity crimes will be held accountable (if at all) and what mechanisms will be utilized or created to accomplish that objective.

Specifically, the parties negotiate the question of whether the peace agreement will be based on amnesty or accountability (in some form). The determination is not binary, and the parties may opt for some form of amnesty coupled with some level of accountability.[16] This may entail an amnesty-based truth commission with accountability for those who do not engage in the truth-telling process.[17] It may also include accountability for those most responsible for the most serious crimes coupled with *de jure*[18] or *de facto*[19] amnesty for lesser offenders. The parties may also agree to amnesty for domestic crimes but leave open the possibility of accountability for international crimes.[20] In some cases, but less so in the past two decades, the agreement may be silent as to the question of amnesty or accountability.[21]

If there is a degree of accountability, the parties negotiate the mechanism(s) that may be used to implement accountability. Do they create a truth commission with the power to grant amnesty?[22] Do they grant or reaffirm the jurisdiction of an international tribunal such as the ICC?[23] Do they create a hybrid internationalized tribunal?[24] Do they create new domestic courts,[25] or empower specialized chambers of existing courts?[26] Notably, there is an increase in the utilization of universal jurisdiction,[27] whose applicability lies outside the scope of a negotiated agreement among the parties.[28]

With respect to crimes to be covered, the matters to negotiate include the core crimes, such as crimes against humanity, war crimes, and genocide. Recently, the crime of aggression has become relevant, as has the crime of ecocide.[29] The parties also face increasing pressure to be specific about crimes against children, and sexual- and gender-based crimes.[30] Other issues to be negotiated include whether state actors, as well as individuals, will be held accountable,[31] the timeline for the jurisdiction of any amnesty or accountability mechanism,[32] and whether there will be retroactive liability.[33]

One constant theme that runs through relating to amnesty/accountability is moral equivalence. In some conflicts, one party is clearly the perpetrator of atrocity crimes,[34] while in others both sides tend to be responsible for a high level of atrocity crimes.[35] In nearly all cases, however, there is a propensity for third parties to seek blame on all sides and establish a moral equivalence which, in their view, facilitates a negotiated peace.[36]

One final dimension is that, in addition to whatever the parties may pursue with respect to amnesty or accountability, the international community or the mediator may have a preferential view for either amnesty or accountability, which may be determined by a variety of factors.[37]

Age of Accountability

Historically, negotiating justice commonly led to an agreement that amnesty and impunity were necessary to achieve peace.[38] Blanket amnesties have been afforded to Turkish forces considered to be responsible for crimes committed against Armenians during World War I,[39] to the French for crimes in Algeria in the 1960s,[40] to perpetrators in Argentina,[41] Chile,[42] El Salvador,[43] Guatemala,[44] Uruguay,[45] Angola,[46] Democratic Republic of the Congo,[47] Haiti,[48] Mozambique,[49] and others. The list goes on all throughout the 20th century.

The blanket amnesties incorporated in these agreements may have contributed to an initial peace, in that they helped to end conflict,[50] but in many instances, it was not a durable peace as it often resulted in perpetrators returning to positions of power and recommitting atrocities.[51] Or it led to lingering societal resentments that then led to a lack of social cohesion and a renewal of conflict.[52]

Indeed, the UN High Commissioner for Human Rights concluded in its report on amnesties that:

> [t]he amnesties that exempt from criminal sanction those responsible for atrocious crimes in the hope of securing peace have often failed to achieve their aim and have instead emboldened their beneficiaries to commit further crimes. Conversely, peace agreements have been reached without amnesty provisions in some situations where amnesty had been said to be a necessary condition of peace and where many had feared that indictments would prolong the conflict.[53]

Recently, however, the international community has increasingly recognized that securing justice helps create stable, peaceful societies after conflict by: (1) establishing individual responsibility and denying collective guilt, (2) delegitimizing institutions and holding war criminals responsible for the commission of atrocities, (3) establishing an accurate historical record, (4) providing victim catharsis, and (5) promoting deterrence.[54]

Negotiating Justice and International Law

Over the last decades, the international legal infrastructure has been gradually developing and transforming from an environment of impunity and peace without justice to one of accountability. Key international legal instruments establish a strong foundation for furthering accountability and resisting pressure that enables impunity.

From a treaty perspective, the First Geneva Convention provides that its parties are under an obligation to search for, prosecute, and punish perpetrators of war crimes committed during international armed conflicts.[55] Moreover, the International Covenant to Civil and Political Rights, in Article 2(3), provides that each State Party to the Convention shall "ensure that any person whose rights or freedoms [recognized in the Convention] shall have an effective remedy, notwithstanding that the violation has been committed by persons acting in an official capacity" and that State Parties will set up and enforce the justice mechanisms necessary to achieve an effective resolution.[56] The European Convention on Human Rights, in Article 13, contains a similar provision.[57]

Dealing with the question of amnesties, international criminal courts, and human rights bodies have also essentially reached a consensus that amnesties may not be provided for certain crimes. Although such courts and human rights bodies have diverged as to the rationale that underlies the amnesty prohibition, the specific crimes for which this principle applies, and whether the prohibition is absolute or permits exceptions in special cases, they all generally agree that providing amnesties for very serious crimes is inconsistent with international law.[58] For instance, the Extraordinary Chambers in the Courts of Cambodia have overruled challenges to its jurisdiction based on a broad amnesty provision, stating that "an emerging consensus prohibits amnesties in relation to serious international crimes, based on a duty to investigate and prosecute these crimes and to punish their perpetrators."[59]

While the European Court on Human Rights (ECtHR) has rejected the view that rights protected by the European Convention of Human Rights entitle the victims of the violations to seek criminal punishment of persons responsible, the ECtHR has criticized amnesty laws on account of the interests of the society as a whole in deterring criminals, preventing the recurrence of abuses, and defending the rule of law.[60] In a number of cases against Turkey involving the discontinuation of criminal proceedings against state officials, the ECtHR emphasized that measures providing immunity to state agents, including amnesties, were unacceptable because they undermined the deterrent effect of criminal sanctions.[61] Moreover, the ECtHR declared that amnesties, pardons, or statutes of limitations should not apply to criminal cases involving torture and ill-treatment since the prosecution of such crimes was essential in maintaining public confidence in justice systems and in preventing any appearance of collusion or tolerance of unlawful acts.[62]

Further, in a particularly elaborate judgment by the Inter-American Court of Human Rights (IACtHR) in the *Gelman v. Uruguay* case,[63] the Court examined amnesty laws, international and domestic decisions, and opinio juris on the topic of amnesties in-depth. The Court concluded that amnesty laws that prevent the investigation, prosecution, and punishment of serious human rights violations are inconsistent with a state's obligations to uphold human rights under international law.[64] Notably, the case concerned an amnesty law that was adopted through a democratic process and was even challenged during a national referendum, in which only 47.7% of the votes supported its nullification.[65] This notwithstanding, the IACtHR underscored that a democratic process and a democratic regime do not mean that a state can relieve itself of the obligation to prosecute human rights violations.[66]

Furthering Accountability Around the Globe

Already at the end of the twentieth century, there were indications that justice was becoming the preferred approach. On May 25, 1993, in response to the documentation of grave violations of international humanitarian law and human rights abuses in the former Yugoslavia, the UN Security Council adopted Resolution 827, establishing the International Criminal Tribunal for the former Yugoslavia (Yugoslavia Tribunal).[67] The purpose of the Yugoslavia Tribunal was to restore peace in the war-torn region,[68] which was an exceptional move after decades of peace agreements affording amnesty to perpetrators of atrocity crimes. In fact, in 1995, Justice Richard Goldstone, the appointed Chief Prosecutor for the Yugoslavia Tribunal, urged Richard Holbrooke, who was mediating the Dayton Accords, to include accountability provisions in the final language of the peace agreement.[69] While the Dayton Accords reflected only a fraction of the language on war crimes sought by the Bosnian delegation, the Accords did not include any form of de jure amnesty for atrocity crimes.[70] While there were some provisions that required the parties to provide a minimal level of cooperation with the Yugoslavia Tribunal,[71] there was fairly widespread speculation that President of the Federal Republic of Yugoslavia Slobodan Milošević had been granted some level of informal de facto amnesty in exchange for his signature on the Accords.[72]

At the time of the signing of the Dayton Accords, Bosnian Serb political and military leaders Radovan Karadžić and Ratko Mladić had already been indicted by the Yugoslavia Tribunal,[73] and hence were excluded from the negotiations of the Dayton Accords.[74] On the other hand, Momčilo Krajišnik[75] and Slobodan Milošević,[76] both of whom were the signatories of the Dayton Accords, were later indicted by the Yugoslavia Tribunal for crimes committed during the war.[77]

In the same vein, the Rambouillet Accords did not provide an amnesty for the grave human rights abuses and international crimes committed in Kosovo during the late 1990s.[78] Indeed, President of Serbia, Milan Milutinović and Deputy Prime Minister of the Federal Republic of Yugoslavia, both of whom headed the Serbian delegation during the Rambouillet talks, were indicted by the Yugoslavia Tribunal along with Slobodan Milošević in 1999.[79] Following a similar approach, the 1990s genocide against the Tutsis in Rwanda concluded with the establishment of the International Criminal Tribunal for Rwanda recognizing the stark need for justice.[80]

Sierra Leone initially opted for amnesty; however, upon the resumption of hostilities after signing the Lomé Agreement, the Sierra Leone President decided to request the assistance of the UN with the establishment of a Special Court for Sierra Leone.[81] Similarly, the Peace Agreement for Cambodia originally provided a de facto amnesty for the Khmer Rouge leaders, under whose watch nearly two million people died.[82] After more years of political turmoil, Cambodia too was forced to request the help of the UN in setting up a hybrid tribunal to prosecute those responsible for the crimes committed during the Khmer Rouge leadership.[83]

The UN was also asked to establish a tribunal for the situation in Lebanon after the assassination of the Lebanese Prime Minister in 2005 and a series of other explosions and assassinations that occurred in the early 2000s.[84] The Special Tribunal for Lebanon was thereafter established and began its operations in 2009.[85]

Iraq and Colombia are two other contexts where judicial mechanisms were established to address conflict situations. In 2003, the transitional government in Iraq decided to establish an Iraqi Special Tribunal to try Iraqi nationals or residents of Iraq accused of genocide, crimes against humanity, war crimes, or violations of certain Iraqi laws during Saddam Hussein's rule.[86] The peace agreement between Colombia's government and the guerrilla group FARC likewise provided for the establishment of the Special Jurisdiction for Peace to exercise investigative and prosecutorial jurisdiction over four categories of people: members or collaborators of FARC, members of the Colombian military or police, state officials, and civilians who funded or cooperated with paramilitary groups.[87]

Further, cognizant of the relevance of addressing the causes and legacy of the human rights violations and atrocities committed during the South Sudanese civil war, parties to the conflict in this context agreed not only to refrain from granting amnesty but, in fact, envisioned a comprehensive transitional justice process. The South Sudanese peace agreement of 2018 includes the development of a truth commission, a hybrid court, and a compensation and reparation mechanism.[88] While continuous political instability and lack of resources have prevented the establishment of all three mechanisms according to the timeline enshrined in the peace agreement, South Sudanese civil society and certain domestic and international actors continue to contribute significant efforts to accomplishing the South Sudanese transitional justice goals.

Lastly, despite the lack of a dedicated tribunal to address the crimes committed in Syria and against the Muslim minority Rohingya in Myanmar, both populations have sought justice ever since the atrocities erupted. The UN thus far has responded to these demands by establishing permanent investigative mechanisms[89] and universal jurisdiction cases have been launched in certain third states to provide justice to the victims.[90] For the Rohingya, genocide and crimes against humanity cases have also been opened before the ICC[91] and the International Court of Justice.[92]

All the above exemplify that conflict and post-conflict societies have learned the pitfalls and risks of peace without justice. Even where negotiations have initially concluded with an amnesty or impunity, as in Sierra Leone and Cambodia, or where existing governments refuse to address their ongoing or past atrocities, as in Syria and Myanmar, the domestic and international societies continue to seek ways to punish the perpetrators of crimes and achieve a durable peace with justice.

Ukraine: Peace With Justice

Along with the broader international pivot to accountability, Ukraine is also finding itself in a completely transformed environment where there is less room for accommodation and appeasement.[93] After agreeing to include amnesty provisions in both Minsk I and Minsk II, which aimed to conclude the Russian armed conflict in Ukraine after the events in 2014, Ukraine has learned its lesson about the pitfalls of peace without justice.

The Minsk I Protocol was signed in September 2014 by the representatives of the OSCE (Ambassador Heidi Tagliavini), Ukraine (former President Leonid Kuchma), Russia (former Ambassador Mikhail Zurabov), the DPR (leader Alexander Zakharchenko), and the LPR (leader Igor Plotnitsky).[94] Paragraph 6 of the Minsk Protocol called for the enactment of "a law prohibiting the prosecution and punishment of persons in connection with the events that took place in certain areas of the Donetsk and Luhansk regions of Ukraine."[95]

After the Minsk I agreement collapsed by early 2015, the OSCE, Russia, Ukraine, DPR, and LPR again signed an agreement (the Minsk II Agreement), which did not amend the earlier amnesty provision. Instead, it called for the "exemption from punishment, prosecution, and discrimination for persons involved in the events that have taken place in certain areas of the Donetsk and Luhansk regions."[96] Likewise, paragraph 5 of Minsk II contains similar language to that of Minsk I stating that parties shall "ensure pardon and amnesty by enacting the law prohibiting the prosecution and punishment of persons in connection with the events that took place in certain areas of the Donetsk and Lugansk regions of Ukraine."[97] Despite this second attempt at peace, neither of the Minsk agreements was observed or implemented,[98] instead paving the way for the Russian full-scale invasion in 2022.

Ukraine-led Momentum for Justice

Even with the amnesty provisions in Minsk I and II, Ukraine continued pursuing justice by issuing two declarations to the ICC recognizing the Court's jurisdiction over crimes against humanity and war crimes committed by officials of the Russian Federation related to events since November 2013.[99] After the issuance of these declarations, the ICC announced the launch of preliminary examinations into the situation.[100] Nonetheless, before 2022, little progress had been made in advancing the ICC's work in Ukraine.

This situation has now completely changed since the 2022 full-scale invasion. The ICC Office of the Prosecutor formally opened an investigation in Ukraine on March 2, 2022, after 39 States Parties to the ICC made referrals asking for this step.[101] Subsequently, the Prosecutor issued indictments against President Putin and Russia's Children's Rights Commissioner, Maria

Lvova-Belova in March 2023 for alleged war crimes of unlawful deportation of children.[102] This indictment against a permanent member state of the UN Security Council was an expected, yet unprecedented move by the ICC Prosecutor. The ICC Office of the Prosecutor had issued an indictment against a sitting head of state before in the situation in Darfur.[103] However, it had thus far shied away from issuing arrest warrants against the permanent Security Council members.[104] The change of approach in this situation can in part be explained by the undeniably strong case that the Prosecutor has likely gathered against Putin for the war crime of deportation of children, and the overwhelming international support that the ICC has received for the advancing the situation in Ukraine.[105]

The ICC indictment against Putin was positively received by many in the West and especially in Ukraine, despite predictable criticism from states such as China and, of course, Russia.[106] For Ukraine, the move was seen as the first tangible step forward in achieving justice for the crimes Russia has been committing in Ukraine since 2014 and restored the faith of many in the international community's ability to deliver justice.[107]

This faith was thereafter reinforced on March 5, 2024, when the ICC Prosecutor issued two additional indictments against a Lieutenant General of the Russian Armed Forces, Sergei Kobylash, and an Admiral of the Russian Navy, Viktor Sokolov, for their alleged responsibility for the war crime of directing attacks at civilian objects, specifically focusing on the targeting of the Ukrainian electric infrastructure.[108]

In addition to the efforts at the ICC, Ukraine has also filed several complaints against Russia before the International Court of Justice (ICJ). These cases alleged Russia's violation of international conventions on the suppression of the financing of terrorism, the elimination of all forms of racial discrimination, and genocide. The first two complaints were lodged in 2017 claiming Russia breached the financing of terrorism and elimination of all forms of racial discrimination conventions by financing pro-Russian separatists in Ukraine's east and carrying out a "cultural eradication campaign" against Crimean Tatars with a view to "Russifying" civilians.[109] Even though the International Court of Justice already issued its judgment in this 2017 case, which is largely seen as a loss in Ukraine,[110] the judges did find certain breaches of the two conventions by Russia, which have established a non-disputable historical record.

The most prominent International Court of Justice case, which has received significant international attention, is the case Ukraine lodged in the wake of the Russian full-scale invasion in February 2022. This complaint alleges Russia's breach of the Genocide Convention for using a claim that Ukraine was committing a genocide in the Donbas as a pretext for the invasion, thereby misrepresenting the convention.[111] Similarly to the earlier International Court of Justice complaints, the Court issued its preliminary observations, which Ukrainians see as a failure. Instead of deciding to move forward with assessing Russia's actions, the Court decided that it will investigate whether Ukraine did indeed commit genocide in its eastern regions.[112] Despite the slightly disappointing decisions, they still represent the advancement of justice in Ukraine.

Ukraine itself has firmly established its negotiating justice position in the Peace Formula that the Ukrainian President Volodymyr Zelenskyy announced in November 2022.[113] Specifically, point seven of the ten-point formula calls for the "establishment of the Special Tribunal regarding the crime of Russia's aggression against Ukraine and the creation of an international mechanism to compensate for all the damages caused by this war."[114]

To this end, Ukraine has established a Register of Damages caused by the aggression of the Russian Federation against Ukraine to allow Ukraine to properly record and verify the war-related damage, including damage to its environment, as a first step towards the creation of an international compensation mechanism.[115]

Moreover, ever since the outbreak of the full-scale invasion, many in the international community, spearheaded by Ukraine, have been calling for a special tribunal for the crime of aggression.[116] Many proposals have been put forth for what it could look like and how it could be established. In February 2023, the European Union made the first step toward the prosecution of the crime of aggression by establishing an International Centre for the Prosecution of the Crime of Aggression in Ukraine in The Hague, which can help collect evidence for use in future prosecutions.[117]

In April 2024, a group of 44 states from around the world issued a ministerial declaration "Restoring Justice for Ukraine," reaffirming their commitment to establishing a special tribunal for the prosecution of the crime of aggression against Ukraine and reiterating the need for the UN General Assembly to create an international mechanism for reparation for Russia's wrongful acts in Ukraine.[118] The declaration also confirmed that Russian frozen assets will remain immobilized for as long as Russia continues its aggression and does not make reparations to Ukraine.[119]

In addition to these steps taken to pursue justice on the international level, certain prosecutions have already begun on the domestic level in Ukraine and in other countries. The Ukrainian Office of the Prosecutor General has opened hundreds of investigation cases and issued indictments against Russian military and political officials.[120] War crimes trials have already concluded in over two dozen cities against hundreds of military personnel with judgments being issued regularly by Ukrainian courts.[121]

Other states, some of which have historically been passive and hesitant to pursue accountability efforts,[122] have also begun investigations into the Russian crimes in Ukraine. For instance, the United States has developed a war crimes accountability team to investigate cases that may have a US nexus, allowing cases to proceed in US courts under new legal authorities from US Congress.[123] Estonia, France, Germany, Lithuania, Sweden, Spain, Poland, Slovakia, Latvia, Norway, and Switzerland have all already launched investigations of international crimes committed by Russia in Ukraine under the universal jurisdiction principle.[124]

What is more, 47 states, including Colombia, Guatemala, the Marshall Islands, Japan, the Republic of Korea, the United States, the United Kingdom, and many others from around the world,[125] and a delegation from the European Union, have joined the Group of Friends of Accountability following the Aggression against Ukraine to share information and engage all of the international community in an effort to pursue justice for Ukraine.[126]

Justice Surpassing the Scope of Negotiation

Bearing in mind the above-mentioned initiatives that have already been launched to further justice in Ukraine, what they mean for how negotiations between Ukraine and Russia could look like. It must be noted, however, that at present Ukraine is committed to winning the war militarily and without negotiations with Russia. President Zelenskyy has explicitly declared that Ukraine's position is not to negotiate with Russia.[127] Instead, Ukraine is focused on negotiating with the international community, excluding Russia, on the steps to achieve durable peace in Ukraine.

Should this primary goal of reaching peace in Ukraine without direct negotiations with Russia fail, several highly complex questions will be put on the table not only by Ukraine and Russia but also by certain other international actors.

Ukraine's Position

Ukraine's negotiating position is discussed in the Zelenskyy's ten-point peace formula.[128] If and when negotiations between Ukraine and Russia take place, Ukraine will enter them with clear demands for: restoring its territorial integrity; releasing all prisoners of war, civilian prisoners, and deported children; restoring food, energy, and nuclear security; prosecuting all those responsible for the commission of crimes in Ukraine and compensating for the damage done to Ukrainian territory during the war.[129] Other matters that could be raised during the negotiations are Ukraine's membership in Western organizations such as the North Atlantic Treaty Organization and the European Union.

The legal basis for all of Ukraine's claims is strong. Russia should respect Ukraine's sovereignty and territorial integrity, cease attacks on nuclear and energy infrastructure, allow the transportation of food and other goods, release all prisoners of war and civilians, including children, prosecute those responsible for crimes, and compensate for all the damage it has inflicted on Ukrainian cities and the population. Nonetheless, it can be expected that Russia will put up a fierce fight against each of Ukraine's demands.

Russia's Position

Russia's negotiating position can be inferred from the numerous statements its officials have made and from a Telegram message by Russia's former President and Prime Minister and current Deputy Chairman of the Security Council of the Russian Federation, Dmitry Medvedev, published in March 2024.[130]

Russia can be expected to request that Crimea and the territories in Donbas remain within the Russian Federation (although Dmitry Medvedev went as far as to call on all of Ukraine to be re-incorporated into the Russian Federation). Additionally, Russia will want all the frozen Russian state and private assets to be released and a blanket amnesty to be issued for all Russian soldiers and state officials. As part of Russia's demand for amnesty, it can also be assumed it will ask that the ICC reverse its indictments against Vladimir Putin, Maria Lvova-Belova, Sergei Kobylash, and Viktor Sokolov.

Other Positions

The war in Ukraine has become not just a Ukrainian and Russian concern; it has impacted the entire world, pulling usually silent members of the international community to attempt to mediate the situation and put forth suggested terms for peace. From the European Union's opening of negotiation talks with Ukraine about its membership in the organization,[131] to the African goal of enforcing food security,[132] to Chinese interest in fostering favorable economic conditions to ensure its continued growth.[133] All these are indications that the future of Ukraine is a matter of global concern. And it thus means that any negotiations between Ukraine and Russia would likely be influenced by the interests of third parties.

For example, "China's Position on the Political Settlement of the Ukraine Crisis," in addition to negotiating positions already elaborated by Ukraine and/or Russia, adds that the resolution of the war should also include measures for maintaining "the existing world economic system and [opposing the use of the] world economy as a tool or weapon for political purposes."[134] China has also called for the cessation of the use of unilateral sanctions as a means to resolve disputes,[135] which, contrastingly, the states in the West would likely oppose due to the role of sanctions as the primary means of punishing violators of international law. Importantly for the purposes of this chapter, China's position for negotiating justice in Ukraine will likely align with that of Russia's. China has criticized the ICC for issuing an arrest warrant against Putin, demanding that the ICC take "an objective and just position, respect the jurisdictional immunity of a head of state under international law, prudently exercise its mandate in accordance with the law, interpret and apply international law in good faith, and not engage in politicization or use double standards."[136]

African states will certainly put significant attention and effort into ensuring that any peace agreement includes measures for the maintenance of secure supply chains and the safe passage of foodstuffs in the Black Sea.[137] In fact, the peace proposal from the African Peace Delegation consisting of Comoros, Congo-Brazzaville, Egypt, Senegal, Uganda, Zambia, and South Africa asks that African states be kept engaged in any peace process in Ukraine.[138]

While most of the Western states call for justice in Ukraine, neither China nor the African Peace Delegation pays much attention to the matter. They have presented plans that fail to incorporate justice for the crimes committed during the war.[139] Given the eagerness of both China and the African countries to achieve a quick peace so as to restore positive economic conditions and functioning supply chains,[140] it can be expected that the peace efforts stemming from these actors would prioritize postponing discussions on anything as complex as developing accountability mechanisms for atrocity crimes committed in Ukraine. Indeed, Chinese spokespersons have repeatedly reiterated their calls for negotiations and dialogue opposing the efforts from the ICC and others at bringing the perpetrators of international crimes in Ukraine to justice.[141] Moreover, the African continent's primary objective is to restore the supply of grain from Ukraine to Africa to avoid an escalating food crisis – after Russian military vessels blocked Ukrainian ports in the Black Sea for grain exports from Ukraine, the fifth-largest grain exporter in the world – and it perceives any push for justice as a barrier to this objective.[142]

The Battle for Justice

While Ukraine has a strong legal basis for all its positions, including territorial integrity, the return of children, and requesting reparations from Russia, none of the Peace Formula's ten points is as irreversible as point seven: "Justice." If Ukraine decided to change its position, it could still agree to give up Crimea and Donbas, cease pursuing ways to extract reparations from Russia, and allow the forcibly transferred children to decide for themselves whether they wish to return to Ukraine. While doing so would be political suicide for the Ukrainian government and run counter to the fundamental principles the international community and Ukraine have stood for ever since World War II, there is little other states could do to counteract Ukraine's decision.

The situation is far less dependent on Ukraine's position when it comes to justice and accountability. Namely, the nature of ICC indictments and universal jurisdiction is such that, even if Ukraine agrees to amnesty in a peace agreement with Russia, this peace agreement will not be binding upon the

ICC or any state willing to invoke universal jurisdiction to prosecute those responsible for crimes committed in Ukraine.

Particularly, any Ukrainian amnesty granted to Russian perpetrators of atrocities would be inconsistent with Ukraine's previous allegations and statements granting the ICC jurisdiction,[143] and therefore would likely be disregarded by the ICC.

The ICC has refused to recognize grants of amnesty for crimes in the past. In the Saif Al-Islam Gaddafi case,[144] Gaddafi (son of Muammar Gaddafi) was charged with murder and crimes against humanity allegedly committed during the violent suppression of civilian demonstrations in February 2011. He challenged the ICC's jurisdiction, arguing in part that he had been granted amnesty under Libyan law. The ICC Pre-Trial Chamber found that the Libyan amnesty laws did not apply to Gaddafi's alleged crimes and proceeded to further explain that such amnesty provisions would, regardless, be in violation of international law. The ICC Appeals Chamber later affirmed that decision, albeit softening the ICC position on the status of amnesty under international law.[145]

Additionally, amnesty provisions in domestic law came into conflict with ICC jurisdiction in Uganda. Despite the existence of an Amnesty Act of 2000, the ICC proceeded to issue arrest warrants in 2005 against five senior leaders of the Lord's Resistance Army.[146] It must be noted that the ICC's move was influenced in large part by a Ugandan ratification of the Rome Statute and subsequent referral of the situation in Northern Uganda in 2004 for examination of the Court.[147] Later, Uganda also issued the ICC Act, giving force of law to most provisions of the Rome Statute. When considering the ICC Act's conflict with Uganda's earlier Amnesty Act of 2000, the Ugandan Parliament decided that, under the principle of complementarity, while amnesty granted in accordance with Ugandan law can be invoked at the domestic level, it cannot be invoked when a person is indicted before the ICC.[148]

The ICC itself has clarified in its publications that an amnesty law is inadmissible as a defense before the Court and would not bar the ICC's jurisdiction.[149] As such, even if Ukraine were to negotiate away from justice in a peace agreement with Russia, it is unlikely that the ICC would honor such an amnesty and reverse its indictments against Vladimir Putin or other senior Russian officials.

Likewise, a negotiated amnesty provision would not prevent other states from prosecuting the perpetrators of atrocity crimes. Even if a state chooses to grant amnesty, foreign states can still prosecute individuals for select offenses under the principle of universal jurisdiction.[150] Universal jurisdiction provides that war crimes, crimes against humanity, and other serious offenses can be tried in foreign courts. Therefore, even if Ukraine were to grant amnesty to Russian perpetrators of atrocity crimes, that amnesty would not preclude any other state or international mechanism with jurisdiction over those perpetrators from prosecuting them.

As mentioned above, universal jurisdiction cases for crimes in Ukraine have already been initiated in several states. A peace agreement between Ukraine and Russia would not be able to terminate these investigations and prosecutions, which means Ukraine does not, in fact, have the power to negotiate away justice entirely.

Slightly less straightforward cases, although still worth noting, arise regarding negotiating justice for those perpetrators already prosecuted under Ukrainian domestic jurisdiction and those that may be indicted should a special tribunal for the crime of aggression be established. In theory, even those cases that have already been concluded before Ukrainian courts with convictions could be reversed and the perpetrators pardoned because of negotiations. What comes into play in this situation is the interpretation of "justice". An important pillar of any justice efforts is the acknowledgment of the existence of the crimes and the resulting victim catharsis.[151] Without question, the release of convicted perpetrators could retraumatize those who have been victimized by those perpetrators, however, the recognition of the victims' grievance and the establishment of a historical judicial record of the existence of these crimes has already happened and cannot be reversed. For instance, even when the South African Truth Commission provided amnesty in return for perpetrators' testimony, the overall effect of establishing the truth about the apartheid-era crimes functioned as a healing and reconciliation mechanism for society.[152]

When it comes to the special tribunal for the crime of aggression, at the moment, Ukraine's contribution and efforts for its establishment are imperative due to the lack of UN Security Council action in this regard and the added legitimacy Ukraine's commitment provides to moving forward on this matter. Nonetheless, if the foundational structures of the special tribunal were established by the time of the negotiations between Ukraine and Russia, a negotiated amnesty would no longer apply to the jurisdiction of the special tribunal.

Indeed, amnesty provisions were considered in cases before earlier ad hoc and hybrid tribunals in Sierra Leone and Cambodia, both of which were established under the auspices of the UN. In *Prosecutor v. Morris Kallon and Brima Bazzy Kamara*, the Special Court for Sierra Leone (SCSL) Prosecutor indicted Morris Kallon and Brima Bazzy Kamara for crimes against humanity, violations of Common Article 3 to the Geneva Conventions, violations of Additional Protocol II, and other serious violations of international humanitarian law.[153]

In the appeal of their convictions, Kallon and Kamara argued that the Government of Sierra Leone was bound to observe the amnesty granted under Article IX of the Peace Agreement between the Government of Sierra Leone and the Revolutionary United Front of Sierra Leone (Lomé Agreement),[154] and that the amnesty granted by the Lomé Agreement amounted to an unconditional pardon for any of their alleged offenses. Accordingly, they argued, the SCSL had no jurisdiction over them.

The SCSL Appeals Chamber found that the Lomé Agreement "created neither rights nor obligations capable of being regulated by international law,"[155] and that the legal status of a treaty or international agreement is determined by its treatment under international law—not by the classification of the transaction by a state.[156] As such, the SCSL held that the amnesty granted by Sierra Leone could not cover atrocity crimes, which are subject to universal jurisdiction under international law.[157]

In the same vein, the Extraordinary Chambers in the Courts of Cambodia (ECCC) declined to honor a pardon and amnesty granted by King Sihanouk via royal decree on September 14, 1996, under the 1994 Law on the Outlawing of the Democratic Kampuchea Group.[158] The ECCC reasoned that treaties[159] and customary rules of international law require the prosecution of such crimes and that there is a prohibition on enforcing amnesties relating to them.[160]

These rulings indicate that it is highly likely that a special tribunal for the crime of aggression in Ukraine would adopt a similar position and dismiss any pardons or amnesties negotiated between Ukraine and Russia. The notable strides already made towards establishing this special tribunal[161] also indicate that, by the time of negotiations, it may be too late for Ukraine or Russia to stop its development. Many states around the world view Russia's aggression against Ukraine not just as an attack on Ukraine but as an attack on the international order, which cannot go unpunished.[162] This conviction might signal that, even without Ukraine's active support and participation, the international community would continue pursuing the development of a special tribunal for the crime of aggression, in which case an amnesty would not be able to prevent it.

Lastly, notwithstanding the fact that the International Court of Justice cases are about state responsibility, rather than individual accountability, they have already been concluded or have advanced to the merits stage. This means that they have already established Russian responsibility for certain acts, which a negotiated settlement will not be able to erase from the historical record.

This is all to say that the circumstances in which Ukraine will find itself if and when it enters negotiations with Russia will be largely unprecedented. Even if Russia has the upper hand in all the other items to be negotiated, one item where any kind of victory will not change much is justice itself. The indictments against Russian officials, including its President, prosecutions launched in numerous countries, and a looming threat of a special tribunal for the crime of aggression will be on the table, and Russia will most certainly want to negotiate them away. What will make these negotiations interesting is that these are also items where Ukraine has little to no room for accommodation, even if it wanted to.

Conclusion

In an ideal scenario, Ukraine would not need to enter into peace negotiations with Russia and can make its Peace Formula a reality through other means. Nevertheless, the reality is that this might not come true, and it may need to sit across the table from Russia and negotiate the end of this brutal war. The demands Ukraine will bring to the table are more or less clearly reflected in its Peace Formula, most of which Russia and its allies will likely attempt to resist. Some of these demands Ukraine may need to give up. These may include its membership in the Euro-Atlantic security infrastructure, claims for reparations, and possibly also its sovereignty over the occupied territories in Ukraine's east.

The one item that Russia will not be able to pressure Ukraine to negotiate away is justice. Any Ukrainian and Russian peace negotiations would be taking place in an environment where justice processes have already been launched. As much as Russia may wish to try to persuade Ukraine to abolish its plans for accountability, it is unlikely that it will be able to halt these processes. The ICC has already obtained the necessary jurisdiction from Ukraine to move forward with the case against Putin,[163] and the international community has made notable steps toward establishing the mechanisms for prosecuting the crime of aggression and seeking compensation for the damage wrought in Ukraine, which do not depend upon Ukraine and Russia's agreement in a peace negotiation process. As such, both sides will be able to negotiate anything. However, they will no longer be able to negotiate themselves out of accountability already underway.

Notes

1 Parts of this chapter are adapted from Dr. Paul R. Williams & Sindija Beta, Negotiating Environmental Justice in Ukraine, 56 CASE WESTERN RESERVE J. INT'L L. 272–308 (2024) with permission from the Case Western Reserve Journal of International Law.
2 *See, e.g.*, Press Release, Antony J. Blinken, 71st Sec'y of State, Crimes Against Humanity in Ukraine (Feb. 18, 2023), https://www.state.gov/crimes-against-humanity-in-ukraine/.
3 *See, e.g.*, Rome Statute of the International Criminal Court art. 8 bis (2)(b)(iv), July 12, 1999, U.N. Doc. A/CONF.183/9; *see* Clara Gutman-Argemí et al., *Ukrainians Are Accusing Russia of Ecocide. What Does That Mean?*, FOREIGN POL'Y (June 9, 2023, 3:59 PM), https://foreignpolicy.com/2023/06/09/ecocide-ukraine-russia-dam-war-crimes/.
4 General Assembly Resolution ES-11/1, para. 2, U.N. Doc. A/RES/ES-11/1 (Mar. 2, 2022) (stating, *inter alia*, that the General Assembly "*[d]eplores* in the

strongest terms the aggression by the Russian Federation against Ukraine in violation of Article 2(4) of the Charter") (emphasis in original).

5 Int'l Crim. Ct., Situation in Ukraine, https://www.icc-cpi.int/situations/ukraine; Int'l Crim. Ct., Georgia, https://www.icc-cpi.int/georgia.

6 *See* Judgment, Yanukovych (case No. 756/4855/17), Obolonsky District Court, Kyiv, 24 January 2019, http://reyestr.court.gov.ua.

7 *See* CourtMH17.com, About the Case, https://www.courtmh17.com/en/about-the-case/.

8 Press Release, U.N. Off. of the High Comm'r of Human Rights, Independent International Commission of Inquiry on Ukraine to the Human Rights Council: War Crimes Have Been Committed in Ukraine (Sept. 23, 2022), https://www.ohchr.org/en/press-releases/2022/09/independent-international-commission-inquiry-ukraine-human-rights-council; *The First Meeting of the International Working Group on the Environmental Consequences of War Took Place in Kyiv*, Pres. of Ukr. (June 30, 2023, 9:06), https://www.president.gov.ua/en/news/u-kiyevi-vidbulosya-pershe-zasidannya-mizhnarodnoyi-robochoy-83949.

9 *See* Nathan Warters, *Q&A: Prosecuting War Crimes in Ukraine*, W&M News (Feb. 20, 2023), https://news.wm.edu/2023/02/20/qa-prosecuting-russian-war-crimes-in-ukraine/#:~:text=Q%3A%20How%20will%20these%20Russian,prosecute%20them%20through%20domestic%20courts.

10 Verkhovna Rada, Resolution of the Verkhovna Rada of Ukraine: Declaration on the Recognition of the Jurisdiction of the International Criminal Court by Ukraine over Crimes Against Humanity and War Crimes Committed by Senior Officials of the Russian Federation and Leaders of Terrorist Organizations "DNR" and "LNR," Which Led to Extremely Grave Consequences and Mass Murder of Ukrainian Nationals *translated in* Int'l Crim. Ct. (Sep. 8, 2015); Press Release, Int'l Crim. Ct., ICC Prosecutor Extends Preliminary Exam. Of the Situation in Ukr. Following Second Article 12(3) Declaration (Sept. 29, 2015), https://www.icc-cpi.int/news/icc-prosecutor-extends-preliminary-examination-situation-ukraine-following-second-article-123.

11 Jennifer Hansler, *Ukrainians Push for US to Support Special Tribunal to Prosecute Russian Leadership for Crime of Aggression*, CNN (Dec. 14, 2022, 9:56 PM), https://www.cnn.com/2022/12/14/politics/ukraine-special-tribunal-russia-crime-of-aggression/index.html#:~:text=Follow%20CNN%20Politics-,Ukrainians%20push%20for%20US%20to%20support%20special%20tribunal%20to,leadership%20for%20crime%20of%20aggression&text=Ukrainian%20officials%20traveled%20to%20the,for%20the%20crime%20of%20aggression.

12 *See* Nick Grono & Caroline Flintoft, *Negotiating Justice to Understand Accountability*, Int'l Crisis Grp. (June 25, 2007), https://www.crisisgroup.org/global/negotiating-justice-understand-accountability.

13 *See China's Position on the Political Settlement of the Ukraine Crisis*, Ministry of Foreign Affs. of China (Feb. 24, 2023, 9:00), https://www.fmprc.gov.cn/eng/zxxx_662805/202302/t20230224_11030713.html.

14 Catherine Nzuki, *Africa's Peace Delegation: A New Chapter for Africa and the Ukraine War*, Ctr. for Strategic & Int'l Stud. (Jun. 16, 2023), https://www.csis.org/analysis/africas-peace-delegation-new-chapter-africa-and-ukraine-war.

15 *Accountability for Atrocity Crimes*, U.N. Off. on Genocide Prevention & the Resp. to Protect, https://www.un.org/en/genocideprevention/accountability.shtml.

16 *See, e.g.*, Promotion of National Unity and Reconciliation Act No. 34 of 1995 § 20 (S. Afr.).

17 Promotion of National Unity and Reconciliation Act No. 34 of 1995 § 2–3 (S. Afr.).

18 U.N. High Comm'r for Human Rights, Rule-of-Law Tools for Post-Conflict Sates: Truth Commission, 1, HR/PUB/06/01 (2006); William T. Armaline et al., *De Jure vs. De Facto Rights: A Response to "Human Rights: What the United States Might Learn from the Rest of the World and, Yes, from American Sociology,"* 32 Socio. F. 220, 222 (2017).
19 U.N. High Comm'r for Human Rights, Rule-of-Law Tools for Post-Conflict Sates: Truth Commission, 1, HR/PUB/06/01 (2006); William T. Armaline et al., *De Jure vs. De Facto Rights: A Response to "Human Rights: What the United States Might Learn from the Rest of the World and, Yes, from American Sociology,"* 32 Socio. F. 220, 222–23 (2017).
20 *See* U.N. High Comm'r for Hum. Rts, Rule-of-Law Tools for Post-Conflict States: Amnesties, 1, 14, U.N. Doc. HR/PUB/09/1 (2009).
21 *See* Stef Vandeginste & Chandra Lekha Sriram, *Power Sharing and Transitional Justice: A Clash of Paradigms?*, 17 Glob. Governance 489, 491, 494 (2011).
22 *See* U.N. High Comm'r for Human Rights, Rule-of-Law Tools for Post-Conflict Sates: Truth Commission, 1, HR/PUB/06/01 (2006).
23 *See* Alison Bisset, *Rethinking the Powers of Truth Commissions in Light of the ICC Statute*, 7 J. Int'l Crim. L. 963, 964–965 (2009) ("The ICC has not yet assumed jurisdiction in a situation that has been or is being investigated by a truth commission").
24 *See, e.g.*, Rep. of the Secretary-General on the Establishment of a Special Ct. for Sierra Leone, ¶ 1, U.N. Doc. S/2000/915 (Oct. 4, 2000).
25 *See, e.g.*, Janet McKnight, *Accountability in Northern Uganda: Understanding the Conflict, the Parties and the False Dichotomies in International Criminal Law and Transitional Justice*, 59 J. Afr. L. 193, 205 (2015).
26 *See, e.g.*, Memorandum from Amnesty International on Special Chambers in the Democratic Republic of the Congo 1, 3–4 (Feb. 2011), https://www.amnesty.org/en/documents/afr62/003/2011/en/; *see also* Maria Stefania Cataleta, *The Kosovo Specialist Chambers, an International Tribunal Inside the National Judicial System*, 3 J. Int'l Crim. L. 1, 2, 5 (2022).
27 *Basic Facts on Universal Jurisdiction*, Hum. Rts. Watch (Oct. 19, 2009, 8:45 AM), https://www.hrw.org/news/2009/10/19/basic-facts-universal-jurisdiction#:~:text=Over%20the%20last%2015%20years%2C%20as%20states%20and,who%20have%20nowhere%20else%20to%20turn%20for%20redress.
28 Yasmin Naqvi, *Amnesty for War Crimes: Defining the Limits of International Recognition*, 85 Int'l Rev. Red Cross 583, 587 n.15, 594–95.
29 *See* Josie Fischels, *How 165 Words Could Make Mass Environmental Destruction an International Crime*, NPR (Jun. 27, 2021, 8:00 AM), https://www.npr.org/2021/06/27/1010402568/ecocide-environment-destruction-international-crime-criminal-court; Linda Pasquini & Tomasz Janowski, *Switzerland Joins Push for Special Tribunal on 'Aggression' Against Ukraine*, Reuters (Nov. 16, 2023, 8:46 AM), https://www.reuters.com/world/europe/switzerland-joins-push-special-tribunal-aggression-against-ukraine-2023-11-16/.
30 World Health Org. [WHO], *Global Status Report on Preventing Violence Against Children 2020*, at xiii–xiv (2020).
31 *See* Andrew Reiter, *Examining the Use of Amnesties and Pardons as a Response to Internal Armed* Conflict, 47 Isr. L. Rev. 133, 141 (2014).
32 Int'l Ctr. for Transitional Just. & Afghanistan Indep. Hum. Rts. Comm'n, Discussion Paper on the Legality of Amnesties 8 (2010).
33 Int'l Ctr. for Transitional Just. & Afghanistan Indep. Hum. Rts. Comm'n, Discussion Paper on the Legality of Amnesties 8, 1 (2010).
34 *See, e.g.*, S.C. Res. 827 (May 25, 1993).

35 *See, e.g.*, Matthew Lee, *U.S. Finds Both Sides in Sudan Conflict Have Committed Atrocities in Darfur*, PBS (Dec. 6, 2023, 5:57 PM), *https*://www.pbs.org/newshour/politics/u-s-finds-both-sides-in-sudan-conflict-have-committed-atrocities-in-darfur.

36 *See, e.g.*, Matthew Lee, *U.S. Finds Both Sides in Sudan Conflict Have Committed Atrocities in Darfur*, PBS (Dec. 6, 2023, 5:57 PM), https://www.pbs.org/newshour/politics/u-s-finds-both-sides-in-sudan-conflict-have-committed-atrocities-in-darfur; *see also* Christine Bell, *Peace Agreements: Their Nature and Legal Status*, 100 Am. J. Int'l L. 373, 386 (2006).

37 *See, e.g.*, Christine Bell, *Peace Agreements: Their Nature and Legal Status*, 100 Am. J. Int'l L. 373, 387–89 (2006).

38 Keith Doubt, *We Had to Jump over the Moral Bridge: Bosnia and the Pathetic Hegemony of Face-Work*, in The Conceit of Innocence: Losing the Conscience of the West in the War Against Bosnia 120, 121 (Stjepan G. Meštrović ed., 1997).

39 *The Armenian Genocide (1915–16): Overview*, Holocaust Encyclopedia, https://encyclopedia.ushmm.org/content/en/article/the-armenian-genocide-1915-16-overview; Treaty of Peace with Turkey arts. 138–140, 28 L.N.T.S 139 (July 24, 1923).

40 *See* Évian Accords art. II(k–l), Mar. 19, 1962, 507 U.N.T.S. 28, 33.

41 *See generally* Amnesty Int'l, *Argentina; Legal Memorandum: Full Stop and Due Obedience Laws*, AI Index: AMR 13/018/2003 (Dec. 2003).

42 Law No. 2191, 18 April, 1978, Diario Official [D.O.] (Chile).

43 The Comm'n on the Truth for El Salvador, From Madness to Hope: the 12-year War in El Salvador: Report of the Commission on the Truth for El Salvador § III (Jul. 1, 1992).

44 Ley de reconciliacion nacional [National Reconciliation Law] (1996) (Guat.).

45 Law No. 15848 (Uru.) (1986).

46 Memorandum of Understanding, Security Council, Identical letters Dated 25 April 2002 from the Permanent Representative of Angola to the United Nations Addressed to the Secretary-General and the President of the Security Council, § 2, U.N. Doc. S/002/483 (Apr. 26, 2002).

47 Political Negotiations on the Peace Process and on Transition in the DRC, § 3, ¶ 4, Dec. 16, 2002.

48 Accord de Governors Island [Governors Island Agreement], ¶ 6–7, Jul. 3, 1993 (Haiti).

49 *Amnesty: General Peace Agreement for Mozambique*, Univ. of Notre Dame: Kroc Inst. for Int'l Peace Stud., https://peaceaccords.nd.edu/provision/amnesty-general-peace-agreement-for-mozambique.

50 Andrew Reiter, *Examining the Use of Amnesties and Pardons as a Response to Internal Armed* Conflict, 47 Isr. L. Rev. 133, 144–145 (2014).

51 U. N. High Comm'r for Hum. Rts, Rule-of-Law Tools for Post-Conflict States: Amnesties, 3, U.N. Doc. HR/PUB/09/1 (2009).

52 *See, e.g.*, Stephen John Stedman, Implementing Peace Agreements in Civil Wars: Lessons and Recommendations for Policymakers 7 (2001).

53 U. N. High Comm'r for Hum. Rts, Rule-of-Law Tools for Post-Conflict States: Amnesties, U.N. Doc. HR/PUB/09/1 (2009).

54 Michael P. Scharf & Paul R. Williams, *The Functions of Justice and Anti-Justice in the Peace-Building Process*, 35 Case W. Res. J. Int'l L. 161, 170–176 (2003).

55 Geneva Convention for the Amelioration of the Condition of the Wounded and Sick in Armed Forces in the Field, art. 49, Aug. 12, 1949, 6 U.S.T. 3114, 75 U.N.T.S.

56 International Covenant on Civil and Political Rights, art. 2, ¶ 3, Dec. 16, 1966, 999 U.N.T.S. 171.
57 European Convention on Human Rights, art. 13, Nov. 4, 1950, 213 U.N.T.S. 222 ("Everyone whose rights and freedoms as set forth in this Convention are violated shall have an effective remedy before a national authority notwithstanding that the violation has been committed by persons acting in an official capacity.").
58 Josepha Close, *Crafting an International Norm Prohibiting the Grant of Amnesty for Serious Crimes: Convergences and Divergences in the Case-Law of International Courts*, 7 Queen Mary L.J. 109, 112 (2016).
59 Prosecutor v. Nuon, Case No. 002/19-09-2007/ECCCffC, Decision on Ieng Sary's Rule 89 Preliminary Objections, ¶ 53 (2011).
60 Josepha Close, *Crafting an International Norm Prohibiting the Grant of Amnesty for Serious Crimes: Convergences and Divergences in the Case-Law of International Courts*, 7 Queen Mary L.J. 109, 114 (2016).
61 *See, e.g.*, Okkali v. Turkey, App. No. 52067/99, ¶ 76–78 (2003), https://hudoc.echr.coe.int/eng?i=001-77522; *see also* Ali and Ayse Duran v. Turkey, App. No. 42942/02, ¶ 69–72 (2008), https://hudoc.echr.coe.int/eng?i=001-120841; *see also* Terzi and Erkmen v. Turkey, App. No. 31300/05, ¶ 33–36 (2009), https://hudoc.echr.coe.int/eng?i=001-93823; *see also* Baran and Hun v. Turkey, App. No. 30685/05, ¶ 58–62 (2010), https://hudoc.echr.coe.int/eng?i=001-98664; *see also* Yerli v. Turkey, App. no. 59177 /10, ¶ 60–63 (2014), https://hudoc.echr.coe.int/eng?i=001-153058.
62 *See, e.g.*, Okkali v. Turkey, App. No. 52067/99, ¶ 65–66 (2003), https://hudoc.echr.coe.int/eng?i=001-77522; *see also* Ali and Ayse Duran v. Turkey, App. No. 42942/02, ¶ 63–64 (2008), https://hudoc.echr.coe.int/eng?i=001-120841.
63 Gelman v Uruguay, Merits, Reparations, and Judgment, Inter-Am. Ct. H.R. (ser. C) No. 221 (Feb. 24, 2011).
64 Gelman v Uruguay, Merits, Reparations, and Judgment, Inter-Am. Ct. H.R. (ser. C) No. 221, §§ D–E (Feb. 24, 2011).
65 Gelman v Uruguay, Merits, Reparations, and Judgment, Inter-Am. Ct. H.R. (ser. C) No. 221, ¶ 149 (Feb. 24, 2011).
66 Gelman v Uruguay, Merits, Reparations, and Judgment, Inter-Am. Ct. H.R. (ser. C) No. 221 (Feb. 24, 2011).
67 *The Tribunal – Establishment,* U.N. Int'l Crim. Tribunal for the Former Yugoslavia, https://www.icty.org/en/about/tribunal/establishment#:~:text=On%2025%20May%201993%2C%20the,Yugoslavia%2C%20known%20as%20the%20ICTY; S.C. Res. 827 (May 25, 1993).
68 Franca Baroni, *The International Criminal Tribunal for the Former Yugoslavia and Its Mission to Restore Peace*, 12 Pace Int'l L. Rev. 233, 233–34 (2000).
69 Michael P. Scharf, *The Tools for Enforcing International Criminal Justice in the New Millennium: Lessons from the Yugoslavia Tribunal*, 49 DePaul L. Rev. 925, 953, 955 (2000).
70 *See generally* Bosnia and Herzegovina-Croatia-Yugoslavia: General Framework Agreement for Peace in Bosnia and Herzegovina with Annexes, Nov. 21, 1995, A/50/79C.
71 Bosnia and Herzegovina-Croatia-Yugoslavia: General Framework Agreement for Peace in Bosnia and Herzegovina with Annexes, art. X, Nov. 21, 1995, A/50/79C.
72 Jackson Nyamuya Maogoto, *International Justice in the Shadow of Realpolitik: Re-Visiting the Establishment of the Ad Hoc International Criminal Tribunals*, 5 Flinders J. Legal Reform, no. 2, 2001, at 29.

73 Press Release, Radovan Karadzic and Ratko Mladic Accused of Genocide Following the Take-Over of Srebrenica, U.N. ICTY (Nov. 16, 1995), https://www.icty.org/sid/7221.
74 Leon Hartwell, *Conflict Resolution: Lessons from the Dayton Peace Process*, 35 NEGOT. J. 443, 459–60 (2019).
75 ICCTY, CASE INFORMATION SHEET: MOMČ ILO KRAJIŠNIK, https://www.icty.org/x/cases/krajisnik/cis/en/cis_krajisnik_en.pdf.
76 Prosecutor v. Miloševič, Caw No. IT-99-37, Indictment (Int'l Crim. Tib. For the Former Yugoslavia 1999).
77 Prosecutor v. Miloševič, Caw No. IT-99-37, Indictment (Int'l Crim. Tib. For the Former Yugoslavia 1999); CASE INFORMATION SHEET: ICCTY, CASE INFORMATION SHEET: MOMČ ILO KRAJIŠNIK, https://www.icty.org/x/cases/krajisnik/cis/en/cis_krajisnik_en.pdf; Bosnia and Herzegovina-Croatia-Yugoslavia: General Framework Agreement for Peace in Bosnia and Herzegovina with Annexes, Nov. 21, 1995, A/50/79C.
78 *See* Interim Agreement for Peace and Self-Government in Kosovo, Feb. 23, 1999, ¶ 12, U.N. Doc. S/1999/648 (June 7, 1999).
79 Prosecutor v. Miloševič, Caw No. IT-99-37, Indictment (Int'l Crim. Tib. For the Former Yugoslavia 1999).
80 S.C. Res. 955 ¶ 1 (Nov. 8, 1994).
81 U.N. Secretary-General, Letter dated 9 August 2000 from the Permanent Representative of Sierra Leone to the United Nations addressed to the President of the Security Council, U.N. Doc. S/2000/786 (Aug. 10, 2000).
82 *See* Ben Kiernan, *The Demography of Genocide in Southeast Asia: The Death Tolls in Cambodia, 1975-79, and East Timor, 1975-80*, 4 CRITICAL ASIAN STUD. 585, 587 (2003); *see also* Letter dated 30 October 1991 from the Permanent Representatives of France and Indonesia to the United Nations addressed to the Secretary-General, U.N. Doc. A/46/608- S/23177, art. 21–22 (Oct. 30, 1991).
83 U.N. President of the S.C., Letter dated June 23, 1997, from Secretary General to the President of the General Assembly and to the President of the Security Council, U.N. Doc. A/51/93 (June 24, 1997).
84 Annex to the letter dated 13 December 2005 from the Chargé d'affaires a.i. of the Permanent Mission of Lebanon to the United Nations addressed to the Secretary-General, Annex, para. 1, U.N. Doc. S/2005/783/Annex (Dec. 13, 2005). A draft agreement between the U.N. and the Lebanese executive branch to create a Special Tribunal for Lebanon was approved by the Security Council on November 21, 2006. *See* Letter dated 21 November 2006 from the President of the Security Council addressed to the Secretary General, para. 5, U.N. Doc. S/2006/911 (Nov. 24, 2006).
85 See Case No. CH/PTJ/2009/06, Order Regarding the Detention of Persons Detained in Lebanon in Connection With the Case of the Attack Against Prime Minister Rafiq Hariri and Others, ¶ 1 (Apr. 29, 2009).
86 *CPA Order No. 48, Delegation of Authority Regarding Establishment of an Iraqi Special Tribunal* (Iraq, 2003).
87 Santiago Vargas Niño, *Colombia's Special Jurisdiction for Peace Bends the Law to Dub Paramilitaries as State Officials: The Time For Critique is Now*, OpinioJuris (Sept. 16, 2022), https://opiniojuris.org/2022/09/16/colombias-special-jurisdiction-for-peace-bends-the-law-to-dub-paramilitaries-as-state-officials-the-time-for-critique-is-now/.
88 *Revitalized Agreement on the Resolution of the Conflict in the Republic of South Sudan*, art. 5.1.1 (South Sudan, 2018), https://igad.int/programs/115-south-sudan-office/1950-signed-revitalized-agreement-on-the-resolution-of-the-conflict-in-south-sudan [R-ARCSS].

89 International, Impartial and Independent Mechanism, https://iiim.un.org/; Independent Investigative Mechanism for Myanmar, https://iimm.un.org/.

90 *See* Hayley Evans, *A Survey of Recent Developments and Trends in Universal Jurisdiction*, Lawfare (Feb. 9, 2022), https://www.lawfaremedia.org/article/survey-recent-developments-and-trends-universal-jurisdiction.

91 Situation in the People's Republic of Bangladesh/Republic of the Union of Myanmar, International Criminal Court, https://www.icc-cpi.int/bangladesh-myanmar.

92 *Application of the Convention on the Prevention and Punishment of the Crime of Genocide (The Gambia v. Myanmar)*, International Court of Justice, https://www.icj-cij.org/case/178.

93 *See generally* Dennis Soltys, *Appeasement is the Worst Possible Policy for Both Ukraine and Russia*, Atlantic Council (May 21, 2022), https://www.atlanticcouncil.org/blogs/ukrainealert/appeasement-is-the-worst-possible-policy-for-both-ukraine-and-russia/.

94 Protocol on the outcome of consultations of the Trilateral Contact Group on joint steps aimed at the implementation of the Peace Plan of the President of Ukraine, P. Poroshenko, and the initiatives of the President of the Russian Federation, V. Putin, Sept. 1, 2014, S/2014/135; *Protocol on the Outcome of Consultations of the Trilateral Contact Group on Joint Steps Aimed at the Implementation of the Peace Plan of the President of Ukraine, P. Poroshenko, and the Initiatives of the President of the Russian Federation, V. Putin*, Peace Agreements Database, https://www.peaceagreements.org/view/1363.

95 Protocol on the outcome of consultations of the Trilateral Contact Group on joint steps aimed at the implementation of the Peace Plan of the President of Ukraine, P. Poroshenko, and the initiatives of the President of the Russian Federation, V. Putin, Sept. 1, 2014, S/2014/135, ¶ 6.

96 Package of measures for the implementation of the Minsk agreements, 1 (Feb. 12, 2015), https://www.osce.org/ru/cio/140221.

97 Package of measures for the implementation of the Minsk agreements, 1 (Feb. 12, 2015), https://www.osce.org/ru/cio/140221.

98 *See* Lidia Powirksa, *Through the Ashes of the Minsk Agreements*, Harvard Univ.: Epicenter (May 18, 2022), https://epicenter.wcfia.harvard.edu/blog/through-ashes-minsk-agreements.

99 Verkhovna Rada, Resolution of the Verkhovna Rada of Ukraine: Declaration on the Recognition of the Jurisdiction of the International Criminal Court by Ukraine over Crimes Against Humanity and War Crimes Committed by Senior Officials of the Russian Federation and Leaders of Terrorist Organizations "DNR" and "LNR," Which Led to Extremely Grave Consequences and Mass Murder of Ukrainian Nationals *translated in* Int'l Crim. Ct. (Sep. 8, 2015); Press Release, Int'l Crim. Ct., ICC Prosecutor Extends Preliminary Exam. Of the Situation in Ukr. Following Second Article 12(3) Declaration (Sept. 29, 2015), https://www.icc-cpi.int/news/icc-prosecutor-extends-preliminary-examination-situation-ukraine-following-second-article-123.

100 Press Release, Int'l Crim. Ct., ICC Prosecutor Extends Preliminary Exam. Of the Situation in Ukr. Following Second Article 12(3) Declaration (Sept. 29, 2015), https://www.icc-cpi.int/news/icc-prosecutor-extends-preliminary-examination-situation-ukraine-following-second-article-123.

101 Press Release, Int'l Crim. Ct., Statement of ICC Prosecutor, Karim A.A. Khan QC, on the Situation in Ukraine: Receipt of Referrals from 39 States Parties and the Opening of an Investigation (March 2, 2022), https://www.icc-cpi.int/news/statement-icc-prosecutor-karim-aa-khan-qc-situation-ukraine-receipt-referrals-39-states.

102 Press Release, Int'l Crim. Ct., Situation in Ukr.: ICC Judges Issue Arrest Warrants Against Vladimir Vladimirovich Putin & Maria Alekseyevna Lvova-Belova (Mar. 17, 2023), https://www.icc-cpi.int/news/situation-ukraine-icc-judges-issue-arrest-warrants-against-vladimir-vladimirovich-putin-and.

103 *See* The Prosecutor v. Omar Hassan Ahmad Al Bashir, Case No. ICC-02/05-01/09, Warrant of Arrest, (March 5, 2009).

104 During the term of the Former Prosecutor of the ICC Fatou Bensouda, the Office was also looking into the crimes that may have been committed by the United States of America in the Afghanistan situation, which the current Prosecutor Karim Khan eventually abandoned. *ICC Prosecutor Defends Dropping US From Afghan War Crime Probe*, Al Jazeera (Dec. 6, 2021), https://www.aljazeera.com/news/2021/12/6/icc-prosecutor-defends-dropping-us-from-afghan-investigation; In December 2020, the Prosecutor of the ICC decided to conclude the preliminary examination into Iraq/UK and not to request the opening of an investigation. *Iraq/UK*, Int'l Crim. Ct., https://www.icc-cpi.int/iraq; Russia has also been implicated in crimes allegedly committed in Georgia, as well as Ukraine prior to 2022. *ICC Issues Warrants for 2008 Russia-Georgia War Crimes Suspects*, The Guardian (Jun. 30, 2022, 12:32), https://www.theguardian.com/law/2022/jun/30/icc-issues-warrants-for-2008-russia-georgia-war-crimes-suspects.

105 The Ukraine situation was referred to the ICC by 43 States Parties of the ICC following the outbreak of the full-scale invasion. *Ukraine*, Int'l Crim. Ct., https://www.icc-cpi.int/situations/ukraine.

106 *Reactions to ICC's Arrest Warrant for Putin Citing Ukraine War Crimes*, Reuters (Mar. 17, 2023, 3:57 PM), https://www.reuters.com/world/europe/reactions-iccs-arrest-warrant-putin-over-ukraine-war-crimes-2023-03-17/; John Feng, China Says Putin has 'Immunity' From War Crimes Prosecution, Newsweek, https://www.newsweek.com/china-russia-vladimir-putin-icc-war-crimes-ukraine-1788911#:~:text=China%20threw%20its%20considerable%20political,to%20prosecute%20the%20Russian%20president (Mar. 20, 2023, 10:19 PM).

107 *See, e.g.*, PILPG, *Expert Roundtable - Prosecuting Putin: Next Steps*, YouTube, 23:08 (March 24, 2023), https://www.youtube.com/watch?v=B4SP6dejQMo.

108 Press Release, Int'l Crim. Ct. Situation in Ukr.: ICC judges issue arrest warrants against Sergei Ivanovich Kobylash and Viktor Nikolayevich Sokolov (March 5, 2024), *https://www.icc-cpi.int/news/situation-ukraine-icc-judges-issue-arrest-*warrants-against-sergei-ivanovich-kobylash-and#:~:text=Today%2C%205%20March%202024%2C%20Pre,Kobylash%20and%20Mr%20Viktor%20Nikolayevich.

109 *Application of the International Convention for the Suppression of the Financing of Terrorism and of the International Convention on the Elimination of All Forms of Racial Discrimination (Ukraine v. Russian Federation)*, International Court of Justice, https://www.icj-cij.org/case/166

110 Oona A. Hathaway, *Taking Stock of ICJ Decisions in the 'Ukraine v. Russia' Cases—And implications for South Africa's case against Israel*, Just Security (Feb. 5, 2024), https://www.justsecurity.org/91781/taking-stock-of-icj-decisions-in-ukraine-v-russia-cases-and-implications-for-south-africas-case-against-israel/.

111 *Allegations of Genocide under the Convention on the Prevention and Punishment of the Crime of Genocide* (Ukraine v. Russian Federation), International Court of Justice, https://www.icj-cij.org/case/182

112 Oona A. Hathaway, *Taking Stock of ICJ Decisions in the 'Ukraine v. Russia' Cases—And implications for South Africa's case against Israel*, Just Security (Feb.

5, 2024), https://www.justsecurity.org/91781/taking-stock-of-icj-decisions-in-ukraine-v-russia-cases-and-implications-for-south-africas-case-against-israel/.

113 Volodymyr Zelenskyy, President of Ukraine, Address at the G20 Summit (Nov. 15, 2022, 7:31), https://www.president.gov.ua/en/news/ukrayina-zavzhdi-bula-liderom-mirotvorchih-zusil-yaksho-rosi-79141.

114 Volodymyr Zelenskyy, President of Ukraine, Address at the G20 Summit (Nov. 15, 2022, 7:31), https://www.president.gov.ua/en/news/ukrayina-zavzhdi-bula-liderom-mirotvorchih-zusil-yaksho-rosi-79141.

115 *See Council of Europe Summit Creates Register of Damage for Ukraine as First Step Towards an International Compensation Mechanism for Victims of Russian Aggression,* Council of Eur. (May 17, 2023), https://www.coe.int/en/web/portal/-/council-of-europe-summit-creates-register-of-damage-for-ukraine-as-first-step-towards-an-international-compensation-mechanism-for-victims-of-russian-aggression.

116 Volodymyr Zelenskyy, President of Ukraine, Address at the G20 Summit (Nov. 15, 2022, 7:31), https://www.president.gov.ua/en/news/ukrayina-zavzhdi-bula-liderom-mirotvorchih-zusil-yaksho-rosi-79141; Irina Paliashvili, *Calls Mount for Russia to Face Tribunal for Aggression Against Ukraine*, Atlantic Council (Feb. 28, 2023), https://www.atlanticcouncil.org/blogs/ukrainealert/calls-mount-for-russia-to-face-tribunal-for-aggression-against-ukraine/.

117 Charlotte van Campenhout & Stephanie van den Berg, *EU: Centre for Prosecution of 'Aggression' Crimes in Ukraine to Be Set Up in The Hague*, Reuters (Feb. 2, 2023, 9:46 AM EST), https://www.reuters.com/world/europe/eu-centre-prosecution-aggression-crimes-ukraine-be-set-up-hague-2023-02-02/.

118 Political Declaration of the Ministerial Restoring Justice for Ukraine Conference (Apr. 2, 2024), https://www.government.nl/binaries/government/documenten/diplomatic-statements/2024/04/02/political-declaration-of-the-ministerial-restoring-justice-for-ukraine-conference/Restoring+Justice+for+Ukraine+Conference+-+Political+Declaration.pdf.

119 Political Declaration of the Ministerial Restoring Justice for Ukraine Conference (Apr. 2, 2024), https://www.government.nl/binaries/government/documenten/diplomatic-statements/2024/04/02/political-declaration-of-the-ministerial-restoring-justice-for-ukraine-conference/Restoring+Justice+for+Ukraine+Conference+-+Political+Declaration.pdf.

120 Oleksii Kovalenko, *Q&A: Ukraine's Prosecutor General Discussed Accountability for Putin's War Crimes*, VOA News (April 27, 2023, 2:28 PM), https://www.voanews.com/a/ukraine-prosecutor-general-discusses-accountability-for-putin-war-crimes/7069088.html.

121 JusticeInfoNet.com, *Map of War Crimes Trials in Ukraine* (Dec. 6, 2022), https://www.justiceinfo.net/en/109654-map-of-war-crimes-trials-in-ukraine.html

122 *See, e.g.*, Sara Sirota, *U.S. Demands Russian War Crime Prosecution While Neglecting Its Own Accountability*, The Intercept (May 11, 2022, 1:12 PM), https://theintercept.com/2022/05/11/russian-war-crime-prosecution-accountability/.

123 Special Briefing, Online Press Briefing with Ambassador-at-Large for Global Criminal Justice Beth Van Schaack, U.S. Dep't of State (June 27, 2023), https://www.state.gov/online-press-briefing-with-ambassador-at-large-for-global-criminal-justice-beth-van-schaack/.

124 Yvonne M. Dutton, *Prosecuting Atrocities Committed in Ukraine: A New Era for Universal Jurisdiction?*, 55 Case W. Rsrv. J. Int'l L. 391, 392–93 (2023).

125 Paul Bekkers, Ambassador, Kingdom of the Netherlands, Joint Statement of the Group of Friends of Accountability Following the Aggression Against Ukraine:

Interactive Dialogue on Ukraine with the UN High Commissioner for Human Rights (July 12, 2023), https://geneva.usmission.gov/2023/07/12/joint-statement-of-the-group-of-friends-of-accountability-following-the-aggression-against-ukraine-hrc53/.

126 *High-Level Launch Meeting of the Group of Friends of Accountability Following the Aggression Against Ukraine*, Int'l Peace Inst. (Mar. 25, 2022), https://www.ipinst.org/2022/03/high-level-launch-meeting-of-group-of-friends-of-accountability-for-ukraine#12.

127 *Zelensky explains why he won't negotiate with Putin*, The Economist (Jan. 1, 2024), https://www.economist.com/films/2024/01/01/zelensky-explains-why-he-wont-negotiate-with-putin

128 Volodymyr Zelenskyy, President of Ukraine, Address at the G20 Summit (Nov. 15, 2022, 7:31), https://www.president.gov.ua/en/news/ukrayina-zavzhdi-bula-liderom-mirotvorchih-zusil-yaksho-rosi-79141.

129 Volodymyr Zelenskyy, President of Ukraine, Address at the G20 Summit (Nov. 15, 2022, 7:31), https://www.president.gov.ua/en/news/ukrayina-zavzhdi-bula-liderom-mirotvorchih-zusil-yaksho-rosi-79141.

130 *О «формуле мира» киевских нацu, швейцарских «мирных конференциях» и реальной основе переговоров*, Дмитрий Медведев, Telegram, https://t.me/medvedev_telegram/464.

131 European Commission, Ukraine's path towards EU accession, https://eu-solidarity-ukraine.ec.europa.eu/ukraines-path-towards-eu-accession_en.

132 Catherine Nzuki, *Africa's Peace Delegation: A New Chapter for Africa and the Ukraine War*, Ctr. for Strategic & Int'l Stud. (Jun. 16, 2023), https://www.csis.org/analysis/africas-peace-delegation-new-chapter-africa-and-ukraine-war.

133 Yang Jiang, *The economic meaning of the Russia-Ukraine war for China*, Danish Institute for International Studies (Dec. 14, 2022), https://www.diis.dk/en/research/the-economic-meaning-of-the-russia-ukraine-war-china.

134 *China's Position on the Political Settlement of the Ukraine Crisis*, Ministry of Foreign Affs. of China (Feb. 24, 2023, 9:00), https://www.fmprc.gov.cn/eng/zxxx_662805/202302/t20230224_11030713.html.

135 *China's Position on the Political Settlement of the Ukraine Crisis*, Ministry of Foreign Affs. of China (Feb. 24, 2023, 9:00), https://www.fmprc.gov.cn/eng/zxxx_662805/202302/t20230224_11030713.html.

136 *Foreign Ministry Spokesperson Wang Wenbin's Regular Press Conference on March 20, 2023*, Ministry of Foreign Affs. of the People's Republic of China (Mar. 20, 2023, 21:40), https://www.fmprc.gov.cn/mfa_eng/xwfw_665399/s2510_665401/2511_665403/202303/t20230320_11045296.html

137 Denys Reva and Priyal Singh, *African peace mission: one step forward, one step back?*, Institute for Security Studies (June 23, 2023), https://issafrica.org/iss-today/african-peace-mission-one-step-forward-one-step-back.

138 African peace mission's 10-point proposal, https://issafrica.s3.amazonaws.com/site/multimedia/2023-06-23-text-box-iss-today-01.png.

139 *See*, Miłosz Bartosiewicz & Krzysztof Nieczypor, *Grain Comes First: The African Peace Initiative for Ukraine*, Ctr. for Eastern Stud. (June 21, 2023), https://www.osw.waw.pl/en/publikacje/analyses/2023-06-21/grain-comes-first-african-peace-initiative-ukraine; *China's Position on the Political Settlement of the Ukraine Crisis*, Ministry of Foreign Affs. of China (Feb. 24, 2023, 9:00), https://www.fmprc.gov.cn/eng/zxxx_662805/202302/t20230224_11030713.html.

140 *See* Miłosz Bartosiewicz, Krzysztof Nieczypor, *Grain comes first: the African peace initiative for Ukraine,* Centre For Eastern Studies (OSW) (June 21,

2023),https://www.osw.waw.pl/en/publikacje/analyses/2023-06-21/grain-comes-first-african-peace-initiative-ukraine; *see also China's Position on the Political Settlement of the Ukraine Crisis*, MINISTRY OF FOREIGN AFFS. OF CHINA (Feb. 24, 2023, 9:00), https://www.fmprc.gov.cn/eng/zxxx_662805/202302/t20230224_11030713.html.

141 *Foreign Ministry Spokesperson Wang Wenbin's Regular Press Conference on March 20, 2023*, MINISTRY OF FOREIGN AFFS. OF THE PEOPLE'S REPUBLIC OF CHINA (Mar. 20, 2023, 21:40), https://www.fmprc.gov.cn/mfa_eng/xwfw_665399/s2510_665401/2511_665403/202303/t20230320_11045296.html ("Our position has always been that dialogue and negotiation provides the fundamental way out for the Ukraine crisis, and that the international community needs to play a constructive role in peacefully resolving the Ukraine crisis, and do more in ways that are conducive to talks for peace, deescalation and mediation efforts. The ICC needs to take an objective and just position, respect the jurisdictional immunity of a head of state under international law, prudently exercise its mandate in accordance with the law, interpret and apply international law in good faith, and not engage in politicization or use double standards."); *see also Ministry of Foreign Aff. of China, Foreign Ministry Spokesperson Wang Wenbin's Regular Press Conference on March 21, 2023,* MINISTRY OF FOREIGN AFFS. OF THE PEOPLE'S REPUBLIC OF CHINA (March 21, 2023, 21:40), https://www.fmprc.gov.cn/mfa_eng/xwfw_665399/s2510_665401/2511_665403/202303/t20230321_11045969.htm.

142 Miłosz Bartosiewicz, Krzysztof Nieczypor, *Grain comes first: the African peace initiative for Ukraine*, CENTRE FOR EASTERN STUDIES (OSW) (June 21, 2023),https://www.osw.waw.pl/en/publikacje/analyses/2023-06-21/grain-comes-first-african-peace-initiative-ukraine.

143 Press Release, Int'l Crim. Ct., Ukraine accepts ICC jurisdiction over alleged crimes committed since 20 February 2014 (Sept. 8, 2015), https://www.icc-cpi.int/Pages/item.aspx?name=pr1146&ln=en.

144 Prosecutor v. Gaddafi, Case No. ICC-01/11-01/11, Judgment on the appeal of Mr Saif Al-Islam Gaddafi against the decision of Pre-Trial Chamber I entitled 'Decision on the "Admissibility Challenge by Dr. Saif Al Islam Gadafi pursuant to Articles 17(1)(c), 19 and 20(3) of the Rome Statute"' of 5 April (Mar. 9, 2020); *see also* Josepha Close, *The ICC refrains from affirming a general ban on amnesties in the Gaddafi admissibility appeal decision*, International Law Blog (Apr. 20, 2020).

145 Prosecutor v. Gaddafi, Case No. ICC-01/11-01/11, Judgment on the appeal of Mr Saif Al-Islam Gaddafi against the decision of Pre-Trial Chamber I entitled 'Decision on the "Admissibility Challenge by Dr. Saif Al-Islam Gadafi pursuant to Articles 17(1)(c), 19 and 20(3) of the Rome Statute"' of 5 April, ¶¶ 94, 96 (Mar. 9, 2020).

146 H. Abigail Moy, *The International Criminal Court's Arrest Warrants and Uganda's Lord's Resistance Army: Renewing the Debate over Amnesty and Complementarity*, 19 Harv. Hum. Rts. J. (2006), https://journals.law.harvard.edu/hrj/wp-content/uploads/sites/83/2020/06/19HHRJ267-Moy.pdf

147 Int'l Crim. Ct., Situation in Uganda, https://www.icc-cpi.int/situations/uganda

148 For a more detailed discussion on this point, *see* The Official Report of the Parliament of Uganda (Hansard) (March 10, 2010).

149 Int'l Crim. Ct., *Understanding the International Criminal Court*, https://www.icc-cpi.int/sites/default/files/Publications/understanding-the-icc.pdf

150 *Prosecutor v. Furundzija*, Case No. IT-95-17/1-T, Judgment, ¶ 155 (Dec. 10, 1998), http://www.icty.org/x/cases/furundzija/tjug/en/fur-tj981210e.pdf; *see*

also Office of the United Nations High Commissioner for Human Rights, Rule of Law Tools for Post-Conflict States: Amnesties, 29–30 (2009); Afghanistan Independent Human Rights Commission, Discussion Paper on Legality of Amnesties, 8 (Feb. 21, 2010).

151 Michael P. Scharf and Paul R. Williams, *Functions of Justice and Anti-Justice in the Peace-Building Process*, 35 Case W. Res. J. Int'l L. 161, 175 (2003), https://core.ac.uk/download/pdf/214078795.pdf.

152 Michael P. Scharf and Paul R. Williams, *Functions of Justice and Anti-Justice in the Peace-Building Process*, 35 Case W. Res. J. Int'l L. 161, 175 (2003), https://core.ac.uk/download/pdf/214078795.pdf.

153 *Prosecutor v. Morris Kallon and Brima Bazzy Kamara*, Case Nos. SCSL-2004-15-AR72(E) and SCSL-2004-16-AR72(E), Appeals Judgment, ¶¶ 86–90 (Mar. 13, 2004).

154 *See* Peace Agreement between the Government of Sierra Leone and the Revolutionary United Front of Sierra Leone (RUF/SL), Lome, July 7, 1999; *Prosecutor v. Morris Kallon and Brima Buzzy Kamara*, SCSL-2004-15-AR72(E) and SCSL-2004-16-AR72(E), Appeals Judgment, ¶ 1, Mar. 13, 2004.

155 *Prosecutor v. Morris Kallon and Brima Bazzy Kamara*, Case Nos. SCSL-2004-15-AR72(E) and SCSL-2004-16-AR72(E), Appeals Judgment, ¶ 42 (Mar. 13, 2004).

156 *Prosecutor v. Morris Kallon and Brima Bazzy Kamara*, Case Nos. SCSL-2004-15-AR72(E) and SCSL-2004-16-AR72(E), Appeals Judgment, ¶ 43 (Mar. 13, 2004).

157 *Prosecutor v. Morris Kallon and Brima Bazzy Kamara*, Case Nos. SCSL-2004-15-AR72(E) and SCSL-2004-16-AR72(E), Appeals Judgment, ¶¶ 67, 70 (Mar. 13, 2004), (citing *Attorney General of the Government of Israel v. Eichmann*).

158 Decision on Ieng Sary's Rule 89 Preliminary Objections, Case No. 002/19-09-2007/ECCC/TC, Judgment, ¶ 37 (2011), https://www.eccc.gov.kh/sites/default/files/documents/courtdoc/E51_15_EN.PDF.

159 The ECCC observed that Cambodia is a party to a number of treaties, including the four Geneva Conventions, which impose an "absolute duty" to prosecute certain international crimes. Decision on Ieng Sary's Rule 89 Preliminary Objections, Case No. 002/19-09-2007/ECCC/TC, Judgment, ¶ 38 (2011), https://www.eccc.gov.kh/sites/default/files/documents/courtdoc/E51_15_EN.PDF.

160 Decision on Ieng Sary's Rule 89 Preliminary Objections, Case No. 002/19-09-2007/ECCC/TC, Judgment, ¶ 37 (2011), https://www.eccc.gov.kh/sites/default/files/documents/courtdoc/E51_15_EN.PDF.

161 As mentioned above, an International Centre for the Prosecution of the Crime of Aggression in Ukraine has already been established. *See* Charlotte van Campenhout & Stephanie van den Berg, *EU: Centre for Prosecution of 'Aggression' Crimes in Ukraine to Be Set Up in The Hague*, Reuters (Feb. 2, 2023, 9:46 AM EST), https://www.reuters.com/world/europe/eu-centre-prosecution-aggression-crimes-ukraine-be-set-up-hague-2023-02-02/. And states frequently reaffirm their commitment to the establishment of the special tribunal. *See* Political Declaration of the Ministerial Restoring Justice for Ukraine Conference (Apr. 2, 2024), https://www.government.nl/binaries/government/documenten/diplomatic-statements/2024/04/02/political-declaration-of-the-ministerial-restoring-justice-for-ukraine-conference/Restoring+Justice+for+Ukraine+Conference+-+Political+Declaration.pdf. *See also* Dr. Patrick Butchard, *Conflict in Ukraine: A Special Tribunal on the Crime of Aggression*, Research Briefing, House of Commons Library (Feb. 22, 2024), https://researchbriefings.files.parliament.uk/documents/CBP-9968/CBP-9968.pdf.

162 Permanent Mission of the Republic of Latvia to the United Nations, FREQUENTLY ASKED QUESTIONS A Special Tribunal for the Crime of Aggression against Ukraine (March 5, 2024), https://www2.mfa.gov.lv/en/newyork/news/69560-frequently-asked-questions-a-special-tribunal-for-the-crime-of-aggression-against-ukraine.

163 The Ukraine situation was referred to the ICC by 43 States Parties of the ICC following the outbreak of the full-scale invasion. *Ukraine*, INT'L CRIM. CT., https://www.icc-cpi.int/situations/ukraine.

13

CONCLUSION

The Ukraine Conflict as a Grotian Moment

By Michael P. Scharf

Introduction

As the most intense global conflict of the past decade, the Russia-Ukraine war has been a laboratory for the development of new international law and institutions. Drawing from the earlier chapters, this concluding chapter describes how the international community's response to the war has amounted to a "Grotian Moment" – a paradigm shifting[1] development leading to accelerated formation of customary international law and novel re-interpretations of treaty law.

Professor Myers McDougal famously described the customary international law formation process as one of continuous claim and response.[2] Out of this process of claim and response, and third-party state support, acquiescence or repudiation, rules emerge or are superseded. Just "as pearls are produced by the irritant of a piece of grit entering an oyster's shell, so the interactions and mutual accommodations of States produce the pearl — so to speak — of customary law."[3] Like the slow creation of a pearl, usually the process of customary international law formation takes many decades or centuries.[4] Under the traditional view, the formation of customary rules is so gradual that it is often described as "crystallization."[5] But sometimes world events are such that customary international law develops quite rapidly.[6] Those instances have come to be known as "Grotian Moments."[7]

By tradition, jurists and scholars have looked exclusively to two factors – (1) widespread state practice, and (2) manifestations of a conviction that the practice is required or permitted by law – to divine whether an emergent rule has attained customary international law status. The Grotian Moment concept

DOI: 10.4324/9781003458166-17

compels consideration of a third factor – a context of fundamental change – that can serve as an accelerating agent, enabling customary international law to form much more rapidly and with less positive state practice than is normally the case.

To understand why a growing number of scholars use the term "Grotian Moments" to describe this phenomenon, one must know something about Hugo Grotius (1583–1645). The brilliant Dutch scholar and diplomat has been called the "father" of modern international law and has been lauded for having "recorded the creation of order out of chaos in the great sphere of international relations."[8] In the mid-1600s, at the time that the nation-state was formally recognized as having emerged into the fundamental political unit of Europe, Grotius "offered a new concept of international law designed to reflect that new reality."[9]

Although some believe that Grotius' actual contribution has been exaggerated and distorted through the ages, the prevailing view today is that his treatise On the Law of War and Peace had an extraordinary impact as the first formulation of a comprehensive legal order of interstate relations based on mutual respect and equality of sovereign states.[10] In "semiotic" terms,[11] the "Grotian tradition" has come to symbolize the advent of the modern international legal regime, characterized by positive law and state consent, which was first codified in the Peace of Westphalia.[12]

The term "Grotian Moment," on the other hand, is a relatively recent creation, coined by Princeton Professor Richard Falk in 1985.[13] Since then, scholars and even the UN Secretary-General have employed the term in a variety of ways,[14] but ever more frequently it has been used to denote a transformative development in which new rules and doctrines of customary international law or radical reinterpretation of treaty law emerge with unusual rapidity and acceptance.[15] Usually this happens during a period of upheaval, like the end of European feudalism in the time of Grotius "when new norms, procedures, and institutions had to be devised to cope with the then decline of the Church and the emergence of the secular state."[16]

Grotian Moments that have been the catalyst for rapid formation of customary international law and radical reinterpretation of treaty law include the creation and judgment of the Nuremberg Tribunal after World War II, the technological access to the continental shelf and outer space in the 1950s and 60s, the leap in international humanitarian law brought about by the creation of the Yugoslavia Tribunal and its first Appeals Chamber decision in 2005, and the international community's response to the ISIS terrorist organization attacks in 2014. After reviewing what these historic cases have in common, this chapter explores whether the Russian-Ukraine war constitutes a Grotian Moment and what novel developments of customary and conventional law have resulted therefrom.

Nuremberg as a Prototypical Grotian Moment

While the post-WWII Nuremberg war crimes trials were not without criticism, there can be no question that Nuremberg represented a paradigm-shifting development in international law. The International Law Commission (ILC) has recognized that the Nuremberg Charter and Judgment gave birth to the entire international paradigm of individual criminal responsibility. Prior to Nuremberg, the concept of international criminal responsibility of individuals did not exist, and what a state did to its own citizens within its own borders was deemed its own business. Nuremberg fundamentally altered that conception. "International law now protects individual citizens against abuses of power by their governments [and] imposes individual liability on government officials who commit grave war crimes, genocide, and crimes against humanity."[17] The ILC has described the principle of individual responsibility and punishment for crimes under international law recognized at Nuremberg as the "cornerstone of international criminal law" and the "enduring legacy of the Charter and Judgment of the Nuremberg Tribunal."[18]

Importantly, on December 11, 1946, in one of the first actions of the newly formed UN, the General Assembly unanimously affirmed the principles from the Nuremberg Charter and judgments in Resolution 95(I).[19] This General Assembly Resolution had all the attributes of a resolution entitled to great weight as a declaration of customary international law[20]: It was labeled an "affirmation" of legal principles; it dealt with inherently legal questions; it was passed by a unanimous vote; and none of the members expressed the position that it was merely a political statement.[21]

Despite the fact that Nuremberg and its Control Council Law #10 progeny consisted of only a dozen separate cases tried by a handful of courts over a period of just three years, the International Court of Justice (ICJ),[22] the International Criminal Tribunal for the Former Yugoslavia,[23] the European Court of Human Rights,[24] and several domestic courts[25] have cited the General Assembly Resolution affirming the principles of the Nuremberg Charter and judgments as an authoritative declaration of customary international law.

Nuremberg, then, represented a prototypical Grotian Moment. The Tribunal's formation was in response to the most heinous atrocity in the history of humankind— the extermination of six million Jews and several million other "undesirables" by the Nazi regime. From a conventional view of customary international law formation, the amount of state practice was quite limited, consisting only of the negotiation of the Nuremberg Charter by four states, its accession by nineteen others, the judgment of the Tribunal, and a General Assembly Resolution endorsing (though not enumerating) its principles. Moreover, the time period from the end of the war to the General Assembly endorsement of the Nuremberg Principles was a mere year, a drop in the bucket compared to the amount of time it ordinarily takes to crystallize customary international law. Yet, despite the limited state practice and minimal time, the ICJ, European Court of Human Rights, and four international criminal tribunals have confirmed that the Nuremberg Charter and Judgment immediately ripened into customary international law.[26]

The Grotian Moment concept rationalizes this outcome. Nuremberg reflected a novel solution to unprecedented atrocity in the context of history's most devastating war. Beyond the Nuremberg trial, there was a great need for universal implementation of the Nuremberg Principles. Yet, on the eve of the Cold War, it was clear that a widely ratified multilateral convention would not be a practicable near-term solution. In fact, it would take half a century before the international community was able to conclude a widely ratified treaty transforming the Nuremberg model into a permanent international criminal court. It is this context of fundamental change and great need for a timely response that explains how Nuremberg could so quickly and universally be accepted as customary international law.

Examples of Grotian Moments since World War II

As the Max Planck Encyclopedia of Public International Law has observed, "recent developments show that customary rules may come into existence rapidly."[27] The venerable publication goes on to explain: "This can be due to the urgency of coping with new developments of technology, such as, for instance, drilling technology as regards the rules on the continental shelf, or space technology as regards the rule on the freedom of extra-atmospheric space. Or it may be due to the urgency of coping with widespread sentiments of moral outrage regarding crimes committed in conflicts such as those in Rwanda and Yugoslavia that brought about the rapid formation of a set of customary rules concerning crimes committed in internal conflicts."[28]

These are not the only examples of Grotian Moments since World War II, but each follows the pattern of Nuremberg. Let us examine each of these examples in turn, beginning with the rapid formation of the law of the continental shelf. In 1945, US President Truman issued a proclamation that the resources on the continental shelf off the coast of the United States belonged to the United States.[29] This represented a major departure from the existing customary international law of the sea, under which the seabed outside of 12 nautical miles was considered free for exploitation by any state.[30] The Proclamation was driven by technological developments enabling exploitation of offshore oil and gas supplies, and the intense post-war demand for such resources for a rebuilding world.[31] Though the United States recognized that it was acting as a custom pioneer,[32] it was careful to couch its justification in legal terms that would render the action easier to accept and replicate by other states. Despite the far-reaching change it represented, the Truman Proclamation was met with no protest[33]; rather, within five years, half of the world's coastal states had made similar claims to the resources of their continental shelves,[34] leading commentators to declare that the continental shelf concept had become virtually instant customary international law.[35] By 1969, the ICJ had confirmed that the Truman Declaration quickly generated customary international law binding on states that had not ratified the 1958 Law of the Sea Convention.[36]

Next, let us look at the formation of outer space law, which rapidly emerged from the great leaps in rocket technology in the 1960s, led by the Soviet Union and the United States, inaugurating the era of space flight. Rather than treat outer space like the high seas (open to unregulated exploitation), the international community embraced a unique set of rules to govern this new area as codified in the General Assembly Declaration on Outer Space, which was unanimously approved in 1963.[37] Though the amount of state practice was limited to a few dozen space flights launched by two states and the lack of protest by the states over which these rockets passed, states and scholars have concluded that the 1963 Declaration represented an authoritative statement of customary international law that rapidly formed in response to new technologies requiring a new international law paradigm.[38]

Finally, let us turn to the customary international humanitarian law that rapidly emerged from the Yugoslavia Tribunal in the 1990s. The establishment of the Yugoslavia Tribunal was made possible because of a unique constellation of events at the end of the Cold War, which included the break-up of the Soviet Union, Russia's assumption of the Soviet seat in the Security Council, and the return of genocide to Europe for the first time since Nazi Germany. In its inaugural case, the Appeals Chamber of the Yugoslavia Tribunal rendered a revolutionary decision that for the first time held that individuals could be held criminally liable for violations of Common Article 3 and Additional Protocol II of the Geneva Conventions for war crimes committed in internal conflict.[39] This decision closed a gaping gap in the coverage of international humanitarian law and was soon thereafter affirmed by the Rwanda Tribunal[40] and Special Court for Sierra Leone.[41] It was codified in the 1998 Statute of the International Criminal Court, which has been ratified by 125 states.[42]

While there are no legal consequences to calling something a Grotian Moment, these case studies suggest that the Grotian Moment concept has several practical applications. It can explain the rapid formation of customary rules in times of flux, thereby imbuing those rules with greater repute. It can counsel governments when to seek the path of a UN General Assembly resolution as a means of facilitating the formation of customary international law, and how to craft such a resolution to ensure that it is viewed as a capstone in the formation of such customary rules. It can, in apt circumstances, strengthen the case for litigants arguing the existence of a new customary international rule. It can also furnish international courts and international organizations the confidence to recognize new rules of customary international law in appropriate cases despite a relative paucity and short duration of state practice. That is what happened in the case of use of force against ISIS.

Syria and Use of Force Against Non-State Actors

Had the Max Planck Encyclopedia been written today, it would no doubt have added the international community's about face on the legality of the use of force against non-state actors in the context of the Syrian conflict as another example of a Grotian Moment. As the authors describe in their prior book, The Syrian Conflict's Impact on International Law,[43] in 2014, a militant group calling itself ISIS rapidly took over more than thirty percent of the territory of Syria and Iraq. In the process, it captured billions of dollars (US) worth of oil fields and refineries, bank assets and antiquities, tanks and armaments, and became one of the greatest threats to peace and security in the Middle East. In an effort to "degrade and defeat" ISIS, the United States, assisted by a handful of other Western and Arab countries, launched thousands of bombing sorties and cruise missile attacks against ISIS targets in Iraq and Syria starting in August 2014.[44] While the Iraqi government had consented to foreign military action against ISIS within Iraq, the Syrian government did not.[45] Rather, Syria protested that the air strikes in Syrian territory were an unjustifiable violation of international law.[46]

The United States claimed that the airstrikes in Syria were lawful acts of collective self-defense on behalf of the government of Iraq.[47] Use of force in self-defense has traditionally not been viewed as lawful against non state actors in a third state unless they are under the effective control of that state,[48] but the United States argued that since the infamous 9/11 attacks by al Qaeda, such force can be justified where a government is unable or unwilling to suppress the threat posed by the non-state actors operating within its borders.[49]

At first, the United States was isolated in its position. Its allies pointed out that the International Court of Justice had repeatedly held that, unless the acts of non-state actors are attributable to the territorial state, the use of force against non-state actors in that state is unlawful. Reaffirming its previous precedent, in its 2005 Armed Activities in the Congo case, the ICJ required the responsibility of the Congo for the attacks of Ugandan rebels operating from the Congolese territory in order to find Uganda's right to self-defense lawful.[50] The post 9/11 case signaled the ICJ's "determination to counter a more permissive reading of Article 51" brought on by the international community's reaction to 9/11.[51]

Scholars[52] and certain members of the International Court of Justice were highly critical of the ICJ's continued insistence after 9/11 that self-defense can only be claimed in cases where the attack by non-state actors can be attributed to the territorial state. Writing separately in the Congo case, Judge Koojimans noted that in the era of al Qaeda, it is "unreasonable to deny the attacked State the right to self-defense merely because there is no attacker State."[53]Judge Simma similarly concluded in his separate opinion in the Congo case that "Security Council resolutions 1368 (2001) and 1373 (2001) cannot but be read as affirmations of the view that large-scale attacks by non-State actors can qualify as 'armed attacks' within the meaning of Article 51."[54]

Yet, it was not until ISIS bombed a Russian jetliner over the Sinai desert on October 31, 2015, and attacked a Paris stadium and concert hall on November 13, 2015, that the situation was ripe for a Grotian Moment. A week after these attacks, the UN Security Council unanimously adopted Resolution 2249, which determined that ISIS is "a global and unprecedented threat to international peace and security," and called for "all necessary measures" to "eradicate the safe haven [ISIS] established" in Syria.[55]

The October 31 and November 13 ISIS attacks were a game changer, killing and injuring over 824 nationals of Russia, France, and twenty-two other countries. They showed that ISIS — the richest and most technologically advanced terrorist organization in the world — was no longer confining its objectives to territorial acquisition in Syria and Iraq, but had adopted the tactics of other terrorist groups, focusing on attacking vulnerable targets outside the Levant. Moreover, Russia was now just as much a target as the West.

It is important to recognize that Resolution 2249 did not provide a new stand-alone legal basis or authorization for the use of force against ISIS in Syria.[56] Unlike past Security Council resolutions that have authorized force, Resolution 2249 does not mention Article 42, or even Chapter VII, of the UN Charter, which is the Article and Chapter under which the Security Council can permit states to use force as an exception to Article 2(4) of the UN Charter. Nor does the Resolution use the word "authorizes" or even "decides" in relation to use of force. These textual differences led Professor Mark Weller to conclude that "this language suggests that the resolution does not grant any fresh authority for states seeking to take action."[57]

But the resolution does stand as a confirmation by the Security Council that the use of force against ISIS in Syria is permissible under the inherent right of self-defense. Importantly, the French Security Council Representative, who had sponsored Resolution 2249, stated in his explanation of vote on the resolution that "collective action could now be based on Article 51 [self-defense] of the United Nations Charter."[58] With a unanimous confirmation, Resolution 2249 has played an important role in crystallizing the new rule of customary international law regarding use of force in self-defense against non-state actors — a phenomenon colorfully described by Professor David Koplow as "helping to midwife the development of new norms of customary international law."[59]

Resolution 2249 had an immediate effect in changing government attitudes about the legality of use of force against autonomous non-state actors.

Within two weeks of its adoption, the UK parliament voted to approve (by a vote of 397 to 223) participating in airstrikes against ISIS in Syria despite the earlier views of many of those same MPs that such action could not be legally justified.[60] Immediately thereafter, the UK joined the United States and several other states in bombing ISIS targets throughout Syria.[61]

The changing law governing the use of force against non-state actors follows the pattern of history's other Grotian Moments. ISIS and al Qaeda were widely viewed as representing a new kind of threat, in which a non-state actor possesses many of the attributes of a state: massive wealth, large numbers of personnel, sophisticated training and organization, and access to destructive weaponry. To respond to the fundamental change presented by these uber-terrorist groups, the United States argued that it is now lawful to attack such non-state actors when they are present in States that are unable or unwilling to curb them. While states and the International Court of Justice were initially reluctant to embrace this new view of self-defense, in the aftermath of the attacks against the Russian airliner and Paris disco and stadium, Security Council Resolution 2249 confirmed that use of force in self-defense is permissible against non-state actors where the territorial state is unable to suppress the threat that they pose. In the words of the Institute of International Law, "where a rule of customary law is (merely) emerging or there is still some doubt as to its status" a unanimous non-binding resolution of the General Assembly or Security Council "can consolidate the custom and remove doubts which might have existed."[62] Resolution 2249 capped a Grotian Moment and reaffirmed the importance of this concept in international law.

Developments in International Law Arising out of the Russia-Ukraine War

Without the benefit of years of hindsight, there is always a risk of perceiving turning points or paradigm shifts that do not ultimately manifest. Even so, three years after the Russian invasion of Ukraine, the authors believe this book has captured a Grotian Moment during its formation. As summarized below, the contributors to this book have described several ways the Russia-Ukraine war has sparked the formation of new customary international law, novel interpretations of treaties, and the creation of new international mechanisms.

Following the historic scene setter by Milena Sterio, my contribution in Chapter 4 describes how the Russian invasion prompted the UN General Assembly to dust off and employ the Uniting for Peace mechanism for the first time in fifty years. This mechanism, which has no explicit foundation in the UN Charter, enables the General Assembly to end-run the Security Council when the Council is paralyzed by a Permanent Member veto. Many experts had believed the mechanism had long become defunct in light of the great powers' concerns about the risk of abuse by the General Assembly.

Yet, not only did the Russian invasion of Ukraine engender a resurrection of the Uniting for Peace mechanism, but it was used in ways never before contemplated, such as labeling Russia's invasion an unlawful act of aggression, declaring that the plebiscites in Russian-occupied territories were invalid, suspending Russia from the UN Human Rights Council, and establishing a Registry to catalogue damages from the invasion that Russia would have to pay (presumably out of frozen assets).

The series of General Assembly resolutions based on the Uniting for Peace mechanism in 2022–2024 represents a fundamental reinterpretation of the UN Charter with potentially significant implications beyond the Russia-Ukraine war. They reflect a major power shift from the UN Security Council to the General Assembly in response to perceived abuse of the veto. Once Pandora's box had been reopened, the General Assembly began to employ its newfound power in other parts of the world. For example, the General Assembly used the mechanism to adopt a resolution on May 10, 2024, upgrading Palestine's participation in the United Nations,[63] and another on September 18, 2024, calling on States to take measures to prevent their nationals, companies, and entities under their jurisdiction from engaging in activities that support or sustain Israel's occupation of Palestine.[64] Where this will lead is anyone's guess, but it is clear that the United Nations was fundamentally changed by the Russia-Ukraine war.

The International Criminal Court's issuance of an arrest warrant in March 2023 for Russian President Vladimir Putin for the crime of child abduction in Ukraine, as described in Chapter 5 by Patrick Keenan, constitutes another manifestation of this Grotian Moment. This was the first time the International Criminal Court (ICC) issued an arrest warrant for the head of one of the most powerful states in the world, a veto-wielding permanent member of the Security Council. As Keenan explains, the action signaled that the Prosecutor would not be intimidated by Putin, despite his efforts to punish ICC officials with sanctions similar to what Donald Trump imposed on the Court during his first term in office. As with the International Court of Justice's decision to hold the United States responsible for trying to overthrow the Sandinista government in 1986, this was the moment the ICC was transformed from a fledgling to a mature institution. Much is on the line for the Court, but Ukraine will undoubtedly be viewed as a turning point in its history.

The international community's efforts to establish an ad hoc aggression tribunal, as described in Chapter 6 by NYU Professor Jennifer Trahan, are an unprecedented and novel response to the Russian-Ukraine war. The crime of aggression was the worst of the international crimes associated with Russia's 2022 invasion of Ukraine, setting in motion all the other international crimes that followed. While the 2010 Kampala amendments added the crime of aggression to the ICC's jurisdiction, they were worded in a way that rendered it impossible for the ICC to prosecute Putin for that offense. In her chapter, Trahan describes the efforts of the international community to establish an ad hoc aggression-specific tribunal for the situation of Ukraine. As this book goes to press, several of the proposals seem to be gaining momentum. If any are adopted, this will be the first international effort to prosecute the crime of aggression since WWII. It will provide refinement to the elements of the crime of aggression, test the contours of Head of State immunity, and send a signal that the crime of aggression has teeth in the 21st Century.

Meanwhile, the idea of prosecuting the crime of aggression and other war crimes before a special Ukraine Court, described by Dr. Greg Noone and Kateryna Kyrychenko in Chapter 7, has the potential to reshape the national approach to war crimes prosecutions across the globe. Known as an internationalized domestic court, the proposal drafted by the Public International Law & Policy Group in partnership with a group of Ukrainian jurists would enable Ukraine to draw upon international expertise and assistance in prosecuting aggression and war crimes in a special domestic court, similar to the War Crimes Chamber in Bosnia and Herzegovina, Piracy Chambers in Mauritius and Seychelles, and the Iraqi High Tribunal that Iraq created to prosecute Saddam Hussein. As a Head of State, Putin would be immune from prosecution by such a court, but his generals, advisors, and members of the Russian parliament could be tried in person or in absentia. Ukraine has a successful model for such a court, having recently launched the High Anti-Corruption Court of Ukraine. In their chapter, Noone and Kyrychenko explore the potential benefits and obstacles to creating an internationalized domestic court – an initiative that could serve as a model for a hybrid domestic-international approach to war crimes prosecutions across the globe.

While universal jurisdiction has been used infrequently, as described by Dr. Yvonne Dutton in Chapter 8, Ukraine war crimes have sparked renewed interest in this mode of accountability and new approaches to its prosecution at the national level. Universal jurisdiction prosecutions usually labor under evidentiary difficulties, but in the case of Russian war crimes in Ukraine there has been unparalleled cooperation among states and organizations in sharing evidence, as described in Chapter 11 by Mark S. Ellis. And although the ICC must focus on top level offenders who are least likely to be prosecuted in the near-term, Dutton predicts that states will use universal jurisdiction to prosecute lower-level offenders who are more likely to be brought to justice. Since at least some of these cases will precede those of the ICC, they will take on heightened precedential importance.

One of the most important areas in which the Russia-Ukraine war is fueling the rapid development of new international law is related to criminal responsibility for attacks against the environment, as described in Chapter 9 by Michael J. Kelly. More than in any other conflict in modern times, Russia has targeted Ukraine's environment as part of its war strategy. From blowing up the Kakhovka Dam to burning forests, polluting riverways, and killing Black Sea dolphins, these acts have shocked the international community in a way few other war crimes have. For that reason, the ICC and Ukraine have each made the investigation and prosecution of Russian environmental crimes a top priority. While the ICC can prosecute attacks against the environment as war crimes or crimes against humanity, Ukraine is one of the first countries in the world to enact a law to prosecute the distinct crime of "ecocide," defined as "mass destruction of flora or fauna, poisoning of the atmosphere or water resources, as well as committing other actions that may cause an ecological disaster shall be punishable by imprisonment for a term of eight to fifteen years." The world will be watching closely how Ukraine's courts interpret that crime, how they apply modes of criminal responsibility to the perpetrators, and how they deal with Russia's defense of military necessity. The resulting precedents will likely have a profound impact on the evolution of international law related to attacks against the environment.

Chapter 10 by the President Elect of the American Society of International Law, Oona A. Hathaway, and her co-author Maggie M. Mills, examines novel legal issues related to the freezing of Russian assets and potential use of those assets for reparations of damages in Ukraine. Russia's illegal assault on Ukraine has resulted in extraordinary damage to the country, requiring an estimated $486 billion (US) for it to recover. To date, governments around the world have frozen nearly half of Russia's foreign reserves, amounting to over $300 billion (US). Hathaway points out that directly using that money as reparations would run afoul of the doctrine of foreign sovereign immunity. Instead, she advocates leveraging the frozen Russian assets as "collective countermeasures" to induce Russia to provides reparations to Ukraine after the war – a model that could alter the approach to war reparations for years to come.

In Chapter 11, Mark Ellis, the Executive Director of the International Bar Association, describes various investigative and prosecutorial cooperation initiatives that have been developed between Ukraine and regional and international authorities. Ellis says war crimes in Ukraine are the most extensively documented in history, and much of it is video evidence taken on cell phones. With the possibility of deepfakes and impediments to authentication, however, technology is not a panacea. In response to the challenge, Ellis describes the development of the IBA's "eyeWitness To Atrocities" App, which enables cell phone videos to be uploaded to a secure web-accessible database, self-authenticated, and checked for reliability using imbedded metatags. In this way, the Russia-Ukraine war is not only transforming law but also the way technology is used in the prosecution of war crimes.

Finally, in Chapter 12, Dr. Paul R. Williams, President of the Public International Law & Policy Group, and Sindija Beta examine whether the Ukraine crisis is the catalyst for an emerging new world order based on concepts of justice. Whereas, traditionally, all issues are on the table in a peace negotiation, Williams and Beta point out that any Ukrainian-Russian peace negotiations would be taking place in an environment where domestic and international justice processes have already been launched. As much as Russia may wish to try to persuade Ukraine and the international community to trade away their accountability initiatives for peace, it is unlikely that Russia will be able to bring a halt to these processes. The ICC has already launched its case against Putin and the international community has made notable steps toward establishing the mechanisms for prosecuting the crime of aggression and seeking compensation for the damage to Ukraine's territory, infrastructure, and citizens. As such, neither side will be able to negotiate away the accountability already underway.

Final Thoughts

When Russia invaded Ukraine in February 2022, many feared the international security and legal system had been irreparably broken.[65] Instead, as this book documents, it turned out to be a period when states and international institutions came together and embraced novel ways to address the problem of a permanent member of the Security Council gone rogue. Rather than serve as an emblem for failure, as Mark Ellis observed in his chapter, "Ukraine emerged as a beacon for accountability."

As such, the Russian invasion of Ukraine will be remembered as one of history's Grotian Moments – a time of rapid development of customary international law and new interpretations of conventional law in response to an extraordinary global challenge. As detailed in this book, the crisis engendered a power shift from the UN Security Council to the General Assembly, the insertion of the International Criminal Court into world politics at the highest level, the formation of new types of investigatory mechanisms and tribunals, the development of international law related to the crime of aggression and attacks on the environment, the deployment of new regimes for collecting evidence, seizing assets, and providing post-war reparations, and perhaps even the emergence of a new global order based on justice.

Notes

1 As defined by Thomas Kuhn in his influential book, THE STRUCTURE OF SCIENTIFIC REVOLUTIONS 150 (1970), a paradigm shift is a change in the basic assumptions within the ruling theory of science. While Kuhn opined that the term should be confined to the context of pure science, it has since been widely used in numerous nonscientific contexts to describe a profound change in a fundamental model or perception of events.

2 *See generally* M.S. McDougal & N.A. Schlei, *The Hydrogen Bomb Tests in Perspective: Lawful Measures for Security*, 64 YALE L. J. 648 (1955).

3 Maurice H. Mendelson, The Formation of Customary International Law 190 (1998).

4 See Vincy Fon & Francesco Parisi, *The Formation of Customary Law* 5 (George Mason Univ. Law, Working Paper No. 02–24, 2000), *available at* www.law.gmu.edu/assets/files/publications/working_papers/02-24.pdf (last visited Feb. 22, 2014); G.I. Tunkin, *Remarks on the Judicial Nature of Customary Norms in International Law*, 49 Calif. L. Rev. 419, 420 (1961); Manley O. Hudson, *Special Rapporteur on Article 24 of the Statute of the Int'l Law Comm'n, Ways and Means for Making the Evidence of Customary International Law More Readily Available*, Y.B. Int'l L. Comm'n, U.N. Doc. A/CN.4/16 (Mar. 3, 1950).

5 Michael P. Scharf, Customary International Law in Times of Fundamental Change: Recognizing Grotian Moments 211 (2013).

6 International Law Commission, Draft Conclusions on Identification of Customary International Law, with Commentaries, Conclusion 8(2), at 136 (2018) ("Provided that the practice is general, no particular duration is required"); North Sea Continental Shelf (Ger. v. Den., Ger. v. Neth.), Merits, 1969 I.C.J. 3, ¶¶ 71, 73–74 (Feb. 20). Rapid formation of customary international law during a Grotian Moment is not the same as so-called "instant custom." Both State practice and *Opinio Juris* are required, though the time period may be quite brief.

7 See generally Michael P. Scharf, Customary International Law in Times of Fundamental Change: Recognizing Grotian Moments (2013); and Michael P. Scharf, Milena Sterio and Paul R. Williams, The Syrian Conflict's Impact on International Law (2020). Other scholars have called these "international constitutional moments." See e.g., Leila Nadya Sadat, *Enemy Combatants after Hamdan v Rumsfeld: Extraordinary Rendition, Torture and Other Nightmares from the War on Terror*, 75 Geo. Wash. L. Rev. 1200, 1206–07 (2007) (describing Nuremberg as an "international Constitutional Moment"); Anne-Marie Slaughter & William Burke-White, *An International Constitutional Moment*, 43 Harv. Int'l L. J. 1,2 (2002) (describing 9/11 as an "international Constitutional Moment").

8 *See* Charles S. Edwards, Hugo Grotius, the Miracle of Holland (1981).

9 John W. Head, *Throwing Eggs at Windows: Legal and Institutional Globalization in the 21st Century Economy*, 50 Kan. L. Rev. 731, 771 (2002).

10 Benedict Kingsbury, *A Grotian Tradition of Theory and Practice? Grotius, Law, and Moral Skepticism in the Thought of Hedley Bull*, 17 Quinnipiac L. Rev. 3, 10 (1997).

11 Semiotics is the study of how the meaning of signs, symbols, and language is constructed and understood. Semiotics explains that terms such as "The Peace of Westphalia" or "the Grotian tradition" are not historic artifacts whose meaning remains static over time. Rather, the meaning of such terms changes over time along with the interpretive community or communities. Michael P. Scharf, *International Law in Crisis: A Qualitative Empirical Contribution to the Compliance Debate*, 31 Cardozo L. Rev. 45, 50 (2009) (citing Charles Sanders Peirce, Collected Papers of Charles Sanders Pierce: Pragmatism and Pragmaticism (Charles Hartshorne & Paul Weiss eds., 1935).

12 Michael P. Scharf, *Earned Sovereignty: Juridical Underpinnings,* 31 Denver J. Int'l L. 373, 373 n. 20. The Peace of Westphalia was composed of two separate agreements: (1) the Treaty of Osnabrück concluded between the Protestant Queen of Sweden and her allies on one side, and the Holy Roman Habsburg Emperor and the German Princes on the other; and (2) the Treaty of Munster concluded between the Catholic King of France and his allies on the one side, and the Holy Roman Habsburg Emperor and the German Princes on the other. The Conventional view of the Peace of Westphalia is that by recognizing the German

Princes as sovereign, these treaties signaled the beginning of a new era. But in fact, the power to conclude alliances formally recognized at Westphalia was not unqualified and was in fact a power that the German Princes had already possessed for almost half a century. Furthermore, although the treaties eroded some of the authority of the Habsburg Emperor, the Empire remained a key actor according to the terms of the treaties. For example, the Imperial Diet retained the powers of legislation, warfare, and taxation, and it was through Imperial bodies, such as the Diet and the Courts, that religious safeguards mandated by the Treaty were imposed on the German Princes.

13 THE GROTIAN MOMENT IN INTERNATIONAL LAW: A CONTEMPORARY PERSPECTIVE 7 (Richard Falk et al, Eds., 1985), excerpt reprinted in BURNS H. WESTON ET AL, INTERNATIONAL LAW AND WORLD ORDER 1087–92 (Thomson/West 2d ed. 1990). *See also* INTERNATIONAL LAW AND WORLD ORDER 1265–86 (Burns H. Weston, Richard A. Falk, Hilary Charlesworth & Andrew K. Strauss eds., Thomson/West 4th ed. 2006). For the early seeds of this concept of a changing paradigm in Falk's work, see Richard A. Falk, *The Interplay of Westphalia and Charter Conceptions of International Legal Order,* in 1 THE FUTURE OF THE INTERNATIONAL LEGAL ORDER 32 (R. Falk & C. Black eds 1969).

14 Boutros Boutros-Ghali, *The Role of International Law in the Twenty-First Century: A Grotian Moment,* 18 FORDHAM INT'L L. J. 1609, 1613 (1995) (referring to the establishment of the International Tribunal for the former Yugoslavia as part of the process of building a new international system for the 21st century).

15 Saul Mendlovitz & Marev Datan, *Judge Weeramantry's Grotian Quest,* 7 TRANSNATIONAL L. & CONTEMP. PROBS. 401, 402 (defining the term "Grotian moment"); Milena Sterio, *Humanitarian Intervention Post-Syria: A Grotian Moment,* 20 ILSA JOURNAL OF INTERNATIONAL & COMPARATIVE LAW (2014).

16 BURNS H. WESTON, INTERNATIONAL LAW AND WORLD ORDER, 1369 (3d ed. 1997), B.S. Chimni, *The Eighth Annual Grotius Lecture: A Just World Under Law: A View from the South,* 22 AM. U. INT'L L. REV. 199, 202 (2007).

17 Anne-Marie Slaughter & William Burke-White, *An International Constitutional Moment,* 43 HARVARD INTERNATIONAL LAW JOURNAL 1, 13 (2002).

18 *See* Rep. of the Int'l Law Comm'n on the Work of its Forty-Eighth Session, 51st Sess., May 6–July 26, 1996, U.N. Doc. A/51/10; GAOR, 51st Sess., Supp. No. 10 (1996), *available at* http://legal.un.org/ilc/documentation/english/A_51_10.pdf (last visited Feb. 22, 2014).

19 Affirmation of the Principles of International Law Recognized by the Charter of the Nürnberg Tribunal, G.A. Res. 95(I), U.N. GAOR, 1st Sess., U.N. Doc A/236, pt. 2, at 1144, (Dec. 11, 1946), *available at* http://www.un.org/en/ga/search/view_doc.asp?symbol=A/RES/95(I)&Lang= E&Area=RESOLUTION(last visited Feb. 22, 2014). The Resolution states in whole:

The General Assembly,

Recognizes the obligation laid upon it by Article 13, paragraph 1, sub-paragraph a, of the Charter, to initiate studies and make recommendations for the purpose of encouraging the progressive development of international law and its codification;

Takes note of the Agreement for the establishment of an International Military Tribunal for the prosecution and punishment of the major war criminals of the European Axis signed in London on 8 August 1945, and of the Charter annexed thereto, and of the fact that similar principles have been adopted in the Charter of the International Military Tribunal for the trial of the major war criminals in the Far East, proclaimed at Tokyo on 19 January 1946;

Therefore,

Affirms the principles of international law recognized by the Charter of the Nuremberg Tribunal and the judgment of the Tribunal;

Directs the Committee on the codification of international law established by the resolution of the General Assembly of 11 December 1946, to treat as a matter of primary importance plans for the formulation, in the context of a general codification of offenses against the peace and security of mankind, or of an International Criminal Code, of the principles recognized in the Charter of the Nuremberg Tribunal and in the judgment of the Tribunal. *Id.*

20 In deciding whether to treat a particular General Assembly resolution as evidence of an emergent rule of customary international law, the International Court of Justice has stated that "it is necessary to look at its content and the conditions of its adoption." *Legality of the Threat or Use of Nuclear Weapons*, ICJ Reports 1996, pp. 254–5. For a discussion of and authorities related to the importance of wording, vote outcome, and explanation of votes in this regard, see MICHAEL P. SCHARF, CUSTOMARY INTERNATIONAL LAW IN TIMES OF FUNDAMENTAL CHANGE: RECOGNIZING GROTIAN MOMENTS, 54–56 (2013).

21 Affirmation of the Principles of International Law Recognized by the Charter of the Nürnberg Tribunal, G.A. Res. 95(I), U.N. GAOR, 1st Sess., U.N. Doc A/236, pt. 2, at 1144, (Dec. 11, 1946), *available at* http://www.un.org/en/ga/search/view_doc.asp?symbol=A/RES/95(I)&Lang= E&Area=RESOLUTION(last visited Feb. 22, 2014).

22 Legal Consequences of the Construction of a Wall in Occupied Palestinian Territory, Advisory Opinion, 2004 I.C.J. 136, 172 (July 9).

23 Prosecutor v. Tadic, Case No. IT-94-1-I, Opinion and Judgment, Trial Chamber, ¶ 623 (Int'l Crim. Trib. for the Former Yugoslavia May 7, 1997); Prosecutor v. Tadic, Case No. IT-94-1-I, Decision on the Defence Motion for Interlocutory Appeal on Jurisdiction, ¶141 (Int'l Crim. Trib. for the Former Yugoslavia Oct. 2, 1995).

24 The European Court of Human Rights recognized the "universal validity" of the Nuremberg principles in *Kolk and Kislyiy v. Estonia*, which stated:

Although the Nuremberg Tribunal was established for trying the major war criminals of the European Axis countries for the offences they had committed before or during the Second World War, the Court notes that the universal validity of the principles concerning crimes against humanity was subsequently confirmed by, *inter alia*, resolution 95 of the United Nations General Assembly (11 December 1946), and later by the International Law Commission.

Kolk and Kislyiy v. Estonia, App. No. 23052/04, 24018/04, Decision on Admissibility, Eur. Ct. H.R. (Jan. 17, 2006).

25 The General Assembly resolution affirming the Nuremberg Principles has been cited as evidence of customary international law in cases in Canada, Bosnia, France, and Israel. *See R. v. Finta*, [1994], 1 S.C.C. 701 (Can.); *Prosecutor v. Ivica Vrdoljak*, Court of Bosnia and Herzegovina, 10 July 2008; *see generally* Leila Sadat Wexler, *The Interpretation of the Nuremberg Principles by the French Court of Cassation: From Touvier to Barbie and Back Again*, 32 Colum. J. Transnat'l L. 289 (1994) (summarizing the *Touvier* and *Barbie* cases in French courts).

26 *See* ANN L. HOLLICK, U.S. FOREIGN POLICY AND THE LAW OF THE SEA30 (Princeton Univ. Press, 1981) (citing Unpublished, National Archives Record Group 48); BARRY BUZAN, SEABED POLITICS 8 (Praeger Publishers, 1976); JAMES B. MORELL, THE LAW OF THE SEA: AN HISTORICAL ANALYSIS OF THE 1982 TREATY AND ITS REJECTION BY THE UNITED STATES2 (McFarland & Co., 1992); Hersch Lauterpacht, *Sovereignty over Submarine Areas* 27 BRITISH YEAR BOOK OF INTERNATIONAL LAW 377 (1950).

27 Tullio Treves, Customary International Law, Max Planck Encyclopedia of Public International Law (2012) at ¶ 24; *accord* REPORT OF THE INTERNATIONAL LAW ASSOCIATION, COMMITTEE ON FORMATION OF CUSTOMARY (GENERAL) INTERNATIONAL LAW, LONDON CONFERENCE (2000), at 20.

28 *Id.*
29 Proclamation 2667 of September 28, 1945, Policy of the United States with Respect to the Natural Resources of the Subsoil and Sea Bed of the Continental Shelf, 10 Fed. Reg. 12,305 (1945).
30 Barry Buzan, Seabed Politics 8 (Praeger Publishers, 1976).
31 James B. Morell, The Law of the Sea: An Historical Analysis of the 1982 Treaty and its Rejection by the United States4 (McFarland & Co., 1992); Barry Buzan, Seabed Politics7 (Praeger Publishers, 1976).
32 Ann L. Hollick, U.S. Foreign Policy and the Law of the Sea30 (Princeton Univ. Press, 1981) (citing Unpublished, National Archives Record Group 48).
33 Barry Buzan, Seabed Politics 8 (Praeger Publishers, 1976).
34 James B. Morell, The Law of the Sea: An Historical Analysis of the 1982 Treaty and its Rejection by the United States2 (McFarland & Co., 1992).
35 Hersch Lauterpacht, *Sovereignty over Submarine Areas* 27 British Year Book of International Law 377 (1950).
36 *North Sea Continental Shelf* (*Federal Republic of Germany v. Denmark*; *Federal Republic of Germany v. Netherlands*), Merits, 20 February 1969, ICJ Rep. 3, North Sea Continental Shelf Case, I.C.J. Reports (1969), pp. 33–34, para. 47.
37 United Nations General Assembly Resolution 1962 (XVIII), Declaration of Legal Principles Governing the Activities of States in the Exploration and Use of Outer Space, December 13, 1963, available at: http://www.oosa.unvienna.org/oosa/en /SpaceLaw/gares/html/gares_18_1962.html
38 MANFRED LACHS, THE LAW OF OUTER SPACE: AN EXPERIENCE IN CONTEMPORARY LAW-MAKING 138 (1972).
39 Prosecutor v. Tadic, Appeals Chamber, Decision on the Defense Motion for Interlocutory Appeal on Jurisdiction, Case No. IT-94-1-AR72 (Oct. 2, 1995), reprinted in 35 I.L.M. 32 (1996), at para. 89.
40 Report of the Secretary General Pursuant to Paragraph 5 of Security Council Resolution 955, 13 February 1995, U.N. Doc. S/1995/134, at para. 12.
41 Statute of the Special Court for Sierra Leone, Art. 3, (16 January 2002), available at: http://www.sc-sl.org/LinkClick.aspx?fileticket=uClnd1MJeEw%3d&tabid =176.
42 Rome Statute of the International Criminal Court, Art. 8, July 17, 1998, 2187 U.N.T.S. 90 (distinguishing between "international armed conflict" in paragraph 2(b) and "armed conflict not of an international character" in paragraphs 2(c)–(f)).
43 Michael Scharf, Milena Sterio, and Paul R. Williams, The Syrian Conflict's Impact on International Law (Cambridge University Press, 2020).
44 Claire Mills and Louisa Brooke-Holland, *House of Commons Briefing Paper No. 06995, ISIS/Daesh: The Military Response in Iraq and Syria*, July 7, 2015, at 4–7.
45 House of Commons Library, *ISIS and the Sectarian Conflict in the Middle East, Research Paper 15/16*, March 19, 2015, at 55. The United States did warn the Assad regime about the imminent launch of airstrikes in September 2014 but did not request the regime's permission.
46 House of Commons Library, *ISIS and the Sectarian Conflict in the Middle East, Research Paper 15/16*, March 19, 2015, at 55.
47 Samantha J. Power, Representative of the United States of America to the United Nations, Note to Ban Ki-moon, Secretary-General of the United Nations, September 23, 2014.
48 Military and Paramilitary Activities in and against Nicaragua (Nicaragua v. United States) (merits), para. 195, 1986 I.C.J. 14, 195 (June 26); Oil Platforms (Iran v. United States) 2003 I.C.J. 161, 195 (Nov. 6); The Construction of a Wall in the Occupied Palestinian Territory, Advisory Opinion, 2003 I.C.J. 136, 139 (July 9); Armed Activities on the Territory of the Congo (Democratic Republic of the Congo v. Uganda) 2005 I.C.J. 168 (December 19).

49 Ashley S. Deeks, *Unwilling or Unable: Toward a Normative Framework for Extraterritorial Self-Defense*, 52 Virginia Journal of International Law 483, 497 (2012).
50 Armed Activities on the Territory of the Congo (Dem. Rep. Congo v. Uganda), 2005 I.C.J. 168 (holding that Uganda could not rely on self-defense to justify its military operation in the Congo because (1) Uganda did not immediately report to the Security Council following its use of force as required by Article 51, (2) Uganda's actions were vastly disproportionate to the threat, and (3) there was no evidence from which to impute the attacks against Ugandan villages by rebel groups operating out of the Congo to the government of Congo).
51 Theresa Reinold, *State Weakness, Irregular Warfare, and the Right to Self-Defense Post-9/11*, 105 American Journal of International Law 244, 261 (2011).
52 See R.Y. Jennings, *The Caroline and McLeod Cases*, 32 American Journal of International Law 82, 82–89 (1938) (quoting 61 Parliamentary Papers (1843).
53 Armed Activities on the Territory of the Congo (Dem. Rep. Congo v. Uganda), 2005 I.C.J. 168 (Separate Opinion of Judge Koojimans), para. 28.
54 Armed Activities on the Territory of the Congo (Dem. Rep. Congo v. Uganda), 45 I.L.M. 271, 308–09, Dec. 19, 2005 (DRC v. Uganda) (separate opinion of Judge Simma), para. 11.
55 S.C. Res. 2249 (Nov. 20, 2015).
56 Arabella Lang, Legal Basis for UK Military Action in Syria, House of Commons Library Briefing Paper No. 7404, Dec. 1, 2015, at 8, available at https://www.voltairenet.org/IMG/pdf/CBP-7404.pdf [https://perma.cc/FH4P-NPMH].
57 Arabella Lang, Legal Basis for UK Military Action in Syria, House of Commons Library Briefing Paper No. 7404, Dec. 1, 2015, at 8 (quoting Weller), available at https://www.voltairenet.org/IMG/pdf/CBP-7404.pdf [https://perma.cc/FH4P-NPMH].
58 Security Council "Unequivocally" Condemns ISIL Terrorist Attacks, Unanimously Adopting Text that Determines Extremist Group Poses "Unprecedented" Threat, U.N. Press Release, (Nov. 20, 2015), http://www.un.org/press/en/2015/sc12132.doc.htm [https://perma.cc/2B2L-CJPF] (last visited Dec. 20, 2015).
59 David Kaplow, International Legal Standards and the Weaponization of Outer Space, in SPACE: THE NEXT GENERATION — CONFERENCE REPORT, 31 MARCH–1 APRIL 2008, UNITED NATIONS INSTITUTE FOR DISARMAMENT RESEARCH 162 (2008).
60 Steven Erlanger & Stephen Castle, British Jets Hit ISIS in Syria After Parliament Authorizes Airstrikes, N. Y. TIMES, Dec. 3, 2015, A16, available at http://www.nytimes.com/2015/12/03/world/europe/britainparliament-syria-airstrikes-vote.html?_r=0 [https://perma.cc/N4722RB6] (last visited Dec. 18, 2015).
61 Steven Erlanger & Stephen Castle, British Jets Hit ISIS in Syria After Parliament Authorizes Airstrikes, N. Y. TIMES, Dec. 3, 2015, A16, available at http://www.nytimes.com/2015/12/03/world/europe/britainparliament-syria-airstrikes-vote.html?_r=0 [https://perma.cc/N4722RB6] (last visited Dec. 18, 2015).
62 Committee on Formation of Customary (General) International Law, Conference Report London, INT'L L. ASS'N 25 (2000), available at http://www.ila-hq.org/en/committees/index.cfm/cid/30 [https://perma.cc/QG73-RLMH].
63 UN News, May 10, 2024, available at: https://news.un.org/en/story/2024/05/1149596
64 UN News, September 28, 2024, available at: https://news.un.org/en/story/2024/09/1154496
65 Andreas Umland, *How Russia's Ukraine War Is Undermining World Order*, The National Interest, May 7, 2024.

APPENDIX: DRAFT HIGH WAR CRIMES COURT LEGISLATION FOR UKRAINE

Prepared By The Public International Law & Policy Group

Introductory Note

The International Criminal Court (ICC) has opened an investigation and will likely prosecute a handful of high-level perpetrators of atrocity crimes committed in Ukraine. Since the ICC does not have jurisdiction over the crime of aggression with respect to Ukraine, there are proposals to establish a hybrid international or regional tribunal to prosecute high-level Russians for the crime of aggression currently under discussion. Because these international mechanisms are designed to prosecute a small number of individuals, there is recognition that most of the perpetrators will need to be prosecuted by domestic courts in Ukraine. Yet, history has shown that without international assistance and involvement, it is inherently difficult to fairly and effectively prosecute foreign nationals and separatists in ordinary domestic courts during and in the aftermath of an armed conflict.

This draft Law, prepared by the Public International Law & Policy Group, Weil, Gotshal & Manges LLP, and a number of consulted experts, draws from the Law on the High Anti-Corruption Court of Ukraine and best practices of other States to provide the template for a Ukrainian High War Crimes Court to prosecute atrocity crimes committed in Ukraine since November 2013. It is a discussion draft intended to inform the formulation of a domestic prosecutorial mechanism that will complement the efforts by existing domestic courts, the ICC, and any future hybrid international tribunal for the crime of aggression.[1] The footnotes include options and explanations for the proposed provisions.

Draft Law Of Ukraine

On the High War Crimes Court

Contents

Chapter I. GENERAL PROVISIONS

Article 1. Definitions

For the purposes of this legislation, the following terms shall mean:

Atrocity crimes: are those international crimes recognized in the Amended Statute of the International Criminal Court ("ICC"), namely war crimes, crimes against humanity, genocide, and crimes of aggression.

Gender: refers to the two sexes, male and female, within the context of society.

International armed conflicts: exist when two or more States resort to armed force.[2]

International humanitarian law: the set of rules seeking, for humanitarian reasons, to limit the effects of international armed conflicts and non-international armed conflicts. It protects persons who have not or are no longer participating in the hostilities and restricts the means and methods of warfare.[3]

Non-international armed conflicts: protracted armed confrontations occurring between governmental armed forces and the forces of one or more armed groups, or between such groups arising on the territory of a State party to the Geneva Conventions. The armed confrontation must reach a minimum level of intensity and the parties involved in the conflict must show a minimum of organization.[4] Situations of internal disturbances and tensions, such as riots, isolated and sporadic acts of violence or other acts of a similar nature are excluded.[5]

Article 2. The status of the High War Crimes Court

1. The High War Crimes Court is a highly specialized court in the judicial system of Ukraine, consisting of Trial Chambers and an Appeals Chamber similar to the High Anti-Corruption Court of Ukraine. It will have an initial duration of 10 years that may be extended in accordance with Ukrainian law.
2. The High War Crimes Court is a legal entity, has a seal with the National Emblem of Ukraine and its name on it.
3. The High War Crimes Court is located in the city of Kyiv, Ukraine. The Court may relocate to and conduct proceedings elsewhere in Ukraine when appropriate and feasible.

Article 3. The language of the High War Crimes Court

The official language of the Court shall be Ukrainian. Working languages of the Court shall include English and Ukrainian.[6] In the event of any discrepancies between documents, the Ukrainian version of the document will prevail.[7] The Court will make sure that the necessary translations of documents and simultaneous interpretations during oral proceedings are available.[8]

Article 4. The legislative framework of the functioning of the High War Crimes Court.

4. The legislative framework of the functioning of the High War Crimes Court consists of the Constitution of Ukraine, the Law of Ukraine "On the Judiciary and the Status of Judges," this Law and other laws of Ukraine, international treaties in force, consented by the Verhovna Rada of Ukraine as binding.
5. Amendments to this Law may be made exclusively by laws on the introduction of changes to the Law of Ukraine "On the High War Crimes Court."

Article 5. Objectives of the High War Crimes Court

6. The objective of the High War Crimes Court is the administration of justice in accordance with the principles and procedures of the judiciary prescribed by the law with the view to protect individuals and society from war crimes, crimes against humanity, genocide, the crime of aggression, and related crimes recognized by Ukraine. Additionally, the High War Crimes Court will have judicial oversight over pre-trial investigation of these crimes,

and observance of rights, freedoms and interests of individuals in a criminal proceeding.

7. As a matter of policy,[9] the main purpose of the High War Crimes Court is to prosecute those persons most responsible for committing atrocity crimes in Ukraine since November 2013. For the purposes of this Law, "persons most responsible" means a person or persons who were knowingly responsible for any or all of the following acts: planning, instigating, inciting, funding, ordering or providing other logistics which directly or indirectly facilitated the commission of crimes falling within the jurisdiction of the Court; in determining whether a person or persons falls within this category for purposes of bringing charges, the Prosecutor[10] shall have regard to factors including the leadership role or level of authority or decision making power or influence of the person concerned and the gravity, severity, seriousness or scale of the crime committed.[11]

Chapter II. ORGANIZATION OF THE FUNCTIONING OF THE HIGH WAR CRIMES COURT

Article 6. Powers and Jurisdiction of the High War Crimes Court

8. The High War Crimes Court shall:Administer justice as the first-instance and appeal court in criminal proceedings concerning crimes within its jurisdiction according to procedural law as well as by means of performing, in cases and pursuant to the procedure prescribed by the law, judicial oversight over observance of rights, freedoms and interests of individuals in such criminal proceedings; analyze judicial statistics, study and generalize judicial practice in criminal proceedings within its jurisdiction, inform the Supreme Court on the results of such generalization and provide it with proposals for conclusions on draft legislative acts pertaining to the organization and activity of the High War Crimes Court, special requirements to the judges of this court and guarantees of their activity, as well as publish them on its official website.

9. Territorial jurisdiction of the High War Crimes Court shall cover the entire territory of Ukraine.[12]

10. The Court shall have subject matter jurisdiction over atrocity crimes, in particular, the following:[13]

a) – The Crime of Genocide[14]

i. Article 442 of the Ukrainian Criminal Code defines genocide as "a willfully committed act for the purpose of total or partial destruction of any national, ethnic, racial, or religious group by extermination of members of any such group or inflicting grave bodily injuries on them, creation of life conditions calculated for total or pratial physical destruction of the group, decrease or prevention of childbearing in the group, or forceful transferring of children from one group to another... and also making any materials with calls to genocide for the purpose of distribution, or distribution of such materials."

ii. Under principles of international law recognized by the Ukraine contained in the Convention on the Prevention and Punishment of the Crime of Genocide, dated December 9, 1948, "genocide" means any of the following acts committed with intent to destroy, in whole or in part, a national, ethnical, racial or religious group, as such:

1) killing members of the group;
2) causing serious bodily or mental harm to members of the group;
3) deliberately inflicting on the group conditions of life calculated to bring about its physical destruction in whole or in part;
4) imposing measures intended to prevent births within the group; and
5) forcibly transferring children of the group to another group.

iii. The following acts shall be punishable:

1) genocide;
2) conspiracy to commit genocide;
3) direct and public incitement to commit genocide;
4) attempt to commit genocide; and
5) complicity in genocide.

b) – Crimes against Humanity[15]

i. According to internationally recognized principles of customary international law codified in the Rome Statute for an International Criminal Court, and reflected in various provisions of the Ukraine Criminal Code, "crimes against humanity" means any of the following acts when committed as part of a widespread or systematic attack directed against any civilian population, with knowledge of the attack:

1) Murder;[16]
2) Extermination;[17]
3) Enslavement;
4) Deportation or forcible transfer of population;[18]
5) Imprisonment or other severe deprivation of physical liberty in violation of fundamental norms of international law;[19]
6) Torture;[20]
7) Rape,[21] sexual slavery, enforced prostitution,[22] forced pregnancy, or any other form of sexual violence of comparable gravity;

8) Persecution against any identifiable group or collectivity on political, racial, national, ethnic, cultural, religious, gender or other grounds that are universally recognized as impermissible under international law, in connection with any act referred to in this paragraph or any crime within the jurisdiction of the Tribunal;
9) Enforced disappearance of persons;[23] and
10) Other inhumane acts of a similar character intentionally causing great suffering, or serious injury to body or to mental or physical health.

ii. For the purposes of paragraph i):

1) "Attack directed against any civilian population" means a course of conduct involving the multiple commission of acts referred to in paragraph a) against any civilian population, pursuant to or in furtherance of a State or organizational policy to commit such attack;
2) "Extermination" includes the intentional infliction of conditions of life, such as the deprivation of access to food and medicine, calculated to bring about the destruction of part of a population;
3) "Enslavement" means the exercise of any or all of the powers attaching to the right of ownership over a person and includes the exercise of such power in the course of trafficking in persons, in particular women and children;
4) "Deportation or forcible transfer of population" means forced displacement of the persons concerned by expulsion or other coercive acts from the area in which they are lawfully present, without grounds permitted under international law;
5) "Torture" means the intentional infliction of severe pain or suffering, whether physical or mental, upon a person in the custody or under the control of the accused; except that torture shall not include pain or suffering arising only from, inherent in or incidental to lawful sanctions;
6) "Persecution" means the intentional and severe deprivation of fundamental rights contrary to international law by reason of the identity of the group or collectivity; and
7) "Enforced disappearance of persons" means the arrest, detention or abduction of persons by, or with the authorization, support or acquiescence of, a State or a political organization, followed by a refusal to acknowledge that deprivation of freedom or to give information on the fate or whereabouts of those persons, with the intention of removing them from the protection of the law for a prolonged period of time.

c) – War Crimes[24]

Article 438 of the Criminal Code of Ukraine on Violations of the Rule of the Warfare defines war crimes as consisting of "cruel treatment of prisoners of war or civilians, deportation of civilian population for forced labor, pillage of national treasures on occupied territories, use of methods of the warfare prohibited by international instruments, or any other violations of rules of the warfare recognized by international instruments consented to by binding by the Verkhovna Rada (Parliament) of Ukraine, and also giving an order to commit any such actions."

For the purposes of Article 438[25] of the Criminal Code "methods of the warfare prohibited by international instruments, or any other violations of rules of the warfare recognized by international instruments consented to by binding by the Verkhovna Rada," "war crimes" means:

i. Grave breaches of the Geneva Conventions of 12 August 1949, namely, any of the following acts against persons or property protected under the provisions of the relevant Geneva Convention:

1) Willful killing;
2) Torture or inhuman treatment, including biological experiments;[26]
3) Willfully causing great suffering, or serious injury to body or health;[27]
4) Extensive destruction and appropriation of property, not justified by military necessity and carried out unlawfully and wantonly;
5) Compelling a prisoner of war or other protected person to serve in the forces of a hostile power;
6) Willfully depriving a prisoner of war or other protected person of the rights of fair and regular trial;
7) Unlawful deportation or transfer or unlawful confinement; and
8) Taking of hostages.[28]

ii. Other serious violations of the laws and customs applicable in international armed conflict, within the established framework of international law, namely, any of the following acts:

1) Intentionally directing attacks against the civilian population as such or against individual civilians not taking direct part in hostilities;
2) Intentionally directing attacks against civilian objects, that is, objects which are not military objectives;
3) Intentionally directing attacks against personnel, installations, material, units or vehicles involved in a peacekeeping mission in accordance with the Charter of the United Nations or in a humanitarian assistance mission, as long as they are entitled to the protection given to civilians or civilian objects under the international law of armed conflict;

4) Intentionally launching an attack in the knowledge that such attack will cause incidental loss of life or injury to civilians or damage to civilian objects or widespread, long-term and severe damage to the natural environment which would be clearly excessive in relation to the concrete and direct overall military advantage anticipated;
5) Attacking or bombarding, by whatever means, towns, villages, dwellings or buildings which are undefended and which are not military objectives;
6) Killing or wounding a combatant who, having laid down his arms or having no longer means of defense, has surrendered at discretion;
7) Making improper use of a flag of truce, of the flag or of the military insignia and uniform of the enemy or of the United Nations, as well as of the distinctive emblems of the Geneva Conventions, resulting in death or serious personal injury;
8) The transfer, directly or indirectly, by the occupying power of parts of its own civilian population into the territory it occupies, or the deportation or transfer of all or parts of the population of the occupied territory within or outside this territory;
9) Intentionally directing attacks against buildings dedicated to religion,[29] education, art, science or charitable purposes, historic monuments,[30] hospitals and places where the sick and wounded are collected, provided they are not military objectives;
10) Subjecting persons who are in the power of an adverse party to physical mutilation or to medical or scientific experiments of any kind that are neither justified by the medical, dental or hospital treatment of the person concerned nor carried out in his or her interest, and which cause death to or seriously endanger the health of such person or persons;
11) Killing or wounding treacherously individuals belonging to the hostile nation or army;
12) Declaring that no quarter will be given;
13) Destroying or seizing the enemy's property unless such destruction or seizure be imperatively demanded by the necessities of war;
14) Declaring abolished, suspended or inadmissible in a court of law, or otherwise depriving, the rights and actions of the nationals of the hostile party;
15) Compelling the nationals of the hostile party to take part in the operations of war directed against their own country, even if they were in the belligerent's service before the commencement of the war;
16) Pillaging a town or place, even when taken by assault;
17) Employing poison or poisoned weapons;
18) Employing asphyxiating, poisonous or other gasses, and all analogous liquids, materials or devices;

19) Employing bullets which expand or flatten easily in the human body, such as bullets with a hard envelope which does not entirely cover the core or is pierced with incisions;
20) Committing outrages upon personal dignity, in particular humiliating and degrading treatment;
21) Committing rape,[31] sexual slavery, enforced prostitution,[32] forced pregnancy, or any other form of sexual violence of comparable gravity;
22) Utilizing the presence of a civilian or other protected person to render certain points, areas or military forces immune from military operations;
23) Intentionally directing attacks against buildings, material, medical units and transport, and personnel using the distinctive emblems of the Geneva Conventions in conformity with international law;
24) Intentionally using starvation of civilians as a method of warfare by depriving them of objects indispensable to their survival, including wilfully impeding relief supplies as provided for under international law; and
25) Conscripting or enlisting children under the age of fifteen years into the national armed forces or using them to participate actively in hostilities.

iii. In the case of an armed conflict not of an international character, any of the following acts committed against persons taking no active part in the hostilities, including members of armed forces who have laid down their arms and those placed hors de combat by sickness, wounds, detention or any other cause:

1) Violence to life and person, in particular murder of all kinds, mutilation, cruel treatment[33] and torture;
2) Committing outrages upon personal dignity, in particular humiliating and degrading treatment;
3) Taking of hostages; and
4) The passing of sentences and the carrying out of executions without previous judgment pronounced by a regularly constituted court, affording all judicial guarantees which are generally recognized as indispensable.

iv. Other serious violations of the laws and customs of war applicable in armed conflict not of an international character, within the established framework of international law, namely, any of the following acts:

1) Intentionally directing attacks against the civilian population as such or against individual civilians not taking direct part in hostilities;
2) Intentionally directing attacks against buildings, material, medical units and transport, and personnel using the distinctive emblems of the Geneva Conventions in conformity with international law;

3) Intentionally directing attacks against personnel, installations, material, units, or vehicles involved in a peacekeeping mission in accordance with the Charter of the United Nations or in a humanitarian assistance mission, as long as they are entitled to the protection given to civilians or civilian objects under the international law of armed conflict;
4) Intentionally directing attacks against buildings that are dedicated to religion,[34] education, art, science, or charitable purposes, historic monuments,[35] hospitals and places where the sick and wounded are collected, provided they are not military objectives;
5) Pillaging a town or place,[36] even when taken by assault;
6) Committing rape,[37] sexual slavery, enforced prostitution,[38] forced pregnancy, or any other form of sexual violence of comparable gravity;
7) Conscripting or enlisting children under the age of fifteen years into armed forces or groups or using them to participate actively in hostilities;
8) Ordering the displacement of the civilian population for reasons related to the conflict, unless the security of the civilians involved or imperative military reasons so demand;
9) Killing or wounding treacherously a combatant adversary;
10) Declaring that no quarter will be given;
11) Subjecting persons who are in the power of another party to the conflict to physical mutilation or to medical or scientific experiments of any kind that are neither justified by the medical, dental or hospital treatment of the person concerned nor carried out in his or her interest, and which cause death to or seriously endanger the health of such person or persons;
12) Destroying or seizing the property of an adversary, unless such destruction or seizure be imperatively demanded by the necessities of the conflict;
13) Employing poison or poisoned weapons;
14) Employing asphyxiating, poisonous or other gases, and all analogous liquids, materials or devices; and
15) Employing bullets which expand or flatten easily in the human body, such as bullets with a hard envelope which does not entirely cover the core or is pierced with incisions.

d) – Crime of Aggression[39]

i. According to Article 437[40] of the Criminal Code of Ukraine on Planning, Preparation, and Waging of an Aggressive War– the "[p]lanning, preparation or waging of an aggressive war or armed conflict, or conspiring for any such purposes, - shall be punishable by imprisonment for a term of seven to twelve years" and "[c]onducting an aggressive war or aggressive military operations, - shall be punishable by imprisonment for a term of ten to fifteen years."

ii. In addition, under international law recognized by Ukraine, the "crime of aggression" means the planning, preparation, initiation or execution, by a person in a position effectively to exercise control over or to direct the political or military action of a State, of an act of aggression which, by its character, gravity and scale, constitutes a manifest violation of the Charter of the United Nations.

iii. For the purpose of paragraph a), "act of aggression" means the use of armed force by a State against the sovereignty, territorial integrity or political independence of another State, or in any other manner inconsistent with the Charter of the United Nations. Any of the following acts, regardless of a declaration of war, shall, in accordance with United Nations General Assembly resolution 3314 (XXIX) of 14 December 1974, qualify as an act of aggression:

1) The invasion or attack by the armed forces of a State of the territory of another State, or any military occupation, however temporary, resulting from such invasion or attack, or any annexation by the use of force of the territory of another State or part thereof;
2) Bombardment by the armed forces of a State against the territory of another State or the use of any weapons by a State against the territory of another State;
3) The blockade of the ports or coasts of a State by the armed forces of another State;
4) An attack by the armed forces of a State on the land, sea or air forces, or marine and air fleets of another State;
5) The use of armed forces of one State which are within the territory of another State with the agreement of the receiving State, in contravention of the conditions provided for in the agreement or any extension of their presence in such territory beyond the termination of the agreement;
6) The action of a State in allowing its territory, which it has placed at the disposal of another State, to be used by that other State for perpetrating an act of aggression against a third State; and
7) The sending by or on behalf of a State of armed bands, groups, irregulars or mercenaries, which carry out acts of armed force against another State of such gravity as to amount to the acts listed above, or its substantial involvement therein.

11. The Court shall have jurisdiction for crimes committed in Ukraine since November 2013.

12. In interpreting the crimes within its jurisdiction, theories of liability, evidentiary matters, and standards for sentencing, the Court may consider rulings of international courts to help inform its decision.

Article 7. Composition of the High War Crimes Court

13. The number of judges of the High War Crimes Court shall be determined in accordance with the Law of Ukraine "On the Judiciary and the Status of Judges" keeping in mind the financial means of the High War Crimes Court, and include a specific number of judges for the Appeal Chamber of the High War Crimes Court.[41]

14. In order to perform judicial oversight over observance of rights, freedoms and interests of individuals in criminal proceedings within the jurisdiction of the High War Crimes Court, investigative judges shall be elected from among the staff of this court for the period of one year without the right to be re-elected for the position of the investigative judge two years in a row.

15. A judge of the Appeal Chamber of the High War Crimes Court may not be elected for the position of the investigative judge.

16. Determination of the number of investigative judges in the High War Crimes Court, their election, performance of duties of a judge of the first instance in the High War Crimes Court shall be carried out pursuant to the procedure prescribed by the Law of Ukraine "On the Judiciary and Status of Judges" for the purposes of determination of the number of investigative judges, their election and performance of duties of a judge in local courts.

Article 8. The Chief of the High War Crimes Court, Deputy Chief, the Chief of the Appeal Chamber of the High War Crimes Court

17. The Chief Judge of the Appeal Chamber of the High War Crimes Court shall be the Chief of the High War Crimes Court. He or she exercises administrative powers prescribed by the Law of Ukraine "On the Judiciary and Status of Judges" and this Law.
18. The Chief of the High War Crimes Court shall have one deputy exercising administrative powers determined by the Chief of the High War Crimes Court.
19. The position of the Chief or Deputy Chief of the High War Crimes Court shall not grant a judge of the High War Crimes Court relief from exercising the powers of a judge prescribed by the law nor suspend this judge

from work in the respective judicial chamber or duties of the secretary of a judicial chamber of the High War Crimes Court.

20. The Chief Judge of the Appeal Chamber of the High War Crimes Court and the Chief Judge of the trial court of the High War Crimes Court shall be elected pursuant to the procedure and exercise powers prescribed by the Law of Ukraine "On the Judiciary and Status of Judges."

Chapter III. PROCEDURE OF TAKING THE POSITION OF A JUDGE OF THE HIGH WAR CRIMES COURT

Article 9. Special requirements to a judge of the High War Crime's Court

21. An individual complying with the requirements to the candidates for the position of a judge defined by the Constitution of Ukraine and the Law of Ukraine "On the Judiciary and Status of Judges"[42] as well as additional special requirements established by this article may be a judge of the High War Crimes Court.
22. A citizen of Ukraine may be appointed for the position of a judge of the High War Crimes Court if he or she complies with the requirements to the candidates for the position of a judge specified in the Law of Ukraine "On the Judiciary and Status of Judges" and possesses knowledge and practical skills necessary for performing judicial functions in international humanitarian law, international law or human rights related cases, as well as complies with any of the following requirements:

a) has at least five years of experience as a judge;
b) holds a law degree and has at least seven years of scholarly experience in law;
c) has at least seven years of professional experience as a defense attorney, including representation in court and/or defense from criminal charges;
d) has at least seven years of total experience of work (professional activity) for items a-c of this paragraph.

23. For the purposes of paragraph 2 of this Article, the terms "professional experience in law," "scholarly experience," "degree" are used in the meaning prescribed in Article 69, paragraph 6, of the Law of Ukraine "On the Judiciary and Status of Judges."
24. An individual shall not be eligible for the position of a judge if:

a) within the ten years prior to the appointment, this individual:

has worked (served) in bodies of interior affairs of Ukraine, the Armed Forces of Ukraine, the National Police of Ukraine, the State Investigation Bureau, other law enforcement agencies, tax police, the Security Service of Ukraine, customs bodies, the National War Crimes Bureau of Ukraine, has held political office or a representative mandate.

b) within the past five years, the individual has been among the top management of a political party or had labor or other contractual relationship with a political party;
c) the individual has been a member of the High Qualification Commission of Judges of Ukraine or the High Council of Justice before the Law of Ukraine "On the Restoration of Trust in the Judicial Power in Ukraine" came into effect;
d) a court verdict which came into force and prohibits the individual to hold office or engage in activity connected with the performance of functions of the state or local self-government (with the exception of rehabilitated individuals) regardless of such a conviction having been expunged or removed from official records, or if the individual had a criminal record for any intentional crime regardless of such a conviction having been expunged or removed from official records.

Article 10. Competition for the position of a judge of the High War Crimes Court

25. The competition for the position of a judge of the High War Crimes Court shall take place pursuant to the procedure determined by the Constitution of Ukraine and the Law of Ukraine "On the Judiciary and Status of Judges," taking into account the peculiarities prescribed by this Article.
26. The transfer of judges of other courts to the positions of judges of the High War Crimes Court without competition or within disciplinary measures shall not be permitted.
27. To be admitted to the qualification assessment to participate in the competition for the position of a judge of the High War Crimes Court pursuant to the special procedure, a candidate for the position of a judge submits to the High Qualification Commission of Judges of Ukraine, in addition to the documents defined by the Law of Ukraine "On the Judiciary and the Status of Judges," documents confirming the compliance with the requirements provided in Article 9, paragraph 22 of this Law as well as a statement on the absence of circumstances stated in Article 9, paragraph 24 of this Law.

28. In order to assist the High Qualification Commission of Judges of Ukraine in the establishment of compliance of the candidates for the positions of judges of the High War Crimes Court with the criteria of integrity (morality, honesty, incorruptibility) for the purposes of qualification assessment, namely in terms of lawfulness of the origin of sources of the candidate's property, correspondence of the standard of living of the candidate or his or her family members with the declared income, correspondence of the candidate's lifestyle to his or her status, knowledge and practical skills that the candidate possesses for the consideration of cases within the jurisdiction of the High War Crimes Court, the Public Council of International Experts shall be formed. The Public Integrity Council, established and acting in accordance with the Law of Ukraine "On the Judiciary and the Status of Judges," shall not be involved in the establishment of compliance of the candidates for the positions of judges of the High War Crimes Court to the criteria prescribed by the Law for the purposes of qualification assessment for the duration of activity of the Public Council of International Experts.
29. Upon initiative of at least three members of the Public Council of International Experts, the question of compliance of any candidate for the position of a judge of the High War Crimes Court with the criteria established in paragraph 4 of this Article, shall be reviewed at a special joint meeting of the High Qualification Commission of Judges of Ukraine and the Public Council of International Experts. The decision on compliance of this candidate with these criteria shall be approved by the majority of the joint composition of the High Qualification Commission of Judges of Ukraine and the Public Council of International Experts provided that at least half of the members of the Public Council of International Experts voted in favour of it. Shall such a decision not be taken, the candidate is considered to cease participation in the competition. Such special joint meeting shall be held no later than thirty days from the day of announcement of the examination results taken by the candidates for the establishment of their compliance with the professional competence criteria for the position of a judge.

At the request of at least three members of the Public Council of International Experts, before the special joint meeting of the High Qualification Commission of Judges of Ukraine and the Public Council of International Experts, a prior interview may be held with the candidates for the position of a judge of the High War Crimes Court, in which at least six members of the High Qualification Commission of Judges of Ukraine shall take part.

30. In case of the same position in the ranking compiled on the basis of the qualification assessment for participation in the competition for the

position of a judge of the Appeal Chamber of the High War Crimes Court, preference shall be given to the participant who has received a greater score for the practical part of the exam taken as part of the qualification assessment, and if the score is identical, as a rule, to the participant who has more work experience on the position of a judge of an appeal or cassation court. If participants of the competition for the position of a judge of the Appeal Chamber of the High War Crimes Court have equal experience on the position of a judge in appeal or cassation courts or do not have any such experience, preference shall be given to the candidate who has more experience on the position of a judge, if experience on the position of a judge is equal for both participants – to the participant who holds a scholarly degree, if both have it or neither does – to the participant with greater professional experience in law.

In case of the same position in the ranking compiled on the basis of the qualification assessment for participation in the competition for the position of a general judge of the High War Crimes Court, preference shall be given to the participant who has received a greater score for the practical part of the exam taken as part of the qualification assessment, and if the score is identical, as a rule, to the participant who has more work experience on the position of a judge. If the participants of the competition for the position of a judge of the High War Crimes Court have equal experience on the position of a judge or do not have any such experience, preference shall be given to the participant who holds a scholarly degree, if both have it or neither does – to the participant with greater professional experience in law.

31. At every stage of the qualification assessment of the candidates for the position of a judge of the High War Crimes Court and during the assessment of the results of such qualification assessment by the secretariat of the High Qualification Commission of Judges of Ukraine, video and audio recording and live broadcast of the respective meetings of the High Qualification Commission of Judges of Ukraine shall be published on the official website of the High Qualification Commission of Judges of Ukraine, and those of the Public Council of International Experts – on the official website of the State Judicial Administration of Ukraine.
32. When the High Council of Justice reviews the matter of the submission of a motion on the appointment of a judge of the High War Crimes Court to the President of Ukraine and takes a decision concerning the candidate for the position of a judge of the High War Crimes Court, video and audio recording and live broadcast of the respective meetings of the High Council of Justice shall be published on the official website of the High Council of Justice provided by the secretariat of the High Council of Justice.

Article 11. The Public Council of International Experts

33. The Public Council of International Experts shall be formed for the period of six years by the High Qualification Commission of Judges of Ukraine to facilitate it in the preparation of decisions on the appointment of judges of the High War Crimes Court and shall be a subsidiary body.
34. The Public Council of International Experts shall exercise its powers in the composition of six members appointed by the High Qualification Commission of Judges of Ukraine exclusively based on the nominations of international organizations with which Ukraine cooperates in the area of international humanitarian law, human rights and international peace and in accordance with international treaties of Ukraine.[43]

Every such international organization may suggest to the High Qualification Commission of Judges of Ukraine at least two candidates to the Public Council of International Experts.
The High Qualification Commission of Judges of Ukraine shall decide on the appointment of the members of the Public Council of International Experts if the number of nominated candidates to the Public Council of International Experts at least twice exceeds the number of vacant positions.Decision on the appointment of the members of the Public Council of International Experts shall be taken at the meeting of the High Qualification Commission of Judges of Ukraine.

35. Citizens of Ukraine or foreigners with impeccable business standing, high professional and moral qualities, respect in the society, at least five years of experience in other countries in procedural management, support of public prosecution in court or administration of justice in international war crimes and crimes against humanity-related cases may be members of the Public Council of International Experts.
36. Individuals who fail to comply with the requirements provided in Article 9, paragraph 24 of this Law may not be members of the Public Council of International Experts.
37. Members of the Public Council of International Experts shall be appointed for the term of office of two years and may not be reappointed.
38. For the period of participation of the members of the Public Council of International Experts in the procedure of the selection of candidates for the positions of judges of the High War Crimes Court they shall be assigned compensation in the amount of the fixed official salary of a Supreme Court judge. Members of the Public Council of International Experts who do not reside in Ukraine shall have the right for refund of their transport and accommodation expenses.

39. Powers of a member of the Public Council of International Experts shall be terminated early in case of:

a) submission of a personal letter of resignation from the position of a member of the Public Council of International Experts;
b) submission of a proposal on premature termination of powers of a member by the Public Council of International Experts;
c) entrance into force of a court's verdict against her/him;
d) recognition of the member of the Public Council of International Experts as legally incapable or gone missing;
e) discovery of failure of the member of the Public Council of International Experts to comply with the criteria established by this Law;
f) his or her death;
g) end of term prescribed in paragraph 5 of this Article.

40. The decision on the removal of a member of the Public Council of International Experts shall be taken by the High Qualification Commission of Judges of Ukraine, which, within ten days after taking it, shall take measures to appoint a new member of the Public Council of International Experts.

41. The Public Council of International Experts shall:

a) collect, verify and analyze information on candidates for the positions of judges of the High War Crimes Court;b) provide the High Qualification Commission of Judges of Ukraine with information on candidates for the positions of judges of the High War Crimes Court;c) participate in a special joint meeting in situations prescribed by this Law;d) take measures to protect personal data, information with restricted access that came to the knowledge of the Public Council of International Experts and its members in connection with their professional activity.

42. In order to exercise powers established by this Article, the members of the Public Council of International Experts shall be entitled to access open state registers for free.
43. A member of the Public Council of International Experts shall be obliged:

a) to participate in its work personally without the right to delegate his or her powers to other individuals, including other members of the Public Council of International Experts;
b) not to use personal data and other information that became known to him or her in connection with the work in the Public Council of International Experts for any other purposes than the professional duties as a member

of the Public Council of International Experts. Any violation of this requirement shall entail responsibility prescribed by the law;

c) to refuse to participate in the collection of information on the candidate, reviewing the compliance of a candidate for the position of a judge of the High War Crimes Court with the criteria established in Article 9, paragraph 24 of this Law if the member of the Public Council of International Experts has or had any personal or business relationship with the candidate for the position of a judge of the High War Crimes Court, is involved in cases that are or were reviewed by the judge who is a candidate for the position of a judge of the High War Crimes Court and/or in the event of any other conflict of interest or circumstances which may affect the objectivity and impartiality during the decision-making process by the member of the Public Council of International Experts concerning the candidate for the position of a judge of the High War Crimes Court.

44. Organizational and technical support of the activity of the Public Council of International Experts shall be provided by the State Judicial Administration of Ukraine. The activity of the Public Council of International Experts may be financed with the help of international technical assistance and through a special donors committee established in accordance with this Law.

Article 12. International Legal Advisors

45. In addition to the duties in Article 41, the Public Council of International Experts shall facilitate the appointment of international legal advisors in the field of international humanitarian law and international criminal law. The advisors shall assist and advise the court on matters concerning international humanitarian law, international criminal law, and the experience of similar tribunals (whether international or otherwise) at all stages of the proceedings. To that effect, the international legal advisors shall conduct any research, assist with the drafting of decisions, and provide assistance during trials and appeals to the judges of the High War Crimes Court. The Public Council shall propose a list of legal advisors to the Chief of the High War Crimes Court.
46. The Chief of the High War Crimes Court shall select from the selected list of nominees at least one international legal advisor per chamber of the court, or in their discretion as many advisors as they see fit depending on the caseload and needs of each chamber but in each case at least one advisor.[44] The same method shall be used to appoint international advisors for the investigative judges, the prosecution, and the defense. The Chief of the High War Crimes Court shall guarantee that the prosecution and

the defense in each case have their own respective international advisors. Specifically, international advisors shall assist prosecutors with research, drafting indictments, motions, opening and closing arguments, questions for witnesses, and appellate briefs. The international advisors shall be persons of high moral character, impartiality, and integrity. Preference shall be given to international advisors with the following experience: (i) experience in either a judicial, prosecutorial, or defense capacity in his or her respective country, or (ii) experience in international war crimes trials or tribunals.

47. International legal advisors to the High Crimes Court shall provide impartial and confidential consultations and recommendations. International legal advisors assigned to the defense shall not perform any service that may result into a relationship, such as a relationship between an attorney and his or her client, or accused individual, or to represent any individual in any proceedings before the High War Crimes Court.

Chapter IV. PECULIARITIES OF THE STATUS OF JUDGES OF THE HIGH WAR CRIMES COURT

Article 13. Additional guarantees of safety of judges of the High War Crimes Court

48. The judges of the High War Crimes Court, in connection with the administration of justice in the criminal proceedings concerning war crimes and crimes against humanity related offenses shall be provided, alongside the guarantees established by the Constitution of Ukraine and the Law of Ukraine "On the Judiciary and the Status of Judges," with additional guarantees of their personal security as well as personal security of their family members and preservation of their property.
49. A judge of the High War Crimes Court and, if necessary upon the judge's motion, his or her family members, shall be provided with round-the-clock security escort. At the motion of a judge of the High War Crimes Court, round-the-clock guard force shall be provided to the personal or official residence of the judge.
50. The home of a judge shall be equipped with security alarm and panic buttons.
51. Security of a judge of the High War Crimes Court, his or her family members and home shall be provided by the Judicial Security Service.
52. If the life or health of a judge of the High War Crimes Court or his or her family members come into jeopardy, the Judicial Security Service, at the request of the judge, shall provide temporary housing of such individuals in places where their safety can be guaranteed.

53. Official premises of the High War Crimes Court shall be equipped with modern security measures which guarantee judges' personal safety, preservation of documentation of the High War Crimes Court, and prevention of illegal access to the premises.

Article 14. Enhancement of the professional competence of a judge of the High War Crimes Court

54. Judges of the High War Crimes Court, alongside the measures of maintenance of professional qualifications of judges set forth in the Law of Ukraine "On the Judiciary and the Status of Judges," shall be provided with conditions for satisfaction of the individual needs for personal professional growth, increasing the level of professional competence on justice in the area of crimes against humanity, new international war crimes standards and best practices in the area of international justice.
55. A judge of the High War Crimes Court shall regularly, but no less than once a year, undergo obligatory further training on the judiciary in the area of crimes against humanity and war crimes.
56. The National School of Judges of Ukraine shall organize regular training for judges of the High War Crimes Court in order to solidify and update necessary knowledge and skills, deliver workshops to study up-to-date international practices of the judiciary in the area of war crimes and crimes against humanity, including those involving representatives of international organizations and foreign educational institutions.

Article 15. Provision of housing to a judge of the High War Crimes Court

57. A judge of the High War Crimes Court who is not provided with housing shall be provided by the government with official accommodation for the term of office.
58. Housing allocated for judges of the High War Crimes Court shall be state-owned. Removal of the premises provided to the judges of the High War Crimes Court for the term of office from the list of official housing and their alienation shall not be permitted.

Chapter V. SPECIAL SUPPORT OF ACTIVITY OF THE HIGH WAR CRIMES COURT

Article 16. Financial support of the activity of the High War Crimes Court

59. The High War Crime Court shall be the principal manager of the funds of the national budget of Ukraine allocated for financial support of its activity and the special donor committee created for this purpose.
60. The expenses for maintenance of the Appeal Chamber of the High War Crimes Court shall constitute a separate item in the national budget of Ukraine and the special donors committee created for this purpose.
61. The Special Donors Committee shall be permitted to accept international donations to support the operation of the Court subject to ensuring the Court maintains absolute judicial independence and integrity. The Special Donors Committee shall have an Oversight Board made up of an international chair and representatives from the Ukrainian Bar, Parliament, and civil society.

Article 17. Requirements to the location of the High War Crimes Court

62. The Appeal Chamber of the High War Crimes Court and the judicial chambers of the High War Crimes Court for administration of justice in the first instance may not be located in the same building.
63. The High War Crimes Court, its chambers and its administration may not be located in the same building as other courts, national agencies, their territorial, structural units, representative offices, bodies of local self-government, institutions, and organizations.
64. The building housing the High War Crimes Court should be reinforced to the greatest extent possible so as to be strong enough to resist the impact and explosive force of bombs or shells.

Article 18. Organizational Support of the Work of the High War Crimes Court

65. Organizational support of the work of the High War Crimes Court shall be provided by the administration of the High War Crimes Court in accordance with the Law of Ukraine "On the Judiciary and the Status of Judges."
66. A separate structural unit shall be established in the administration of the High War Crimes Court for organizational support of the work of the Appeal Chamber of the High War Crimes Court.

67. The Chief of the Appeal Chamber of the High War Crimes Court shall control the efficiency of activity of the separate structural unit providing organizational support to the work of the High War Crimes Court, submit proposals on the appointment of the chief of this unit and authorize his or her dismissal, submit motions on his or her recognition or application of disciplinary measures in accordance with the law, approve draft regulation on this structural unit and amendments to this regulation.

Article 19. Protection of Victims and Witnesses

68. The High War Crimes Court shall provide for the protection of victims and witnesses. Such protection measures shall include, but shall not be limited to, the conduct of in camera proceedings and the protection of the victim's identity.[45]

Chapter VI. ENFORCEMENT

Article 20 Enforcement[46]

71. Imprisonment shall be served in prisons in Ukraine. In the case that is not feasible, sentences may be served in any state on a list of states that have indicated their willingness to accept persons convicted by the Court that meet Ukrainian standards.
72. No authority outside the High War Crimes Court of Appeal may grant a pardon or mitigate the punishment issued by the Court.

Chapter VII. CORE PRINCIPLES OF THE HIGH WAR CRIMES COURT

Article 21. Independence of the High War Crimes Court

73. In exercising justice, the Court shall be independent of any improper influence, and administer justice proceeding from this Law and the laws of Ukraine.
74. The Court shall not consider appeals to the court by citizens, organizations, or officials who are not party to the trial.
75. Interference with the Court's administration of justice, or influence on the Courts or Judges shall be prohibited.
76. In order to protect professional interests of judges and address issues of internal functioning of courts in accordance with this Law, judicial self-government shall operate.

Article 22. The Right to a Fair Trial

77. Every person shall be guaranteed protection of their rights, freedoms and interests within reasonable time frames by an independent, impartial and fair trial, established by this Law and Ukrainian law.
78. Accessibility of justice shall be ensured under the purview of the Court.

Article 23. Equality Before the Law and the Court

79. Justice shall be exercised based on the principles of equality of all parties in a trial before the law and the court, regardless of race, color, political, religious and other beliefs, gender, ethnic or social origin, property status, residence, language and other characteristics.

80. The Court shall establish an environment where each party to a proceeding is guaranteed equality in the exercise of the granted procedural rights and in the performance of judicial duties, as determined by the procedural law.

Article 24. Professional Legal Assistance in the Implementation of the Right to a Fair Trial

81. Every person shall have the right to professional legal assistance.
82. The accused may employ their own private legal counsel at their cost, or select from the Court's roster of available defense counsel free of charge.

Article 25. Transparency and Openness of Court Proceedings

83. Court decisions, hearings and information on cases considered by the High War Crimes Court shall be open. No one may be restricted in their right to receive in-hearing oral or written information about the results of consideration of their trial. All parties shall be entitled to free access to the judgment in the manner specified by Ukrainian law.
84. Consideration of cases before the High War Crimes Court shall be open, except in cases stipulated by Ukrainian law. Any person may be present at an open hearing. However, where a person has committed acts demonstrating disrespect to the Court or to parties to a case, such person, upon a substantiated decision of the Court, shall be removed from the courtroom.
85. The High Court Judges shall promulgate rules guiding the televising of proceedings, and retain discretion to close the proceedings from the public for good cause where publicity would prejudice the interests of justice.

86. The Court shall allow the presence of international observers provided by the international community. Such international observers shall monitor the protection by the Court of general due process of law standards.

Chapter VIII. FINAL AND TRANSITIONAL PROVISIONS

87. This Law shall come into force on the next day after its publication.
88. The following changes shall be made in the following legislative acts of Ukraine: [To be drafted by specialized Ukrainian legislative council at the appropriate time.]
89. Within 12 months after this law comes into force, the following shall be done:

a) the High War Crimes Court shall be formed according to the procedure and in the composition stipulated by this law;
b) a competition for the vacancies of judges of the High War Crimes Court's Appeal Chamber and other judges of the High War Crimes Court shall be announced and held according to the law of Ukraine "On the Judiciary and Status of Judges" and according to this law. As a result of this competition, judges of the High War Crimes Court shall be appointed.
c) a new class of prosecutors with international criminal law knowledge shall be authorized to bring criminal proceedings before the High War Crimes Court. To that effect, a new Office of Prosecutors for the High War Crimes Court shall be created within the Department of War of the General Prosecutor's Office of Ukraine. The Office shall be assisted by international experts consistent with the other provisions of this law.
d) The day when the High War Crimes Court, in the composition determined by this law, starts its operation shall be determined by the decision of a meeting of this court, and the decision shall be published on the judiciary web-portal and in *Holos Ukraiiny* paper.
e) The High War Crimes Court shall start its operation provided at least [number] of judges of the High War Crimes Court have been appointed based on the results of the competition held in accordance with the Law of Ukraine "On the Judiciary and the Status of Judges" and this Law, including at least [number] judges of the Appeal Chamber of the High War Crimes Court.
f) Within thirty calendar days of the day of appointment of the judges of the High War Crimes Court in the number specified in item d) of this chapter, the oldest judge of the High War Crimes Court shall convoke a meeting of judges of the High War Crimes Court to decide on the day of the start of operation of the High War Crimes Court, resolve organizational issues of the court's activity and elect investigative judges.

g) If investigative judges are not elected before the day when the High War Crimes Court starts its operation, their duties shall be performed by three judges of the High War Crimes Court selected by means of drawing lots at a meeting of judges of the High War Crimes Court. Judges of the Appeal Chamber of the High War Crimes Court shall not participate in such drawing of lots.
h) The President of Ukraine shall be proposed to submit a draft law on the creation of the High War Crimes Court in accordance with the established procedure.

President of Ukraine	*V. ZELENSKYY*

Kyiv
[date]
No. [ ]

Notes

1 Appendix Notes
Ukraine is not a member of the International Criminal Court (ICC); however, it has accepted the court's limited jurisdiction over alleged crimes committed on its territory since November 2013. The ICC could exercise jurisdiction over individuals accused of war crimes, crimes against humanity and genocide in cases in which domestic courts are unable or unwilling to prosecute, such as if high-level accused perpetrators are present in a third country which is unwilling to extradite him to Ukraine for prosecution. Because of its limited capacity and the number of other situations it is currently investigating and prosecuting, the ICC traditionally asserts jurisdiction over only a handful of the highest-level defendants, so there would still be a need for the High War Crimes Court of Ukraine to prosecute the next level of culpable civilian and military leaders. Further, the ICC would not have jurisdiction over the crime of aggression since the Russian Federation has not consented to jurisdiction over that crime pursuant to the 2010 Aggression Amendment to the Rome Statute.

2 This definition was recommended by the International Committee of the Red Cross (ICRC) in its opinion paper "How is the Term 'Armed Conflict' defined in International Humanitarian Law? (March 2008), p. 5, available at: https://www.icrc.org/en/doc/assets/files/other/opinion-paper-armed-conflict.pdf

3 International humanitarian law is also known as the law of war or the law of armed conflict. This definition was taken from ICRC's paper entitled *What is International Humanitarian Law?* (2004), available at: https://www.icrc.org/en/doc/assets/files/other/what_is_ihl.pdf

4 This definition was recommended by the ICRC in its opinion paper "How is the Term 'Armed Conflict' defined in International Humanitarian Law? (March 2008), p.1, p. 5, available at: https://www.icrc.org/en/doc/assets/files/other/opinion-paper-armed-conflict.pdf

5 This language is taken from Article 8(d) of the International Criminal Court (ICC) Statute.

6 Including English as a working language is justified by the fact that the Court will include foreign legal advisors and that evidence may have been gathered in the English language by international humanitarian agencies present in Ukraine.

7 This is to address potential issues in the domestic legislation arising from having English as a working language of the Court.

8 Article 12(3) of the Law of Ukraine On the Judiciary and Status of Judges reads: "Courts shall use the official language in the course of the judicial proceedings and guarantee citizens' right to use their native language, or the language they speak, in the course of the proceedings." With respect to whether this Article is limited to Ukrainian citizens, it appears it does not. According to Article 7(2) of the same law (the right to a fair trial), "[f]oreigners, stateless persons and foreign legal entities shall be entitled to judicial protection in Ukraine on equal basis with the citizens and legal entities of Ukraine." In any case, the Court should have whatever translators necessary on its staff at all times to facilitate the smooth conduction of the proceedings. Further, According to the experience of the International Criminal Tribunal for Rwanda ("ICTR"), switching to simultaneous translation during oral proceedings (as opposed to consecutive interpretation), has resulted in a 25% time saving.

9 It is envisioned that the Prosecutors' Office will select which war crimes cases will be tried by ordinary Ukrainian courts and which will be directed to the High War Crimes Court.

10 It is understood that the prosecutors acting before the High War Crimes Court are to be special prosecutors trained in international criminal law, and assisted by international experts. Such a category of special prosecutors shall be created within the General Prosecutor's office by an amendment to the applicable law.

11 This is the definition of the Special Tribunal for Kenya Bill of "persons bearing the greatest responsibility." We understand that the "persons most responsible" is a broader concept targeting not only the top ranking officials but also middle level officials. We believe this definition, however, might be broad enough to accomplish such goal. The Kenyan Tribunal was never created but the bill was drafted following the experience of the Special Court for Sierra Leone (SCSL), which encountered various jurisdictional challenges based on the "persons bearing the greatest responsibility" language. In fact, in the context of the creation of the SCSL the United Nations' Secretary-General suggested to the United Nations Security Council to use the alternative terms "persons most responsible" to replace the "greatest responsibility" language. He stated: "[w]hile those 'most responsible' obviously include the political or military leadership, others in command authority down the chain of command may also be regarded 'most responsible' judging by the severity of the crime or its massive scale. 'Most responsible[,]' therefore, denotes either a leadership or authority position of the accused, and a sense of the gravity, seriousness or massive scale of the crime. It must be seen, however, not as a test criterion or a distinct jurisdictional threshold, but as a guidance to the Prosecutor in the adoption of a prosecution strategy and in making decisions to prosecute in individual cases." Taking all the above into account, the prosecution of the "most responsible" is included here in the objectives of the High Court as a matter of policy instead of in the article dealing with jurisdiction.

12 This includes areas of Ukraine currently under the control of a foreign State.

13 In addition to these four internationally recognized atrocity crimes, the High War Crimes Court would have jurisdiction over related crimes contained in the Criminal Code of Ukraine such as: Article 109 (actions aimed at forceful change or overthrow of the constitutional order or take-over of government), Article 110 (trespass against territorial integrity and inviolability of Ukraine), Article 110-2 (financing of actions committed for the purpose of forcible change or overthrow

of the constitutional order or take-over of government, change of boundaries of the territory or state border of Ukraine), Article 112 (trespass against life of a statesman or a public figure), Article 155 (murder), Article 127 (torture), Article 146 (illegal confinement or abduction of a person), Article 146-1 (hostage taking), Article 152 (rape), Article 332-2 (illegal crossing of the state border of Ukraine), Article 349 (hostage taking of a representative of government authorities or a law enforcement officer), Article 437 (planning, preparation and waging of an aggressive war), Article 438 (violation of rules of the warfare), Article 439 (use of weapons of mass destruction), and Article 447 (use of mercenaries).

14 The definition of the crime of genocide in this Law is based on Articles II and III of the Convention on the Prevention and Punishment of the Crime of Genocide.

15 The definition of crimes against humanity in this Law is based on Article 7 of the ICC Statute, excluding the crimes of apartheid and enforced sterilization, which do not appear applicable in the context of the armed conflict in Ukraine. This definition is widely viewed as reflecting customary international law. The Criminal Code of Ukraine does not have a specific Article on Crimes Against Humanity, but various Articles of the Code do reflect the types of crimes recognized as a Crime Against Humanity when committed on a systematic and widespread basis. Nevertheless, it is recommended that the Criminal Code of Ukraine be amended to add a specific Article on Crimes Against Humanity so that Ukraine can satisfy the obligations it has undertaken to the International Criminal Court.

16 Under Article 115 of the Ukrainian Criminal Code, murder is defined as the "willful unlawful causing death of another person."

17 The Nuremburg Tribunal held that if one murder is unlawful, then mass murder is also unlawful. Similarly, since Article 115 prohibits murder under Ukrainian law, then mass murder, or extermination, must also be unlawful under the current law of Ukraine.

18 Article 146 of the Ukrainian Criminal Code forbids the illegal confinement or abduction of a person. Similarly, Article 147 of the Code prohibits hostage taking which it defines as the "[t]aking or holding a person as a hostage with the intent to induce relatives of the hostage, any government agency or other institution, business or organization, any natural person or any official to make or refrain from any action as a condition for release of the hostage." Additionally, Article 149 of the Code proscribes the trafficking in human beings or other illegal transfer deals with respect to a human being. It defines the trafficking of human beings as the "[s]ale, other transfer for payment or any other illegal deals with regard to a person, involving legal or illegal movement of that person, with or without his/her consent, across the border of Ukraine for further sale or other transfer to any person (or persons) for the purpose of sexual exploitation, use in pornobusiness, engagement in criminal activities, peonage, adoption for commercial purposes, use in armed conflicts, labor exploitation..."

19 Article 146 of the Ukrainian Criminal Code prohibits the illegal confinement or abduction of a person.

20 The Ukrainian Criminal Code forbids battery and torture in Article 126. It defines such conduct as "[i]ntended blows, battery or other violent acts which caused physical pain but no bodily injury." Article 127 of the Code further proscribes torture, defining it as the "willful causing of severe physical pain or physical or mental suffering by way of battery, martyrizing or other violent actions for the purpose of inducing the victim or any other person to commit involuntary actions."

21 Article 152 of the Ukrianian Criminal Code prohibits rape and defines it as "sexual intercourse combined with violence, threats of violence, or committed by taking advantage of the victim's helpless condition." The Code also outlaws the

"violent unnatural gratification of sexual desire" in Article 153. It defines such conduct as the "[v]iolent unnatural gratification of sexual desire combined with physical violence, or threats of violence, or committed by taking advantage of the victim's helpless condition." Additionally, Article 154 proscribes "compulsion to sexual intercourse" which is defined as "compulsion of a female or male to natural or unnatural sexual intercourse by a person on whom such female or male is financially or officially dependent." Article 155 of the Code further outlaws sexual intercourse with a sexually immature person.

22 Article 303 of the Ukrainian Criminal Code outlaws prostitution or the "compelling to and engaging in prostitution." It defines such conduct as the provision of "sexual services for a fee by use of violence or threats of violence or destruction or endamagement of property, or by blackmail or deceit."

23 The Ukrainian Criminal Code proscribes the illegal confinement or abduction of a person in Article 146. Similarly, in Article 147 the Code prohibits hostage taking. It defines such conduct as the "[t]aking or holding a person as a hostage with the intent to induce relatives of the hostage, any government agency or other institution, business or organization, any natural person or any official to make or refrain from any action as a condition for release of the hostage." The Code also outlaws the trafficking in human beings or other illegal transfer deals with respect to a human being. Article 149 defines such conduct as the "[s]ale, other transfer for payment or any other illegal deals with regard to a person, involving legal or illegal movement of that person, with or without his/her consent, across the border of Ukraine for further sale or other transfer to any person (or persons) for the purpose of sexual exploitation, use in pornobusiness, engagement in criminal activities, peonage, adoption for commercial purposes, use in armed conflicts, labor exploitation."

24 The definition of war crimes in this Law is based on Article 8, paragraph 2, of the ICC Statute. This includes both war crimes committed in an international armed conflict (Article 8, paragraphs 2 (a) and 2(b)) and war crimes committed in an armed conflict not of an international character (Article 8, paragraphs 2 (c), 2 (d), 2 (e) and 2 (f)).

25 Article 438 of the Ukrainian Criminal Code states: Cruel treatment of prisoners of war or civilians, deportation of civilian population for forced labor, pillage of national treasures on occupied territories, use of methods of the warfare prohibited by international instruments, or any other violations of rules of the warfare recognized by international instruments consented to by binding by the Verkhovna Rada (Parliament) of Ukraine, and also giving an order to commit any such actions, - shall be punishable by imprisonment for a term of eight to twelve years. 2. The same acts accompanied with a murder, - shall be punishable by imprisonment for a term of ten to fifteen years, or life imprisonment.

26 Article 127 of the Ukrianian Criminal Code defines torture as a "willful causing of severe physical pain or physical or mental suffering by way of battery, martyrizing or other violent actions for the purpose of inducing the victim or any other person to commit involuntary actions."

27 Article 121 of the Ukrainian Criminal Code defines intended grievous bodily injury as "a willful bodily injury which is dangerous to life at the time of infliction, or resulted in a loss of any organ or its functions, or caused a mental disease or any other health disorder attended with a persisting loss of not less than one-third of working capability, or interruption of pregnancy, or permanent disfigurement of face."

28 Article 147 of the Ukrainian Criminal Code defines hostage taking as "[t]aking or holding a person as a hostage with the intent to induce relatives of the hostage, any government agency or other institution, business or organization, any natural

person or any official to make or refrain from any action as a condition for release of the hostage."

29 The Ukrainian Criminal Code Article 197 prescribes punishment for "the illegal retention, desecration, or destruction of religious sanctities."

30 Article 289 of the Ukrainian Criminal Code prescribes punishment for "willful spoiling, destruction of or impairment of historical or cultural monuments."

31 Rape is defined as "sexual intercourse combined with violence, threats of violence, or committed by taking advantage of the victim's helpless condition" under Article 152 of the Ukrainian Criminal Code.

32 Article 152 of the Ukrainian Criminal Code defines enforced prostitution as "provid[ing] sexual services for a fee by use of violence or threats of violence or destruction or endamagement of property, or by blackmail or deceit."

33 Article 438 of the Ukrainian Criminal Code prohibits cruel treatment of civilians.

34 Article 179 of the Ukrainian Criminal Code prescribes punishment for "the illegal retention, desecration, or destruction of religious sanctities."

35 Article 289 of the Ukrainian Criminal Code outlines punishment for "willful spoiling, destruction of or impairment of historical or cultural monuments."

36 Article 179 of the Ukrainian Criminal Code prohibits the "pillag[ing] of national treasures on occupied territories."

37 The Ukrainian Criminal Code defines rape in Article 152, as "sexual intercourse combined with violence, threats of violence, or committed by taking advantage of the victim's helpless condition."

38 Article 152 of the Ukrainian Criminal Code defines enforced prostitution as "provid[ing] sexual services for a fee by use of violence or threats of violence or destruction or endamagement of property, or by blackmail or deceit."

39 The definition of the crime of aggression in this Statute is based on Article 8 of the ICC Statute.

40 Article 437 of the Ukrainian Criminal Code states that (1) "planning, preparation or waging of an aggressive war or armed conflict, or conspiring for any such purposes, - shall be punishable by imprisonment for a term of seven to twelve years" and (2) "conducting an aggressive war or aggressive military operations, - shall be punishable by imprisonment for a term of ten to fifteen years."

41 With regard to the number of chambers of the Court, Article 31 of the Law of Ukraine "On the Judiciary and Status of Judges" reads: "[t]he decision on establishing a judicial chamber, its composition and on election of the Secretary of the Chamber shall be adopted by the meeting of judges of the respective high specialized court, upon the proposal of the Chief Judge." With regard to the term of the Chief judges, Article 20 of Section 2 Chapter 1 of the Law of Ukraine "The Chief Judge of the trial court, their Deputy, Chief Judge of the appellate court, their Deputies, Chief Judge of the high specialized court and their Deputies shall be elected to their position by meeting of judges by secret ballot by a majority of the judges of a relevant court for a three-year term but not exceeding the term of office of a judge within the procedure established by law."

42 Chapter 4 Section 2 of the Law of Ukraine "On the Judiciary and Status of Judges" is devoted to "High specialized courts," including the High Anti-Corruption Court.

43 Examples of such organizations are the United Nations, the International Committee of the Red Cross (ICRC), Council of Europe, and International Federation for Human Rights (FIDH).

44 The revised statute for the Iraqi High Criminal Court (IHCC) allows for the discretionary appointment of non-Iraqi experts to act in advisory capacities. It defined their role as providing "assistance with respect to international law and the experience of similar Courts (whether international or otherwise)." M. Cherif

Bassiouni, *Ceding the High Ground: The Iraqi High Criminal Court Statute and the Trial of Saddam Hussein*, Case Western Reserve Journal of International Law, Volume 39 Issue 1 2006-2007, at p.58, available at: https://scholarlycommons.law.case.edu/cgi/viewcontent.cgi?article=1302&context=jil

45 This is separated into its own section in order to highlight its importance, rather than including it in the section on rights of the judges, where it seems out of place.

46 Penalties shall be in accordance with Ukrainian law. It is understood that the highest enforcement for war crimes is a life sentence (See: Criminal Code of Ukraine, Article 12, Classification of Criminal Offenses). If Ukrainian Law is amended to provide for confiscation and forfeiture as a penalty for the crimes within the jurisdiction of the High War Crimes Court, that penalty shall also be an option in cases before the High War Crimes Court.

INDEX

Made in the USA
Monee, IL
13 September 2026

62980179R00201